RUSSIA AND BLACK AFRICA BEFORE WORLD WAR II

RUSSIA and BLACK AFRICA before World War II

Edward Thomas Wilson

HM Holmes & Meier Publishers, New York & London

Published in the United States of America 1974
by Holmes & Meier Publishers, Inc.
101 Fifth Avenue
New York, N.Y. 10003

Great Britain
Holmes & Meier Publishers, Ltd.
Hillsview House
1, Hallswelle Parade
Finchley Road, London NW11

Printed in the United States of America

Library of Congress Cataloging in Publication Data

Wilson, Edward Thomas.
    Russia and black Africa before World War II.

    "Slightly edited version of a dissertation accepted
by the Johns Hopkins University in May, 1972."
    Bibliography: p.
    1. Africa, Sub-Saharan--Foreign relations--Russia.
2. Russia--Foreign relations--Africa, Sub-Saharan.
I. Title.
DT38.9.R8W54 1974   327.47'067   73-84939
ISBN 0-8419-0109-0

TO MY MOTHER AND MY WIFE,
each in a different way, sources
of life and inspiration for this
book and its author.

Foreword

Sovietologists in the past decade have produced several meritorious analyses of Soviet policy toward the countries of Africa south of the Sahara. It is commonplace for these studies to contend that contacts between Russia and Black Africa were minimal before African colonies began to attain their independence in the late 1950's. Undaunted by such contentions Edward Wilson has explored these earlier links in depth to determine whether they were really as negligible as often portrayed.

The author has dug deeply into Russian, Western and African source materials, many of them hitherto unused. In doing so, he has uncovered a surprising number of missing details, which are really an original contribution to our knowledge. Writing with clarity and precision, he is judicious in assessing the significance of his material. While he demonstrates fully that there were more early contacts between Africans and Russians than is generally realized, he is careful to avoid the trap of allowing his evidence to draw him into loose exaggerations of the extent of Russian penetration of Africa.

The study is primarily an historical survey of Russian initiatives in Black Africa especially in the fifty years before World War II. It reconsiders the repeated efforts of Czarist governments to establish a Red Sea outpost on the African coast, and to support Ethiopian resistance to British and Italian imperialism.

Of special interest is the author's account of Soviet attempts, mainly through the Comintern and especially between 1928 and 1935, to foment anti-colonial revolts in British and French Africa, and to prevent the use of Black African troops in imperialist ventures against the Soviet Union.

Stressing the basic continuities in the uninterrupted pursuit of national security by both Czarist and Soviet leaders, the author concludes that both regimes found in Black African nationalist movements a useful instrument for promoting the objectives of Russian foreign policy.

The publishers are to be congratulated, in these days of higher costs and lower markets, for publishing the full text of a long but worthy manuscript which will remain the standard work on the subject for the foreseeable future.

VERNON MCKAY   APRIL 9, 1973

Contents

List of Abbreviations

ABB	African Blood Brotherhood
ANLC	American Negro Labor Congress
ANSSSR	Academy of Sciences of the U.S.S.R.
ARPS	Aborigines' Rights Protection Society
AWUN	African Workers' Union of Nigeria
CDRN	Comité de Défense de la Race Nègre
CGT	Confédération Générale du Travail
CGTU	Confédération Générale du Travail Unitaire
CPGB	Communist Party of Great Britain
CPSA	Communist Party of South Africa
CPSU	Communist Party of the Soviet Union
CPUSA	Communist Party of the U.S.A.
ECCI	Executive Committee of the Communist International
IASB	International African Service Bureau
ILD	International Labor Defense
ISH	International of Seamen and Harbor Workers
ITUC-NW	International Trade Union Committee of Negro Workers
KPD	German Communist Party
KUTV	Communist University of the Toilers of the East, known also as "Kutvu" and as "Stalin" University
LAI	League Against Imperialism
LDRN	Ligue de Défense de la Race Nègre
NAACP	National Association for the Advancement of Colored People
NCBWA	National Congress of British West Africa
NIANKP	Scientific Research Association for the Study of National and Colonial Problems
NWA	Negro Welfare Association
PCB	Belgian Communist Party
PCF	French Communist Party
RDA	Rassemblement Démocratique Africain
RILU	Red International of Labor Unions (Profintern)
UNIA	Universal Negro Improvement Association
UTN	Union des Travailleurs Nègres
WANS	West African National Secretariat
WASU	West African Students' Union
WAYL	West African Youth League

Preface

In the early 1960's, shortly after most countries in Black Africa had been granted independence, many Western journalists and scholars were surprised by the initial success of Soviet efforts to penetrate the region. This surprise reflected the widely-held view that the Russian government had no contact or experience with African politics prior to World War II.

This study disputes this view by demonstrating that the recent involvement of Russia in Black Africa is rooted in policies that reach back more than two centuries. An examination of official Russian accounts and other Russian sources reveals a history of selective involvement in sub-Saharan Africa which dates to an expedition to Ethiopia in 1888–89, and indeed even earlier if one counts the efforts of Czar Peter I to establish commercial relations with the "highly esteemed king and owner of the glorious Island of Magaskar" in 1723.

The analysis of Russian involvement in Black Africa is presented chronologically, beginning with its earliest and tentative manifestations. After a brief review of the record before 1889, the bulk of the study is devoted to the half-century prior to the outbreak of World War II and falls into three subdivisions: 1) the Czarist period, 1889–1917; 2) the early Soviet period, 1917–27; and 3) the later Soviet period, 1928–39. This chronological survey is followed by an analytical assessment of Russian involvement, highlighting its major characteristics and its impact on Soviet policy toward Black Africa since 1945.

The study traces three interwoven elements in Russia's approach to Africa. First, it examines the character and extent of Russia's commercial and strategic interest in this distant region. Second, it analyzes the campaign to spread Russian ideological influence and undermine Western authority in Africa. Third, it focuses on the strategy and tactics used by the Kremlin to pursue its ideological and political objectives.

In the Czarist period, Russian strategy concentrated on Ethiopia and the region surrounding the Red Sea. By securing a foothold in these areas, it was believed that Russia could protect its maritime links with the Far East and at the same time sabotage the British route to India. In further attempts to weaken British imperial strength, the Czar supported the French in their effort to gain control of the Nile, and the Boers in their unsuccessful war in South Africa (1899–1905).

During the Soviet period, special attention is given to the multiple activities of the Comintern designed to confuse, demoralize, and eventually drive out the British, French, and Belgians from Africa. The principal target was always the British, the arch-typical imperialists in the communist lexicon. Various forms of agitation and propaganda were employed to stimulate educated Africans to move against colonial authorities, including the clandestine distribution of Comintern periodicals in English and French and the training of selected leaders for specific kinds of political activity. Even American Negroes were courted as standard bearers in the cause of African liberation.

The geographical scope of this study is confined to Black Africa because it is a region clearly distinguishable from Arab North Africa and because the Russians themselves consistently treated it as such. Further, the area has a distinct heritage of racial identity and a common experience with European colonial rule. A word needs to be said, however, about the inclusion of Ethiopia within Black Africa. Certainly there are valid ethnic, cultural, and historical reasons for viewing Ethiopia as a separate entity. Yet geographically, and in terms of Russia's interest, it fits easily into the larger region. Indeed, just as West Africa was the primary focus of Russian efforts during the Soviet period, the "black empire" of Ethiopia was the major focal point of Russian concern during the last thirty years of Czarist rule.

The emphasis throughout is on Russian policy, although wherever possible reference is made to the African response to Russian initiatives. Particularly in assessing the post-World War II implications of Russia's historical experience, a special attempt is made to underscore the importance of the Kremlin's efforts in accelerating the pace of African political development.

Although Russian sources—notably primary accounts by pre-revolutionary travellers and official Soviet documents—were heavily relied upon, African sources such as early nationalist newspapers were also exploited. The archives of the British and French colonial ministries were invaluable as sources both of African publications and of correspondence relating to political developments within the colonies. The task of piecing together the story of Russian involvement in Black Africa was made difficult both by the absence of any centralized source of primary information and by the paucity of reliable secondary materials on the subject. The research effort was rendered even more challenging by the veils of secrecy which the principal actors consistently sought to draw around their movements and intentions in Africa. Accounts authorized by the governments of Britain, France, and Russia consciously disguised the real nature and extent of official strategic interests in the continent. In the case of British and French colonial authorities, an effort was even made to manipulate the flow of information to and from Africa and to destroy large amounts of documentation revealing the proportions of communist influence and indigenous unrest.

The scope of this book is limited to Russian policy toward Black Africa, yet it covers more than half a century and spans two very disparate Russian political systems. Thus, it hopefully contributes to an understanding of Czarist and Soviet foreign policy. Among other things, it demonstrates a remarkable continuity in policy and purpose between the two Russian regimes toward the largest single land mass in the Third World. By examining the admixture of strategic and ideological factors that motivated the Kremlin, it invites comparison with Russian approaches to the underdeveloped regions of Asia and Latin America.

For these reasons, the book is addressed both to historians and to political scientists interested in Russian foreign policy and African affairs. In addition, since it explores the roots of anti-colonial sentiment in Black Africa, it is addressed to those concerned with the early development of Third World nationalism and with the struggle of indigenous peoples for independence from external rule.

The present work is a slightly edited version of a dissertation accepted by The Johns Hopkins University in May, 1972. I wish to thank in the first instance Dr. Vernon McKay, Professor of African Studies at The Johns Hopkins School of Advanced International Studies, Washington, D.C., for his patient reading of the text and above all for his continuing belief in the merit of the project. I am also indebted to Dr. Robert Osgood and to Dean Francis Wilcox of SAIS for their interest in the study and to Dr. Herbert Dinerstein, SAIS Professor of Soviet Studies for his guidance as my dissertation adviser. I would like to add a special note of thanks to Dr. Ernest Lefever of the Brookings Institution for his valuable editorial advice on creating a book from a dissertation and to Dr. Sergius Yakobson, former Chief of the Slavic and Eastern European Section of the Library of Congress, whose longstanding and scholarly enthusiasm for the subject I was fortunate to absorb and whose suggestions on sources, particularly for the Czarist period, were invaluable. More than to any other person, I owe my original interst in Russia and its history to George Gabritchevsky, my first Russian teacher, who cheerfully assisted his former pupil in several difficult translations from old Russian.

A number of librarians and archivists—notably at the Slavic Section of the Library of Congress and the Colonial Archives in London and Paris—share credit for the research effort represented in this volume. Space here permits the mention of only one, Madame Maurin, at the Overseas Section of the French National Archives, whose selfless assistance typified the contributions of many. The staggering logistical burden of typing, photocopying, and proofreading was largely borne by Mrs. Joan DeAngelis, Mrs. Ruby Blackstone, and by two unsuspecting fathers—The Honorable Edward Foss Wilson and the Reverend James Salango. Last—and most—I want to thank my wife who shared the joys and frustrations of this project as thoroughly as I and who alone can ever know the extent of her contribution to its success.

PART I

THE ORIGINS AND DEVELOPMENT OF RUSSIAN CONCERN FOR SUB-SAHARAN AFRICA: THE CZARIST EXPERIENCE

A discernible manifestation of the rise of a nation to the status of a great power is a marked increase in its awareness of peoples beyond the confines of its own borders and a heightened ability to relate their interests to its own. At first this awareness is apt to be limited to adjacent regions. However, the most farsighted and successful rulers have usually been quick to recognize opportunities to secure the economic and political advantages of associating with foreigners— even in the most distant lands. This was certainly the case with several of the first great rulers of modern Russia, who allowed their imaginations, and sometimes their nation's energies, to travel to the very limits of the known world. Not even Africa, the least known of all continents, was exempt from their attentions. As early as the seventeenth century the Czarist government began to display an interest in Africa which was to expand progressively until the very eve of the Bolshevik Revolution.

Between the years 1889 and 1903 the Czarist government pursued a course of comparatively active involvement in Ethiopia and the regions surrounding the Red Sea. The peculiar Czarist concern for northeastern Africa at the end of the nineteenth century was a combined product of Russia's proselytizing impulses, its hatred of the British, and its desire to secure, through Egypt, uninhibited access to India and the Far East. Although Czarist activity did not result in any lasting Russian presence on the African continent, it did precondition Russians to think of Africa in terms of their own national security. Thus, whether or not the Kremlin was successful in achieving its objectives during the Czarist period, its experience did provide important precedents for Russian involvement in Africa in the years after 1917.

1

Russian Interest in Africa Prior to 1889

ORIGINAL MOTIVATIONS

Russia's commercial and strategic interest in India and the Far East, together with its desire to win allies against the Ottoman Empire, were largely responsible for Russia's first contacts with the African continent. Both factors served to direct Czarist attention southward to the Mediterranean and to underscore the significance of northeastern Africa as an area of Russian strategic concern.

The earliest foreign relations of the Czarist government had a distinctly southern orientation.[1] In the wake of Russia's religious, economic, and cultural attachment to Constantinople came Orthodox anxiety over Turkey's control of Jerusalem and its dominion over "the second Rome." To this motive for channeling Czarist energies southward, Peter I (1682–1725) added new geopolitical considerations. Russia's entrée as a naval power, he was convinced, depended upon the nation's ability to secure both a warm water port in the South and a share in the lucrative trade of the Indies.

Although Russia was very much a latecomer in the quest for a commercial stake in India, Russians were no less eager than were their Western European counterparts to obtain access to the Indian treasure-house.* When efforts to reach the subcontinent by land proved fruitless, Peter I turned to the idea of achieving the same objective by circumnavigating Africa. The first practical step in establishing such a route, he concluded, was the erection of a Russian post at some point along the extended trajectory between Bengal and

---

* Indeed their zeal in this direction sometimes reached fantastic proportions. Peter I, in an attempt to compete with the British in India, contemplated everything from a diversion of the Amur Darya River to a route through the Arctic Ocean. Nearly a century later, Czar Paul, in cooperation with the French against the British, even sent a Russian army on an abortive mission to the Indus. (See Sergius Yakobson, "Russia and Africa," in the *Slavonic and East European Review*, XVII, no. 51 [April, 1939]: 14; and George Curzon, *Russia in Central Asia* [London, 1889, reprinted 1967]: 324.)

St. Petersburg. With its strategic location at the crossroads of Indian Ocean trade routes, the island of Madagascar seemed to recommend itself for this purpose.

Accordingly, in December, 1723, Peter dispatched two vessels under Vice Admiral Wilster on a mission to establish friendly relations with the "highly esteemed king and owner of the glorious Island of Magaskar [sic.]."[2] Admiral Wilster himself anticipated that a Russian colony would eventually take root on the island, and, in the event there was no king, he expected Peter to select an appropriate individual to govern it.[3] The ultimate goal of his mission was, however, Bengal, where Peter hoped to "persuade the Mogul ruler to enter into commercial relations with Russia."[4] Thus, "Madagascar . . . was needed by Peter, not for itself, but as a convenient way station in the trade relations between St. Petersburg and the place which was luring all of the European world—India."[5]

Although one of the vessels sprang a leak and the expedition was obliged to return immediately to Russia,[6] the conditions under which it was undertaken shed light on the political motivations which prompted Russian interest in Africa. The long-range objective of the mission was to provide Russia with an accessible route to India. Yet the immediate impetus for the project was an intelligence report to the effect that Russia's Swedish rivals planned to establish a colony in Madagascar themselves. The mission was to be one of utmost secrecy, hidden from the knowledge not only of the Swedish but also of the British.[7] Thus, preventive imperialist instincts and hostility toward Britain—attitudes which were to become characteristic of Czarist involvement in Africa—were apparent as early as the eighteenth century Madagascar project of Peter the Great.

It is possible that one of Peter's successors, Czar Paul I (1796–1801), also thought in terms of establishing a secure maritime route to India—this time one which would skirt Africa's northern shores. Not only did Czar Paul plot a joint conquest of India with Napoleon, but while the French were seizing Egypt and thereby convincing Britain of the strategic importance of the shorter Mediterranean route to India he appeared to be showing particular interest in securing for Russia valuable pieces of Mediterranean real estate. Thus, in the face of British and French schemes to gain control of Malta, he became "Grand Master of the Order of Malta" and, between 1797 and 1800, seemed to be on the verge of winning the island for Russia.[8] At approximately the same time, moreover, one of his admirals seized the Ionian Islands at the mouth of the Aegean, thereby giving Russia effective control over that strategic area.[9] Clearly, if his intention was to establish Russia's own fortified route to India, Czar Paul came much closer to achieving this objective than had his more illustrious predecessor, Peter.

Russia's interest in maritime routes to India served to draw Czarist attention to Madagascar and the Mediterranean shores of the African continent. At the same time, Russia's desire to win allies against Turkey focused the sights of the Kremlin upon Africa's northern shores. Indeed, by the mid-eighteenth century, Russians had already come to recognize that the support of indigenous nationalism within the empires of rival powers constituted a powerful weapon both for winning allies to Russia's cause and for weakening the positions of Russia's adversaries.

The policy of supporting nationalism for its disintegrative effects on empires south of Russian borders became an active policy of the Kremlin during the reign of Catherine the Great (1762–96). In an effort to undermine Turkish power, Catherine sent Count Alexis Orlov and a Russian fleet to the Aegean in 1770 for the purpose, among other things, of rescuing "the Greek peoples who are looking to the shore of the Neva for their freedom."[10] Although Orlov was not successful in liberating the Greeks, he was able to win a major engagement with the Turkish fleet, thereby establishing Russian power in the Mediterranean.

As a result of Orlov's naval success, the entire Mediterranean area acquired increased significance for Russia and consequently the northern shores of the African continent began to fall within the scope of the Kremlin's strategic interest. Russian naval officers began to visit points as far away as Tunis, and, if the experience of M. G. Kokovtsov is any indication, their exploratory ventures yielded information of political as well as potential military value. Introduced to the Bey of Tunis simply as "a Russian noble in search of curiosities," Kokovtsov succeeded both in reporting the Bey's desire to conclude a peace treaty with the Russian sovereign and in taking careful note of local rivalries which might be exploited by his countrymen. Furthermore, "under the guise of fishing," he proceeded to take soundings of the harbor at Tunis. On a second visit to North Africa in 1777, Kokovtsov was obliged to pose as a Frenchman, a step indicative of the problems in store for a nation which, lacking diplomatic status in Africa, would be forced to rely upon secret agents and clandestine missions.[11]

Although Catherine's support of the Greeks brought about certain preliminary contacts between Russia and the African continent, the Czarina's activities on behalf of the Mameluks in Egypt were even more directly related to the emergence of Russian interest in Africa. Certainly if Catherine found it expedient to encourage dissent among Turkey's Greek subjects, it made equally good sense to fan the flames of separatism in Egypt. Indeed, in the rebellious Mameluk Beys, Russia saw potential anti-Turkish allies of no little significance.[12]

In 1772 Count Orlov sent two Russian officers disguised as Englishmen to the Mameluk leader, Ali Bey, with arms and ammunition. Later the same year he went so far as to dispatch a naval squadron to help the Mameluks besiege the Turks at Jaffa.[13] Although in 1774 Catherine attempted to lend respectability to her new association with the Mameluks by dispatching Russia's first diplomatic representative to Egypt,[14] it was essentially in the framework of a clandestine military alliance that the doors were first opened to a significant Russian involvement on the African continent.

There seems little question that the objective of Catherine's efforts was "to encourage the Beys to make themselves independent of the Porte and to place themselves under the protection of [the Russian] sovereign."[15] Certainly the behavior of Baron de Thonus, Russia's consul in Alexandria, suggests that this was the case. In 1783 and 1784 de Thonus was active in negotiating an agreement whereby Russia would officially recognize the independence of the Mameluks in return for the right to quarter Russian troops in Alexandria, Rosetta, and Damietta.[16] Evidently he was successful not only in planting young Russian officers in the households of such Mameluk leaders as Ibrahim Bey, but in promoting a general influx of Russian military forces into Egypt. So great was this influx, in fact, that by 1786 it was estimated that one fourth of the entire Egyptian militia was composed of Czarist troops.[17]

Angered by such intrigues, the Ottomans declared war on Russia and took action to quell the revolt of their Egyptian subjects. Despite further offers of men and money from de Thonus, and even a letter from Catherine herself pledging virtually unlimited Russian support for the insurgency, the Mameluk cause was crushed at the hands of the Ottomans in 1788.[18] Thus, Russia proved unsuccessful in its immediate objective of dislodging the Turks from Egypt. However, in a broader sense, Catherine's adventures with the Mameluks were not altogether unproductive. In the course of the 1780's an impressive Russian presence in Egypt had been established. As a result, moreover, the Czarist government felt that it had acquired sufficient influence in the region to enable it to offer the Mameluks not only political and military advice, but also diplomatic protection. Perhaps most important, it was able to create the impression among other European governments that Russia would eventually be in a position to take control of Egypt.[19]

Certainly such an impression was of value to Russia quite apart from any erosive effect which Catherine's Egyptian enterprises may have had upon Turkish power. In an age when geographical competition between imperial powers was a familiar feature of the international political scene, it made sense to establish positions of strength, or apparent strength, even in unlikely corners of the globe. Catherine's government probably believed that should the Ottoman Empire fall prey to dismemberment at the hands of European powers, a pied-à-terre in Egypt might serve as a useful asset to be bargained for Russia's most coveted geographical prize—a controlling position on the Bosphorus. References to a Russian proposal for a joint Franco-Russian expedition to Egypt (c. 1788), as well as reports of approaches made by Catherine to Louis XVI of France regarding a possible division of Ottoman spoils, tally well with such a supposition.[20]

In sum, Catherine's maneuvers in Egypt succeeded in creating among other powers a certain respect for Russia's interests in the region. Great Britain in particular displayed an awareness of these interests when it turned to the Czarist government for support in its plan to oust Napoleon from Egypt in 1801. To this end, the British Ambassador in St. Petersburg was instructed to learn "whether Russia was disposed to guarantee jointly with His Majesty's Government the province of Egypt to Turkey in the event of the expulsion of the French."[21] Possibly out of concern that Russian forces might again be deployed in Egypt, the British were also anxious that such an agreement include a stipulation regarding the proportion of military forces to be used by each power for the subsequent defense of Egypt.[22] Thereafter it was clear, as Dr. Sergius Yakobson observes, that "the right of Russia to have some say in the fate of Egypt was not only safeguarded, but also recognized by the other European powers as legitimate."[23]

THE BEGINNINGS OF RUSSIAN INVOLVEMENT IN ETHIOPIA

Early Interest in Russo-Ethiopian Ties

The search for allies against the Ottoman Empire also led the rulers of Russia to become interested in Ethiopia—the land which was destined to be the central focus of Czarist activity in sub-Saharan Africa. In fact, nearly a century before Catherine began to play Greeks against Turks, the second Romanov, Czar Alexis (1645–76), toyed with the idea of using the Christian Ethiopians for joint military action against the Ottoman infidels. The concept of an alliance for this purpose probably originated with the Saxon scholar Iovus Ludolfus who published a book, *The History of Abyssinia*, in 1681 and who reportedly was able to induce his sovereign, Duke Ernst of Saxony, to make a formal proposal to the Russian Czar in 1674 for a joint anti-Turkish coalition which would include Ethiopia.[24] Although the death of Alexis two years later put an end to any immediate plans to "arouse a new enemy against Turkey," the idea of an alliance with Abyssinia remained under active discussion in the Kremlin throughout the following decade and was periodically revived under Alexis' successors.[25]

Under the reign of Peter the Great there seemed to be a particularly marked renewal of interest in establishing ties with Ethiopia. At Peter's behest, a group of scholars translated Ludolfus' book on Ethiopia into Russian, thereby providing the Russian government with its first source of detailed information on the country.[26] Subsequently Peter obtained a more direct source of information concerning the region by acquiring the services of a former Ethiopian slave named Ibrahim.* Thus endowed with what must have been a

---

* Ibrahim (also known by the name of Hannibal) had been bought by Peter in Constantinople and had been attached to the Russian court. He later became a successful and probably intimate protégé of the Czar, rising to the rank of general. As Pushkin's great-grandfather he also served as the subject of the first Russian historical novel as well as the focal point for the first popular Russian interest in Black Africa. (See Harold Acton, "Pushkin and Peter the Great's Negro", in Nancy Cunard, ed., *Negro Anthology* [London, 1934]; and Czeslaw Jesman, *The Russians in Ethiopia* [London, 1958]: 31–34.)

comparatively well-informed interest in Ethiopia, Peter proceeded to explore the possibilities of establishing ties with the country through the good offices of the Orthodox Patriarch of Alexandria, Cosmos II.[27] It is also possible that toward the end of his reign (c. 1718) he promoted a plan whereby a "scientific expedition" would go from Russia to Ethiopia via Persia.[28]

Again in the mid-nineteenth century the notion of a Russo-Ethiopian combination against Turkey was revived, this time at the initiative of the Ethiopians. In 1855 Emperor Theodore II, with visions of a joint crusade against the infidels, sent a message to Nicholas I suggesting a Russo-Ethiopian alliance against Turkey and Egypt.[29] This demarche was followed up by Theodore's successor, Johannes IV, who communicated with Alexander II, addressing him as a "fellow enemy of the Turks."[30] Although no tangible results appear to have come of any of these initiatives, they did indicate that the idea of diplomatic ties, and even military alliance, held a certain appeal both for Russians and for Ethiopians. Even more important, they contributed to the evolution of the belief that somehow Orthodox Russia had a unique role to play in the political future of northeastern Africa.

The Theoretical Case for Russian Involvement in Ethiopia

Although the political advantages of establishing friendly relations with Ethiopia were recognized by Russians as early as the seventeenth century, it was not until the 1860's that the case for Russian involvement in Ethiopia was fully articulated. While the concept of religious rapprochement as a basis for political cooperation had been advocated for some time by members of Russia's religious hierarchy, it remained for the Orthodox monk, Porfiry Uspensky (1804–85) to set forth in convincing terms the rationale for Russian religious and political penetration of Ethiopia. In effect, Uspensky's writings on Ethiopia established the theoretical basis for all of Czarism's subsequent activity in sub-Saharan Africa.[31]

As a prominent church figure dedicated to the promotion of Russian influence in the Middle East, Uspensky was chosen by the Procurator of the Holy Synod to head a Russian spiritual mission in Jerusalem between 1848 and 1854. Although this mission was surrounded by an air of secrecy, Uspensky does reveal that its tasks included "studying the history of the Ethiopian church from books and gathering information on contemporary events in Ethiopia from Ethiopians themselves and from Copts."[32] Such activities were possible in Jerusalem, for in that city was to be found an Ethiopian religious community—the sole foreign outpost of the Ethiopian Empire and one of its few channels of communication with the outside world.

It is obvious from Uspensky's writings that early Russian interest in Ethiopia was grounded in more than theological curiosity. Since at the time of Uspensky's mission the Ethiopian religious community was rebelling against its Armenian protectors, the question of the political status of Ethiopians in Jerusalem was open to dispute. In light of the British and French challenge to Russia's position as protector of Orthodox Christians in the Ottoman Empire (on the eve of the Crimean War), it was inevitable that the head of the Russian spiritual mission to Jerusalem would approach Ethiopians as often in political as in ecclesiastical terms.[33] Thus in his article "Ecclesiastical and Political Status of Abyssinia from Earliest Times until the Present," published in *Trudy Kievskoi Dukhovnoi Akademii* in 1866, Uspensky included a detailed analysis of Ethiopia's political history which in its final portions amounted to political reporting of the kind usually performed by diplomatic representatives.[34]

In point of fact, Uspensky actually did engage in political reporting on numerous occasions. In the course of various communications with Russia's diplomatic establishment he stressed the growing political power of Ethiopia and the importance of establishing ties between the two Orthodox empires.* After returning to Russia from Jerusalem he devised a detailed plan for the consolidation of Russo-Ethiopian relations. The essential outlines of this plan appeared in

---

* On April 10, 1854, he made a report to Liubimov, Director of the Asian Department of the Russian Foreign Ministry (the department which was ultimately to become responsible for Ethiopian affairs) regarding the consolidation of the power of the Ethiopian Emperor Theodore II and its implications for European diplomacy. Earlier (in 1851) Uspensky had written to the Russian Consul General in Beirut, Mr. Bazili, emphasizing the importance of Ethiopia "as a point of departure for our activity for the glory of God and the interests of Holy Orthodoxy." (Porfiry Uspensky, "Tserkovnoe i Politicheskoe Sostoianie Abissinii s Drevneishikh Vremen do Nashikhe Dnei", in *Trudy Kievskoi Dukhovnoi Akademii*, 1866, no. 5: 13–14, 9–11.) As an initial measure he had in mind the establishment of some kind of Orthodox religious society in Ethiopia and offered to go there himself "in the capacity of a traveler and observer" if this met with the approval of his superiors. To his regret, however, his letter remained unanswered. (*Ibid.*: 10.)

August, 1866, in an article entitled "Russia's Role in the Destiny of Ethiopia."[35] The following year, Uspensky presented a memorandum along the same lines to the Holy Synod which became, according to Czeslaw Jesman, "the cornerstone of Russian ecclesiastical policy in Africa."[36]

Arguing that Ethiopians were qualified for the friendship of Russia by virtue of their long history, their distinguished culture and religion, their unified political status, and "above all [by virtue of] their struggles with the Mohammedans,"[37] Uspensky was convinced that Ethiopia offered the best possible base from which to launch a Christian civilizing mission in Africa. Since Christianity had already raised the people of Ethiopia above their barbarian neighbors, he maintained, that country could be looked to as a source of political as well as religious leadership for the rest of the African continent.

Briefly stated, Russia's task, according to Uspensky, was a three-fold one: to study all aspects of Ethiopia's national life; to prepare Ethiopia for political rapprochement with Russia; and, finally, to use Ethiopia as a base from which to disseminate the message of Orthodox Christianity throughout the interior of Africa.

According to his formula, the first practical steps toward an active relationship between Russia and Ethiopia would be essentially inves-tigative in nature. Russian missions to the country, he advised, should be extremely discrete so as not to attract the attention of the Egyp-tians and other hostile Arabs. By the same token, these missions should at all times be careful not to provoke unfriendly reactions on the part of European powers with diplomatic representation in Ethio-pia. As a preliminary move, Uspensky anticipated that the Russian government might simultaneously dispatch two lesser officials to Ethiopia. The first, sent as chargé d'affairs for a short period of time, could propose to the Ethiopian Emperor a political alliance and the exchange of plenipotentiary ambassadors. The second, traveling under the guise of tourism, could make a prolonged journey through-out the country and gather detailed information which would be useful to the Ministry of Foreign Affairs. This latter individual, pre-ferably enlisted from the ranks of minor Russian clergy, would be expected to ascertain such strategic items as which Red Sea ports belonged to Ethiopia and whether Emperor Theodore intended to obtain other outlets to the Indian Ocean. He might also learn some-thing of the political situation in the neighboring kingdoms of Black

Africa and collect data concerning the workings of the Ethiopian church.[38]

A primary objective of Russia's emissaries to Ethiopia would be to cultivate attitudes among Ethiopians which would be conducive to the development of a working Russo-Ethiopian entente. Indeed, the importance of Ethiopia as a potential ally of Russia was a central theme in Uspensky's writing. Not only had the country proven its internal political strength, but Ethiopia had demonstrated its ability to extend its influence beyond the confines of its original territorial patrimony. Already, he noted, the enterprising merchants of Harrar had established a network of trade routes into the interior of Africa which could well serve the interests of European penetration.[39] Moreover, Emperor Theodore II had shown remarkable energy in consolidating his power beyond Adowa. It only remained, therefore, for Russia to encourage this process and more specifically:

> to determine the strength and the religio-political aspirations of the kingdoms adjacent to Ethiopia—Adel, Senaar, Kordofan, Darfur, Kambat—and to help Abyssinia annex these kingdoms by providing (in case it is necessary and opportune) advice, arms and money in the interest of spreading Christian enlightenment inside Africa and linking Abyssinia with Timbuktu and Senegambia by means of railroads.[40]

Uspensky felt, moreover, that Russian policy should be aimed at preparing Ethiopia not only for a preeminent political role in the rest of Black Africa, but ultimately for the conquest of Egypt as well.[41]

In order to enhance Ethiopia's power and assist it in the accomplishment of so ambitious a task, Uspensky insisted that Russian policy give consistent support to the Ethiopian monarchy. In particular, he advised the Russian government to treat gifted members of the Ethiopian nobility with special kindness and to do everything possible to protect the family of the Negus (the Ethiopian Emperor). In addition, he suggested that it could help by training mining experts, foundrymen, and gunpowder specialists—in order that Ethiopia might be able to produce independently the implements of modern warfare. This type of assistance, Uspensky noted, Russia was particularly well qualified to give and the Ethiopians were especially anxious to receive.[42]

Thus, by the dispatch of investigative missions and by the extension of material support, Russia could expect to promote political rapprochement with Ethiopia. Such a rapprochement was to serve, in turn, as a foundation for the fulfillment of what Uspensky considered to be the most exalted aspect of Russia's threefold task in Africa— the dissemination of Orthodox Christianity. Indeed, to Uspensky, Russian investigative and political pursuits in Ethiopia were simply preliminary to the spiritual mission which he firmly regarded as Russia's highest calling in Africa.

The conduit for Russia's contribution to the evangelization of the Dark Continent was to be a "reunification" of the Russian and Ethiopian churches. According to such a plan, Ethiopia would establish a church hierarchy independent of the Egyptian Coptic church and fuse its eparchial line with that of Russia.[43] The Holy Synod would then be in a position "to veto" important decisions of the Ethiopian church and, in effect, to assume a controlling influence over the religious affairs of the country.[44] Finally, it was hoped, Russian guidance would serve to stimulate Ethiopian missionary work in the adjoining countries of central Africa.[45]

What were some of the factors which induced Uspensky to come forward in 1866 with his proposal for the development of an active Russo-Ethiopian relationship? By and large, they were related more to international politics than to strictly evangelical considerations. Uspensky's unfriendly references to the ambition of the British Bishop, Samuel Goba, to establish an Ethiopian Protestant church in Jerusalem and his jaundiced view of the attention given by Britain's Consul in Jerusalem to the Ethiopian community there suggest, for example, that the Russian interest in "reunification" awoke within the context of the general hostility then prevalent between Britain and Russia. Uspensky hardly disguised his opinion of the British, who, in his words, were "inclined to interfere everywhere and to provoke quarrels among everyone."[46] What provoked his most intense sarcasm, however, was their supposed interest in religious rapprochement with the Orthodox Ethiopians. "And so," he observed, "the children of Luther have started to pursue unification."[47]

Another development which appears to have prompted Uspensky's desire to see a Russian evangelization of Black Africa was the contemporary effort of the Roman Catholic church to win converts in the region. A mission appointed by Pope Gregory IV had recently established headquarters in Khartoum under the leadership of a certain Father Rylo. It aspired, according to Uspensky's understanding, to a sphere of activity which spanned the continent from Guinea to

Abyssinia.[48] Even more ominous, Father Rylo's mission was suspected in Russia of having political and commercial objectives.[49]

Certainly Uspensky was not likely to believe that other powers would be immune to the tendency to combine religious and political objectives which his own plans for Russian activity in Africa seemed to betray. The work of Roman Catholic and Protestant missionaries in Ethiopia during the first part of the nineteenth century and the activity of the European diplomats who followed in their footsteps called forth his careful scrutiny and, apparently, his apprehension. Such activities seemed, moreover, to arouse in him a thirst for competition. "France, England, Austria, and even Greece in our times have put out their hand to Christian Abyssinia," he observed—"should not Russia make friends with her?"[50] To Uspensky the answer to this question was clear: "Following the example of these leading powers, Russia must also establish a presence in Ethiopia."[51]

As plans progressed for the construction of the Suez Canal, European attention was attracted as never before to the entire vicinity of northeastern Africa, injecting an element of particular urgency into Uspensky's proposals. He was concerned, for example, about the danger of a "coming confrontation between England and France in the region of the Suez Isthmus and the Red Sea,"[52] and he undoubtedly understood that this rivalry over Suez had a bearing upon the newly awakened desire of European powers to "rush to Abyssinia."[53] Britain, in particular, had just appointed a permanent Consul General in Ethiopia, prompting Uspensky to observe: "There is reason to think that England, having occupied the Island of Perim which is located opposite Abyssinia, will soon turn that country [Ethiopia] into a warehouse for its products."[54]

Despite the intensified efforts of Britain, France, and other European powers to establish a foothold in Ethiopia in the 1860's, Uspensky nonetheless believed that Russia, by virtue of its Orthodox Christian faith, possessed a unique advantage in relation to these powers which it could successfully exploit in the emerging competition for power and influence in northeastern Africa. For a variety of reasons he felt that the time was particularly opportune for Russia to make use of its special position vis-à-vis Ethiopia.

In the first place, Uspensky was concerned that Ethiopia might fare badly in the scramble of European states for territory in northeastern Africa. Thus he felt it was a matter of some urgency that "a first-rate power [i.e. Russia], by foreseeing future events in the depths of Africa and by carefully manipulating them . . . [be in a position] to eliminate any difficulties [for Ethiopia] at a time when events could force her to rush to the gates of Alexandria or to the ports of Massawa."[55] As suggested in this passage, Uspensky was probably apprehensive lest the Ethiopians, encouraged by visions of Russian support, embark upon a premature war with Egypt. (He understood, for example, that Emperor Theodore had entertained a Syrian Greek who posed as an ambassador from the Russian Czar and that this had very nearly embroiled Ethiopia in a war with its Muslim neighbor.)[56]

A second and probably more important factor in Uspensky's reasoning was the reported desire of the Ethiopian Emperor "to strengthen the independence of the Abyssinian church from the Coptic Patriarch in Cairo and to establish a new [church] hierarchy."[57] According to Uspensky, "this circumstance" was "so propitious for the reunification of the Abyssinian church with ours that it behooves us to take advantage of it without delay."[58] "Given the identity of our faiths and the same bases in our church administrations," he confidently predicted, "the preponderance of influence over the Abyssinian church will fall to us."[59]

As a final consideration, Uspensky realized that through his work in Jerusalem, as well as through the work of his successor, Bishop Cyril, Russia had earned a good name among the Ethiopian clergy. He understood that the warm sentiments which the Ethiopian community in Jerusalem held for Russia had been communicated to the Ethiopian Emperor himself, and that Theodore "was anxious to receive an ambassador from Russia."[60] In short, the time was ripe for the inauguration of close ties—both ecclesiastical and diplomatic —between Russia and Ethiopia. And, in Uspensky's mind, the two clearly went hand in hand.

Coming at a time of budding strategic interest in Ethiopia and its surrounding territory, Uspensky's proposals for Russo-Ethiopian relations could only have been regarded as politically subversive by Great Britain. This would have been true, it might be added, even had the proposals been confined to lesser ecclesiastical matters. But Uspensky was, in effect, raising an issue of no smaller magnitude to Anglo-Russian relations than the virtual reorientation of Ethiopia's religious establishment toward Russia. Certainly the suspicion with which Britain regarded subsequent discussion of church reunification suggests that the British attitude toward this project was considerably less than accommodating.[61]

It was possibly out of fear of Britain's reaction that the Czarist government chose to make no direct political moves toward Ethiopia for another quarter century. The failure of Russia to embark upon immediate implementation of Uspensky's recommendations, however, does not detract materially from the importance of this ecclesiastical figure as the prophet of Czarist involvement in Africa. Certain features of his proposals were subsequently put into effect during the period of most intensive Russian contact with northeastern Africa. Moreover, in large part as a result of his efforts, the Holy Synod ultimately became the institution in Russia most eager for the establishment of close Russo-Ethiopian ties. Finally, perhaps Uspensky's most meaningful contribution to the development of Russian interest in Africa consisted in his having systematically developed the background of thought and information necessary for the subsequent establishment of political relations between St. Petersburg and Addis Ababa. However unrealistic were his hopes for Ethiopia's Christian mission in Africa, Uspensky's conviction that a strong Ethiopia would be a real asset to Russia was destined to become the touchstone of the Czarist government's policy in Africa.

The Emergence of Official Strategic Interest in Ethiopia

The government of Nicholas I (1825–55), which was obliged on more than one occasion to confront Egyptian troops in its battles with the Ottomans, developed an early interest in the military capabilities of Egypt's southern neighbors and frequent enemies, the Ethiopians.[62] Thus, when it received an appeal from Mohammed Ali of Egypt for a Russian mining engineer to assist him in the development of gold deposits along his southern frontier near Ethiopia, the Russian government weighed seriously the advantages of an uncharacteristically cooperative approach to the Egyptian ruler. As Foreign Minister Nesselrode observed to Vronchenko, the Imperial Minister of Finance, "a favorable response to the solicitation of Mohammed Ali would be entirely useful from a political standpoint and in addition would secure for our officer [of the engineering corps] the opportunity of penetrating a region little known to Europeans."[63] On the basis of such considerations, the government decided to comply with Mohammed Ali's request. Accordingly, in 1847, a "scientific expedition" under the leadership of Lieutenant Colonel E. P. Kovalevsky was dispatched to the Upper Nile (Eastern Sudan), thus launching Russia's first venture into Black Africa.

After successfully initiating operations at the gold deposits, Kovalevsky continued southward along a tributary of the Blue Nile, the Tumat River, into Ethiopia. There he was able to gather firsthand information concerning the country which had for so long been of interest to his government. Although Kovalevsky's observations undoubtedly did represent a contribution to general knowledge, he was no casual observer whose talents were dedicated solely to the service of universal science. Instead, Kovalevsky was one of a long line of Russian travelers to northeastern Africa, who, like Kokovstsov, were actually emissaries of a far more political character than either Imperial Russian or Soviet sources are inclined to disclose.

Kovalevsky's expedition, while it was ostensibly conducted under the auspices of the Imperial Russian Geographical Society, was essentially an official undertaking. In fact, the Society itself, although in theory independent of the government and primarily scientific in purpose, was in reality very much a creature of the Russian state. Established in 1845 with the cooperation of the Minister of the Interior, the Society, from its inception, received regular annual subsidies from the Imperial Treasury and cooperated closely with the research agencies of the Russian General Staff.[64] In addition, it enjoyed the patronage of members of the immediate family of the Czar as well as the advice of numerous prominent government officials, who served as its directors. (Kovalevsky himself served as Vice-Chairman of the Society between 1856 and 1862.)[65] In effect, identification with the Imperial Russian Geographical Society was one of the principal ways in which the political purposes of Russia's missions in Africa were camouflaged.

In Kovalevsky's case there was additional evidence to identify him as a political agent of the Russian government in Africa. He was known, prior to his departure for the Nile, to have "repeatedly carried out assignments of the Ministry of Foreign Affairs in a fully satisfactory manner."[66] While in Africa between 1847 and 1848, he remained in the pay of the Russian government, despite an offer on the part of the Egyptian government to support him.[67] Moreover, after returning to Russia and receiving a decoration from the Czar, he presented reports to Nicholas I describing "A Project for Russian Trade with Egypt" and "The Contemporary Political Situation in the Sudan and Abyssinia."[68] His identification with the Russian government's official interest in Africa is further suggested by his subsequent assumption of the directorship of the Asian Department of the Ministry of Foreign Affairs—the department which ultimately assumed responsibility for Russian involvement in Ethiopia.[69]

Whatever Kovalevsky's official status at the time of his visit to Africa, his contribution to the evolution of an African policy on the part of the Czarist government was a sizable one. As a result of his African experience, Kovalevsky was able, for example, to draw the attention of the Russian government to the commercial advantages of trading with northeastern Africa. Moreover, his observations concerning the capabilities of the two thousand Egyptian troops entrusted to his expedition by the Egyptian "Governor General of the Sudan" furnished the Russian government with new information for a comparative evaluation of Egyptian and Ethiopian military strength.[70] Finally, Kovalevsky's eyewitness accounts were an important source of information for Porfiry Uspensky in formulating his own proposals, not only with regard to commercial contacts with Ethiopia, but also with respect to Russia's Christianizing role in Black Africa.*

In the final analysis, however, Kovalevsky's most significant

---

* Uspensky met Kovalevsky in Bethlehem on August 18, 1848, when the latter was returning to Russia. After this meeting Uspensky noted in his diary: "His [Kovalevsky's] observations and opinions on these black tribes were useful to me in forming my own views." (Uspensky, *Kniga Bytiia Moego* [St. Petersburg, 1896]: 303.) Together they discussed whether Negroes were in fact inferior beings. Although Uspensky had been impressed with the Ethiopians, before the meeting with Kovalevsky he appeared to have shared the conviction then current in Europe that Negroes "because of [their] color could not have descended from Adam, but from a black creation of the Lord, created, along with the animals, earlier than this first man—as a transition between him and monkeys." (*Ibid.*: 308.) Kovalevsky, on the other hand, felt that this view was "incompatible with that brotherhood to which the words of the Gospel commend men." (Kovalevsky, *Puteshestvie vo Vnutrenniuiu Afriku* [2 vols.; St. Petersburg, 1849], II: 86.) Moreover, his comparatively detailed observations of Negroes in Africa led him to reject the notion that Negroes were physiologically inferior to Europeans and to deny the assumption that they had been altogether ignored by civilization. (*Ibid.*: 81–108. This section of Kovalevsky's book, together with the article "Negritsiia" ["Negritude"] which Kovalevsky published concurrently in the famous Russian liberal journal *Otechestvennye Zapiski* ["Notes of the Fatherland," vol. 62 (1849): 119ff.], contain what is probably the first systematic treatment of such racial issues in Russian.)

achievement was to launch Russia into the international competition to discover the sources of the Nile River—a geographical enigma which had, by the latter half of the nineteenth century, captured the imagination of all of Europe.

The energies of Europeans were drawn to the headwaters of the Nile by more than the simple romance of discovery. At least since the time of Herodotus, they had recognized the strategic importance of the sources of the river to which Egypt owed her livelihood. Emperor Nero had sent detachments of Roman soldiers upstream in a futile attempt to locate its origins. Albuquerque, the great Portuguese colonizer, had conceived of a plan to divert the Nile into the Red Sea in order to discourage other nations from approaching India through Egypt. In brief, as Alan Moorehead observes, "the idea that the Blue Nile might be blocked or poisoned at its source in Ethiopia as a means of destroying Egypt had been canvassed in every age."[71]

It is possible that an awareness of these strategic considerations was responsible for the Russian decision to send Kovalevsky to the Upper Nile. Several factors, in fact, suggest that this was the case. In the first place, Kovalevsky was entirely knowledgeable concerning earlier plans (including that of Albuquerque) to use the river as a strategic device. His account of his explorations supplies ample evidence that he fully understood the implications of a successful diversion of the Nile. Had this been accomplished, he observed, "it would not be so impossible for Egypt to be converted into a desert."[72]

In the second place, Kovalevsky's expedition appears to have been intentionally organized with an eye to acquainting Russia with the region of the Nile sources. Attached to the expedition was L. S. Tsenkovskii, who was assigned by the Russian Geographical Society to undertake a detailed geographical survey of the area.[73] Left by Kovalevsky in the region of the lower Blue Nile, Tsenkovskii spent some time exploring that river as well as the Nile's adjacent tributary, the Tumat. During his relatively prolonged sojourn in Africa, Tsenkovskii supplied the Russian Geographical Society with field reports, and, upon his return to Russia in 1850, reported to the organization in person.[74]

Finally, Kovalevsky's own accounts of the expedition suggest that one of its primary objectives was to solve the mystery of the Nile's yet unexplored sources. As he confessed, "my thoughts, my eyes [were] strained toward the south, to the sources of the White Nile, about which I heard from no one, regardless of all my questioning."[75] One of the first to suggest looking for major Nile sources in a south-westerly direction, Kovalevsky sought through his explorations in this area to dispel certain misconceptions concerning the status of the Niger River as a tributary of the Nile.[76] Although he was obliged to turn back before he was able to fulfill entirely his objective in this regard, he was successful in placing his own country's mark on the map of African discovery. As the first European to visit this particular region, he felt entitled to christen a small river near the Tumat the "Little Neva," and the area south of Fadasi (now in Ethiopia) "Nicholas country"—so that, in his words, the names "might serve as an indication of how far a European traveler had gone and to what nation he belonged."[77] Such patriotism, it might be observed, was not out of keeping with sentiment in Kovalevsky's native land. Indeed, in all probability Kovalevsky's African exploits provided the stimulus for the well-known Slavophile poet, Fedor Tiutchev, to include the Nile in the list of "Russian rivers" mentioned in his poem "Russian Geography."[78]

In sum, Kovalevsky's efforts, undertaken in the prevailing atmosphere of international competition, were an important element in encouraging subsequent interest in Africa on the part of the Czarist government. Not only was the information which he brought back from his travels of value to Russia's military strategists, but his experiences fostered enthusiasm for Africa on the part of Russian observers in commercial, ecclesiastical, and cultural circles as well. Although Kovalevsky himself was not successful in transversing the African continent or in satisfying his country's curiosity concerning the sources of the Nile River, the spirit of competitive adventurism which he helped to spark was an important ingredient in persuading Russians in the 1890's to take up once more the banner of African exploration.*

---

* Kovalevsky's call for the exploration of Africa did in fact evoke an immediate response on the part of V. V. Junker, who undertook an excursion along the Blue Nile in 1876 and contributed valuable ethnological observations concerning certain tribes in the neighboring regions. It is particularly interesting that Junker obtained, as did few other Europeans, a firsthand exposure to the political developments which shook this part of Africa during the 1880's. Not only did he have an opportunity to meet Gordon, the famous Governor General of the Sudan, but he visited Gordon's fort on the Sobat River—a point of considerable strategic importance during the following decade. (See Junker's travel diaries, *Puteshestviia V. V. IUunkera po Afrike*, edited by E. IU. Petri [St. Petersburg, 1893]: 68ff.)

While it can be said that Czarist interest in the discovery of the Nile's sources was enhanced by Kovalevsky's travels in Africa, it must be pointed out that this interest was primarily a product, not of Russian exploration, but of British activity in the Nile region. Since the seventeenth century England had been aware of the strategic importance of Ethiopia's position astride the headwaters of the Blue Nile, the best known of the Nile sources.[79] With the intensification of British involvement in Egypt in the mid-nineteenth century and the beginning of construction on the Suez Canal in the 1860's, Britain's interest in Ethiopia was inevitably renewed. As Alan Moorehead observes, "now, less than ever, could England afford to have an enemy in control of Ethiopia and the Red Sea ports."[80] As a result of such considerations, Captain Charles Cameron of the Indian Service was sent to Ethiopia in 1862 to suggest a treaty of friendship to Emperor Theodore. The same year, Samuel Baker was making his celebrated explorations along the great river.

Russians were certainly not immune to the general fascination with the Nile which prevailed in Europe after the publication of Baker's study, *The Nile Tributaries of Abyssinia*. Just as they did among Western Europeans, Baker's findings awakened among Russians a general recognition of the importance of the Nile basin. His publications were reproduced in numerous Russian editions, and his experiences as Governor General of Equatoria and as leader of the Egyptian expedition "to curtail the slave trade in the Sudan" were followed with particular attention in Russia.[81]

Lord Napier's expedition to Ethiopia in 1867–68, ostensibly to rescue British Consul Cameron from incarceration at the hands of "mad" Emperor Theodore, was the subject of even closer Russian surveillance. Three comprehensive articles covering "The March of the English into Abyssinia" appeared in 1870–71 issues of *Voennyi Sbornik*, a journal published under the supervision of the Ministry of War and edited by Lieutenant General Men'kov of the Russian General Staff.[82] Although these articles dealt primarily with questions of tactics, they did indicate that the strategic lessons of Lord Napier's enterprise were not lost upon Russian military planners.

Indeed, it was apparent that Lord Napier had accomplished far more than the rescue of Britain's Consul in Ethiopia. By defeating Theodore at the Battle of Magdala (1868), he had virtually eliminated all effective resistance to British expansion up the Nile Valley and had opened up the possibility of future British control over Ethiopia. In light of Britain's growing stake in Egypt, this was decidedly an important achievement. Like the hegemons of ancient times, the masters of "modern Egypt" had come to realize that the foundations of their power rested upon their ability to control the flow of the Nile.

If the British were thus conscious of the need to extend their influence into Ethiopia and the regions south of Egypt, it seems safe to assume that the Russian government was aware of the wider strategic significance of the British government's Ethiopian maneuvers. In the course of the nineteenth century, Britain had in fact come to supplant Turkey as Russia's principal imperial adversary. While the power of the Ottomans steadily declined, Britain was forging the world's mightiest empire—notably in the coveted realm of India. In addition to inspiring the imperial jealousy of Russia, Britain had won Russia's enmity with its victory over Czarist forces in the Crimean War (1854–56). When, therefore, British attention turned to northeastern Africa as a critical midpoint in the imperial chain between Britain and India, Russian eyes inevitably followed.

In effect, rivalry with Britain provided the crucible in which Russia's active involvement in northeastern Africa was prepared. The marked increase in Anglo-Russian hostility which became apparent in the years following the opening of the Suez Canal in 1869 constituted, in fact, the primary stimulus for Russian efforts to establish relations with Ethiopia at the end of the nineteenth century. During the twenty-year period ending in 1889 two factors combined to produce this unprecedented Russian concern for the politics of northeastern Africa. The first was Britain's success in establishing suzerainty over Egypt and in seizing effective control over the Suez Canal. The second was the British failure to defeat the forces of the Mahdi at Khartoum and the consequent Czarist desire to exploit Britain's weakness in Africa in order to strengthen the Russian position in Central Asia.

The importance of the Suez Canal to Russia and the role of the waterway in Russia's growing hostility toward Britain should not be underestimated. A strong supporter of the Suez project when it was initiated as a French undertaking,* the Russian government was

---

* The French canal builder, de Lesseps, was enthusiastically received in Russia in 1858 when he traveled to Odessa to obtain support for his plan for the Suez Canal. Not only did Russians purchase shares in his canal company and elect

eager to take advantage of the benefits which the shorter route to India provided. From a commercial point of view the significance of the canal was overwhelming. At one stroke the distance between Odessa and Bombay was reduced by seventy percent. Finding themselves in a position to compete favorably with British enterprises in supplying Indian cotton and Chinese tea to Russian markets, Russian steamship lines extended their route to Bombay and Shanghai, making Russia by 1871 the eighth largest client of the canal.[83] Even more important than its commercial value, however, was the strategic function of the Suez Canal in linking Russia's European and Asiatic extremities. With the expansion of Russian influence into the Far East during the mid-nineteenth century, there was a commensurate increase in the demand for an efficient means of transcontinental communication.[84] In brief, the dramatic maritime shortcut through Suez at once satisfied both the commercial demand for improved access to India and the strategic need to enhance the integrity of the far-flung Russian empire.

In light of such considerations it was understandable that Russia would not accept with equanimity Britain's purchase of a controlling share in the Suez enterprise in 1875. The British themselves were uneasy about the possibility of an adverse Russian response to Disraeli's Egyptian coup. In fact public opinion in England was inclined to regard the canal purchase both as an insurance against a takeover by Russia and as a barrier to the eastward shipment of Russian arms.[85] Whether or not he shared such views, Disraeli was probably aware that the Russian government might well see the canal purchase as another move in the Anglo-Russian maritime contest initiated by the

---

one of their compatriots to its board of directors, but they seemed fully aware of the commercial advantages which they would realize upon completion of the Suez project. (D. A. Farnie, *East and West of Suez* [Oxford, 1969]: 51.) Further evidence of Russian enthusiasm for the canal was the presence at the opening ceremonies of several members of the Czar's family, a score of Russian diplomatic observers, and representatives of Russian commercial interests. (See D. A. Skal'kovskii, *Suezskii Kanal i Ego Znachenie dlia Russkoi Torgovli* [St. Petersburg, 1870]: 197–207, 316, and Vladimir Sollogub, *Novyi Egipet* [St. Petersburg, 1871]: 159, both of whom represented Russia at the opening of the canal.) According to Cox ("Khedive Ismail and Panslavism," *Slavonic and East European Review*, December, 1953: 159), Czar Alexander II also sent his brother, Grand Duke Michael, to the inauguration ceremonies. Farnie (*op. cit.*: 150) notes, moreover, that Grand Duke Nicholas, although ostensibly traveling incognito, made a visit which amounted to a "royal procession" and that in 1872 Grand Duke Alexis became the first European prince to travel through the canal.

Crimean War—a kind of retaliation for Russia's renunciation of the Black Sea clause of the Treaty of Paris.*

In this context, the presence in Egypt of a Russian general named Fadeyev provoked particular anxiety on the part of the British government. At the very moment that England's strategic interest in Egypt was reaching full bloom, here was a Russian who was not only an influential military advisor to the Khedive, but a potential commander in chief of the Egyptian army.[86] Although the British may have been correct in assuming that the primary purpose of Fadeyev's mission was to frustrate their growing position of power in Egypt,[87] they could not conclude that this was the sole reason for the Russian general's presence at the court of the Khedive. Instead, Fadeyev's efforts appear to have been simultaneously directed toward the traditional Russian aim of inciting Egyptian revolt against the Turks. On this occasion the attempted subversion of the Ottoman Empire through Egypt proved scarcely more successful than it had in the days of Baron de Thonus. The utter failure of the Russian move became dramatically apparent with the advent of the Russo-Turkish War of 1877, in the course of which Russia was obliged to witness the use by its enemy of a sizable contingent of Egyptian troops.[88]

It was this same conflict which first brought to prominence the question of the international legal status of the Suez Canal and inspired new awareness in Europe of the waterway's strategic importance in international politics. For the Czarist government, the conflict meant the realization of its worst fears regarding Suez: just when Russia was becoming one of the canal's principal clients, the locks clanged shut, forcing the virtual suspension of Russian use of the new route to the east.[89] Although the first British warning requested only that Russia exclude the canal from the arena of military operations, subsequent measures taken by the Khedive in accordance with the wishes of England resulted in the denial of entry to all Russian vessels.[90]

Thus, the Russo-Turkish War of 1877–78 served to convince the

---

* Britain seemed particularly concerned lest Russia in some way sabotage the canal. Thus when an Armenian with a chest of dynamite was arrested by Egyptian authorities, the British associated this plot with subversive Russian intentions. (See "Russia. 'Lock Ahoy!'," *Punch*, June 16, 1877: 271.) This and similar episodes explain Britain's heightened interest in canal security after 1877.

Czarist government that free access to the Suez Canal was indeed vital to Russian national security. Despite its insistence that no foreign power should exercize unilateral control over a waterway of such "extreme importance for Russia's maritime connections with the Far East,"[91] however, the Imperial government lacked effective power to prevent Britain from progressively establishing control over Suez. Undisputed British authority over the canal was attained in July, 1882, with the advent of British military occupation of Egypt. Although Russia and France were able in the Constantinople Convention of 1888 to force Britain to recognize both the neutrality of the canal and its inclusion within the sphere of Egyptian sovereignty, it was nonetheless painfully apparent, as the Russian Foreign Minister Lobanov-Rostovsky observed in 1896, that "passage [through Suez will] depend upon the goodwill of England as long as she occupies Egypt."[92]

If Britain was largely successful in establishing its power in Egypt, the same cannot be said of British efforts in Central Asia and the Sudan. During the early 1880's, while English forces were tied down along the banks of the Nile, Russians had begun to move southward toward India, and by 1884 had gone so far as to capture the Merv Oasis on the border of Afghanistan.[93] Following closely upon the heels of this Russian victory came news in 1885 of General Gordon's defeat by the forces of the Mahdi at Khartoum. As Queen Victoria herself became "ill" with indignation, statesmen everywhere began to question the extent of Britain's imperial resources and the depth of its imperial resolve. Gladstone's government, in part out of fear of exposing Britain's flank to Russia in Afghanistan, was unwilling to save the British position in the Sudan. After an inconclusive move from Suakin against the rear of the Mahdi's forces, most British troops were withdrawn from the southern coast of the Red Sea. The Italian occupation of the Eritrean port of Massawa was then promoted by the British government in hopes that through the efforts of a friendly power Britain could secure by proxy what it had failed to achieve by more direct means.

The withdrawal of British troops from the Red Sea served to redirect Russian attention to north eastern Africa as an area from which to threaten British imperial strength. Indeed, if the English could see the strategic link between Afghanistan and Eritrea, so could the Russians. In many ways the Red Sea coast provided an inviting alternative to the geographically arduous path toward India via Merv and Herat. Certainly it provided a valuable strategic location for sabotaging the British position in Egypt and for interfering with Britain's all-important line of communication with India.* Neighboring Ethiopia, moreover, which was known to be kindly disposed toward Russia, possessed similar strategic attributes—an historically recognized potential for threatening Egypt and geographical proximity to the Suez route. As the Berlin correspondent for *Moskovskiia Viedomosti* put it, "a reawakened Abyssinia could become a watchman for the southern gates of the Red Sea."[94] Thus Ethiopia and the surrounding territories promised to become an area in which Russia's anti-British maneuvers might find political and strategic rewards. As such, this area was destined to provide the stage for Russia's first entrance into the politics of sub-Saharan Africa.

---

* In this connection it is interesting to note that Czar Alexander III (1881–1894) was not above serious consideration of a fantastic anti-British scheme whereby the Suez Canal would be filled in, fresh water would be diverted from the capital of Egypt, 100,000 Sudanese tribesmen would be sent into action, and India and Afghanistan would be provoked into rebellion. (See diplomatic dispatch from Russian Ambassador in Constantinople, A. I. Nelidov, cited in V. N. Lamsdorff, *Dnevnik* ["*Diary*"], *1886–1890* [Moscow, 1926]: 108.)

2

Imperial Intrigue in Sub-Saharan
Africa: 1889-1917

THE DEVELOPMENT OF RUSSIA'S POLITICAL STAKE
IN NORTHEASTERN AFRICA

The Ashinov Expedition to Ethiopia: 1888–1889
In this climate of international competition the man most responsible
for initiating active Russian involvement in northeastern Africa
made his appearance on the African scene. This Russian, a Cossack
named N. I. Ashinov, was only the first in a series of Russian officers
who led expeditions to Ethiopia at the end of the nineteenth century.
Yet his activity between 1888 and 1889 as promoter of an abortive
attempt to establish a "New Moscow" at the mouth of the Red Sea
constituted the real starting point for Russia's sub-Saharan enterprises.*

However frequently Ashinov has been depicted by his detractors
as an ignorant adventurer, there is good reason to believe that he was
personally very much aware of the wider international political setting and the strategic factors which surrounded his African project.
Even before his expedition had set forth for Tajura Bay (the proposed
location of New Moscow), Ashinov had advanced a series of appealing strategic arguments for Russian involvement in the northeastern

---

* Ashinov had made a previous visit to northeastern Africa, arriving in Massawa
in 1885. The circumstances surrounding this earlier expedition suggest its basically political character. Not only were Ashinov's relations with the newly
arrived Italians of a very unfriendly nature, he lost little time in making contact
with the Mahdists. According to one source, Ashinov was able to meet personally
with Osman Digna, the Mahdi's principal lieutenant and empire builder in the
eastern Sudan. This account even suggests that Ashinov went so far as to act as
an intermediary in an attempt to establish direct relations between the Mahdi
and the Czar, returning to Russia carrying gifts from the Sudanese leader and
in the company of a Sudanese sheik. The same source reports that while in
Africa, Ashinov received an official commission from Emperor Johannes IV of
Ethiopia to obtain modern weapons for the Ethiopian army—an undertaking
assumed by a number of subsequent Russian visitors to Ethiopia. (Vicomte de
Constantin, "Une Expédition Réligieuse en Abyssinie," *Nouvelle Revue*, February
1, 1891: 464–65.)

corner of the continent. First, a Russian presence on the Suez route would serve as a threat to Britain and as security for passage between eastern and western Russia. Second, a favorable Russian position at the mouth of the Red Sea might somehow be used as a bargaining point for promoting Russian interests on the Bosphorus. Finally, a Russian port at Tajura Bay would provide a point of departure from which future Russian contacts with Ethiopia could be developed. In particular, Russia could, from this sanctuary, strengthen Ethiopia and, in turn, rely upon that country to oppose the British, both in the Red Sea region and in the interior of the African continent.[1]

Ashinov seemed to envisage a joint Franco-Russian effort which would fortify the Ethiopian state as a bulwark against the advance of Britain and Italy. As Ashinov made final preparations for his colonial expedition in 1888, it became apparent that he intended to obtain, with the help of French financiers, modern armaments for Ethiopia in quantities hitherto unknown in northeastern Africa.[2] This threatened to have a significant effect on the balance of power in the region. In a statement made in 1888 at Nizhni Novgorod, Ashinov described the strategic effect these arms would ideally produce. "The Negus," he explained, "thus empowered by Russia and France, will succeed in uniting the peoples of Africa and in blocking the path of Anglo-Italian movement."[3]

Ashinov's ideas coincided with significant currents of opinion within Russia. The notion of a shift of interest from the Balkans to Africa appealed to many Slavophiles, who were becoming increasingly frustrated with the pace of Russian expansion southward toward the Bosphorus.[4] His thinking, moreover, was developed at a time of intensified Russian concern over British control of the Suez Canal—demonstrated by the Imperial government's lobbying effort in behalf of the Suez Canal Convention of 1888. Furthermore, the Ashinov scheme was devised during a period when many people in both France and Russia were awakening to the importance of "creating at the heart of the Red Sea an independent and civilized nation [Ethiopia], capable of being the guardian of a straits which must henceforth play in the policy of the maritime powers a role no less considerable than that of the Bosphorus and the Dardanelles."[5]

The popularity of Ashinov's ideas explains in large part the surprising degree of support accorded his ambitious African project.

Sympathy for Ashinov was to be found not only among Russian Slavophiles, but within the very highest circles of the Imperial Russian government.

Official interest in Ashinov's plans was aroused after his preliminary visit to Eritrea and Ethiopia in 1888. Leaving six Russians and a temporary encampment at Tajura Bay,[6] Ashinov returned to Russia escorting two Ethiopian priests who had come to attend the 900th anniversary celebration of Russian Christianity. Constantine Pobedonostsev, Procurator of the Holy Synod and Alexander III's most influential advisor, received this delegation. Realizing that Ethiopia had "since olden times . . . maintained itself in Eastern Christianity," and had long "nourished a sympathy for Russia," Pobedonostsev urged his sovereign to see Ashinov and the Ethiopians himself.[7] In so counseling the Czar, it appeared that Pobedonostsev was making more than purely religious calculations. His letter to Alexander included the following observation:

> As regards Ashinov he is of course an adventurist, but in the present circumstances he serves as the sole Russian person to have penetrated Abyssinia. [Pobedonostsev was apparently ignorant of Kovalevsky's travels.] It would be worth at least seriously questioning him in order to hear, in his own words, about that enterprise which he has already initiated on the banks of the Red Sea. By all indications it can have for us no little importance . . . In such enterprises the most convenient tools are cutthroats of the likes of Ashinov.[8]

Alexander complied with Pobedonostsev's advice and granted an audience to the unusual delegation. At approximately the same time, the Czar received a proposal which would have drawn him even further into Ashinov's schemes. This proposal came from N. M. Baranov, Governor General of Nizhni Novgorod and an enthusiastic supporter of Ashinov. Baranov urged the Czar to support the formation of a "Russo-African Company" along the lines of the colonial enterprises of other European powers. Using a fortified Russian settlement at Tajura as a base, the company, it was hoped, would be in a position to exploit the economic resources of the region.[9]

According to Baranov's plan, the Czar could reap his reward for assisting the enterprise by taking control, at a politically appropriate moment, of all military, naval, and administrative functions of the Tajura colony.[10] Such a policy, in the opinion of Baranov, promised certain strategic advantages for Russia in its struggle against the

British. "At a time when nearly all governments, one after another, and often at great sacrifice . . . are striving to seize points along the African coast," he observed, "a handful of Russian Cossacks occupied the shore of Tajura Bay, recognizing not only the geographical, but particularly the strategic importance of this bay in the event of war with England."[11]

Baranov's request for Imperial authorization to form a Russo-African Company was forwarded to Alexander by Pobedonostsev on October 9, 1888, eliciting from the Russian sovereign the response, "I will see what can be done about this."[12] Apparently the Czar was sufficiently interested in the military implications of the scheme to seek the opinion of his Minister of the Navy, Admiral Shestakov.[13] The latter, for his part, seemed to be sympathetic to the project, but advised that before commencing any governmental involvement at Tajura Bay, it would be necessary to send some reliable Russian sailor to familiarize himself with the situation existing there.[14] According to Jesman, Shestakov ultimately supported the endeavor to the extent that he sent a Russian gunboat to the Red Sea in order to give naval protection to Russia's colonists.[15]

It is interesting to note that these preliminary attempts to establish a direct Russian stake in Africa were made in the face of the most persistent opposition on the part of the Foreign Ministry. Foreign Minister de Giers and the officials directly responsible to him feared the adverse reactions which Ashinov's schemes might create on the part of European powers which had interests in the Tajura region. In particular, they were concerned about the attitude of France, whose budding friendship with Russia was being assiduously cultivated. Thus, from the outset, Russia's official diplomatic establishment made repeated attempts to discredit Ashinov and to prevent him from reaching the Czar.[16]

The voices of caution within the government, however, clearly lacked sufficient power to prevent the Russian sovereign from heeding the call of the expansionists. One suspects, in fact, that Alexander III shared to a certain extent the sympathies then prevalent among the higher commercial and ecclesiastical circles in Russian society. In any event, it was difficult for him to ignore and impossible for him to repudiate the current of Slavophile sentiment which existed within Russia. This broad wave of nationalist zeal, which held Orthodoxy to be Russia's unique gift to humanity, was the moving spirit behind

Great Russian expansion during the latter part of the nineteenth century.

Slavophilism also appeared to be guiding Russian energies in the direction of Africa as it stimulated the revival of Russian projects in the Holy Land during this period.[17] After the disastrous defeat of Russian diplomacy and military strategy in the Crimean War, the Imperial Russian government came increasingly to rely upon the efforts of Slavophiles to advance its interests in the Middle East. Ostensibly nonpolitical Slavophile bodies such as the Slavonic Society and the Palestine Society began to be used by the Russian government for the most purely political of purposes.[18] Religion, never free from politics, saw increasing service as a cloak for the foreign policy maneuvers of the Russian state.

Such was the context within which Ashinov's projects must be viewed. At the time these projects received their most serious consideration by the Russian government, Slavophiles were taking their turn at the helm of Russian policy. It is important to note that the Palestine Society, headed by the Czar's brother, Slavophile Grand Duke Sergei Alexandrovich, actually collected the funds which made it possible for Ashinov and 175 Russian settlers to set sail from Odessa in December, 1888, bound for Africa.[19] In brief, the colonization of northeastern Africa had become simply another, although admittedly one of the most ambitious, of Slavophilism's expansionist plans for Russia.

No one was more thoroughly identified with the Ashinov expedition than was the most prominent Slavophile of his day, Pobedonostsev.[20] By arranging for the expedition to include a spiritual mission, he was responsible for endowing it with a mantle of religious respectability.[21] The Procurator of the Holy Synod evidently took a personal hand in selecting the individual who was to lead this mission, Father Paissi.[22] The political interests and background of this priest* suggest moreover, that Pobedonostsev was acting in

---

* Father Paissi was one whose past hardly inclined him toward uniquely spiritual pursuits. At his previous post in Constantinople, where he had looked after Russian pilgrims on their way to the Holy Land, Father Paissi had been looked upon as "Russia's guardian at the gates of the Orient"—a title he had earned as much by his behavior as by his position. At the time of the Russo-Turkish War of 1877–78, for example, this pious figure "seemed to forget his cloth and, recalling his Cossack valour, stood ready to guide Russian columns in case they stormed Istanbul." (F. Volgin, *V Strane Chernykh Khristian* [St. Petersburg, 1895]: 59–60.)

accordance with the political orientation which had characterized Uspensky's original conception of Russian ecclesiastical contacts with Ethiopia.

Given the enthusiasm of Russian Slavophiles for Ashinov, the Czar must surely have been tempted indeed to give his endorsement to the Tajura project. Daring Russian exploits in an exotic portion of the globe offered real promise of rendering a service to the throne if only by capturing the popular imagination and diverting it from the dangerous pathways of revolution. Yet despite the encouragement given to Ashinov by members of the Imperial family and the enthusiasm for his cause displayed by Pobedonostsev and other Slavophile members of the Imperial cabinet, Alexander's attitude remained one of caution. Whether it was by instinct, or by virtue of warnings given him by the Foreign Ministry, the Czar retained a healthy suspicion of the adventurous Cossack. On January 12, 1889, he observed to Pobedonostsev: "I think this sly old fox Ashinov will dupe everyone, rob everyone, and throw them out."[23]

But what is perhaps more interesting is that Alexander appeared to be highly reluctant to make any move which would interfere with the realization of Ashinov's schemes. Although he probably had small hope for its success, the Czar seemed quite content to adopt a wait-and-see attitude with regard to Ashinov's project. Such behavior clearly invites speculation as to the possible Russian response had something substantial materialized at Tajura Bay. It is possible that in such an event, the government might have assumed leadership over the enterprise, developing it along the lines anticipated by Governor Baranov.

History, however, was to decide otherwise. Russian Slavophiles displayed a dangerous ignorance of the workings of European colonialism when they argued that so modest a colonial beginning as the occupation of a site in Africa by a band of Cossacks was unlikely to arouse the suspicions of other powers.[24] Both Britain and Italy were overtly hostile to Ashinov's schemes from the start. Not only did their diplomatic representatives in St. Petersburg make repeated efforts to prevent the embarkation of the New Moscow expedition, but once the Russians had arrived in the Red Sea the Italians managed to follow them with gunboats and even to plant a spy in their midst.[25]

Apparently the governments of Italy and Britain, with stakes of their own in the region, were uneasy about the possibility of Russian colonial ventures along the Red Sea coast. What seemed to cause them equal disquietude was the thought of new arms shipments being made to indigenous African forces—especially of the variety which Ashinov intended to make to Ethiopia. The convening of the Brussels Conference of 1888–89, where France and Russia were asked to join a general restriction on arms deliveries to Africa, was probably prompted by such considerations. It is also likely that the same motivation induced Britain and Italy to remind France of its territorial claims in the vicinity of Tajura and to urge the French to deal harshly with Ashinov and his settlers.[26]

France, however, was a potential supporter of the Russian expedition. Not only had Ashinov been careful to echo pro-French sentiments, but his political ambitions in northeastern Africa coincided in many ways with those of the Third Republic. This coincidence of purpose might best be explained in terms of the community of interests which was emerging in Franco-Russian relations at the end of the 1880's. During this decade both powers were forced to witness the consolidation of the British route to India and to endure the frustration of having their Mediterranean projects blocked by Britain and the Triple Alliance. France and Russia had discovered an equally fundamental bond in the hostility they shared toward British power in Asia. By August, 1891, therefore, the two powers allowed their friendship to develop into an acknowledged entente. This was sealed in January, 1894, by the conclusion of a formal military alliance.[27]

By aligning itself with France, the Czarist government was able to benefit from France's far-flung territorial rivalry with Britain. With the help of the French, the Russian government was in a position to threaten the British, knowing that "with the Russians in the Pamirs and the French on the Mekong, India was indeed caught between two fires."[28] Other terrain for anti-British maneuvers was also opened to Russian foreign policy. Northeast Africa was a conspicuous case in point. Indeed, the political fact of Franco-Russian amity underlies the entire record of Imperial Russian involvement in Ethiopia and the region surrounding the mouth of the Red Sea.

Although there was no Franco-Russian alliance when Ashinov came to Paris in 1888 seeking support for his African projects, French political sympathies were already well enough established to ensure a warm reception for this Russian traveler. According to one source, the French cabinet even discussed the idea of giving some kind of assistance to Ashinov's expedition.[29] No decision to this effect was taken but the government of France, like that of the Czar, appears to have been at least initially willing to reserve judgment on the Cossack.[30]

In 1862 France had occupied Obok, a port on Tajura Bay, and by 1888 it was actively extending its jurisdiction among the Somali tribes along the coast. Although it had significant territorial interests in the area, France, through its authorities in Obok, apparently offered no interference when Ashinov's party disembarked and began to occupy an abandoned fortress at nearby Sagallo. It seemed that as long as Ashinov was willing to recognize France's ultimate sovereignty in the region, these authorities were prepared to leave him in peace and to allow him to proceed with the construction of New Moscow.[31] When, however, Ashinov balked on the critical issue of raising a French flag over the establishment and implied to French officials that he recognized only the authority of the local Danakil chieftain, Mohammed Leita, with whom he had independently established friendly relations,* suspicions were aroused.[32] Thus, the sovereignty-conscious French, fearing competitive encroachments in the area, probably took the first available opportunity to protest to the Russian government.

At this juncture it became apparent that the fears of Foreign Minister de Giers had in fact materialized. In light of Ashinov's apparent readiness to defy France, the Russian government realized that any further identification with the Cossack was apt to prove highly embarrassing. It therefore instructed its Chargé d'Affairs in Paris to inform the French Foreign Minister that the Russian government "was absolutely not privy to Ashinov's adventure, which was

---

* Members of Ashinov's party were obviously inclined to doubt French claims to the territory surrounding Sagallo. They failed to observe "any indications of an actual protectorate" there and tended to regard the local sultan as "an independent sovereign." (L. Nikolaev, *Ashinovskaia Ekspeditsiia* [Odessa, 1889]: 32f.) Friendly relations with this sultan had been established in the course of Ashinov's visit to the area early in 1888. The Russians who remained at Tajura until the arrival of the settlers the following year appear to have maintained friendly relations with the Danakil leader, who seemed to be anxiously awaiting the return of Ashinov. It is possible that the two had agreed to trade a certain amount of territory in the mountains above Sagallo in return for Russian rifles. One of the members of the expedition, Nikolaev, asserts that this is what Ashinov told his followers. (*Ibid.*: 33f.) When the Russians subsequently became embroiled with the French naval forces at Sagallo, Leita reportedly offered to come to their support with 500 of his tribesmen. (*Ibid.*: 54.)

conducted on his own responsibility and at his own risk," that it was "entirely ignorant" of the agreement Ashinov reportedly signed with the local authorities concerning Sagallo, and that if the locality fell "under the protectorate of France," then Ashinov would have to "submit" to the laws existing there.[33] Foreign Minister de Giers also found an opportunity to inform the French Ambassador in St. Petersburg that Russia would find it "natural and legitimate" for France to take measures to assert its rights vis-à-vis Ashinov.[34]

Czar Alexander, who at the outset had not seemed overly concerned that Ashinov might provoke the French in Obok, was soon receiving reports of the Cossack's misbehavior both from his ambassador in Paris and from officers in his own navy.[35] Quickly coming around to de Giers' point of view, the Czar decided that it was "absolutely necessary to pull this beast Ashinov out of there [Tajura] as soon as possible."[36] Accordingly, it was resolved that a Russian gunboat should proceed to Tajura Bay to retrieve Russia's knight errant.[37]

The diplomatic correspondence between Russia and France indicates that the latter was perfectly willing to allow Russia to discipline Ashinov.[38] It is understandable, however, that France interpreted de Giers' earlier assurances as an indication that Russia would not stand in the way should French forces undertake the forcible expulsion of the Cossack. Orders were therefore issued to Admiral Orly's Red Sea squadron to do so.[39] These orders were hurriedly countermanded when it was learned that the Russians had decided to deal with Ashinov themselves.[40] Ironically, the Russian decision was not communicated to the French Foreign Minister until February 17, 1889, the day on which Admiral Orly bombarded New Moscow, killing several Russian settlers and abruptly ending Russia's only colonial venture in Africa.[41]

What significance did the Ashinov expedition hold for the future of Imperial Russia's involvement in northeastern Africa? What were the political implications of this shooting incident between French and Russians on African shores?

Perhaps the most conspicious result of the Sagallo incident was its effect on relations between France and Russia. Contrary to the opinion of Jesman,[42] the Ashinov affair did not constitute a serious threat to the new entente between the two powers. As French diplomatic sources clearly reveal, the only real problem between the two governments was one of communications. Not only had France and Russia virtually agreed upon a common policy with regard to Ashinov before the incident occurred, but their behavior in the course of Sagallo's aftermath was the very model of accommodation and amity.

The Czar personally harbored little sympathy for the unsuccessful Ashinov. Upon hearing the news of Sagallo, he pronounced it "a sad and stupid comedy."[43] More important, Alexander insisted publicly that Ashinov, and not the French authorities in Obok, should bear the responsibility for the affair. He went so far as to authorize his government to publish an official statement which recognized French sovereignty over Sagallo and which reaffirmed the opinion that the French had acted entirely within their rights in forcing Ashinov to respect the laws of the locality.[44] No effort was spared to make known the Russian government's disgust with Ashinov and to expose him as a useless ruffian.[45]

The government of France was equally prompt and solicitous in its pronouncements. Regrets were hurriedly expressed to the Russians for the loss of life, and the French National Assembly even took the unusual step of passing a vote of sympathy.[46] In order to repair as much damage as possible, the French were quick to draw the distinction between their opposition to Ashinov and their attitude toward the Russian spiritual mission. So as to emphasize their friendly disposition toward the latter, French authorities in Obok reportedly offered Father Paissi a caravan to facilitate his voyage to Ethiopia.[47]

In sum, there is good reason to believe that the net result of Sagallo was to enhance Franco-Russian amity. Given the cooperative and obliging manner in which the issue was treated by both powers, it is possible to regard the Ashinov affair as a successful test of the viability of the Franco-Russian rapprochement. As such it did much to create a favorable climate for the close Franco-Russian cooperation which characterized the entire record of Imperial Russian involvement in north eastern Africa.

However fortunate its final outcome may have been in terms of relations with France, internally, the Russian government's experience with Ashinov was largely an unsettling one. For one thing, it brought into focus the startling lack of concert among the various branches of the Russian government involved with the country's foreign relations. To the consternation of the Russian Foreign

Ministry, other administrative units such as the Ministries of War and the Navy were embarking upon relatively independent policies, and even semi-official bodies such as the Palestine Society were acting as autonomous agents, promoting an entire series of Slavophile intrigues in the Middle East. To more than one high official of the Foreign Ministry, the Ashinov episode was sad evidence that "we have departments, but not a government."[48]

At the same time the failure of the Ashinov enterprise did appear to vindicate the position of the Foreign Ministry and to represent a significant defeat for the Slavophiles. This failure was a source of acute personal embarrassment to Pobedonostsev who had strongly supported Ashinov.[49] The Procurator did further damage to his standing within the Imperial government by spuriously denying that he had had any hand whatsoever in the Ashinov affair and by attempting to lay blame at the feet of General Richter and the late Admiral Shestakov.[50]

Yet, by promoting Ashinov's expedition, the Slavophiles were responsible for bringing northeastern Africa into the realm of Russian public consciousness in a way they might scarcely have anticipated. When Russian blood was spilled on African soil, the region inevitably acquired new and special status in the eyes of the Russian public. To some, Ashinov suddenly became a hero, a true Russian "patriot" who had made "valiant efforts to establish close relations with Abyssinia."[51] Other influential Russians, who wished for no repetition of the Ashinov experience, nonetheless held hopes for Father Paissi's continued progress toward Ethiopia and expected their government to take steps to put its relations with Africa on a more satisfactory footing.[52] More numerous still were those who concluded from the Ashinov episode that Russian prestige in the Red Sea area was at a low ebb and that Italian presence in the region constituted a growing threat to Russian interests.[53] Such a climate of opinion induced Lamsdorff (then First Secretary of the Foreign Ministry) to wonder whether "in spite of the recently experienced scandal, attempts at new adventures might not be repeated."[54]

Certainly the Russian government could not afford to remain altogether oblivious to the more reasonable expectations aroused by the Ashinov fiasco. If it never had before, Russia was now forced to take seriously the question of its prestige in Ethiopia. A diplomatic dispatch from the Russian Consul General in Cairo not long after the Sagallo incident indicated that this was the case.[55] Commenting upon the Consul General's description of the harm which Ashinov's appearance in Ethiopia might have done to Russian prestige, the Czar made the remark: "thank the Lord he did not get to Abyssinia."[56]

Thus the Russian sovereign appeared to have been not only intensely annoyed with Ashinov, but also considerably relieved at the thought that Russia's knight errant had been unable to penetrate the African interior. Did this perhaps imply that Alexander was beginning to harbor some definite ambitions with regard to northeastern Africa? Did Russia already have something on the Ethiopian fire which could have been spoiled by premature moves such as those the impetuous Ashinov was likely to make? The subsequent behavior of the Russian government clearly suggests that it did.

The Mashkov Missions: 1889, 1891–1892
At least one of the highest officials of the Imperial Russian government, General Vannovski, the Minister of War, was reluctant to support the Ashinov expedition for the very reason that he had other plans for establishing contact with Ethiopia. Some time before the unexpected termination of the Ashinov expedition, General Vannovski had decided to explore Ethiopia's potential as a weapon in Russia's strategic struggle with Britain. His first move was to send a Russian officer on a reconnaissance mission to Ethiopia in early 1889.[57] Thus, while the Imperial government was still preoccupied with the diplomatic confusion left by Ashinov's adventures, the Ministry of War was pursuing an alternative, but probably more reliable avenue toward initiating Russian relations with Ethiopia.

Vannovski's interest in Ethiopia appears to have arisen within the context of the Anglo-Russian confrontation in Afghanistan (1884–85). As the *Times* of London was careful to point out, when the Russian advance halted at Merv, "the Komaroff [*sic*.] war fever gave rise to the idea of creating Russian interests in Africa with a view to harass England in the event of hostilities breaking out between the two countries."[58] In short, the Russian Minister of War had undoubtedly come to the conclusion that in Africa it was possible "to hamper the British government more effectively than [was] . . . feasible either in Afghanistan or in India."[59]

Vannovski's strategic motivations are further suggested by his decision to use for the African mission an officer who had previously been assigned to the Afghan frontier. The individual chosen, Lieutenant V. F. Mashkov, was a veteran of Russia's Central Asian campaigns against the British and was regarded by the latter as capable of zealous Anglophobia.[60] Even more significant, Lieutenant Mashkov was a person who had done considerable thinking about the strategic importance of northeastern Africa, had studied the people and geography of the region, and had advanced what was, in effect, a fully developed plan for the establishment of a Russian position of strength in the area.

Under the pseudonym of V. Fedorov, Mashkov had written a book entitled, *Abyssinia: An Historical-Geographical Essay with a Map of Abyssinia and the Tajura Inlet,*[61] which described this plan and emphasized its strategic importance. Leaving aside the question of any overt Russian colonialism in the region (Mashkov's reference to this option serves as a reminder that the idea was then current in Russia), Mashkov made a comprehensive argument for securing not only religious, but also military and economic control over Ethiopia.[62] In this context he makes an interesting case for the economic advantages of a Russian presence in Ethiopia, citing the importance of a new market and a firsthand source of colonial products for the stability of the ruble and the welfare of the Russian population.[63]

In enumerating the political benefits of Russian dominance in Ethiopia, Mashkov emphasized essentially three points. In the first place, by becoming "a kind of neighbor" of Egypt, Russia would find itself in a position to check that country's capabilities for supplying the Ottomans with auxiliary military forces. Instead of being forced to witness Egyptian troops fighting Russians, Russia might, with the help of the Ethiopians, "give Egypt a job to do [militarily] in its own back yard."[64] In the event Egypt should be transferred altogether into the hands of Britain, such tactics would be equally useful for ensnaring British power along the Nile valley.[65]

In the second place, Ethiopia's quarrel with Italy, in Mashkov's opinion, held real promise of diverting a portion of Italian strength from the European war theatre. A development of this kind would represent a significant victory for Russian interests, given Italy's membership in the anti-Russian Triple Alliance.[66]

A final reward for Russian association with Ethiopia, Mashkov anticipated, might be the acquisition of a port on the Red Sea. Since "belicose Ethiopia" was inevitably bound to cut its way to the Red Sea and to conquer Africa's Red Sea coastline, Russia "might easily obtain from her one of the ports to the south" which Ethiopia needed least.[67] A facility of this kind would be valuable to Russia as a much needed coaling station. But more significantly, such a port would provide an installation from which Russian torpedo boats and privateers could "at any given moment close the Red Sea trade route to English vessels," forcing the English commercial fleet to make the circuitous and not altogether secure trip around the entire African continent.*[68] Hence Russia's position on the Red Sea would serve, in Mashkov's words, as "an eternal threat to the welfare and consequently to the power of England. . . . The capability of shutting this route would force the proud English to drop their pervasively hostile tone towards us, and possibly, might assist in the solution of the Eastern Question in a desirable sense for Russia."[69]

Arguments such as these must have seemed appealing to Russia's anti-British Minister of War. One source indicates that General Vannovski received Mashkov personally on several occasions.[70] This source refers, moreover, to a scheme, submitted in writing by Mashkov to Vannovski, which corresponded almost identically to the plan outlined in *Abyssinia*.[71] That Mashkov subsequently departed on a secret mission to Ethiopia, reportedly with the Russian War Minister's financial authorization, implies that Vannovski was amenable to Mashkov's thinking and was prepared to proceed at least initially with his plan for Ethiopia.

Arriving in Abyssinia in October, 1889, the members of Mashkov's party presented gifts to Menelik II and were warmly received by the Ethiopian sovereign as "military representatives of his brother, the

---

* Mashkov also discussed the importance of the Suez Canal to the British economy. His analysis of the workings of British capitalism convinced him that even a temporary closure of the Canal held great promise of bringing England to its knees. In his words: "Contemporary England draws its strength from far-reaching trade, from developed production, and from the juices of its numerous wealthy colonies. But sources of its strength also represent its Achilles heel." (Mashkov [writing as V. Fedorov], *Abissiniia* [St. Petersburg, 1886]: 48.) Hence, in Mashkov's opinion, if the all-important manufacture of raw materials were blocked, "English production would be curtailed and nine-tenths of the population would be left without work and without bread." (*Loc. cit.*) Mashkov insisted that the British themselves knew this full well and had therefore already been active in endeavoring to protect the security of the Red Sea route. (*Loc. cit.*)

Negus of Muscovy."[72] It is possible that the occasion of this first direct communication between the governments of Russia and Ethiopia was utilized to discuss the question of Russian assistance in Ethiopia's impending struggle with Italy.[73] In any event, the Russians promptly returned to St. Petersburg, reportedly carrying a personal letter from Menelik to Czar Alexander.[74]

Although Mashkov's first assignment in Africa was carried out in extreme secrecy, British observers were quick to recognize the official character and political significance of the undertaking. The activity of the expedition was inconspicuous and its proportions modest, yet the London *Times* was prompted to predict that, "incredible as it may appear, the outcome of the expedition seems likely to be infinitely more wide-reaching and enduring than our own armed enterprise of 1868 [referring to the Napier expedition]."[75]

The Russians themselves attached considerable importance to Mashkov's preliminary visit. The attitude of the Imperial government emerges most graphically from a remark made by Alexander III on the question of Russian intentions in Ethiopia. "We will hear out Mashkov himself, review this matter very carefully and make a final decision," he wrote on the margin of a dispatch from one of his diplomats.[76] Evidently the Czar was awaiting the return of the Russian officer to determine whether he would enter into close relations with the Ethiopians.

When Mashkov did appear in St. Petersburg, the Czar granted him a lengthy private audience, in the course of which a secret map of Abyssinia prepared by the Italian General Staff was reportedly consulted.[77] In addition, Mashkov received a decoration from the Russian sovereign which was regarded as unusually important for an officer of his rank.[78] In brief, the Czar did not appear to be in any way adverse to Mashkov's plans for Ethiopia.

The Czar's affirmative reaction to Mashkov's initial investigation was even more obvious in his decision to send this officer back to Ethiopia in early 1891. Alexander seemed prepared at this time to commit himself to the principle of Russo-Ethiopian friendship. Not only did he address a letter to Menelik expressing his readiness to extend "a brotherly helping hand to Ethiopia in case of need,"[79] but he also entrusted Mashkov with rifles for the Ethiopian ruler—perhaps as a token of what Russian assistance might yield in the future.[80]

A larger expedition was organized for Mashkov's second visit to Africa. Although this expedition was ostensibly of a "scientific" nature and was conducted under the auspices of the Imperial Russian Geographical Society, it received the firm support of key organs within the Russian government. In addition to the Ministry of War —the Ministry of Finance, the Holy Synod, and even the Ministry of Foreign Affairs participated in determining the expedition's composition, its tasks, and its financing.[81] Contrary to its position with regard to Ashinov, the Ministry of Foreign Affairs, and particularly its Asian Department, enthusiastically endorsed the efforts of Lieutenant Mashkov. So dramatic was the change of position on the part of this Ministry that the London *Times* was prompted to observe:

> The value set upon the political results anticipated from Mr. Mashkov's mission may be accurately gauged by the keen interest displayed by the cautious Ministry of Foreign Affairs, which is credited with a considerable degree of squeamishness in matters of this kind.[82]

Indeed, in many respects, the Foreign Ministry gave positive assistance to the Mashkov mission. Not only did it occupy itself with dispatches from the field concerning the mission, but it made very definite diplomatic moves to clear the way for Mashkov's activities in Africa. Stressing the unarmed nature of the enterprise, Foreign Minister de Giers went out of his way to recommend that French authorities in Africa welcome Russia's second "traveler" to Ethiopia.[83] Moreover, the Foreign Ministry took even greater pains to convince the Italian government that the expedition was primarily scientific in nature. First Secretary Lamsdorff carefully explained to the Italian Ambassador in St. Petersburg that the mission had "no political character."[84] Yet, curiously enough, the Russian government in virtually the same breath made known its refusal to accept Italy's self-assumed role as a "go-between" in Ethiopia's relations with the outside world.[85] Mashkov's departure for Ethiopia was made the occasion for announcing Russia's intention to take a firm position in behalf of Ethiopian independence.

Menelik II, who had used Italian arms in his successful bid for the Ethiopian throne, had been obliged to sign a treaty of friendship with Italy in 1889. The Italian government subsequently interpreted this Treaty of Ucciali, and Article 17 in particular, as legal grounds for asserting an Italian protectorate over Ethiopia. Such an interpretation was contrary to Menelik's understanding of the treaty.

(In fact, the Amharic text of Article 17 asserted that "Ethiopia *may* use the services of Italy in the conduct of its foreign relations," while the Italian text consciously employed the term "is obliged to use the services of Italy.")[86] Thus, when Mashkov arrived in Africa, the question of Ethiopian independence vis-à-vis Italy was uppermost in the mind of Menelik.

The Ethiopian reception of the Mashkov mission was exceedingly warm, almost to the point of embarrassing the Russians.[87] In the tense atmosphere, politics quite naturally became a prominent subject of conversation. By his own account, Mashkov discussed the Treaty of Ucciali in considerable detail with Menelik.[88] Upon learning of Italy's efforts to convince Europe of its claim to an Ethiopian protectorate, Menelik reportedly became indignant, exclaiming, "this has never happened and it never will."[89]

According to Mashkov, the Ethiopian Emperor was extremely grateful that Russia and France had refused to accept the Italian claims.[90] Apparently Russia's diplomatic sympathy prompted Menelik to seek further support. When Mashkov returned to St. Petersburg in August, 1892, he brought with him a request that a Russian artillery officer be sent to Ethiopia to train Ethiopians to operate and repair modern weapons.[91] In addition, Mashkov was accompanied by the son of a noble of Harrar, who was to be trained in a military school in St. Petersburg.[92] Developments of this kind seemed to foreshadow success for Mashkov's plan to "transfer into our hands the armed forces of the country."[93]

While in Ethiopia, Mashkov also sought to promote two other aspects of his strategic design for the assertion of Russian control over the country. Presumably as part of his plan for the eventual subjugation of Ethiopia, Mashkov appeared to be working for the conclusion of a Russo-Ethiopian commercial treaty. According to one source, such an agreement would have been designed to obtain a new outlet for "Russian fire arms, fire-water, and church utensils"— in return, Russia would have received much-coveted Ethiopian gold.[94]

In addition, Mashkov seemed to have been pursuing Porfiry Uspensky's notion of Russian religious hegemony in Ethiopia.[95] Like Ashinov, Mashkov had been accompanied to Ethiopia by a Russian monk, Father Tikon, appointed by the Holy Synod. Together, they apparently had instructions "to mould the religious question into a powerful lever to be used in Abyssinia as it was heretofore employed against the Turks in the Balkan Peninsula."[96] After meeting with the head of the Ethiopian Church, Abuna Petros, Mashkov appeared quite encouraged about the prospects for asserting "Russian protection" over Ethiopia's religious affairs.[97]

However ambitious were his aspirations, the principal tasks entrusted to Mashkov by the Russian government were essentially of the traditional political reporting variety. Important among these was the task of determining the political strength of Ethiopia internally, and assessing its strategic position with regard to neighboring areas.[98]

It was probably in the interest of determining Ethiopia's military strength that Mashkov visited Ankober, where Menelik was grouping his army to oppose the Italian supported pretender, Ras Mangasha.[99] Interest in Ethiopia's relations with the Mahdists may similarly have prompted him to make an "exploring tour" as far north as Khartoum.[100] In any event, one of Mashkov's most valuable services was to obtain a clear impression of the extent of Ethiopia's determination both to resist the Italians and to become a friend of the Russians.

How did other European nations react to Mashkov, his mission, and his ideas? As might have been expected, both the British and the Italians were highly skeptical concerning the motivations underlying the Russian expedition to Ethiopia.

Intense in their hostility to Mashkov's second Ethiopian mission, the Italians were quick to deprecate the cultural and religious aspects of the undertaking. How could Russians bring civilization to Ethiopia, the Italian press asked, when Russia itself did not possess that valuable commodity?[101] Moreover, the Italians warned the Ethiopians to be wary of the motives of the Russians, who, heavily in debt in Europe, were apt to exploit Ethiopian riches for their own selfish benefit. Mashkov observes that while in Ethiopia, he was on numerous occasions confronted by Italian accusations to the effect that the Russians "under the guise of friendship" would subjugate Ethiopia as they had their "small Orthodox neighbors."[102]

The British, known for their perceptivity in such matters, were also inclined to look for ulterior motives on the part of Russia. They were hardly deceived by the veil of scientific inquiry which had been drawn around Mashkov's enterprise. In a tone of caustic certitude, the *Times* of London declared:

As a matter of sober fact, the astronomic, geological, meteorological, botanical and zoological observations which the Geographic Society can reasonably anticipate from Lt. Mashkov and his devoted comrades will prove about as valuable to science generally as were the startling archaeological discoveries of the conscientious Mr. Pickwick, as expounded to the learned club that bore that worthy scholar's name.[103]

Instead, the British clearly recognized that the Imperial Russian government was closely connected with the affair and that the Czar would be unable to disassociate himself from Mashkov, as he had from Ashinov.[104] By the same token, British observers attributed considerable political significance to Mashkov's enterprise, going so far as to regard it as an attempt to drive in "the thin edge of an enormous wedge" of Russian influence into Africa.[105] Thus, they were apprehensive lest the Mashkov mission prove to be only the beginning of a series of African victories for Russian diplomacy. "Where will the good fortune of Mr. Mashkov himself end," asked the London *Times*, "welcomed as he will be by the Aboona [head of the Ethiopian Church], beloved by the Negus, and befriended by the clergy and the people?"[106]

What caused the British particular anxiety was the perennial question of their security in Egypt. Indeed the thought of a renascent or a rearmed Ethiopia was a disquieting one both to the Egyptians and to their English overlords. Since the possibility of Russian military assistance to Ethiopia was currently in the air, the suspicions of the British were aroused lest such benevolences ultimately lead to direct moves against Egypt. In this connection certain ominous historical precedents came to mind. As the *Times* observed:

> Russian diplomatists . . . will not neglect to remind the world that the ill-fated King Theodore firmly intended to assert his rights to Egypt proper at a time when British interests there could scarcely be said to exist.[107]

Thus was Russian activity fitted into the context of Franco-Russian opposition to British power. It was felt in Britain that France would probably welcome the influx of Russian influence in Ethiopia. It was feared, moreover, that the French would see in the success of Mashkov a means by which to recover their lost position in Egypt. Perhaps, the British concluded, the establishment of Russo-Ethiopian relations was itself a manifestation of a joint intention on the part of Russia and France to "draw a sponge over the late history of Egypt."[108]

Certainly the attitude which the French government took toward the Mashkov expedition did nothing to dispel British fears. On the contrary, the apparent solicitude of the French for Mashkov's every step deepened the British conviction that the French were "expecting a fair percentage on their investment" in a program of collusion with Russia.[109] Everywhere, Mashkov was received in a friendly fashion by French officials. Not only did the French in Africa provide his expedition with much useful advice for its journey inland, but they reportedly supplied it with an armed escort of Senegalese troops.[110]

That British fears regarding the Mashkov expedition were justified is in fact suggested by Lamsdorff's own diary. Conceding the mendacity of the official Russian statement to the Italian government, this diary reveals:

> The Mashkov expedition, although officially purely scientific in character, in fact pursued political objectives. The French and Russian governments repeatedly sought to strengthen their influence in Abyssinia in the first place in order to counterbalance the designs of Italian imperialism there; and in the second place . . . to threaten the Upper Nile and thus the very position of the English in Egypt.[111]

The political significance of the Mashkov missions in the development of Russian relations with Ethiopia has been largely overlooked by scholars.[112] Whatever celebrity or notoriety was acquired by Ashinov in the course of his African adventures, Lt. V. F. Mashkov should be regarded as the individual who laid the foundations for the initiation of direct relations between Ethiopia and Russia. His two visits to the court of Menelik made possible the first direct and reciprocal exchange of messages between the rulers of the two countries. Although Ethiopian monarchs had on several occasions sought to enter into direct communications with the Russian Czar, Mashkov's second visit to Ethiopia marked the first Imperial response to Ethiopian overtures.

Although it may be true, as K. S. Zviagin points out, that Mashkov's success in Ethiopia was to a certain extent hindered by his lack of fluency in local languages and by illness,[113] it is nonetheless certain that Mashkov was able to return to Russia in 1892, after nearly a year in Ethiopia, with the confidence of having won, for himself and for his country, the friendship of Ethiopia's sovereign. Through his conversations with Menelik, he had suggested that friendship with Russia could well serve as a diplomatic avenue for Ethiopia to assert

its independence from the Italians. Moreover, as a result of Mashkov's second mission, Ethiopia possessed for the first time tangible
assurance of the Czar's support—something Menelik had good reason
to remember in the course of his ensuing struggle with the Italians.

In contrast to earlier Russian ventures in Africa, Mashkov's activities appear to have conformed to a consistent and well-developed
strategic plan. If his first visit to Ethiopia had been only exploratory
in nature, his second mission represented an officially considered
move on the part of the Russian government. As a well-informed
traveler, Mashkov was able to explain to Russians the nature of the
political situation in northeastern Africa. As one of the first political
observers of Africa to recognize the plight of underdeveloped peoples
when confronted with the onslaught of European civilization, he was
able to stimulate Russian sympathy and support for Ethiopians.
Finally, as writer and lecturer, Mashkov, upon his return from
Ethiopia, was able to spark popular enthusiasm for a land and for
peoples far beyond the confines of Russia's traditional sphere of
interest.

The Eliseev Expedition to Ethiopia: 1895

Although several years elapsed before Russians reappeared in Ethiopia, this period did not represent a hiatus in Russia's growing interest
in the African continent. In 1893, for example, a particularly dramatic attempt was made by a Russian officer, Captain A. V. Eliseev,
to reach the headquarters of the Mahdists in the Sudan.[114] Eliseev
was also a medical doctor who had learned on earlier visits to North
Africa that the instruments of his profession gave him a far better
entrée among local inhabitants than did the arms used by other
Europeans in their African travels. No evidence has yet come to light
to indicate conclusively whether Eliseev's Sudan mission was undertaken at the explicit behest of the Russian government. Nonetheless,
the expedition does appear to have been conducted in the spirit of an
anti-British intelligence operation and to have yielded information of
value to the Russian government in assessing the strength of the
British position in Egypt and along the Nile.*

---

* Disguised as an Arab and taking a devious route toward the Sudan in order to
leave Egypt "unnoticed by English spies," Eliseev was able to penetrate some
distance into the territory of the Mahdists before he was forced to turn back by

It was in the context of continued Russian interest in Mahdism that Eliseev returned to Africa in 1895, at the head of a Russian expedition bound for Ethiopia and the Sudan.* [115] In many ways this expedition appeared to fit clearly into the pattern of Russo-Ethiopian exchanges which had been established by Mashkov. Members of the mission may have described their undertaking as a "modest scientific enterprise,"[116] but, like Mashkov's visit to Ethiopia in 1891–92, their expedition had a distinctly political flavor.

In addition to Eliseev, two other members of the expedition, K. S. Zviagin and N. S. Leontiev, held commissions in the Russian army. That they were given leave of absence for an African journey in itself implies that their objective was more than purely scientific in nature. Moreover, both the Ministry of War and the Ministry of Foreign Affairs evinced a definite interest in the success of the undertaking. Vannovski's Ministry outfitted the expedition with weapons and

---

local brigands. (A. V. Eliseev, "Makhdism i Sovremennoe Polozhenie Del v Sudane". Russkoe Geograficheskoe Obshchestvo, *Izvestiia*, XXX [1894], no. 4 605ff.) Although he failed to reach the Mahdists' capital at Omdurman, Eliseev did succeed in obtaining a rather accurate impression of their military capabilities. Mahdist chances of successfully opposing the Egyptians under British command, he concluded, were not good. In fact, Mahdism, weakened by widespread famine and internal disaffection, could, in his opinion, be expected to disintegrate of its own accord. (*Ibid.*: 665–66.) On May 25, 1894, Eliseev reported these findings to the Russian Geographical Society. Among his most interesting observations were those concerning the affinity between Russia's Muslim populations and those of Africa. One of the first in a long line of Russians who pointed to the inability of "millions of Muslim citizens in Russia to remain indifferent" to the politics of Islam in Africa, Eliseev noted that Mahdism had already gained a certain number of adherents among Muslims in the Ural area of Russia. (*Ibid.*: 605.)

---

* It seems certain that this expedition was conceived at least in part as another attempt to reach the Mahdists. (A. V. Eliseev, *Po Belu-Svetu*, [St. Petersburg, 1898]: 268.) Although there is no indication that any members of Eliseev's expedition ever did get to the Sudan, they were able to obtain much useful information about Mahdism from Father Rossinoli, who had recently escaped from prison there. (K. S. Zviagin, *Ocherk Sovremennoi Abissinii*. [St. Petersburg 1895]: 8.) It is apparent that Eliseev's political sentiments lay clearly on the side of these Muslim opponents of Britain. Upon arriving in Africa he wrote home: "I am heartily glad of the advance of the Mahdists along Wadi Halfa, and of the failure of the Italians [to extend their conquests into Ethiopia] which I had predicted long ago. The Manifesto of the Mahdi [actually the Caliph Abdullah, the Mahdi's successor] is excellent and promises much that is excellent in the future. Discontent with the English is growing in Egypt." (Letter of Eliseev from Egypt, dated January 6, 1895, cited in V. Y. Golant, 'A. V. Yeliseyev, Writer and Traveller' [from material in the Central State Military-Historical Archive], in *Russia and Africa* [Moscow, 1966]: 151.)

scientific instruments, while de Giers and his colleagues arranged for
the cooperation of the French government, as they had done in the
case of the Mashkov expedition.[117] The Holy Synod, following the
now established pattern, appointed an ecclesiastical representative
(Father Efrem) to accompany Eliseev and to pursue the objective of
unifying the Ethiopian and Russian churches.[118]

Thus, whether or not the decision to support Eliseev's venture
represented a conscious effort on the part of the Russian government
to pursue the political projects begun by Mashkov, in effect Russia
was proceeding along the path prescribed by that earlier African
traveler. Eliseev's own desire to visit Ethiopia may even have been
inspired by reading the works of Mashkov. At any rate, by corresponding with Mashkov before his departure for Africa, Eliseev was
able to absorb much from the experience of the Russian expedition of
1891–92.[119]

Even if Eliseev's party had been anxious to avoid altogether the
concerns of international politics, the circumstances surrounding its
arrival in Ethiopia would have made this impossible. The appearance
of the Russians coincided with a severe deterioration in Ethiopia's
relations with the Italians. By 1895 an all-out military confrontation
between Ethiopia and Italy was becoming inevitable.

In his new capital, Addis Ababa, Menelik had been eagerly awaiting news of the return of his friends the Muscovites.[120] Undoubtedly
he was thinking in terms of the services which these sympathetic
northerners—themselves no friends of the Italians—could render
Ethiopia.[121] When word finally came that the Russians were again
visiting his country, Menelik was obviously very much pleased.
Before they had penetrated Ethiopia further than the provincial
capital of Harrar, the members of Eliseev's expedition were treated
to an official welcome of proportions unprecedented for any European visitor in the country.[122]

In the course of the ceremonies, the Russians met with Ras Makonnen, Menelik's principle lieutenant and designated successor, who
had come to greet them in behalf of the Ethiopian sovereign. Before
very long it became apparent that the Ethiopians desired a significant
and rapid expansion in their official relations with Russia. In this
connection they indicated that they were prepared to dispatch a high
level embassy to Russia.[123] Would this be acceptable to the Czar?

It was decided that Eliseev should himself return immediately to

St. Petersburg to make the necessary preparations, while Leontiev and the other members of the expedition would proceed to the court of Menelik.[124] The new Czar, Nicholas II (1894–1917), received the Russian officer upon his return, and on May 10, 1895, twelve days before his death, Eliseev reported on his journey to the Russian Geographical Society, the official sponsor of his expedition.[125]

England and Italy, seeing in the Eliseev expedition a new step toward Russo-Ethiopian rapprochement, exhibited no less hostility toward the enterprise than they had toward that of Mashkov. The French Governor of Djibouti, M. Lagarde, even became concerned lest agents of these powers bribe the natives into attacking the expedition on its journey inland across the Danakil Desert.[126] In such a situation, the promise of the French Ambassador in St. Petersburg that France "will see your expedition through to the very borders of Ethiopia,"[127] was fulfilled with particular care.

The experience of A. V. Eliseev thus served as a further illustration of Franco-Russian cooperation in north eastern Africa. But it was significant for other reasons as well. Although Eliseev himself never reached the court of Menelik and his expedition did not come equipped with much-needed military supplies for Ethiopia, Eliseev was able to assert with certain justification that he and his companion had "served to a certain extent as pioneers in the establishment of various kinds of relations with Abyssinia."[128] One member in particular, Captain Leontiev, played a significant role in the further development of Russo-Ethiopian ties. Probably as a result of his utility to Menelik as an expert on military tactics and on the modernization of the Ethiopian army, Leontiev rapidly acquired considerable influence at the Ethiopian court.[129] Having equally close ties in Russian court circles, he was able to act as liaison in subsequent exchanges between the two governments.

Eliseev's repeated efforts to gather intelligence on Mahdism suggest that Russia was aware of the value of that movement as an indigenous force capable of disrupting the plans of British and Italian imperialism in Africa. Yet in the wake of the Eliseev expedition of 1895 it became apparent that Ethiopia was of far more immediate value to Russia as an anti-Italian, anti-British force. It was equally apparent, moreover, that the Ethiopians were willing and able to enter into close relations with Russia.

If he did nothing else, Eliseev contributed significantly to the

prompt inauguration of Russo-Ethiopian relations by appearing in
Ethiopia at the most favorable psychological moment. His visit provided a timely opportunity for the Ethiopians to manifest their
friendly attitudes toward Russia and it encouraged them to send
their first official mission to St. Petersburg. In a political sense, the
Eliseev expedition marked the beginning of the period of greatest
intimacy between Imperial Russia and Ethiopia.

The Ethiopian Mission to Russia: 1895
Captain Leontiev and Father Efrem had been at the court of Menelik
only a short time before they were asked to escort Ethiopia's first full-
scale mission to Russia. This they did, arriving in St. Petersburg in
June, 1895.

Menelik's unprecedented decision to send an embassy to Russia
was undoubtedly based on a variety of considerations. Ostensibly he
felt obliged to render homage to the memory of Alexander III, whose
friendship had been extended to him via a personal communication
brought to Ethiopia by Mashkov. In addition, there was the continuing question of religious rapprochement between Russia and
Ethiopia. Not only did this factor prompt Menelik to choose an
Ethiopian bishop to be one of the members of his embassy, but it
allowed him to draw an ecclesiastical veil over much of the embassy's
official activity in Russia.

Although Ras Makonnen had previously assured Eliseev that
Ethiopians "neither ask nor expect anything from Russia: the sole
desire of all of us is that she treat us sympathetically, believing in the
friendship of a people sharing her faith,"[130] one suspects that from
the Ethiopian point of view the most pressing arguments for sending
a mission to Russia were political and military in nature. In 1895 one
political fact seemed to overshadow all else: Ethiopia was on the
verge of an all-out war with Italy. In such a situation, the country
needed every manner of military assistance available in order to
fight a modern European army. Menelik's pointed reference to
Alexander III may, in fact, have been intended as a discrete hint
that Ethiopia could now use that assistance which the late Czar had
promised.

All diplomatic symbolism aside, it was obvious from the composition and rank of Menelik's embassy that the Ethiopians had come to

discuss critical affairs of state. In addition to his first cousin, Prince Damto (an important military leader who served as "Extraordinary Ambassador"), and another relative, Prince Beliakio, Menelik sent with the mission to Russia his personal secretary, a general of the Ethiopian cavalry, and two additional officers of the Ethiopian army.[131]

Further indications of the embassy's particular interest in military matters can be gleaned from observing its itinerary in Russia. In addition to their repeated contacts with the highest echelons of the Russian military establishment,[132] members of the embassy attended demonstrations of Russian army maneuvers, observed weapons tests, and visited arms factories.[133] Moreover, the Ethiopians' travels ended on a martial note when their Russian hosts evoked, in the course of farewell ceremonies, the memory of the seventeenth century proposals for a Russo-Ethiopian military alliance. As a parting gift, the Ethiopians took with them a number of modern weapons and a large monetary gift for Menelik.[134]

Throughout its stay in Russia, the Ethiopian embassy had been received in a manner which attracted both popular enthusiasm and political attention. The Russian church, aroused as never before to the prospects of union with its Ethiopian counterpart, turned the visit at many junctures into a triumphal and emotional procession.[135] Similarly, the Russian press did much to stimulate genuine popular enthusiasm for Ethiopia.[136] But perhaps the most prominent display of hospitality toward the visiting dignitaries came from the very group of Slavophiles which had been most active in promoting the projects of Ashinov. The unsuspecting Ethiopians were literally showered with invitations—from Pobedonostsev to dine at Tsarkoe Selo, from Grand Duke Sergei Alexandrovich to stay with him in Moscow, and from Governor General Baranov to visit Nizhni Novgorod.[137]

Doors opened, as they did for few visitors, to enable the Ethiopians to meet the highest officials of the Russian government.[138] Finally, on June 30, 1895, the Ethiopian embassy was formally presented to Nicholas II and members of the Imperial family. In a sense, the long series of efforts on the part of Russians and Ethiopians to establish friendly relations between their two countries reached a culmination in this meeting. In the course of the audience, Prince Damto gave the Czar a personal letter from Emperor Menelik[139] and, in effect, formal diplomatic relations were thereupon established between Russia and Ethiopia.

Given Italian pretensions to a protectorate over Ethiopia, such a diplomatic event represented the most open defiance of Italy on the part of the Ethiopians. Quite possibly Menelik sent his embassy to Russia with this very purpose in mind. Whatever his intent, it is clear that as a result of the mission Menelik succeeded in breaking the spell of diplomatic isolation which had hung over Ethiopia since the Treaty of Ucciali. In brief, he had secured official recognition of Ethiopia from one of the major powers. The exceedingly warm reception accorded the Ethiopian mission was tantamount to an open repudiation by Russia of the Italian claims of suzerainty. But equally important, the Russian government chose to make its support of Ethiopia's right to political independence still more explicit. The Russian Foreign Minister as well as Russian diplomats in Italy, chose the occasion of the Ethiopian mission to reiterate in no uncertain terms that Russia had never recognized either the Treaty of Ucciali or any Italian protectorate in Ethiopia.[140]

The success of Menelik's embassy to Russia thus worked to bring Ethiopia's conflict with Italy to a head.[141] It is no exaggeration to say that the favorable Russian reception of the mission contributed significantly to Menelik's determination to pursue a struggle which led to the fateful confrontation at Adowa on March 1, 1896. Some evidence exists which suggests that Menelik deliberately postponed military moves against Italy until the return of his mission to Russia.[142] Although he may not have obtained all the immediate military aid he needed, Menelik did have good reason to believe as a result of his mission, that he could turn to the Russians for assistance in the future. If only in terms of moral support, Menelik had found considerable encouragement in Russia for asserting Ethiopian independence.

RUSSIA AND THE RACE FOR THE NILE: 1896–1898

Menelik was dramatically successful in his confrontation with the Italian army at Adowa. Of the approximately 20,000 Italian troops participating in the battle, over half were killed, wounded, or taken as prisoners by the Ethiopians.[143] As rarely before in the long history of the country, virtually the whole feudal hierarchy of Ethiopia had rallied behind a single national leader to expel a foreign invader.

Certainly Menelik had good reason to rejoice in the final outcome of his life and death struggle with the Italians. It is no exaggeration to say that the question of Ethiopia's very existence had been resolved decisively at Adowa. The battle was also decisive in a much wider sense. Adowa was the first example of the defeat of a major European army on the African continent. As such, it became a prominent point of reference in the cultural heritage of African nationalism. By the same token, it won considerable respect for Menelik among European governments of the day. One government, that of Crispi, was overthrown in the wake of the battle, bringing to an abrupt end Italian claims of suzerainty over Ethiopia. In effect, as a result of Menelik's astounding victory, a number of European powers, particularly those which harbored imperialist intentions for northeastern Africa, felt obliged to undertake hurried reassessments of their policies in the region.

In the opinon of the leaders of these countries, the virtual elimination of Italy from northeastern Africa created a power vacuum which could be exploited to their advantage. Ethiopia itself seemed to recognize that there was room for immediate territorial aggrandizement. This, in turn, served to stimulate the natural proclivity of European imperialists to seek new real estate of their own on the African continent. In brief, the battle of Adowa triggered a rush for territory so energetic and so precipitate that it is appropriate to speak in terms of a "race for the Nile" during the two years after 1896.

The most immediate reaction to the new political situation in northeastern Africa came from Britain. Within days of Italy's defeat at Adowa, Lord Cromer had received authorization from the British government to embark upon the reconquest of the Sudan.[144] Much more was at stake in this decision than simply the longing of Victorian Britain to avenge the memory of its fallen hero, General Gordon. In the first place, the services of Italy could no longer be relied upon to look after British interests in northeastern Africa. Lord Salisbury hardly needed to be reminded that the vital route to India was now exposed to the subversive intentions of England's adversaries.[145] Moreover, as Cromer recognized, Britain could not allow the sources of the Nile to remain unguarded—given its interests in Egypt and its plans for a colonial empire in Africa. Ever an eloquent exponent of the growth of British colonialism, Winston Churchill (who went to cover the Sudan campaign as a young journalist) explained:

> It must not be forgotten that the sources of the Nile are physically as much an integral part of Egypt as the roots are an integral part of the tree.[146]
> Of what use would the roots and rich soil be, if the stem were severed, by which alone their vital essence may find expression in the upper air? Here then is the plain and honest reason for the River War.[147]

Closely related to this concept and perhaps equally important as a rationale for Britain's prominent role in the race for the Nile was the English dream of linking its northern and southern African possessions. The east bank of the Nile south of Khartoum offered the most favorable terrain for the construction of a Cape to Cairo railroad.[148] Although the ownership of this area was uncertain, Ethiopia seemed a likely suzerain unless Britain could acquire the territory first. Extremely disquieting to the English in this regard was the possibility that France, with its increasing influence in Ethiopia, would ultimately find itself in a position to cast a permanent veto upon British attempts to connect its footholds in the African continent.

French strategists were certainly not innocent of such intentions. Experience in Africa had already impressed them with the utility of preempting the British by gaining control of the rivers upon which British possessions were dependent.[149] On the Upper Nile the use of this strategem would not only work against British interests in Egypt, but it might serve the added purpose of frustrating Britain's continental designs. Moreover, if Britain had the audacity to plan a north-south axis of power in Africa, then France, too, was capable of extending its own cordon across the continent in the opposite direction—from east to west.

Ethiopia's victory at Adowa and the subsequent British decision to move southward from Egypt served to convince the French government to proceed with the implementation of its transcontinental plan. Even as Lord Kitchener was making his first preparations to move up the Nile toward Dongola, an expedition of major proportions left France on its way toward the Upper Nile.[150] This expedition, led by the intrepid French explorer, Captain Marchand, had specific instructions to traverse the continent from west to east via French possessions. Relying upon the anti-British sentiments of local Mahdists, it was to secure French claims to the Bahr el Ghazal, an immense and sparsely populated region lying south-west of Khartoum, and thereby to establish French power once and for all on the west bank of the Nile.[151]

An equally important aspect of the French transcontinental plan involved Ethiopia. While Marchand was heading eastward, the Governor of Djibouti, M. Lagarde, was transferred to the court of Menelik. There, he was to make arrangements for two French expeditions to cross Ethiopia and join Marchand from the east.[152] Ultimately, all French forces were to meet at some convenient point such as Fashoda. There, French forts would be constructed on both banks of the White Nile and the river would be sealed off to the British.[153] France ostensibly had no territorial pretensions to the east bank of the Nile. Lagarde was simply instructed to encourage Menelik to make good Ethiopian claims by occupying all the territory lying between his frontier and the river. Thus, when the British arrived, they would find no room for their cherished north-south corridor.

Such was the strategic plan by which the French sought to prevent the extension of British power in Africa. The territorial designs of both France and Britain, emerging clearly in the wake of Adowa, inevitably involved Ethiopia, a nation whose power had lately become of obvious importance. In such a situation, what would be the position of Russia, whose growing sympathy for Ethiopia had reached a highpoint at the time of Menelik's dramatic encounter with Italy?

Although it was not one of the chief protagonists in the drama, as an ally of France and a friend of Ethiopia, Imperial Russia played an active role in the race for the Nile. Russian policy in north-eastern Africa had for many years been oriented toward cooperation with France in the interests of curtailing British power in Egypt and the Red Sea. As an almost inevitable consequence of such a policy, Russia found itself irreversibly aligned with Ethiopia in opposing Italy. Both during and after the battle of Adowa, the Russian government continued to demonstrate clearly its support for Ethiopia and its sympathy for France's anti-British strategy in Africa.

It is important to note that Russia assisted Menelik in his fateful encounter with the Italians. Although French and Russian arms to Ethiopia are thought to have played an influential role in the Adowa battle,[154] perhaps even more significant was Russian advice concerning military tactics.

It is entirely possible that one Russian officer, Captain N. S. Leontiev, was responsible for developing the major outlines of Ethiopian strategy against the Italians. Leontiev, who had come to Ethiopia with the Eliseev expedition of 1895, had, since that time, served as a member of a council which Menelik had formed to discuss the military approach to be used against Italy. In this capacity, he had urged the Ethiopians to apply a strategy similar to that used by the Russians in their victory over Napoleon. By allowing the Italians to penetrate deeply into the country and then by cutting off their line of supply, Ethiopia could, in Leontiev's opinion, use its greatest advantage—geography—to overcome Italy's military strength.[155] This, with certain modifications, was essentially the policy which Menelik followed. Ethiopian geography was used to maximum advantage, while Italian weapon superiority remained ineffectual.[156]

That the Ethiopians associated Leontiev with their success at Adowa was apparent in the tokens of esteem which they bestowed upon him. Not long after the battle, Menelik took the unprecedented step of granting Leontiev an Ethiopian title. In addition he entrusted the Russian officer with the task of returning prisoners to the Italian government and even bade him undertake diplomatic initiatives in connection with the conclusion of an Italo-Ethiopian peace treaty.[157]

In any event, whether it was out of appreciation for specific services rendered by individual Russians, or because of gratitude for a less tangible kind of moral support, Menelik clearly felt that the Russian government, together with that of France, deserved to share his jubilation at victory over the Italians. To this end, he took the trouble of informing immediately both the Czar and the President of France of the successful conclusion of hostilities so that, in his words, "our friends can rejoice with us."[158]

In its own way, the Russian response to Adowa was as prompt and unequivocal as that of Britain. Almost immediately after news of the battle had been received, the Russian Red Cross Society decided to dispatch a medical team to Ethiopia, voting 100,000 rubles for the enterprise.[159] This gesture reflected not only popular enthusiasm for Menelik's cause, but also growing recognition on the part of the Russian government that the time had come to invest materially in Ethiopia's well-being. Russian military officials cooperated with the endeavor by authorizing Lt. General N. K. Shvedov, and four other officers to lead the Red Cross expedition. In all, nearly fifty Russians appeared in Ethiopia in June, 1896,[160] inaugurating the first significant Russian presence in Ethiopia.

As might have been expected, British fears were aroused by this seemingly beneficent Russian mission. As one British observer put it:

> Pills and bandages . . . [are] marking the first footsteps of Russia in Africa, and opening perhaps, under the cloak of charity and humanity, what may become a foundation to build a right to interfere in the politics of Abyssinia and the north-east of Africa and also on our line of commerce to the east.[161]

An even more immediate note of alarm was sounded by the Italian government. On the basis of reports which were no doubt exaggerated, the Italian government came to the conclusion that the mission disguised a direct Russian move to reinforce Ethiopian military strength.[162] Communicating repeatedly with Russian Foreign Minister Lobanov-Rostovsky, the Italian government sought to prevent the departure of the Russian mission from Odessa. Failing that, it announced that it would deny the Russians access to Massawa, their designated point of disembarkation.[163]

Despite Italian attempts to frustrate its progress, the mission arrived in Addis Ababa in July, 1896, receiving a warm welcome from Menelik. As Russian doctors began to treat Ethiopian soldiers, they won ever increasing respect from the Ethiopian sovereign. So badly needed were the services of these doctors that when the time came for the mission to return to Russia, Menelik made known his desire to see the establishment remain in Ethiopia on a continuing basis. Several of the doctors were persuaded to stay in Addis Ababa and a permanent Russian hospital was opened there in 1898.[164] (Although the activity of this hospital ceased in 1906, its work was resumed by the Soviets after World War II.)

It is impossible to estimate with any accuracy the political return which Imperial Russia derived from medical assistance to Ethiopia. Yet, there is little question that this assistance earned considerable goodwill from Menelik personally and from the most influential members of his government. By treating the Emperor and those closest to him, various Russian doctors were able to establish comparatively intimate relationships with Ethiopia and its rulers.[165] If only in terms of knowledge accumulated and information gathered on the scene, Imperial Russia's experience in supplying medical assistance to Ethiopia was a useful beginning for subsequent Russian involvement in sub-Saharan Africa.

Possibly as a result of the friendly attitude engendered by Russia's medical mission, Menelik felt disposed to request that the Russian Czar act as mediator in his peace negotiations with Italy. It is likely that this request, together with a letter of appreciation from Menelik, was delivered to the Russian government by Menelik's personal secretary, Grazmach Iosif, who returned to St. Petersburg in the company of Leontiev in the fall of 1896.[166] Although the Russian government provisionally declined the offer, it did commit itself to aid Ethiopia militarily in the future. Not only did Leontiev go back to Ethiopia with rifles and ammunition, but he carried with him an assurance from the Russian government that a much larger consignment of arms would be forthcoming in the near future.[167] Evidently Russia, like other European powers, had seen in Menelik's victory at Adowa an indication of Ethiopia's potential military strength. As would soon be seen, Russia's response to Adowa involved not merely the extension of medical and military assistance, but also a decision to assign for the first time a fully accredited diplomatic mission to the court of Menelik.

The Russian diplomatic mission to Ethiopia was a direct outgrowth of the Franco-Russian desire to strengthen Ethiopia as a counterweight to British power in Africa. On more than one occasion in the past, Russian and French officials had been tempted "to explore together . . . the most appropriate means of safeguarding the common interests of the two countries in Abyssinia," and to consider the establishment of diplomatic representation there.[168] In this vein, French Foreign Minister Hanotaux discussed with acting Russian Minister Shishkin the possibility of the simultaneous dispatch of official diplomatic missions to Ethiopia which would work jointly to promote the interests of the Franco-Russian entente in the area.[169] Evidently the idea appealed to the new Russian Foreign Minister, Count Muraviev, who, in talks with Hanotaux in January, 1897, announced his intention of sending an official mission to Ethiopia under the leadership of his personal friend, M. Vlassov.[170]

In the fall of 1897, as Vlassov prepared to depart for Ethiopia, the governments of France and Russia took steps to coordinate the specific instructions which their respective envoys would receive and to clarify the concert in their policies toward Ethiopia. That the French government clearly recognized the congruity of interests between the two countries was apparent in a special note which it submitted to the Russian government in September, 1897.[171] Underlining the importance of maintaining Ethiopian strength, the diplomatic note went on to observe:

> It does not seem that on any of these points Russian interests are opposed to our own. They are, on the contrary, identical to ours on all questions of major importance such as the maintenance of the independence and integrity of Abyssinia, a kingdom which serves as a barrier to the unlimited growth of Italian and English [colonial] establishments.[172]

Certainly the French government had made no mistake in assessing the Russian position concerning Ethiopia. Particularly with regard to the question of preventing the north-south extension of British power, the Czarist government saw eye to eye with its French ally. As the Czar told Vlassov before his departure for Africa, the Russian mission should be oriented toward the support of French policy in Ethiopia, "in order that the English might be prevented from establishing themselves in that country thereby uniting their possessions in the south with the political influence they are seeking to establish in the valley of the Nile."[173] By 1897, Russia, along with other European powers, clearly recognized the nature of the contest in Africa. As one member of the Russian mission put it: "Will England be able to accomplish her cherished dream and cut through the entire continent from north to south, laying her hands on the riches of the lands at the center and creating for herself a second India—or will France be able to stop her?"[174] Clearly Russia was hoping that the French would be the victors in this struggle.

As the opposing transcontinental lines of French and English movement emerged with increasing clarity, Ethiopia, or the territory to the west of Ethiopia, attracted new attention in Europe as the most likely point of Anglo-French confrontation. Largely as a result of their earlier cooperation with Ethiopia, the French, together with their Russian supporters, had by 1897 gained a distinct advantage over other powers in the rush to curry favor with Menelik—a monarch who, it was believed, might hold the key to the outcome of the Nile race. Not only were plans afoot to use Ethiopian territory to promote the interests of France's east-west axis in Africa, but proposals were being discussed to erect a French dam on the Nile confluent, the Sobat, so as to "wash out Egyptian civilization" should that ever become necessary.[175]

In this situation the British saw a severe threat to their plans in the Sudan. If this region were to be finally reconquered, they reasoned, then the scope of the Dongola expedition would have to be expanded to include a decisive move against Khartoum. This, in turn, would require that Britain eliminate the Franco-Russian menace in Ethiopia and prepare ground for the expansion of British power southward up the Nile valley.[176] To this end, Britain dispatched, in the spring of 1897, a high level mission to Menelik's court.

This mission, under the leadership of Rennell Rodd, had a difficult assignment indeed. How was it possible to convince Menelik of British friendship when Britain's support of Italy and of Italian claims in Ethiopia was well known to the Ethiopian ruler? To make matters even worse, the Rodd mission had to contend with what appeared to be a strong Russian influence at Menelik's court. A French eyewitness describes vividly the atmosphere of Anglo-Russian confrontation surrounding Rodd's first audience with the Negus:

> The Indian soldiers [forming Rodd's escort] are nearly face to face with two Cossacks brought by Leontiev. And it is not one of the lesser curiosities of the day to observe [these Russian] men dressed in black Circassian uniforms, sabre at the side and dagger in the belt, Astrakhan caps on the head, looking at the Sikh turbans and red uniforms [of the Indian soldiers] opposite them here in Africa at the court of the Emperor of Abyssinia. In Asia they [the Russians] are used to lying in wait for these soldiers from the heights of the Pamirs, looking forward to the opportunity of being allowed to come down to provoke them on the plains of India.[177]

Rodd seemed particularly suspicious of the "considerable influence" at Menelik's court wielded by Count Leontiev, who had recently returned to Ethiopia from Russia. In correspondence with Prime Minister Salisbury, Rodd took note of Leontiev's "keen interest in H.M. government's intentions in the Sudan, as well as in the direction of the Great Lakes."[178] Perhaps aware of earlier Russian flirtations with Mahdism, Rodd seemed distinctly worried about Leontiev's plans to visit the Mahdist headquarters at Omdurman. In particular, he appeared to be concerned lest the Russian officer promote collusion between Menelik and the Khalifa on the eve of Britain's campaign against the Mahdists.[179] This matter was of particular importance to the British at the time since their intelligence had discovered that European weapons were finding their way into the hands of the Mahdists.[180]

Although Rodd himself was able to make a good impression upon Menelik, his mission, politically speaking, was only of limited success. British efforts to divert Menelik's attention from the Nile valley by offering Ethiopia territorial concessions in the north east were to no avail. Moreover, Rodd evidently surmised, from the tenor of his conversations with the Ethiopians, that it was not politic at that time to push for Britain's real objective—control over the territory along the east bank of the Nile.[181] Yet, despite its shortcomings, the Rodd mission did furnish the British government with fresh evidence that a move of its own forces up the Nile was necessary to forestall the east-west designs of the French and the territorial appetites of Menelik.[182] Rodd's recommendations undoubtedly played an important part in convincing Salisbury to hasten the British advance against Khartoum and to make a British move from Uganda toward Fashoda.[183] In brief, after Rodd's mission had returned from Ethiopia, the race for the Nile acquired an irreversible momentum.

There is little question that the French government was aware of the political objectives of the Rodd mission, for even before the English had arrived in Addis Ababa, the French had presented a plan of their own to the Ethiopian Emperor. Lagarde was instructed to warn Menelik of the danger which British ambitions along the Nile represented to his own territorial aspirations in the region. In order to protect himself from territorial encirclement by the British, Menelik should, in the opinion of the French, push his own frontiers westward to the Nile where he would join with the forces of Marchand and link the possessions of France and Ethiopia.[184]

Such thinking must have appealed to Menelik, for on March 20, 1897, on the eve of the arrival of the Rodd mission, he and Lagarde signed a secret Convention on the White Nile.[185] By the terms of this agreement, the French government undertook to assist Ethiopia in establishing itself along the east bank of the Nile. Thus, it was hoped "the colors of His Majesty [the Emperor of Ethiopia] will fly on the right bank of the White Nile while the French standard will be raised on the left bank"[186]—and no room would be left for even so much as a narrow English railroad.

Rodd's obvious interest in the territory between Ethiopia and the Nile served only to strengthen Menelik's desire to realize his own territorial ambitions in that area. Shortly after Rodd's departure, the Ethiopian army began preparations to move westward, and by the end of 1897, over 250,000 Ethiopian troops had been mobilized for the Nile campaign.[187] Indeed, French plans seemed to be developing in the most satisfactory way. Ethiopia—the only missing piece in France's territorial puzzle—was fitting nicely into the grand east-west design.

From the outset Russia was associated with this joint Franco-Ethiopian strategy. Captain Leontiev had, in fact, informed the French in 1896 of Menelik's plans to push his frontier westward to the White Nile and had pointed out the advantages which France might derive from supporting such a move.[188] His own appointment by Menelik to the post of Governor General of Equatoria, the most south westerly province of Ethiopia and a region of considerable strategic significance to Britain's Cape to Cairo scheme, further stimulated French interest in using Ethiopian territory to promote its east-west projects. Terming Leontiev's appointment the result of "a long and wisely prepared policy" on the part of Menelik, the French adventurer, Prince Henri d'Orléans, found in it much encouragement for his own scheme to link up with Marchand via Ethiopia.[189] Together, d'Orléans and Leontiev developed a plan to exploit the new province of Equatoria, and, at the same time, to serve the larger interests of their respective countries.[190]

In Russia too there was optimism that Leontiev's new responsibilities in Ethiopia might provide a means for increasing Russian influence in central Africa.[191] Escorting a second Ethiopian diplomatic mission to Russia in October, 1897, Leontiev was able to tap the same wellsprings of Slavophile sympathy which had endorsed Russian projects for Ethiopia in the past.[192] It could in fact be maintained that at this time Russian ambitions for a political foothold in Ethiopia reached their furthest point. As Count Witte (albeit a critical observer) pointed out:

> There exists in Russia in the highest circles a passion for conquest, or more precisely, for the seizure of that [territory] which is not nailed down. . . . [In the religion of Ethiopia] there are certain rays of Orthodoxy and on that foundation we are anxious to declare Abyssinia under our protectorate and at the proper moment devour it.[193]

Not only was Leontiev granted a personal audience with Czar Nicholas in the fall of 1897, but during the winter of that year, he and d'Orléans were able to raise sufficient funds from Russian and French commercial interests to enable them to organize a large expedition for their return to Ethiopia. The French government, anxious to use d'Orléans and Leontiev to support Marchand, even supplied them with a force of *tirailleurs Sénégalais*, recruited from its colonies in West Africa.[194]

Given such initial success, d'Orléans was justifiably optimistic concerning his plans to frustrate the British in Africa. Unfortunately, however, his accomplice had made one fatal mistake: Leontiev had enlisted British interests in the scheme to exploit Equatoria.

Remembering their unhappy experiences with another Russian adventurer, officials of the Russian Foreign Ministry had for some time been on their guard against Leontiev.[195] In fact, they probably regarded the Vlassov diplomatic mission to Ethiopia, which arrived in Addis Ababa in February, 1898, as a reliable alternative to Leontiev's activities in the sphere of Russo-Ethiopian relations. One of Vlassov's responsibilities in Ethiopia was to control the activities of Leontiev and to investigate the information he was sending to St. Petersburg.[196] Hardly was Vlassov obliged to look very long before he discovered that Britain under the guise of certain financial arrangements with Leontiev, was attempting to establish its control over Ethiopia's strategic southwestern province. By May, 1898, it was possible to sound the alarm.[197]

News of Leontiev's dealings in London struck Paris with considerable force. In the opinion of the French government, something had to be done immediately to prevent the success of the Equatoria scheme. Asking his ambassador in St. Petersburg to make certain that the Imperial government was fully informed of the particulars of the affair, French Foreign Minister Hanotaux suggested that Russia join France in alerting the Ethiopians to the situation.[198] In response, Hanotaux was told that the Russian Foreign Ministry, acting under the express orders of the Czar, had asked the Russian representative in Ethiopia "to admonish Menelik regarding the danger of English interference in the affairs of his country under the cover of these [Leontiev's] arrangements."[199] Shortly thereafter, the Russians were able to calm their French allies with the assurance that Leontiev's influence in Ethiopia was already on the wane.[200] In so responding to the Leontiev affair, the Imperial government displayed an awareness of the strategic importance of Ethiopia's western provinces and, at the same time, demonstrated that it was willing to offer its services in the strategic game against Britain.

For his part, Menelik appeared to welcome assistance from Russia. On the surface, this assistance had certain advantages over aid from France. Russia was geographically remote and lacked any tradition of permanent military involvement in sub-Saharan Africa. Moreover, there seemed to be little chance that Russian imperial routes might traverse Ethiopian territory and thus threaten Ethiopian independence.[201] Finally there was the possibility that Russian assistance, when received simultaneously with aid from France, would enhance the options to Menelik to maneuver freely and to counterbalance foreign influences. Menelik owed much of his strength, in fact, to his uncanny ability to use various European representatives in Ethiopia as foils against one another.

Considerations such as these weighed heavily on the thinking of Menelik in 1897, as he embarked upon his program of territorial expansion. He therefore invited Russian as well as French officers to accompany his forces. In the fulfillment of their duties these officers played a significant role in the Nile campaign. Those belonging to the Russian Imperial Guards had prominent commands in at least two of the three major columns of Menelik's army. They appeared to have been acting not only under the authority of the Ethiopian sovereign, but simultaneously on direct instructions from the Russian government. They reported both to Vlassov, of whose mission they formed a part, and to the Russian General Staff in St. Petersburg. In this sense, the Russian government made a specific, active contribution to the Franco-Ethiopian effort.

The achievements of Russian officers were significant in several respects. In the first place, these officers made valuable discoveries concerning the geography of several of the Nile tributaries important to the Franco-Ethiopian effort. Secondly, they furnished Ethiopia's advancing columns with modern topographic and cartographic data —something which was indispensable to Ethiopian strategic planning. Finally, and perhaps most important, Russian officers were responsible for planting Ethiopian (or French) flags in locations where they were likely to check British territorial advances. Their efforts in this regard were remarkably successful. Indeed, Ethiopia's contemporary boundaries owe many of their contours to the exploits of these Russians.

Of particular value to the Franco-Ethiopian effort was the activity of Captain A. K. Bulatovich. This Russian officer had accompanied the Red Cross mission to Ethiopia in 1896. Taking advantage of the opportunity afforded by this first visit to Ethiopia, he had obtained authorization from the Russian government to investigate the western portions of the country along the Baro tributary of the Nile.[202] Thus knowledgeable concerning the geography of the region, Bulatovich returned to Ethiopia with the Russian diplomatic mission of 1898. After serving as an advance messenger between Vlassov and the Ethiopian sovereign, he undertook to join the army of one of Menelik's lieutenants, Ras Walde Giorgis, which was advancing in a southwesterly direction toward Lake Rudolf.[203]

In January, 1898, soon after setting off with the expedition, Bulatovich discovered a previously unknown mountain range which deflected the waters of the Omo River away from the Nile. With the concurrence of Menelik, the Russian Czar allowed Bulatovich to name it the "Nicholas II Range."[204] In this symbolically anti-British gesture, the Czar undoubtedly found considerable amusement.

Other exploits attributable to Bulatovich had more tangible effects. It is possible that as a result of its confrontation with Ethiopian units under the command of Bulatovich, MacDonald's British expedition decided to abandon its plans to push northward to meet Kitchener at Fashoda.[205] Certainly the Ethiopian forts which Bulatovich constructed on the route to Lake Rudolf made it impossible to extend the frontier of British East Africa into that quarter. In any event, Bulatovich in the space of scarcely four months, assisted in adding over 20,000 square miles to Ethiopian territory. Commenting upon this achievement, he was able to note with considerable satisfaction that: "In the newly conquered territory garrisons are distributed and these provinces must be considered lost once and for all to any other power which might have had claims to them."[206]

The participation of Bulatovich in the Lake Rudolf expedition was, by all appearances, a critical factor in its success.[207] His energy and speed won him the title of "wildfire man" among the Ethiopians. He also earned deep appreciation from Walde Giorgis and from Emperor Menelik. So important were his services that his own commanders in Russia considered it appropriate to grant him a promotion while he was still in Ethiopia.[208] This, in addition to the fact that he reported directly to Vlassov upon his return (who in turn communicated with Muraviev),[209] suggests that Bulatovich was operating under the authorization, if not the specific instructions, of the Russian government.

Considerably less certain, however, was the relationship between the Imperial government and Captain N. S. Leontiev. Although this free-wheeling Russian officer had, at least after 1898, fallen out of favor, his later achievements in behalf of the extension of Ethiopia's boundaries are worthy of note. Whether or not Leontiev was at one point prepared to cooperate with the British, the net effect of his expedition to Lake Rudolf in 1899 was to inhibit the expansion of British territory northward.[210] One account even suggests that he went to the length of replacing British flags with Ethiopian standards as he established the most southerly outposts of the Ethiopian empire.[211] At any rate, his activity in 1899 made it possible for Ethiopia to establish its power firmly on the shores of Lake Rudolf—a position from which no subsequent foreign territorial encroachments have been able to dislodge it.

Historically, the most interesting of all efforts undertaken by Russian officers in behalf of the Ethiopian army were those of Colonel L. K. Artamonov. Under special orders from the Ministry of War, Artamonov came to Ethiopia as a member of the Russian diplomatic mission.[212] Within days of his arrival in Addis Ababa, he received instructions from Vlassov to join the army of Ras Tsesema which was heading due west toward the Nile.[213] As a result of Menelik's request that a Russian officer accompany the expedition, Artamonov was presented by Vlassov to the Ethiopian sovereign on February 25, 1898, to receive instructions. Evidently Menelik was concerned about reports that his general, Tsesema, was conniving with Lagarde to establish a French protectorate along the east bank of the Nile, should France succeed under Marchand in establishing itself along the west bank.[214] He therefore asked Artamonov to report to him personally concerning everything he saw.[215] In this way Menelik would have some means of verifying the real intentions of the French. As the project to "link hands across the Nile" was reaching its final stages, Menelik undoubtedly wanted to make sure that one of those hands, as agreed, would indeed be Ethiopian.

Accompanied by two Cossacks from Vlassov's legation guard,

Artamonov soon caught up with Ras Tsesema. The latter's forces, which at the outset had numbered an impressive 15,000 were, however, weakened by disease and were reluctant to make the final push toward the Nile. According to one eyewitness, it was Artamonov who persuaded Tsesema to fulfill Menelik's instructions by sending a small detachment to complete the journey.[216] Tsesema requested that Artamonov lead this detachment and thus, together with approximately 2,000 soldiers and two very reluctant Frenchmen, he finally arrived on July 23, 1898, at the mouth of the Sobat on the White Nile. The Ethiopian flag was solemnly raised on the river's eastern shore. Since Marchand was nowhere in sight, it was decided that members of the Artamonov detachment should cross the river and raise the French flag on the Nile's western shore in his behalf. The Frenchmen demurred, whereupon Artamonov and his two loyal Cossacks, ignoring the crocodiles, swam the river and hoisted the French flag.[217] Symbolically, at least, they had realized the objective of the Franco-Ethiopian treaty. Menelik was delighted and the Russian Cossacks were officially decorated by both the French government and the Russian Czar.[218]

Unfortunately, however, this Russian heroism bore little fruit politically. Unable to find French forces heading east, Artamonov's detachment had returned to Tsesema's headquarters and had promptly begun the long and arduous journey back to Addis Ababa. Marchand, arriving at the Sobat only a few weeks later, saw the traces of their presence. However, he was too late. When the critical moment of confrontation came on September 19, 1898, Marchand faced Kitchener's Anglo-Egyptian forces alone at Fashoda.

It is interesting to speculate how history might have been changed had Marchand's forces been able to communicate with those of Artamonov. Had the latter known of Marchand's proximity, he no doubt would have maintained his position on the Nile and sent word for reinforcements from Tsesema's troops. Fashoda was essentially no more than a show of force. But how might the British response have differed if Kitchener had been greeted by a thousand or more troops under Artamonov's command? Such questions must, of course, remain unanswered, for when the British arrived at Fashoda, instead of being confronted by an Ethiopian army of formidable proportions, they were threatened by little more than the bedraggled representatives of Marchand's expeditionary force.

The Russian government had followed closely the events leading up to Fashoda.[219] As the fateful moment approached, Count Muraviev reaffirmed the support of the Czarist government for France, assuring French Foreign Minister Delcassé that "in this affair, as in all questions concerning Egypt, the Imperial Government is resolved to act in accord with [France] . . . and to shape its position to conform with that of the French government."[220] Likewise, the Russian press was sympathetic to the French cause. It both criticized the expansion of Anglo-Egyptian power and, at the same time, supported French demands for a port on the Nile.[221] Upon receiving news of the Fashoda encounter the *Novoe Vremia* of St. Petersburg warned:

> The cabinet of St. James cannot suppose that the power allied with France regards the denouement of the Fashoda affair with an indifferent eye. . . . She [Russia] will do everything necessary to convince England that she must consider the logical consequences of this [Russia's pro-French position].[222]

In the tense days following the Fashoda crisis, when war between France and England indeed seemed imminent, Czar Nicholas appeared ready to fulfil such warnings. Convinced that England constituted a real threat to Russian interests and ever prepared to exploit Anglo-Russian hostility, the Czar began to concentrate Russian troops in the Caucuses. As he subsequently explained to the French ambassador, "we made preparations and arrangements for any contingency."[223]

Russian aggressiveness, however, was extremely short-lived. When it began to appear as though France might capitulate to the British, the Imperial government recognized that it was in no position to face Britain alone. Not only was it difficult to employ Russian naval forces during the winter months, but an extraordinary amount of time was required to effectively mobilize the Russian army. In such a situation, caution seemed the most prudent course. Thus, as Russian newspapers pointed out the futility of an Anglo-French war over Fashoda, Count Muraviev preached to Delcassé the virtues of conciliation and Czar Nicholas calmed the volatile Kaiser with assurances that war was not imminent after all.[224]

In the interests of reducing international tension, the Russian government suggested that it would recall its diplomatic representative in Ethiopia, offering the familiar pretext that Russian interests in that country were essentially scientific, rather than political.[225] Although this diplomatic step was not carried out, it was patently apparent that in regard to Russian policy in Ethiopia, calculations of realpolitik had taken precedence over considerations of friendship or ideological affinity. Clearly Russia had, in the latter part of the nineteenth century, established a rather intimate relationship with its black brothers in Ethiopia. History shows, however, that the Czarist government, like that of other imperialist powers, was at all times willing to use this relationship to further its own self-interest in Africa and the Middle East.

It would be a mistake to assume that all Russian activity in Ethiopia ceased after the denouement of the Fashoda crisis. Although this crisis did mark the climax of Russian optimism concerning Ethiopia's future, it did not effectively terminate Imperial Russia's interest in northeastern Africa. The Vlassov mission, for example, remained in Addis Ababa for nearly two years after the Fashoda incident. And, as late as June, 1899, Count Muraviev was cautioning the French against agreeing to the neutralization of Ethiopia lest this preclude subsequent Franco-Russian projects in the country.[226]

Further Russian interest in Ethiopia was no doubt stimulated by Menelik's continuing struggles against British and Italian colonialism. In the critical months following Fashoda, the Emperor's internal authority was seriously threatened by the revolt of Ras Mangasha, a pretender to the Ethiopian throne.[227] Reportedly this revolt in the North was heavily supported by the Italians, who hoped to return to their former position in northeastern Ethiopia, and by the British, who were anxious to prevent Ethiopian expansion toward the Nile.[228]

In this context, Russia's established policy of promoting the integrity of Menelik's empire took on new life. After the British victory over the Mahdists at the battle of Omdurman, the Russian government recognized that Ethiopia was the next target in the path of Britain's imperial machine.[229] Given past associations, it was difficult for the Russians to abandon the Ethiopians. In fact, when French support faltered, Russia, at least for a time, began to think of itself as Ethiopia's principal friend and protector.[230] During the Ethiopian revolt, Vlassov was active, both in warning Menelik of British and Italian moves, and in attempting to make peace between the various feuding princes.[231] More than ever, the Russian diplomatic representative occupied himself with the question of Ethiopia's military capabilities,[232] and once again Russian officers were active behind the scenes in Menelik's military campaigns.[233] As a final gesture, the Russian government even stood in for the French when they failed to produce a loan which had been promised to the Ethiopian Emperor.[234]

Ultimately, however, Menelik was to prove unsuccessful in his attempts to resist the advance of British influence. By 1902, it was clear that England would have its own way in Ethiopia regardless of anything Menelik or Russia might do to prevent it. On March 15, 1902, Menelik was obliged to sign a treaty with Great Britain renouncing his claims to the east bank of the Nile and granting Britain veto power over the construction of installations to divert the waters of Ethiopia's Nile tributaries.[235] Recognition of the futility of Menelik's cause, combined with internal political problems and grave concerns in the Far East, served to divert Russian attention from Ethiopia. By the early years of the twentieth century, Russian activity in northeastern Africa had markedly diminished.

Although Imperial Russia was thus obliged to accept defeat in Ethiopia,* its diplomatic mission in Addis Ababa was retained until the last days of Czarism.[236] Old ambitions regarding Ethiopia were not easily laid to rest. In fact, as late as 1913, there was a curious revival of Russian commercial interest in Ethiopia. In that year Russian Foreign Minister Sazonov received a comprehensive report from one of the members of the Russian mission in Addis Ababa urging Russian economic penetration of the country "as a basis for supporting Ethiopia in a religious and political connection."[237] And, as if there were nothing else to occupy their attention in 1914, Russians prepared to receive in their country the Abuna Matheos, head of the Ethiopian church, to discuss the perennial question of Russo-Ethiopian church union.[238]

An aura of unreality did indeed seem to surround the entire record of relations between the two ancient Christian empires. In retrospect, it seems incredible that Imperial Russia should have allowed itself to extend politically so far into Africa and to pursue ideological

---

* In 1906 Ethiopia was divided into spheres of influence by Britain, France, and Italy. In the opinion of more than one Russian observer, this unhappy event was directly attributable to the fact that "Russia, defeated by Japan, was renouncing its prominent role in world politics, reducing its representation in Abyssinia and its expenditures on Abyssinia and retreating from its earlier position as a friend-protector." (A. I. Kokhanovskii, "Imperator Menelik II; i Sovremennaia Abissiniia," *Novyi Vostok*, no. 1, 1922: 326–27.)

overindulgence for so long a time with its black brethren in Ethiopia. Yet, in the final analysis, it was calculations of realpolitik, more than ideological impulses, which furnished the most powerful motivations for Imperial Russian involvement in Ethiopia. One such motivation —the desire for a port on the Red Sea—was so significant an aspect of Russian involvement in Africa that it merits special consideration.

RUSSIAN ATTEMPTS TO ESTABLISH A PORT ON THE RED SEA

Imperial Russia's ambition to possess a port of its own near the mouth of the Red Sea was a permanent feature of its concern for northeastern Africa at the end of the nineteenth century. Recognizing that an overt Russian seizure of territory along the Red Sea coast was likely to give rise to international complications (Ashinov's attempt furnished a sufficient indication of that), the Russian government looked alternately to both Ethiopia and France as potential sponsors of its territorial objective. As the race for the Nile gained momentum, speculation grew that Russia would receive a territorial reward for its assistance in the French east-west scheme. In Britain, certain observers were convinced that the French government planned to make "territorial sacrifices . . . including Obok and the French sphere of influence on the coast" in return for the services Russia might render to France in Africa.[239] As one British writer subsequently insisted, "Russia's share in the matter, over and above the consciousness of a good and noble action, . . . would have been the seizure of Raheita Bay."[240]

Although it is difficult to know what would have transpired had France's pre-Fashoda plans been successful, it does seem possible that, at least as far as the Russians were concerned, there was a definite connection between their ardor in supporting the Franco-Ethiopian cause and their hopes to see the Russian flag planted on the Red Sea.

The idea of acquiring a Russian port on the Red Sea arose in the context of Anglo-Russian rivalry in the Middle East. This idea, like the notion of Russian involvement in Ethiopia, found its origin in the thinking of Porfiry Uspensky. Recognizing that Russia might itself become involved in the intensifying struggle to control the Suez route to India, Uspensky, as early as 1862, raised the question of securing permanent representation for Russian interests at some point along the Red Sea coast.* [241] This concept was taken up by Mashkov who, in his writings of 1889, developed in full the economic and military rationale for acquiring a Russian Red Sea base.[242]

Certainly if Russia wanted to sabotage the British position in Egypt or India, a fortified position at the mouth of the Red Sea would be a logical point from which to strike at the Suez route and thereby achieve this goal. That a Red Sea port would also serve as a valuable facility for provisioning Russian vessels and for enhancing the security of their journey to the Far East seemed to occur to Russian strategists only as an afterthought.

Throughout the Czarist period, much of the activity of Russians in northeastern Africa was oriented toward preparing the ground for a permanent Russian presence at the mouth of the Red Sea. By and large, this activity was concentrated in the two adjoining locations of Tajura Bay and the Raheita Sultanate.

The disproportionate emphasis which this portion of Africa's coast-line received in Russian literature of the period in itself suggests that plans were afoot for some kind of permanent Russian commitment in the area. Beginning with the Cossack Captain Nesterov, who remained at Tajura to prepare for the arrival of Ashinov's settlers, Russian observers developed special interests in all aspects of the life of the locality.[243] Lt. Mashkov, either on the basis of personal observation or careful scholarship, went so far into detail in discussing the region that he included statistics concerning the depth of the sea off Tajura (presumably for the benefit of any subsequent Russian projects for a port in that location).[244] Others, like A. S. Troianskii, evinced a keen sense of the strategic importance of territory near the mouth of the Red Sea and indicated to readers the eagerness with which other European nations were pursuing territorial claims there.[245]

The political difficulties which attended the Ashinov enterprise of 1888–89 in no way deterred further Russian efforts to establish

---

* The idea that Russia, with its own interests in the Suez route, might want to lay claim to a point on the Red Sea shores occurred, in turn, to Bismark. Evidently hoping to divert Russian attention from Europe, the German Chancellor in 1885 (shortly after Gordon's fall at Khartoum) suggested to the Russian government that it occupy some convenient point on the Red Sea shore such as Massawa. Although there was no immediate response from the Russian government, Ashinov's appearance at Massawa that same year may have been associated with Russian interests along these lines. (Lamsdorff, *Dnevnik, 1886–1890* [Moscow, 1926]: 132, 108.)

influence in the Tajura-Raheita region. In fact, nearly every subsequent Russian expedition to Ethiopia included this region in its itinerary. After visiting Tajura in 1895, Capt. Eliseev spoke in terms of "a brighter future for the shore of Tajura Bay, chosen by the notorious expedition of Ashinov."[246] At this time the rumor was circulating that somehow France would agree to cede territory to Russia in the area—a possibility which caused considerable anxiety to the British in Aden. Not only did these British observers note the arrival of Russian naval vessels in 1895, but simultaneously they received reports that the residents of Obok were preparing to be transferred to the authority of Russian officials who, it was thought, would arrive shortly.[247]

Perhaps even more disquieting to the British was evidence of Russian flirtations with Danakil leaders in the Sultanate of Raheita, a territory of somewhat uncertain political status. In 1895 Captain Eliseev, on his return to Russia from Ethiopia, made a detour in order to visit Raheita.[248] Soon thereafter, British and Italian agents learned that Mohammed Dini, Sultan of this strategic spot, had expressed his open sympathy for Russia and his dissatisfaction with Italy, his nominal protector. So provoked were the Italians with the insubordinate Sultan that, upon learning that he might welcome a Russian landing in Raheita, they sent the Italian navy to capture him.[249]

The Raheita affair of 1895 served only to enhance the growing fear in Europe that Russia, perhaps at the explicit invitation of Menelik, would obtain a protectorate over the entire Danakil region.[250] After Italy's defeat at Adowa the next year, the German government, for one, was concerned lest Russia "seize possession of Massawa and other places along the Red Sea coast in order to take control of the vital route to India."[251] Such fears were no doubt shared by other European governments as well.

Whether France, for its part, was ever convinced that its Russian ally should be allowed to obtain a territorial outpost on the southern shore of the Red Sea is a matter of considerable doubt. Judging from its reaction to Ashinov, there is reason to believe that the French government was jealous of its sovereignty in the region and wary of attempts by Russians to establish suzerainty there. The French reactions to Leontiev's activities in 1897 serve further to substantiate this view.

Among his multifarious activities, Captain Leontiev had reportedly approached both Menelik and Mohammed Dini with the aim of establishing a Russian port at Raheita.[252] Learning of this scheme in early 1897, the French government, which had only a short time previously appealed to the Czar to recall another one of his Russian officers from the same location,[253] understandably felt uncertain regarding Russian ambitions. Although France itself did not lay claim to the Sultanate of Raheita, by 1897 it felt sufficiently suspicious of Leontiev's plans to do what it could to stop his project.[254]

Given Leontiev's tenuous relationship with the Russian government, France could have attributed his activity to independently motivated Russian adventurism. If this were the case, however, then how could they explain the behavior of members of the Vlassov diplomatic mission? Upon its arrival in Djibouti, Lagarde observed with surprise, "half of the mission . . . hastened off to Raheita, which is scarcely the route for Shoa."[255] Moreover, was it not curious that Colonel Artamonov, the Russian officer who was subsequently to distinguish himself in the race for the Nile, should have led this excursion to "conduct ethnographic research in the Sultanate of Raheita?"[256]

The truth of the matter was that Artamonov and three other military members of the mission had orders (presumably from St. Petersburg) to meet with the Sultan of Raheita.[257] Although Artamonov's own description of the meeting offers little insight into what actually transpired during the visit, his reference to Russian sailors "who know it is impossible to sail along the coast of Africa and not have a coaling station there," offers a likely clue.[258]

Finally, at the end of 1898, the French government was able to obtain a more accurate idea of Russian intentions. After a conversation with Vlassov in Addis Ababa, Lagarde discerned a "secret desire" on the part of his Russian colleague that France cede, or at least allow Russia free disposal of one of its ports in the vicinity of Obok.[259] Soon afterwards, the Czarist government overcame its reticence and took up the matter directly with the French Foreign Ministry. On December 30, 1898, it submitted a memorandum to Delcassé which referred specifically to assurances made by the French Ambassador in St. Petersburg that "France was entirely disposed to cede to Russia terrain in the bay of Djibouti (Tajura) for the purpose of establishing a coaling station there."[260] The memorandum announced, moreover, that a Russian cruiser was on its way to Djibouti to "study the question on the spot."[261]

Montebello, the French Ambassador in St. Petersburg, was quick to point out that he had assured Muraviev only that France would favor the establishment of a coaling station at some mutually convenient point. "There was no question of the cession of territory," he insisted.[262] Thus, in response to the direct Russian diplomatic initiative, France's real position became clear. While the French government may have evinced a willingness to grant port facilities to the vessels of its Russian ally, on the issue of ultimate sovereignty, its position was as intractable as it had been at the time of Ashinov's unhappy adventure.

Russia's desire for a pied à terre on the Red Sea coast may be regarded as the only potential point of discord in an essentially untroubled record of Franco-Russian cooperation in Africa. This Russian ambition was treated tactfully on an intergovernmental level, yet, in the end, it inspired much the same suspicion of Russian intentions on the part of the French as it did on the part of the English and Italians.

Certainly the French could understand the Russian desire for secure maritime passage between Europe and Asia. However, as events on the Persian Gulf were soon to reveal, there were certain aggressive overtones to the Russian efforts to establish a port on the Red Sea. When Russian activity along Persia's southern coast followed upon the heels of Russian interest in Raheita and Tajura,[265] it was possible to view the project for an African port in a wider perspective. In this context it appeared as though Russia's age-old ambition for a warm-water outlet on the Indian Ocean had been revived. Thus, aside from its more modest strategic uses, a Russian port at the mouth of the Red Sea might well have been intended to support a Russian naval presence in the Indian Ocean.

Whether or not it was intended as a means to further Russian expansionism southward, the establishment of a permanent shelter for Russian vessels in north eastern Africa would undoubtedly have made good sense from the standpoint of naval communication between European Russia and the Far East. This was dramatically demonstrated at the time of the Russo-Japanese War when Russia's Baltic fleet had to be transferred to the Japanese theater of war. During that conflict, not only were Russian strategic options severely limited by an unfriendly Britain firmly astride the Suez route,[264] but even French ports, including Djibouti, were partially closed to Russian naval vessels.*

Thus, for lack of a safe haven on the African coast, Russian Admiral Rozhdestvensky was obliged to use the high seas both to coal his vessels and to rendezvous his squadrons.[265] These difficulties hardly facilitated his already arduous circumnavigation of Africa to meet the Japanese. In fact, such problems are generally cited by naval historians as contributory factors in explaining the annihilation or Rozhdestvensky's fleet at Tsushima.[266] It is difficult to refrain from wondering how the course of the Russo-Japanese War might have been affected had Russia indeed secured freer passage through Suez and realized its plans for a permanent port at the mouth of the Red Sea.

CZARIST CONCERN FOR SOUTH AFRICA, 1899–1905

Although Russian interest in Africa during the Czarist period was oriented primarily toward Ethiopia and the adjacent lands along the Red Sea, in order to understand more completely Russian attitudes it is important to discuss briefly the response of the Czarist government to political developments in South Africa. In many respects Russian activities in this part of the continent represented a direct continuation of those undertaken earlier in Ethiopia. As in north-eastern Africa they established important precedents for future Russian involvement in the politics of sub-Saharan Africa.

After disappointment over the failure of efforts to frustrate Britain's imperial strength in north-eastern Africa, news of the outbreak of the Boer War at the end of 1899 was greeted with barely disguised satisfaction in Imperial Russia. As the British army suffered a series of surprising defeats, it appeared indeed possible that the victor in the race for the Nile might well become the loser at the other end of the Cape to Cairo line. Lord Kitchener, the triumphant "Sirdar" of the

---

* France, wishing to remain neutral in the conflict, submitted to Japanese pressure and reminded the Russian government that as a neutral nation under international law it could allow only limited stopovers of Russian warships. (Delcassé to Bompard, February 16, 1904, DDF, 2e, IV: 362–64.) On February 18, 1904, Russian Foreign Minister Lamsdorff was forced to order Russian naval vessels in Djibouti to return to Russia. (Loc. cit.)

Sudan campaign, was transferred to the southern extremity of Britain's north-south axis to face what was perhaps the most embarrassing military situation in the long history of British imperialism.

The early Boer successes were not without meaning to Britain's adversaries in Europe. As it became apparent that British military strength had been widely overestimated, European powers, including Russia, saw a new opportunity to exploit weaknesses in Britain's imperial position. Recognition that British power was being seriously challenged in South Africa had a distinct bearing upon the health of Britain's entire imperial system and especially upon the security of its position in India. The future of that dominion, in particular, which had recently been struck by severe famine, was extremely unsure. In such a situation, it appeared to many that the British lion of the Napoleonic era which ushered in the nineteenth century might be obliged to see the century out as a lamb.

Czar Nicholas, not unaware of the implications of Britain's military dilemma, immediately recognized the effect which the South African conflict might have on the British position in India.[267] Realizing that the successes of the Boers had strengthened his own position vis-à-vis Britain, Nicholas felt that the time might be opportune to strike at British power along the Indian border. As the Czar explained to his sister in October, 1899:

> It is pleasant for me to know that the ultimate means of deciding the course of the war in South Africa lies entirely in my hands. It is very simple—just a telegraphic order to all the troops in Turkestan to mobilize and to advance toward the frontier [of India]. Not even the strongest fleet in the world can keep us from striking England in that, her most vulnerable point.[268]

Although the slow development of Russian railroads in Central Asia prevented the Czar from pursuing this "pet project," he did take advantage of the outbreak of the Boer War to undertake military maneuvers in the area of Turkestan.[269] Thus, like Alexander before him, Czar Nicholas exploited the occasion of Britain's dilemma in Africa to threaten its position in India.

In addition to Russian moves against India, other means of exploiting British weakness were considered. Serious attention was devoted by the Russian government to the possibility of occupying the Bosphorus.[270] Moreover, at least at the outset of the war, the Czar and his Foreign Minister thought of forming, together with

France and Germany, some kind of concert for the purpose of "taking common action against the ever increasing aggressions and expansion of England."[271] Although the notion was soon abandoned for lack of a sufficient response on the part of France and Germany, this démarche suggests the tenacity of the Russian ambition to thwart British imperial growth.

As staunch fighters of British imperialism, the Boers were obvious candidates for Russian sympathy and support. When these South Africans continued to prove successful in their efforts to resist British force, initial Russian enthusiasm for their cause ripened into profound respect. Increasingly both the Russian government and the Russian press began to interpret the South African conflict not just as an anti-British struggle in Africa, but as a genuine movement for national independence. Like the war for Greek independence in the early 1800's, the Boer War became a *cause célèbre* in Russia, attracting liberals and conservatives alike.[272] As the *Russkiia Viedomosti* put it:

> Many thousands of people who have never previously heard of the Boers and who cannot even pronounce their names wish them success, if only because they are standing up for their independence.[273]

In such an atmosphere it seemed natural that Russians would want to support directly the efforts of the Boers. By March, 1900, a volunteer corps of approximately thirty Russian soldiers had found service in the area near Bloemfontein.[274] Like many of the Russians active in Ethiopia, the majority of the members of this unit were officers of Russian guard regiments who had been granted reserve status.[275] In addition to volunteer military aid, a Russian medical detachment consisting of twenty-six persons was also sent to South Africa and in 1900 it opened a hospital in New Castle.[276] Although neither of these undertakings appears to have been sponsored directly by the Russian government, official cooperation was in all likelihood requisite to make possible their departure.

Certainly the British had good reason to regard Russian activity with suspicion. The Czarist government may not have been prepared to commit itself openly to assist the Boers, but it did seem to take an inordinate interest in the day-to-day progress of the fighting.[277] Czar Nicholas himself appeared to be responsible for much of this official curiosity. As he admitted to his sister not long after the conflict had begun, "I am entirely absorbed by England's war in the Transvaal. Daily I read through all the details."[278]

Presumably it was this personal interest on the part of the Czar which prompted the Russian General Staff to assign a military agent to the Boer army. On February 28, 1900, Colonel V. I. Romeiko-Gurko presented himself to President Stein of the Boer Transvaal Republic, and immediately thereafter he went to join Boer forces at the front.[279]

The services of this Russian officer were of considerable value to the Czarist government. By serving with Boer forces on the field of battle, Romeiko-Gurko was able to provide Russian authorities with detailed information concerning British military capabilities—something which would have proven extremely useful in the event of direct Anglo-Russian hostilities.[280] Perhaps even more important, the Russian government, by studying the report of this officer,[281] was able to observe both the political miscalculations of the British and the depth of indigenous nationalist feeling in South Africa.[282] In this way, Russia was able, perhaps more readily than other European powers, to recognize the strength of the Boer independence movement as an anti-British force.

Despite the initial Boer successes, British forces, by the end of February, 1900, were beginning to regain their lost position. In an attempt to salvage as much as possible of Boer political fortunes by freezing the military situation in South Africa, the Russian Foreign Ministry approached the French government with the thought that Russia, France and Germany might jointly apply pressure on Britain to end the war "in the interests of humanity."[283] Although Britain flatly rejected all Russian attempts to mediate their conflict with South Africa, the Imperial government seemed to persist in its sympathy for the Boer cause. Even after Boer fortunes had turned, a Russian officer, Lieutenant E. IA. Maksimov, reportedly sought to encourage the President of the Transvaal to continue his struggle against the British.[284] As with Ethiopia, Russian hopes for South Africa were not easily laid to rest.

The war in South Africa had deeply impressed the Russian government with the value of Boer nationalism as an anti-British force. The possibility of using this weapon against Britain in the future was certainly not dismissed. At the time of the Russo-Japanese War, when England adopted a hostile position toward Russian involvement in the conflict, the possibility of using Boer activism to divert British attention was again seriously considered. As the Director of the

Asian Department of the Foreign Ministry reported to Foreign Minister Lamsdorff on February 28, 1904:

> The possibility of a new, ever persistent war in South Africa constitutes a factor of first rank importance in international politics. This factor ultimately would make it possible to exclude England from those powers whose interference in the present war we fear, and thus almost entirely free our hands for energetic activity in the Far East.[285]

Certainly South Africa seemed to be a logical location for the strategic embarrassment of Britain, particularly if it was necessary to do no more than pick up the pieces of a barely moribund conflict. Lamsdorff therefore corresponded with the Minister of War, General Sakharov, concerning ways in which Russia might exploit Boer activism.[286] Although several specific alternatives were suggested, one plan in particular seemed to capture the imagination of the Russian government.

This plan was advanced by the former Boer General, Pinaar-Joubert, who was already known in St. Petersburg for his writings in behalf of the Boer cause.[287] According to Joubert's scheme, discontent among African Negroes would be used to create widespread disturbances. These, in turn, would occupy British forces until, within two or three years, the Boers themselves would be able to mount a major offensive. Although the Negroes whom he had in mind were principally the "Kaffir" peoples of South Africa, Joubert had become convinced in his talks with native leaders throughout Black Africa that the majority of the continent's Negroes could be relied upon to oppose British rule. "I found," he observed, "that all of Africa resembles a huge field covered with dry grass which needs only a match held up to it in order to catch fire, and I intend to be that match."[288]

To encourage the Russian government to provide military equipment and financial assistance to the scheme, Joubert made the extraordinary proposal that Russia accept a protectorate over the political entity to which these plans were to give birth. "Russia must be willing to declare itself suzerain of South and Central Africa," he explained —"a precious stone to add to the crown of Russia."[289]

If anything could have been more astonishing than the plans of General Joubert, it was the initial response of the Imperial government. Not only did it express the desire to learn more about the scheme, but it was inclined to believe, as Lamsdorff pointed out to the Czar, that "in view of the current political situation—especially the not altogether friendly policy of Britain toward Russia—the Joubert proposals might be considered useful."[290] Since the Czar apparently shared Lamsdorff's sentiments, the Russian Ambassador in Lisbon, who was conducting the first interviews with Joubert was informed that "the proposals of Joubert without doubt appear alluring and we are prepared to accept them in principle."[291] Although Lamsdorff agreed to subsidize Joubert's journey to Paris (where the South African could be further questioned by Ambassador Nelidov), he was not prepared to make any specific commitment to the scheme in advance. Rather the Russian Foreign Minister suggested that Joubert be informed that "he may rely upon our material support only upon the realization of his intended undertaking."[292]

Thus Lamsdorff slipped into the same attitude of cunning opportunism which he had been so shocked to observe in the official approach to the Ashinov enterprise a scant sixteen years before. In many respects Joubert did represent another Ashinov. Certainly he stimulated in Russia much the same enthusiasm for adventurism and the same ambition for territorial acquisition. Even more clearly than was the case with Ashinov, Joubert's experience with the Russian government demonstrated the lengths to which Czarism's expansionist proclivities could lead. Moreover, the consideration which the Russian government gave to the notion that its Czar might become "autocrat of all blacks" marked not only an extreme point in Russia's global ambitions, but the weakest moment in its political realism.

In the end, good sense gained the upper hand within the Russian government. Thanks largely to the arguments of Nelidov, to whom the plan had been presented in Paris, the government was brought to the realization that it should be thinking "not about new additions to the imperial title," but rather about ways "to retain in its entirety the old one."[293] At the time of Russia's unsuccessful war in the Far East and the domestic upheaval of the 1905 revolution, it seemed implausible that the Russian government should be debating the merits of new commitments in Africa. In such a situation Nelidov's admonition that "we must occupy ourselves first of all with the restoration of our military and financial strength and carefully avoid all foreign involvements" seemed hardly necessary.[294]

In addition to the scarcity of financial resources, there were also powerful political arguments for refraining from further Russian activity in Africa. The obvious priority which Russia's policy in the Far East was forced to claim was an important consideration. Moreover, Russian officials no doubt recognized that, had they supported the Joubert scheme, its chances of success were at best uncertain. As Nelidov warned Lamsdorff, "British rule on the Dark Continent is established on foundations too firm to be overthrown by a local uprising"—especially if another great power could not be counted upon to divert British forces to other parts of the world.[295] But perhaps most important, there were distinct indications that England had already begun to abandon its position of hostility toward Russia.* Since Britain had been a primary catalyst in stimulating Russian activity in Africa in the first place, the improvement in relations between the two countries served to remove a major practical rationale for further Russian involvement in South Africa.

The arguments which bore upon the final Russian decision to abandon Joubert's scheme were relevant to the whole spectrum of Imperial Russia's activities in Africa. The economic and political considerations which led to a withdrawal of Russian involvement in South Africa in 1905 were virtually the same factors which explain the diminution of Czarist interest in Ethiopia at approximately the same time. For a period it seemed that the basic justifications for Russian activity in Africa had been either removed or supplanted. It was not until after the Bolsheviks had taken over the reins of government that considerations of realpolitik would again direct the attention of Russians to sub-Saharan Africa.

*   *   *

Although Imperial Russia's interest in sub-Saharan Africa never represented a prominent feature of Czarist foreign policy, the Russian government did develop by the latter part of the nineteenth century what can meaningfully be described as an African policy. This involved the support of indigenous nationalism as a means of sabotaging the British Empire. Russia did at times evince a desire to establish a foothold in Africa, but its primary objective seemed to be the prevention of British colonial expansion rather than the promotion of its own territorial aggrandizement. Thus, Imperial Russia can be

---

* British policy did begin to change after 1905. Following the defeat of Russia in the Russo-Japanese War, Britain, the great balancer of power, decided upon a drastic realignment of its position in favor of cooperation with Russia. This culminated in the Anglo-Russian Agreement of 1907.

regarded as a participant in the African contest of preventive imperialism.

Viewed chronologically, the intensity of Russia's concern for sub-Saharan Africa was primarily a function of its enmity toward Britain. Although original Russian interest in Africa was sparked by rivalry with the Ottomans and by the Czarist desire to establish trade routes to India and the Far East, the most active period of Russian activity in Africa (1888-1905) coincided with the years of greatest Anglo-Russian antagonism. It was not until relations between Russia and England began to improve at the beginning of the twentieth century that the Czarist government lost its enthusiasm for African projects.

Ethiopia and the lands adjacent to the Red Sea were able to claim the major share of Russian attention during the Czarist period. That this interest was the product of a conscious policy on the part of the Russian government seems clear. The nature of this policy was perhaps best summarized by Kokhanovskii in a report to Foreign Minister Sazonov in 1913:

> While French and Russian policies were opposed to those of Britain, the political role of Russia in Abyssinia was clear. To establish an Ethiopian Empire as a fortress and bulwark against Egypt, and to prevent the English colonies of Africa from becoming united was a matter of high importance for us.[296]

Thus it was on the basis of calculated self-interest that Russia cultivated the friendship of its co-religionists in Ethiopia. The importance of strengthening Ethiopia as a means to threaten British power was certainly not lost to Russian officials. Given its strategic location, Ethiopia possessed the potential ability to challenge Britain's unilateral control over the Suez route to India and to prevent the implementation of its Cape to Cairo scheme. Moreover, by controlling the sources of the Nile, Ethiopia was in a critical position to threaten British power in the Sudan and in Egypt.[297] Considerations such as these were determinative in the Russian decision to promote Ethiopian independence and to support the Franco-Ethiopian role in the race for the Nile.*

---

* Scholars such as G. N. Sanderson (*England, Europe and the Upper Nile: 1882–1899* [Edinburgh, 1965]) who rely upon the Jesmon account of the Imperial Russian experience in northeastern Africa are inclined to overlook these points altogether. Instead, they define Russian interest in Ethiopia and the Nile valley as little more than the "hobby" of a few individuals in St. Petersburg and deny the existence of any meaningful Franco-Russian collaboration in the region. (See *ibid.*: 384.)

Just as calculations of realpolitik demanded that Russia support Ethiopia as a counterweight to British expansion in Africa, considerations of practical advantage dictated that Russia support France in the implementation of its anti-British policy. Virtually the entire record of Imperial Russian involvement in Africa was characterized by Franco-Russian cooperation. So great was the congruity of interests between the two powers in north-eastern Africa that neither sought to embark upon major moves without informing, consulting, or even, at times, requesting the assistance of the other. It was not until the French had proven unsuccessful in their bid against British power that Russia sought to disassociate itself from France's African ambitions. When both France and Ethiopia had demonstrated their weakness in north eastern Africa, Russia was not slow to redirect its attention to other potential allies—this time to the Boers in South Africa—in its continuing attempt to weaken the British imperial system.

In addition to Russia's anti-British objectives in Africa, other concerns of a practical nature served to stimulate Russia's African projects. Not the least of these was the recurring desire to acquire a territorial foothold for Russia on the African continent. In some of the Russian writings on Abyssinia, such as those of Mashkov, the idea was advanced that Russia might, through the influence of the Orthodox Church and through economic penetration of the country, acquire some type of suzerainty over the entirety of the Ethiopian state. Although there is little indication that Russia's actual activities in Ethiopia were ever directed toward this ambitious objective, Russia did seek to use its friendship with the Ethiopian Emperor Menelik, as well as its amity with France, to establish a permanent political presence on the shores of the Red Sea. The Russian attempt in 1889 to set up a permanent colony at Tajura Bay and later efforts to acquire a port at the mouth of the Red Sea ultimately resulted in failure. Yet these schemes, together with the project to establish a protectorate over Negroes in central and southern Africa, should be viewed not only as attempts to sabotage British power, but as striking examples of Russian expansionist ambitions.

On the surface it appears that the major objectives of Imperial Russian involvement in Africa were never realized. Britain emerged as the undisputed victor in north eastern Africa. It retained control of the vital Suez route to India and was able to proceed with preparations for its Cape to Cairo axis. Even in South Africa, Britain, after a series of surprising defeats, was able to reverse the military tide and quell Boer resistance. In such a situation, what achievements could Russia claim as a result of its involvement in the politics of African imperialism?

Although the resistance of other imperialist powers prevented Russia from achieving its most ambitious objectives, it is wrong to believe that the Czarist government reaped no advantage from its African policy. It could, for example, look back upon its experience in north eastern Africa as having gone some distance in frustrating the expansion of British influence up the Nile valley. Russian efforts had been responsible not only for helping Ethiopia win its key victory at Adowa, but for enabling Menelik to extend his frontiers southward and westward in the face of British pressure. Also in what might be termed a bartering sense, Russia's African activities were comparatively successful. By maintaining a presence in north eastern Africa Russia was able to threaten British power and thereby to win concessions in other parts of the world. Playing upon British fears, Russia was able to use its position in Africa as a bargaining lever to achieve more important foreign policy objectives in Central Asia and the Far East. Nowhere was this practice more apparent than in Russia's participation in the race for the Nile. So concerned was Britain lest Russia increase substantially its contribution to France's anti-British campaign in Africa, that in 1898 it adopted a conciliatory posture toward Russian ambitions in the Far East. As Churchill later observed, conciliation toward Russian diplomacy in China was pursued in order "to influence the impending conflict on the Upper Nile and make it certain, or at least likely, that when Great Britain and France should be placed in direct opposition, France should find herself alone."[298]

Thus, Russia was ever prepared to exploit the predicaments of British imperialism. Points of British weakness in north eastern Africa and South Africa were seized in order to promote Russian objectives elsewhere. That these token moves on the African chessboard reaped certain limited rewards in other parts of the world should not be forgotten in evaluating the significance of Russia's African policy.

In retrospect, however, perhaps the most important result of the Czarist African experience was the precedent it established for subsequent Russian involvement in the politics of African nationalism. In a variety of ways, the Czarist legacy was important in shaping the Soviet approach to sub-Saharan Africa.

In the first place, Czarist experience established a definite pattern of active political involvement in Africa which was oriented toward the pursuit of the national objectives of the Russian state. Contrary to the impression which Soviet writers have sought to convey, the activities of Imperial Russia in Africa fell very much within the pale of European power politics. Although the Czarist government lacked the resources to make a real commitment to colonial expansion in Africa, it was clearly not above taking advantage of the independent achievements of Russian citizens. In the best eclectic tradition of other European *imperia*, Czarist Russia was fully prepared to appropriate the most diverse fruits of Russian expeditions to Africa—even of those associated least directly with the Imperial government. No less than in the case of Britain or France the motto was: "Succeed and we shall recognize you. Fail, and we shall disavow you."299 Thus, although it may not have established any African colonies to bequeath to its Bolshevik successors, Imperial Russia did develop a pragmatic approach to involvement in Africa which was to be of undeniable relevance to Soviet policy in the years ahead.

Moreover, in determining its political objectives in Africa and in choosing the means of achieving these objectives, the Soviet government was to repeat to a remarkable extent the experience of its predecessor. The opportunism of the Czarist approach, the intensity of opposition to British colonial power, the recognition of the disruptive potential of indigenous nationalist movements, and the exploitation of Negro discontent were all to find their echo in postrevolutionary Russian policy. Similarly, the instruments used by the Soviets to disseminate Russian influence among Africans were borrowed in part from the Czarist experience. Certainly the use of clandestine agents and "front organizations" to promote the objectives of Russian policy in Africa was not to find its final expression in the peregrinations of Kovalevsky and Mashkov or in the dissembling activities of the Imperial Russian Geographical Society. Likewise, the programs of military and medical assistance, the training of African students in Russia, and the warm receptions given to visiting African delegations were aspects of Russian policy which were clearly not abandoned in the transition between Czarist and Soviet regimes.

There were, in effect, striking continuities in the Czarist and Soviet approaches to Africa. Underlying these continuities was a remarkable tendency for Russians of both periods to perceive their relationship with Africa in similar ways. In part, this can be regarded as a product of the surprisingly extensive quantity of Russian literature on Africa which emerged at the turn of the century. Without exception, every Imperial Russian expedition included members who kept detailed diaries of their travels. Many of these survived in published form, thus constituting a body of firsthand information upon which the Soviets were able to draw in formulating their own attitudes toward sub-Saharan Africa.

Perhaps the continuity in the Russian view of Africa can be equally well explained, however, in terms of the basic affinity in ideological outlook between Russians of the prerevolutionary and of the post-revolutionary periods. In its messianic qualities, the communist faith was not very different from that of Slavophilism. Both were inherently expansionist in character. Both provided an ideological motivation for the extension of Russian influence into sub-Saharan Africa. Whether it was under the aegis of Slavophilism or that of communism, one theme remained the same: Russia should have a role in the awakening of the colonial world.

PART II

EARLY SOVIET INTEREST IN BLACK AFRICA: 1917-1927

After the fall of the Czarist government, Russia found itself in the hands of new rulers who sought to draw a curtain across the history of the country and to reformulate the interests and objectives of the Russian state. In such an atmosphere of change, one would expect that thoughts of distant Africa, which seemed to so fascinate Czarist Russia, would have been abandoned once and for all by the new regime of the Soviets. To the Bolshevik leadership the African ambitions of the Russian Empire seemed characteristic of the ill-considered adventurism which had led to the downfall of the old regime. For all the machinations of the Imperial government, Russia had clearly failed to establish a permanent territorial foothold on the African continent. With its flavor of unreality and its lack of tangible consequence, Russia's African adventure seemed hardly worthy of further thought.

Even if Czarist involvement in Africa had resulted in net gains for Russian foreign policy, other far more important concerns in the early twenties would have understandably deflected Soviet energies away from Africa toward objectives of far greater priority. The manifold problems created by revolution, civil war, and foreign invasion were sufficient to occupy the attention of Bolshevik leaders during the early days of their rule. Furthermore, in the wake of World War I, Russia's external political interests were unquestionably concentrated in Europe. If Russia had possessed the will and the resources to turn its attention beyond the confines of the former Russian state, it would logically have been to Europe rather than the colonial world that this attention would have turned.

In such circumstances it seems surprising indeed that the Bolsheviks sought to continue and even to enlarge the scope of earlier Russian concern for sub-Saharan Africa. In fact, from the very inception of Soviet power, the new regime displayed, in both its literature and its official policy, an active interest in Black Africa not totally dissimilar from that displayed by the Czarist government.

3

The Bases for Soviet Interest
in Black Africa

Africa first attracted Bolshevik interest as a region in which capitalism's most nefarious practices were given free rein. Karl Marx himself pointed a finger to Africa when he condemned slavery and accused eighteenth century English capitalists of building their prosperity upon the ill-gotten profits of the slave trade.[1] Similarly, it was impossible for early communist writers to remain indifferent to the increasingly intensive race among nineteenth century capitalist empires to carve up the African continent. Marx's colleague, Engels, in particular, was dismayed at the spectacle of "Africa leased directly to companies" in the interests of the European stock exchange.[2] In short, Africa provided a prime example, not just of the evils of eighteenth century slavery, but of the sins of imperialist powers who subdivided colonial areas according to their own advantage.

When Lenin formulated his own thinking on imperialism, it was therefore natural that Africa should have attracted his attention. In *Imperialism: the Highest Stage of Capitalism* (1916) Lenin was interested in explaining the origins of World War I. In so doing he was led to the conclusion that European territorial rivalry in Africa had inevitably led to severe confrontation between capitalist powers. Africa's unique role in the irreversible downward path, according to his thinking, consisted in its having provided the last available terrain for the "free grabbing" of territories.[3] Whereas the last decades of the nineteenth century had witnessed comparatively uninhibited expansion, by the beginning of the twentieth century almost all of the African continent had been claimed. After this point, Lenin concluded, political change had to be by redistribution of territory rather than by new distribution, and the pressures for violent confrontation were accordingly increased. Thus, Lenin's understanding of imperialism led not only to the conclusion that territorial rivalries in Africa had contributed their measure to the outbreak of the great war in Europe, but to the belief that the continent would continue to provide a breeding ground for imperialist war in the future.

There were other equally important reasons for Bolsheviks to develop an interest in the affairs of colonial Africa. For one thing, they readily perceived a strategic connection between the economic health of the capitalist system and the expanding scope of its African enterprises. European capitalism may have been in the process of decay, but its life could well be prolonged by the influx of African raw materials and by reliance upon "super profits" derived from the exploitation of colonial labor. Lenin was particularly concerned about the apparent ability of Cecil Rhodes and other "social chauvinists" to use such resources to bribe the European proletariat and thereby to stifle its revolutionary energies.[4]

Related to this "economic parasitism" was another stratagem for promoting the security and longevity of the capitalist system. This, according to Bolshevik thinking, was the widespread resort by colonial powers to the use of subject armies. Although it was believed that such a practice would eventually prove to be the undoing of the European capitalists,[5] the thought that Africa would, in the immediate future, be increasingly used as a reservoir for the recruitment of mercenary troops was hardly comforting to the embattled Soviet revolutionaries. The thought was especially disquieting in light of the fact that colonial regiments—including Negroes from French Africa—had been stationed on the eastern front in World War I,[6] and were probably used by France during the Allied intervention in the Russian Civil War.* In such a context the issue of African colonialism

---

* As early as the Crimean War France had thrown Senegalese troops into the battle against Russia and it is quite possible that the move was repeated when France decided to join the Allied powers in intervening in the Russian Civil War. (Endré Sik, *Histoire de l'Afrique Noire*, II [Budapest, 1964] : 76.) The Soviets even claimed to have won over at least one French colonial regiment in the struggle against the White forces. (Mikhail Pavlovich [alias Vel'tman], *Voprosy Kolonial'noi i Natsional'noi Politiki i IIIi Internatsional* ["Questions of National and Colonial Politics and the Third International"] [Moscow, Izd. Kommunisticheskogo Internatsionala, 1920]: 59.) It is interesting to note, moreover, that one African Negro, probably a *tirailleur Sénégalais*, reportedly died leading a Red cavalry regiment against Whites near Voronezh. In his poem *Moia Afrika* (Leningrad, 1935), Boris Kornilov describes the incongruous figure of this African cavalry officer who fought the enemies of the revolution during the winter of 1918 "in order to deal a blow to the African capitalists and bourgeoisie." (*Moia Afrika:* 64.) After winning the respect of his fellow combatants, he was buried with honors by the Red Army. Radio Moscow, in a review of the second edition of Kornilov's book (*Moia Afrika*, Leningrad, 1963), referred to

threatened to become one not just of the welfare of the revolutionary movement in Western Europe but of the security of the Soviet Revolution itself.

In light of their belief that Africa was essential to the economic and military position of European capitalist powers it was understandable that Bolsheviks should seek to encourage nationalist discontent within African colonies. As indigenous nationalist movements gathered momentum in the years following World War I, sub-Saharan Africa appeared increasingly attractive as a location for Soviet anti-imperialist designs. In pursuing the Czarist practice of encouraging nationalism in Africa, the Bolsheviks found themselves particularly well equipped.

In the first place, Lenin, as the architect of Marxism's first successful application to national politics, was keenly aware of the value of nationalist sentiment as an instrument of power politics.[7] Alert to opportunities for enhancing the strength of his own movement, Lenin saw in the growth of colonial nationalism a means both for sapping the strength of the colonial powers and for gaining fifth-column support for his new and relatively isolated regime. If the goal of national self-determination had been propounded successfully in the Bolshevik rise to power in Russia, why then could it not be employed with equal effect as an external weapon? Moreover, in contrast to their experience internally, the Bolsheviks, by supporting nationalism outside the confines of the former Russian Empire, would not face the embarrassing necessity of denying in practice rights to secession which had been granted so freely in theory.

In short, advocacy of colonial independence, like so many other platforms of early Soviet foreign policy, was essentially a costless gesture. As Bukharin put it: "If we propound the solution of the right of self-determination for the colonies . . . we lose nothing by it. The most outright national movement is only water for our mill, since it contributes to the destruction of . . . imperialism."[8]

The Bolshevik propensity to support revolution among African and other colonial peoples was reinforced by certain specific ideological needs. The much trumpeted communist ambition to

---

the African eulogized by Kornilov as one of seven Senegalese who had volunteered to fight for the Reds. (Radio Moscow broadcast, February 2, 1964, summarized in British Broadcasting Corporation, *Summary of World Broadcasts and Monitoring Report*, Part I, SU/1480/A5/4.)

universalize the revolution was certainly one of these. Probably more influential, however, was the simple emotional urge to identify with the plight of downtrodden peoples which had long characterized the behavior of Russians. This feeling of empathy, which was apparent in the Czarist attitude toward Africans, accorded remarkably well with the spirit of exuberance prevalent among Russian communists during the first years of the Comintern's career.

Another convincing explanation for the surprising willingness of communists to turn their attention to Africa and the colonial world at the beginning of the twenties can be found in the paucity of alternative targets for their revolutionary energy. When, at the outset of the decade, bitter disappointment came over the failure of revolution to materialize in Germany and Western Europe, it suddenly became necessary to find new terrain for revolutionary activities. At the same time, explanations were needed for inactivity in Europe. The solution was simple. If communists could argue that success in Europe was contingent upon the liberation of capitalism's colonial slaves, then the inevitably slow process of upheaval in the colonies would provide a convenient scapegoat for the failure of revolution elsewhere. Statements were therefore issued from Moscow insisting that as long as colonial oppression existed there could be no freedom for the European worker.[9] Communist theoreticians, in effect, began to substitute colonial revolution for revolution in Europe as the next item on the agenda of world revolution.

Nowhere was this shift in priorities more clearly discernible than in the utterances of Lenin during the final years of his career. His statements before the Second and Third Comintern Congresses (1920 and 1921) placed marked stress upon the importance of encouraging work in the colonies.* In his last article Lenin expressed with unshaken optimism his belief that the Third World would be the decisive element in the victory of the communist revolution. "In the last analysis," he wrote, "the outcome of the struggle will be determined by the fact that Russia, India, China, etc. account for the overwhelming majority of the population of the world."[10]

---

* In a speech at the Third Comintern Congress (July 5, 1921) Lenin had declared: "It is evident that in the decisive battles of the world revolution the movements of the colonial peoples will play a greater revolutionary role than we dare hope." (Cited in *Inprecorr* [International Press Correspondence of the Comintern], VII, no. 17 [February 5, 1927]: 232.)

Concrete evidence of Lenin's eagerness to win support among the peoples of the underdeveloped world can be found as well in the substantial additions to communist theory which he announced at the Second Comintern Congress. In order to render classic Marxist theory more palatable to nonindustrialized peoples, Lenin held out the prospect that the difficult stage of capitalist transformation might be avoided completely. This new shortcut in the route of historical development would be possible for underdeveloped peoples "if the victorious revolutionary proletariat organizes systematic propaganda and the Soviet governments give them all the help they can."[11] In other words, the rudimentary state of development of the proletariat in colonial regions would not necessarily present an impediment to rapid progress towards a socialist order. Russia, in effect, would substitute its own proletariat for the sociological deficiency of less developed societies. However impractical such a gesture may have appeared at the time, it did establish a theoretical basis for all subsequent communist support of revolution in the colonial world.

Thus, early Bolshevik interest in sub-Saharan Africa was founded upon powerful considerations of both a practical and a theoretical nature. At issue was not only the long-term ambition of communist ideology to witness the destruction of the capitalist system, but also an immediate need to protect the security of the Soviet state. All subsequent Soviet behavior toward Africa was to testify to the existence of such basic motivations—both ambitious and conservative in nature. What was remarkable, however, as the following discussion of Bolshevik literature and the development of early Comintern policy should reveal, was that these forces were moving Russia toward involvement in sub-Saharan African from the very beginning of the Soviet era.

4

Bolshevik Literature on Black Africa

In spite of the variety of concerns which occupied the attention of the Soviets during the period of War Communism and NEP, a surprising amount of Bolshevik literature dealing with Africa was published in the years before 1927. This literature, some of which appeared even prior to the revolution, provides an important means for understanding the nature of early Soviet interest in Africa. In examining the literature certain significant features become apparent. First, Bolshevik writing on Africa, both before and after the revolution, represented a direct outgrowth of the African scholarship of the Czarist period. Second, Soviet interest in Africa, as reflected in Bolshevik literature, was stimulated in large part by concern over European colonial rivalry. The view that Africa constituted a major breeding ground for European conflict understandably led Soviet writers to focus attention on the African activities of imperialist powers hostile to Russia. Finally, and perhaps most importantly, a study of Bolshevik literature indicates that Russian observers, from the very beginning of the Soviet period, were aware of the importance of African nationalist sentiment. The attention they devoted to the initial stirrings of Negro discontent after World War I was clear indication of the significance the nationalist issue would assume in the Soviet approach to Africa throughout the interwar period.

EARLY SOVIET WRITINGS—AN OUTGROWTH OF THE CZARIST EXPERIENCE

Bolshevik literature on Africa was very much an offspring of the Czarist era. The fact that Russian writings on Africa during the late Czarist and early Soviet periods were, in certain instances, authored by the same individuals was a revealing indication of the intellectual and cultural linkage between Imperial Russian and Bolshevik scholarship. The work of a number of Russian Africanists embraced both the Czarist and Soviet periods. Certain of these Czarist writers, like Professor B. A. Turaev, established their reputations in the field of African studies prior to the revolution and were republished during the early decades of the Soviet regime.[1] More important still, there remained in Leningrad after the revolution a nucleus of ethnologists and linguists interested in Africa. This group of specialists, part of the tradition of African scholarship which had evolved in Russia at the turn of the century, provided training for Soviet Africanists. Moreover, the prerevolutionary thinking of these scholars was no doubt influential in stimulating interest in Africa on the part of succeeding Soviet writers.*

Continuity of authorship was exemplified not only in the works of Czarist scholars, but, more important, in the Marxist writings of Mikhail Pavlovich, the most influential Soviet writer on Africa during the 1920's. Pavlovich, who was later to serve as member of the Commissariat of Nationalities, adviser to the Commissariat of Foreign Affairs, Chairman of the All-Russian Association of Eastern Studies, and editor of the important periodical *Novyi Vostok*, developed, as early as the turn of the century, an active interest in Africa which he retained until the time of his death in 1927.

Active before the revolution as a journalist and political orator, Pavlovich began to write on Africa at the time of the Boer War and continued throughout the latter years of Czarist rule.[2] The important duties which he assumed in the Soviet regime were no doubt a product of his personal friendship with Lenin and his reputation as one of the early adherents to the Russian revolutionary cause.[3] In any event, Pavlovich, immediately after the revolution, became a resident authority on imperialism for the new Soviet government. In this capacity he was able to continue his writing on Africa and

---

* Thus Professor Turaev's discussion of the transmission of Negro African culture to Europe via Egypt in *Istoriia Drevnogo Vostoka* stimulated Professor Bogaevskii to advocate in 1924 "A solid inclusion of Africa in the sphere of European interest," and an "end to this isolation of the Black Continent from other countries." (B. Bogaevskii, "Negry i Novye Problemy Afrikanisty," *Novyi Vostok*, no. 6, 1924: 389.) A similar connection was apparent in the experience of Professor D. A. Olderogge, subsequently the dean of Soviet African studies, who began his career under the wing of Professor Bogoroz Taz, one of the nucleus of St. Petersburg ethnologists and linguists interested in Africa. (Mary Holdsworth, "Russian African Studies" [MSS].)

promote within Russia a continued study of "the East"—as the Third World, including Africa, was then known in communist parlance.

In stimulating interest in the less developed world Pavlovich's role in establishing and directing the All-Russian Association of Eastern Studies was particularly important. Founded in 1922 upon the initiative of Lenin himself, the Association had as one of its chief goals the promotion of "the study of national revolutionary movements in the black and yellow continents and in the countries of South America."[4] It pursued its tasks by organizing study circles in the Soviet Army, establishing an Institute of Eastern Studies, and, perhaps most effectively, by publishing the monthly periodical, *Novyi Vostok* ("New East"). Pavlovich's role as editor of this periodical, as well as his position as chairman of the Association of Eastern Studies and authority on Eastern questions within the Russian government were, in effect, sufficient to qualify him as the father of Soviet academic interest in the peoples of Africa and Asia.

If the personnel of Soviet Eastern studies seemed to have been largely inherited from the Czarist era, the institutional channels through which Soviet interest in the East was expressed bore uncanny traces of ties to their predecessors as well. *Novyi Vostok*, for example (the name itself was reminiscent of Czarist titles such as Sollogub's *Novyi Egipet*) was the most prominent publication dealing with the politics of Africa and the Third World during the 1920's, yet, in no way did it fit into the usual mold of Soviet periodicals. Not only were many of its contributors holdovers from Czarist days, but the entire format and tone of sophisticated analysis which it projected seemed to have been patterned after Czarist learned journalism. In many respects, it was not unlike the important pre-Soviet periodical, the Russian Geographical Society *News*, which itself managed to maintain uninterrupted publication throughout the period of the revolution.

Institutional continuity was apparent in another way as well. As mentioned previously, there remained in Leningrad a nucleus of ethnographic and linguistic scholarship which had evolved at the time of most intensive Czarist involvement in northeastern Africa. The continued work of this group of scholars was of great importance to the perpetuation of Russian academic interest in Africa.* Not only

---

* No doubt one of the reasons for Pavlovich's success in establishing the All-Russian Association and in editing *Novyi Vostok* was that he openly recognized the value of this old school of Eastern studies and made a conscious effort to

were the individual careers of Soviet students molded by the thinking of this group, but, perhaps more important, its influence led directly to the establishment of such Soviet institutions as the Institute of Spoken Eastern Languages in Leningrad and the Committee of Peoples of the North (an organization designed to promote research on underdeveloped societies).[6]

Thus, in terms of both personalities and institutions, there were distinct linkages between Czarist and Soviet scholarship on Africa. Yet, the most striking and significant tie was apparent in still another respect—in the very nature of the subjects discussed. Just as Czarist observers were concerned with the African activities of European colonial powers whose interests conflicted with those of Russia, Bolshevik writers saw the need to follow closely the African moves of their European adversaries. As it became apparent that the policies of imperialist powers were likely to threaten the success of revolution in Russia, Bolsheviks increasingly recognized that the outcome of European struggles in Africa, as elsewhere, was of critical importance to the future of the communist experiment.

BOLSHEVIK INTEREST IN AFRICA AS THE SCENE OF EUROPEAN COLONIAL RIVALRY

The similarities between Czarist and Bolshevik literature on Africa were perhaps most clearly apparent in the prerevolutionary writings of Pavlovich. In his book *The Great Railroad and Maritime Routes of the Future* (1913), Pavlovich sought to analyze the strategic importance of European competition for communication routes in Africa. Although at the time this book was written Pavlovich was a convinced revolutionary, his interpretation of the significance of colonial rivalry in Africa differed little from that of his Czarist contemporaries. That Pavlovich felt compelled to devote his attention to this subject at a time when his revolutionary energies might logically have been spent in more politically remunerative ways was indication of the importance which colonial activity in Africa assumed in Russian thinking at the end of the Czarist era.

Pavlovich, like other Russian writers of the period, was greatly

recruit former Czarist scholars into the services of the new Soviet regime. (S. Oldenburg, "Pamiat M. P. Pavlovicha," *Novyi Vostok*, no. 18, 1927: 24-26.)

concerned with the effect that African communication routes, particularly railroads, would have on the relative power and influence of European states. Expanding upon earlier Czarist discussions of imperialist activity in Africa, he analyzed, in turn, the projects of Britain, Italy, and France to span the continent with railroads and thereby link Europe with the center of Africa.

Although Pavlovich recognized that the real obstacles to the building of African railroads had far more to do with international politics than with geography or technology,[7] he rejected as economically impractical the Italian scheme to link North Africa with central Africa. The French trans-Saharan project, however, was something different. Whereas the economic wisdom of this project was also questionable, Pavlovich maintained that the strategic advantages accruing to France from construction of the railroad would more than offset the economic problems involved. Believing that of the three transcontinental projects that of France was most likely to see ultimate completion, Pavlovich analyzed the strategic implications of the trans-Saharan scheme.[8] His observations on this subject go far in indicating the nature of early Bolshevik thinking with regard to colonial rivalry in Africa.

According to Pavlovich, France would undoubtedly gain certain important advantages by construction of the trans-Saharan railroad. Completion of the project would give France a head start on its more ambitious scheme to connect Algiers with Capetown by means of railroads and thus would offer France an opportunity to preempt the British in their bid for a Cape to Cairo artery. (In this context Pavlovich viewed the project as a significant step toward the intensification of Anglo-French colonial competition.) But in Pavlovich's mind, much the most important strategic advantage of the trans-Saharan plan lay in the new facility it would provide for the recruitment and deployment of a Negro African army. Was it really worthwhile, he wondered, for the French "to ponder over the empty question of the economic importance of the trans-Saharan railroad when its 'great' military role was so obvious?"[9]

As Pavlovich saw it, France stood to gain materially by using black troops to secure its position in North Africa and other colonial territories. Indeed the *tirailleurs Sénégalais*, as they had to some extent already, could provide a key weapon in stamping out flames of rebellion in French North Africa. Moreover, they could be used for the task of overseeing the conscription of North African Arabs, so as to swell yet further the ranks of French armed forces.[10]

In addition to such uses for West African soldiers within the French Empire, Pavlovich recognized the value which a *force noire* could have with regard to the position of France externally. Not only would this army greatly strengthen France vis-à-vis other powers in Africa, but it promised to enhance significantly France's relative power status in Europe and the world at large. The capability of transferring on comparatively short notice large numbers of colonial troops to European battle fronts was in itself a factor which France's neighbors could ill afford to ignore. Germany, in particular, could not be oblivious to the possibility that France might quickly send Negro Africans to Alsace-Lorraine in the event trouble developed along that disputed frontier.[11]

Although Pavlovich anticipated some of the cultural and psychological problems which would arise from the use of Negro troops, he saw no alternative for France but to take the greatest possible advantage of its West African reservoir of human resources. Revealing a distinct affinity to Lenin's subsequent thinking on the subject, Pavlovich expressed the belief that France, plagued by a steadily declining domestic birthrate and riddled with internal corruption, would find itself increasingly dependent upon those redoubtable Negro soldiers whose "intoxication with gunpowder" and other martial virtues personified the lost qualities which France needed to remain alive as a nation.[12]

The trans-Saharan railroad was viewed in this context as the most efficient method for insuring the full utilization of France's Negro reserves. By establishing a "strategic route for its black army," France would avoid the difficulties of stationing its forces outside West Africa.[13] For a comparatively modest outlay, France would in effect possess an impressive deterrent capability for use in Europe. "In a word," Pavlovich concluded, "the trans-Saharan railroad appears to be an important and strategic route which will greatly enhance the military power of France and its role in international politics."[14]

It was only by including this discussion of the importance of Negro troops that Pavlovich in his prerevolutionary writing on European imperialism differed noticeably from Czarist writers of the same period. Although, as a Marxist, he sought to condemn Russian as well as European colonial endeavors, his analysis of imperialism betrayed the same anxiety over European activity in Africa which had preoccupied Russians since the latter decades of the nineteenth century. This concern for Africa as a scene of colonial conflict, so apparent in the prerevolutionary writing of Pavlovich, continued to represent an important aspect of Bolshevik literature on Africa throughout the early Soviet period.

In particular, this concern was expressed in Bolshevik discussions of the causes of World War I. Lenin himself touched upon the subject of Africa's role in the advent of the war in his work on *Imperialism* (1916). Yet, again, it was in the writings of Pavlovich that the question received most detailed discussion. In a volume entitled *The World and the Struggle for the Division of the Black Continent* (1918),[15] Pavlovich sought to analyze the influence of African territorial rivalries on the political situation in Europe. In so doing he was led to the conclusion that colonial politics in Africa had contributed directly to the outbreak of hostilities in 1914.

Pavlovich regarded the African activities of imperialist powers as a "race for the Nile" writ large, in which the competing transcontinental designs of European states—beginning with Britain's Cape to Cairo scheme and the Boer War—had led down the path to confrontation. When Germany began to dream of a trans-African empire the established colonial powers decided it was preferable to wage war in Europe rather than sacrifice their holdings to the Germans. Singling out for special attention the Moroccan crisis ("an electric button connected to the torpedo lying beneath Europe")[16] and the problem of the Congo (the trigger for Belgian entry in the war),[17] Pavlovich found substantiation for his contention that "the struggle to divide the last remnants of the African continent played an enormous role in the advent of the World War."[18] Although his writings on this subject were not published until two years after the appearance of Lenin's *Imperialism*, Pavlovich's works nonetheless augmented and helped to popularize Lenin's earlier thinking on European imperialism.

The revolution in Russia brought only a brief pause in the evolution of Bolshevik thinking on Africa. As early as 1921 articles dealing with Africa were appearing in Soviet periodicals.* One contributor

---

* At the end of 1921 and the beginning of 1922 a number of articles dealing with the politics of sub-Saharan Africa appeared in *Novyi Vostok*, *Zhizn Natsional'nostei* (the organ of the Commissariat on Nationalities Affairs, published between 1918 and 1924), and *Vestnik Narkomindela* (the journal of the Commissariat of Foreign Affairs).

to *Novyi Vostok* almost seemed compelled to apologize for the interruption in Bolshevik concern for the continent. As he explained it:

> We were too busy in the recent postwar revolutionary years with inter-
> nal, European, and Asian questions to be able to devote the necessary
> attention to the most distant . . . yet altogether important colonies of
> Africa.[19]

Whatever the case, Africa did attract Bolshevik attention in the early
Soviet period. The belief that African territorial conflict had provided
a spark for the outbreak of World War I contributed to this
revived interest. But perhaps even more important was the fear,
increasingly prevalent among security-conscious Soviet observers,
that the situation in Africa would inevitably lead to a recurrence of
global conflict. In the opinion of Pavlovich, as well as of other Soviet
writers on African affairs, the war and the peace settlement had left
Africa in a condition even less stable politically than that which had
existed prior to 1914. In particular, these writiers seemed to anticipate that as a result of the Versailles treaty Russia would once again
be forced to suffer the far-reaching consequences of African colonial
conflict.

Central to Bolshevik thinking was the belief that Britain, as a result
of the war, had made off with alarming gains on the African continent. In the redistribution of Germany's colonies at Versailles, it was
felt, Britain had so benefited as to eliminate every serious colonial
rival in Africa except France. Moreover, although Britain and France
had received in terms of acreage roughly equal shares of the territorial spoils, far the more valuable land had fallen to the British. This
was especially true in that the new acquisitions enabled Britain to
round out its possessions in eastern and southern Africa, thus realizing
—at least in terms of territory—an "uninterrupted link between
Capetown and Cairo."[20]

According to the Bolshevik view, Britain's new position of strength
in Africa greatly increased the possibility of Anglo-French conflict.
It could hardly be expected that France, with its long tradition of
anti-British colonial activity, would remain indifferent to this postwar power configuration. Was not France already preparing to
challenge Britain's strategic position by once again making construction of the trans-Saharan railroad the "order of the day?" In short,
as Pavlovich and his fellow writers concluded, French discontent
over the Versailles division of Africa was bound to produce "new

contradictions between the former allies" thus setting off a whole new round in the imperialist war-spawning game.[21]

The prospect of renewed conflict in Africa was not something which Bolsheviks were inclined to take lightly. Even Pavlovich's friend, Foreign Minister Chicherin, became concerned over the possible repercussions of what he felt would be a period of "actual hate" between France and Britain. "We must think of the security of our coasts and frontiers," he warned—"we dare not let a single detail of the daily play of world antagonisms escape us."[22]

Apparent in the Bolshevik response to the postwar political situation in Africa was not only a fear of renewed colonial conflict, but, equally important, a revived concern (reminiscent of the Czarist period) over the extension of British imperial power. One of the antagonisms which Chicherin undoubtedly had in mind was that between Britain and the Soviet Union over control of India and Central Asia. Although Soviet and Czarist plans for India may have been different, Soviet leaders appeared no less anxious than their predecessors to see Britain deprived both of political claim and of free access to the subcontinent.[23] The British, in turn, eager to establish an overland route from Cairo to Calcutta, were prepared if necessary to take active military measures against Red forces. Thus Pavlovich, who recognized well the historical background of Anglo-Russian hostility was led to the conclusion that "our principal and most dangerous enemy . . . is England, which has always seen in a united and powerful Russia a threat to British hegemony in Persia, Afghanistan and especially in India."[24]

The old story of Anglo-Russian hostility over Egypt and the Upper Nile, which originated in the more fundamental conflict over India, seemed indeed to be repeating itself.* In such an anti-British setting, it was inevitable that Russians would again become concerned over British imperial activity south of the Sahara. Led by Pavlovich, a number of contributors to *Novyi Vostok* took up once more the issue

---

* The British appeared to be as anxious to prevent the Bolsheviks from interfering in the affairs of Egypt as the Bolsheviks, for their part, appeared to be interested in Suez and the perennial question of Britain's control over the Nile waters. (See Theodore Rothstein, *Anglichane v Egipte* [Moscow, 1925] and P. V. Kitaigorodskii, *Ot Kolonial'nogo Rabstva k Natsional'noi Nezavisimosti* [Moscow, 1928, with a preface by Pavlovich]: 77f.) In this context, the Bolsheviks even managed to rekindle earlier Russian sympathies for the Mahdists of the Sudan. (See N. A. Rubakin, *Prikliucheniia v Strane Rabstva: Raskazy o Zharkoi Strane* [Petrograd, 1918]: 109.)

of Britain's Cape to Cairo railroad—discussing it in terms which differed little from those characteristic of Czarist writings.[25]

Similarly, in the early postwar period the trans-Saharan project of France received attention from Bolshevik writers. This project was viewed not only as an instrument for the general enhancement of France's military strength, but more specifically as a weapon to be used against the British position in Africa. By increasing the mobility of French troops, the railroad would, according to Bolshevik writers, provide a means to threaten British military power. Moreover, by diverting trade away from the Suez route, it would serve the additional purpose of weakening British economic strength.[26] Certainly early Soviet observers overestimated the prospects of the French scheme and exaggerated its nearness to completion (in fact, no tracks were ever laid). V. Khudadov, for example, predicted that "the construction of the trans-Saharan railroad will bring with it the exclusive hegemony of France throughout all West Africa,"[27] while Pavlovich himself estimated that the route would assume the pivotal importance of the Bagdad Railroad as a bone of political contention among the European powers.[28] Although somewhat far afield in their predictions, these Soviet accounts of the British and French transcontinental projects are interesting in that they betray the same spirit of apprehension—even ill-founded alarmism—which was a familiar feature of European reporting on Africa in the days before 1917.

In sum, Africanists of both the prerevolutionary and postrevolutionary periods had one thing very much in common—a tendency to see events in Africa as they related to Russian national interests. In this sense, the Leninist proclivity to regard Africa as a breeding ground for imperialist wars—wars which could affect the survival of the Soviet state—represented in some measure a direct continuation of the concerns of the preceding era. A similar observation can be made with regard to Soviet interest in African nationalism. This interest, as expressed in Bolshevik literature, represented in part a carry-over from Czarist writing on indigenous African culture and from the Czarist policy of supporting native discontent within the territories of Russia's imperial adversaries. As will become apparent in the discussion that follows, Russian interest in Africa as a scene of nationalist rebellion was fully articulated during the postrevolutionary period and became increasingly a principal basis for Soviet involvement in the politics of Africa.

BOLSHEVIK INTEREST IN AFRICA AS A BREEDING GROUND
OF NEGRO DISCONTENT AND NATIONALIST SENTIMENT

Russians may have been exposed to Africa principally by the dynamics of European power politics, but their thinking about the continent was certainly not confined solely to European rivalry there. Accustomed to political and economic suffering at home, Russian observers seemed prepared to look at Africa in human terms and to consider seriously the feelings and desires of its inhabitants.

This difference in approach between Russians and many of their European counterparts became particularly noticeable in the course of Russia's prerevolutionary contacts with north-eastern Africa. As their knowledge of this region grew, Russians came to acquire a genuine respect for African cultural and political achievements. Without the burden of devising apologias for the colonial exploits of their own nation, Russian scholars of the Czarist period felt free to argue the merits of the indigenous African civilization.[29] In so doing they made possible the evolution in Russia of remarkably liberal attitudes towards the peoples of Africa. This, in turn, was an important step, not just in stimulating Bolshevik concern for the cultural awakening of the Dark Continent, but in influencing subsequent generations of Russians to become ardent supporters of Africa's political renaissance.

Certainly the writing of Pavlovich in the pre-Soviet period placed him squarely in the camp of liberal Russian thought on Africa. Although he was intensely interested in the exploits of European powers in Africa, he went out of his way to consider the effect European actions would have on Africans themselves. In so doing, Pavlovich left little doubt that his true sympathies lay on the side of the colonized. For them, he observed, "European civilization" meant little more than an updated version of the old system of slavery in which degradation and the grave were the most likely rewards. Whether it was at the hands of the British, French, or German colonizers, the African inevitably became the beast of burden— the victim to be sacrificed upon the altar of European economic progress.[30]

Similarly Pavlovich looked with sympathy on the plight of Africans who were forced to serve in the armies of their European overlords. He described in some detail the sufferings of France's Negro African contingents, noting in particular their high mortality rate and the callous attitude of their French commanders who tended to see Africa as little more than "territory for producing soldiers."[31] In short, Pavlovich concluded, the African continent was undoubtedly "the most unhappy corner of the earth."[32]

But fortunately Negro Africans were not condemned to remain forever in such an unfortunate state. Expressing confidence in "the vitality of the Negro race," Pavlovich predicted that indigenous African peoples would overcome the attempts of the colonizers to keep them in their ignorance and would ultimately alter the status quo in Africa.[33] Displaying his Marxist faith, Pavlovich further suggested that it would be with the help of the very factors which facilitated the imposition of European suzerainty that "the black population can raise itself out of its semi-barbarous state and become acquainted with the benefits of higher civilization."[34]

With such optimistic expectations Pavlovich was understandably alert to signs of colonial unrest in Africa. Indeed as early as 1913 he found evidence of a "new spirit" of rebellion among Negro troops in the Congo,[35] and during World War I he was able to note with satisfaction the problems encountered by France in recruiting its black armies in West Africa.[36] Yet it was only after the war had ended and Negro troops had returned to their homeland that Pavlovich's expectations found substantial confirmation. That Africans would react with surprising hostility to their service in the armies of imperialism was immediately apparent at the war's end. Feelings of discontent aroused by the conflict were indeed the catalysts which led to national revolt against colonial power. Such a fact was not lost upon Soviet observers who saw in nationalism a weapon which could be used against their imperialist adversaries. Before the Soviet response to the nationalist issue in Black Africa can be further discussed, however, it is first necessary to give some indication of the extent to which colonial discontent had already become a political reality in the period immediately following World War I.

The Postwar Political Awakening in Negro Africa
As Pavlovich had anticipated, Negro African troops were used extensively by France, and to a lesser degree by England, during the course of World War I. Over 181,000 soldiers were recruited from

French West Africa alone and many (like those who fought at Verdun) played a critical role in major battles of the war.[37] While contributing their share to the Allied victory, these African contingents bore a disproportionate amount of the suffering in combat. Often placed on the front line in preference to metropolitan troops, many Africans served as cannon fodder. Others escaped death on the battlefield only to succumb to disease during the cold European winters to which they were unaccustomed.[38]

Those colonial troops who did manage to survive the war and return to Africa did so with profoundly altered conceptions of themselves, Europe, and the world. Bitterness at having risked their lives in what many regarded as someone else's war was certainly one aspect of their new attitude. As a result of their much acclaimed performance in European combat many felt a new sense of self-respect both as soldiers and as human beings. For some the exposure to European affairs produced a political awakening as well. Although relatively uneducated, these African soldiers were not altogether unresponsive to the lofty principles which were being invoked by European statesmen at the time. If it was indeed true, as these statesmen maintained, that "democracy, brotherhood, justice only can revive and rehabilitate the nations who shall survive in this titanic struggle," then could it not be anticipated that inevitably "the Negro, like the Lybians of old, will be at the footsteps of these nations demanding his place in the sun?"[39]

In a real sense African nationalism, like the Russian Revolution, was born in the trenches of World War I. As the war came to a close and the Peace Conference began deliberations at Versailles, a strong current of opinion took shape in Africa, as elsewhere in the colonial world, demanding political recompense for the contribution which colonial peoples had made to the war effort. Certainly many of the voices raised sought primarily a reform of colonial practices and an enlightened redefinition of the role of Africans within the French and British imperial systems. Yet, there was a significant element within the new movement which, influenced by the Wilsonian principle of self-determination, commenced political activity which led in the direction of ultimate independence for Black Africa. In a word, modern nationalism had become a force to be reckoned with in the politics of sub-Saharan Africa.

In the English-speaking colonies leadership for the new movement came from the increasing number of Negro lawyers and businessmen living in the coastal cities of West Africa. In these areas it was possible to speak of a distinct body of public opinion which, aroused by the war, was actively interested in shaping future colonial policy.[40] With the establishment of such local papers as the *Gold Coast Independent*, members of the West African educated elite had a means of voicing their discontent and of expressing their political aspirations. "The war has proved our loyalty, our equal sacrifices in lives and money," it was asserted.[41] Now what the West Africans wanted to know was "whether we shall develop as a free people under the 'Union Jack' or be made hewers of wood and drawers of water."[42]

Perhaps the single most significant development in what the *Gold Coast Independent* termed a "growing tide of public indignation" was the organization in March, 1920, in Accra, of the National Congress of British West Africa (NCBWA). Described as "the first modern organization in African politics,"[43] the NCBWA took the lead in defending West African political interests during the twenties and thirties. Although this organization never strayed beyond the bounds of constitutionality, its activities were unquestionably directed toward the eventual achievement of West African independence.* [44]

As had been the case in the British colonies, the experience of participation in World War I caused an outburst of postwar political sentiment among the inhabitants of French-speaking Africa. Perhaps because of their more direct exposure to the war, or because of the greater freedom of expression they were allowed, French African Negroes were even more outspoken in their criticisms than were their

---

* It is probably safe to conclude that African political activity such as that connected with the formation of the NCBWA was a direct response to the discussion of the issue of self-determination at Versailles. In 1921, for example, the National Congress sent a delegation to King George V asking why Africa had been left out in the granting of self-determination to subject peoples. At approximately the same time, moreover, pleas for self-determination were addressed by the NCBWA delegation to the Council of the League of Nations. (Christopher Fyfe, *Sierra Leone Inheritance* [London, 1964]: 316–19.) The statements made at the third meeting of the NCBWA in Gambia, January, 1926 (the second meeting had been held in Sierra Leone in 1923) reflected even further the extent to which the principle of self-determination had influenced the formation of the National Congress. One delegate, after quoting extensively from Wilson's Fourteen Points, went on to explain that the principle of self-determination was not only a concept which "has been brooded over [throughout] almost the whole of our continent," but was "the energizing force which has brought into being the NCBWA." (J. W. Kuye, "The Right of People to Self-Determination [With Special Reference to British West Africa]," reprinted in *Gambia Outlook*, XIV, no. 45 [November 7, 1936] [part 1]: 6, 4.)

counterparts in the British colonies. Among the first voices to be heard came from inhabitants of Madagascar, a colony which had contributed 41,000 troops to the French army during the war and whose insularity had nourished strong traditions of political and cultural autonomy.[45] It was Madagascan intellectuals in Paris who immediately after the war took the initiative in promoting colonial reform. With the purpose of pressuring the French government to grant citizenship and other political rights to black Africans, they inaugurated in 1923 a newspaper entitled *Le Libéré: Tribune du Peuple Malgache*. Although this paper was only published for two years, it presented a series of convincing arguments for radical political change, not only in Madagascar, but throughout Negro Africa. Somehow there was an inescapable logic to its proposition that if "everyone was equal when it came to dying for France," then everyone should have an equal say in the political future of the empire.[46]

This line of thought found an ardent exponent in one West African, Prince Tovalou Houénou of Dahomey—himself a veteran of the war and a product of French cultural "assimilation." A man whose professional and academic attainments constituted living testimony to the ability of African Negroes to absorb the fruits of European civilization,* Houénou took it upon himself to expand upon the efforts of Madagascans and to champion the political cause of Negro Africans. In both his writing and in the work of the organization which he helped to establish, Houénou contributed substantially to the early development of the nationalist movement in French-speaking Africa.

According to Houénou's thinking, France's Negro soldiers had more than fulfilled their responsibilities as French citizens by sacrificing their lives during the world war. Instead of the right that went with citizenship, however, Negroes had, in his words, "only the right to go to the slaughter house."[47] France, with its corrupt and prejudiced administrators, with its harsh labor policies and exactions of financial "contributions," was, moreover, bringing unfettered despotic power to bear on its African subjects in the postwar period. In short, it was the colonizers, not the colonized who were guilty of

---

* The author of two esoteric volumes on *L'Involution des Métamorphoses et des Metapsychoses de l'Univers* (Paris, 1911), Houénou was a professor of linguistics and philosophy at the Ecole des Hautes Etudes Sociales in Paris. In addition he was a medical doctor, a director of the Comédie Française, and a lawyer at the Paris Court of Appeals. (See *Action Coloniale*, V, no. 99 [October 10, 1923]: 1–2.)

savagery and barbarism.[48] Of what value were the mortal sacrifices of Negro African troops in the world war, he asked bitterly—"did they fall so that the chains of the survivors could be riveted more securely?"[49] Houénou believed that the time had come for Africans to present France with a clear-cut ultimatum: "either absolute autonomy . . . or total, integral assimilation without frontiers—without racial distinctions."[50]

In order to promote the rights of Negroes, Houénou, with the help of the Martiniquais René Maran* and other intellectuals in Paris, established in 1924 a political organization known as the *Ligue Universelle de Défense de la Race Nègre* (Universal League for the Defense of the Negro Race [LDRN]). In many respects this organization seemed to have been inspired by the revolutionary movement of Marcus Garvey which was centered in the United States. Not only did the name of the LDRN invoke the image of Garvey's "universal" movement for the improvement of the Negro race, but its stated goals, which included the promotion of solidarity and social improvement among Negro people and support for nations of Black Africa already independent, bore a striking affinity to the Garveyite program.[51] In addition the LDRN, in a variety of ways, sought to publicize Garvey's "plan for Africa" within the French Empire.[52] Houénou's extravagant praise of Garvey himself ("Zionist of the black race . . . the leader who can incite the masses"), as well as his often stated desire to work in conjunction with every existing association in the interests of Negro solidarity and the renaissance of Africa, gave observers still further cause to identify him with Garveyism.[53] Thus the French government, which followed intently Houénou's activities, was prompted to regard his organization as "a Garveyite operation in France."[54]

Despite these similarities, however, the LDRN could be viewed as something more than a European branch of America's black Zionist movement. The objectives of Houénou's organization were clearly directed toward the ultimate political emancipation of France's Negro African colonies.[55] Although its headquarters were

---

* Considered by some to have been the real father of belief in *négritude*, Maran first achieved prominence as the author of *Batouala*, a novel critical of French treatment of colonial Negroes. He subsequently lent support to the Madagascan separatists and turned to Houénou probably in part out of the conviction that the latter was a staunch supporter of the Negro cause. (See René Maran, "La France et Ses Nègres," *Action Coloniale*, VI, no. 101 [November 10, 1923]: 1.)

in Paris, this organization, through the publication of a bimonthly paper, *Les Continents*, made a particular effort to influence indigenous opinion in Africa. As a result of comparatively liberal press laws, as well as the connivance of several sympathetic colonial administrators, this LDRN publication was able to enjoy brief circulation not only in Paris but in Madagascar and West Africa as well.[56]

Although the LDRN under Houénou's leadership may have exerted only limited influence among the Negroes of French Africa, its appearance in 1924, like that of the NCBWA in 1920, did mark a definite beginning in the development of African political consciousness. These organizations provided the first institutional channels through which indigenous opinion in Africa could be mobilized. Their existence symbolized the new spirit of discontent and incipient nationalist feeling which had emerged in the immediate postwar period.

The Soviet Response

Believing that they themselves had gained nothing from participation in World War I, the Soviets were predisposed to sympathize with other peoples whose wartime sacrifices had apparently been in vain. In particular, they were aware of the frustrations of African and other colonial troops who had been forced to serve and to die in a conflict not of their own making. As Trotsky put it in 1919: "the colonial peoples were drawn into the European war on an unprecedented scale: Indians, Negroes, Arabs, and Madagascans fought on the continent—for what?"[57] This was, in effect, the central question which Africans were beginning to ask themselves as they returned from the battlefields of Europe and sought to readjust to their status as colonial subjects.

Indeed Bolshevik observers were to a remarkable degree conscious of the new political forces which were emerging in colonial Africa following World War I. Noting that "the war had produced a marked change in the world view of the Negro educated and semi-educated classes" in Africa, one Bolshevik writer made the perceptive observation that:

A sense of self-respect, a yearning for improved social status, and a desire to have a voice in all questions of internal and external policy are beginning to awaken among the indigenous masses of the African continent.[58]

Much more than a pious wish, this observation was the product of a rather careful—and surprisingly accurate—assessment of the existing political situation. Bolsheviks who devoted attention to Africa in their writings seemed to understand the process by which nationalism was making its appearance. They were correct, for example, in singling out returning African veterans of World War I as the key agents of political change and as potentially disruptive elements in African society. These black troops, Bolsheviks noted, were impressed by their newfound prestige as "heroes of the Marne" and as respected and sometimes even decorated participants in the Allied victory. As a product of their wartime experience these colonial soldiers had acquired a radically new conception of their own strength vis-à-vis Europeans. On the basis of missionary reports one writer, A. Krikkel, went on to observe that secret societies were even being formed among demobilized troops (probably *tirailleurs Sénégalais*) in French Equatorial Africa and the Belgian Congo and that these societies were popularizing militant anti-colonial notions.[59]

Soviet observers were also accurate in perceiving that such principles as the right of self-determination were producing their effect upon the African mentality. In particular, they recognized that such concepts were encouraging the development of a spirit of national awareness among colonial peoples. Possibly because of their belief that British colonial practices were more oppressive than those of France,[60] Bolshevik writers, at least during the immediate postwar years, tended to devote attention to nationalist movements in the English-speaking rather than French-speaking African colonies.

Both Krikkel and Pavlovich welcomed the formation of the NCBWA as a rallying point for nationalist sentiment in West Africa. Rejoicing at the dilemma of the British government (which apparently felt it necessary to discredit the new organization), they recognized that the thrust of the NCBWA's activity was clearly in the direction of "national" autonomy for Negro Africans.[61] Moreover, they noted that a "radical, indigenous press" was making its appearance in Nigeria and the Gold Coast and that this press was conducting a vigorous defense of the NCBWA against British attempts at harassment.[62]

Similarly, the difficulties which Britain was encountering in East Africa did not escape Soviet attention. Articles in the journal of the Commissariat of Nationalities, for example, described in some detail native unrest in Kenya. Not only was discontent taking organized form in this colony, but for the first time agitational literature was being distributed among the indigenous population.[63] When the British arrested the leader of the Kenya movement prompting his supporters to clash with Nairobi police, Bolshevik writers were quick to note the spirit of militancy which prevailed among certain native elements in the colony.[64] In short, political developments of a disruptive nature in both Kenya and West Africa were taken as evidence —not just that the small educated stratum of African society was "applying its own interpretation to the principle of self-determination"[65]—but that ultimately widespread political upheaval against Britain could be expected throughout English-speaking Africa.[66]

Although open manifestations of discontent in colonial Africa captured Russian interest during the immediate postwar years, it was the radical movement of Marcus Garvey, together with the pan-African cause which he promoted, which seemed to attract the most attention from Bolshevik writers during this early period. In an article entitled "On the Black Continent" published in *Zhizn Natsional'nostei* in 1921, I. Trainin undertook for Soviet readers a comparatively detailed description of the Garveyite movement.[67] Referring to Garvey as "a redoubtable revolutionary," Trainin noted that his American-based movement was likely to have political implications in sub-Saharan Africa, especially in appealing to sentiments aroused by African participation in the war.[68]

Similarly, A. Krikkel, in an article written for the *Journal of the Commissariat of Foreign Affairs*, appears to have taken seriously both Garvey and Garveyism.[69] Impressed by the size of Garvey's organization in America (The Universal Negro Improvement Association [UNIA]), Krikkel was perhaps even more intrigued by the ability of the movement to secure cooperation on the part of black nationalists in Africa and thereby to contribute to the radicalization of indigenous opinion. Not only were such recently formed African political organizations as the *Union Congolaise* in the Belgian Congo sending representatives to Garvey's congresses, but Garveyite agitational literature, printed in native dialects, was beginning to penetrate the continent in tens of thousands of copies.[70]

If Garvey was acquiring Bolshevik respect for the inroads he was making into the newly begun political life of sub-Saharan Africa, his objective of creating "Africa for the Africans" seemed all the better calculated to win the esteem of Bolshevik observers. Trainin quotes a passage from one of Garvey's speeches in which the "black Messiah" appears to be casting himself as the very model of the modern revolutionary:

> For the forty million black inhabitants of Africa the time has come not just to ask England, France, Belgium, and Italy "why are you here" but to propose that they clear out altogether . . . One of the bloodiest wars is still ahead. When Europe decides to exact obedience in Asia by force— that will be the appropriate opportunity for the black race, weapons in hand, to conquer Africa for itself.[71]

In effect, by campaigning for the abrupt, even violent termination of imperialist rule in Africa, Garvey appeared to the Soviets to be playing their own hand. Indeed, according to Krikkel, Garvey's followers had authorized him as the newly elected "President of Africa" to conduct armed hostilities against the whites "in alliance with the Bolsheviks."[72]

Garvey's potential as a revolutionary leader probably served to stimulate Bolshevik interest in another strain of American-born Pan-Africanism, the Pan-African congress movement. In particular, the proceedings of the Second Pan-African Congress, held consecutively in London, Brussels, and Paris in the latter part of 1921, were followed closely by Russian observers.[73] Although both Krikkel and Trainin noted certain moderate tendencies within the movement,[74] they were able to discern with satisfaction the emergence of a "progressive" left-wing grouping which sought to direct Pan-Africanism along a more radical course. At the session of the "World Negro Conference" held in London, for example, the leader of the left-wing element, a certain Negro named DuBois, had made the extreme proposal that Europeans either grant Negroes equal rights in Africa or leave the continent entirely and allow the Negro race to follow its own separate path of development.[75] According to Krikkel's account, DuBois continued such agitation at the next session of the Congress in Brussels, forcing the conservative chairman to terminate the proceedings in order to prevent the delegates from adopting a more radical program.[76] In such developments the Bolsheviks saw signs of a mounting revolutionary ferment, the ultimate objective of which would be the expulsion of colonial rule from Africa.

As this initially favorable view of Garveyism indicates, Soviet observers during the early postwar period were surprisingly optimistic concerning the political future of sub-Saharan Africa. Although they recognized that the region still lacked the economic and sociological prerequisites for political struggle on a class basis, they appeared confident that the years ahead would bring ever increasing expansion in the scope of "revolutionary protest."[77] Trainin, for one, felt that the political awakening of Negro Africa was "closely linked to the revolutionary movement which had embraced the East under the influence of the Russian Revolution" and that "sooner or later its avalanche will sweep . . . the power of the Europeans . . . from its path."[78] Going perhaps a step further, Pavlovich concluded that colonialist fears concerning the advent of Bolshevism in Africa were "not without foundation" and that inevitably "African Bolshevism" would have a chance to play its role in the destiny of the continent.[79]

Despite such overly optimistic expectations, Bolshevik scholars were realistic in recognizing that the new political awakening of Africa had already become a factor with which European colonial powers had to reckon in shaping their policies toward the continent. Noting that the press in both England and France abounded with discussions of "the native problem," Bolshevik writers concluded with obvious satisfaction that "the bourgeoisie's peace of mind concerning the security of its colonies had finally been broken—once and for all."[80] With equal satisfaction they went on to predict that the new spirit of Negro discontent in Africa would play an increasingly important role in the external policies of European states. Thus Pavlovich emphasized that if Britain and France were to exclude Germany altogether from sub-Saharan Africa, German revanchists would be able to undercut the latter's colonial position by supporting Pan-Africanism.[81] In a similar vein, Krikkel discussed the increasing role which the African population would play in Anglo-French colonial rivalry. Although he noted that heretofore indigenous Negro peoples had been forced to passively observe political events in their own territories, he predicted that these peoples in the future would play an "enormous role" in determining the outcome of imperialist conflict in Africa. This was especially true, he added, in portions of the continent where the European population was comparatively sparse.[82]

Such observations indicate that Bolshevik writers were keenly aware of the emergence of indigenous nationalism as a new political force in Negro Africa. By no means a cause for regret on their part, this new voice against imperialism was a source of considerable satisfaction. In describing contemporary events in colonial Africa Bolshevik authors made a special effort to express their understanding of the factors which brought about the first efflorescence of African nationalist sentiment. More important still, they went out of their way to welcome openly the first organized expressions of Negro discontent.

In this way, Bolshevik writers helped to set the stage for subsequent Soviet involvement in the politics of sub-Saharan Africa. More than simply a continuation of Czarist concern over the interplay of European colonial schemes, their interest marked the beginning of what was destined to become a significant relationship between Russia and the leaders of modern African nationalism.

5

The Development of an Active Comintern Policy Toward Black Africa

BACKGROUND TO THE COMINTERN APPROACH

The Communist International was officially formed on March 4, 1919, at the initiative of the leaders of the Russian Communist Party with the purpose of assisting their revolutionary colleagues in other countries to promote proletarian upheaval. Very soon after the new organization had commenced operations, however, it began to lose sight of its more ecumenical responsibilities and to fall under the spell of the Russian bureaucracy. By the time of the Fourth Comintern Congress (held in Moscow, November 5 through December 5, 1922) it had become quite clear that the Comintern no longer existed to serve the interests of the struggling movements in the rest of the world, but rather to enlist their support in the task of defending the security and the foreign policy interests of the Soviet state. In other words, there had occurred what E. H. Carr describes as a "reversal of obligation": Russian domination of the Communist International had passed a point of no return.[1]

The conversion of the officially constituted organ of the international communist movement into an arm of Soviet statecraft was reflected as much in the Comintern's relationship with Africa and the colonial world as it was in its policies toward Europe and the industrialized West.[2] In fact, after the Fourth Comintern Congress it became impossible to distinguish between the official Russian and the Comintern approach to colonial areas. For this reason, the record of Russian relations with sub-Saharan Africa, at least after 1922, must be discussed in terms of the African concerns of the international communist movement.

From the earliest years of its existence the Comintern displayed a distinct interest in the affairs of sub-Saharan Africa. Although Asia, among the regions of the Third World, received the greatest share of its attention, the Comintern's universalist pretensions led inevitably, to the conviction that "the teeming millions of the Dark Continent" would "come under its wing" as well. Such ambitious designs might be discounted as pure chimera were it not that two aspects of the Comintern's approach to world politics actually did show promise of involving sub-Saharan Africa in communism's activist plans. The first was a growing Comintern concern for the problems of the colonial world; the second was an increasing interest in the Negro race as a particularly unfortunate victim of capitalist exploitation.

During the early twenties the Comintern devoted a remarkable amount of attention to both Negro and colonial problems. Sometimes the "Negro Question" was considered under the wider rubric of colonial issues, while on other occasions the two subjects were deemed worthy of separate discussion. Whether discussed independently or subsumed under the same general category, however, these two dimensions of early Comintern interest inevitably touched upon the peoples of Black Africa. As both Negroes and as colonial subjects these peoples were destined to become the objects of specific concern on the part of communist leaders.

It was at the Second Congress of the Comintern in July, 1920, that the theoretical bases for communist involvement in the colonial world were first enunciated. Departing markedly from traditional Marxist theory, Lenin, in his well-known "Theses on the National and Colonial Questions" described to the Congress the relationship between colonial emancipation and the proletarian revolution in Europe.* If, as Lenin seemed to be saying, communist victory in Europe was contingent upon the prior success of revolutionary movements in the colonial world, then a reorientation of Comintern policy in the direction of a "union of the proletariat with the colonial slaves" seemed indeed to be in order.[4]

Lenin himself appeared convinced of the tactical advisability of such an important departure in policy. Not only did he tend to view the colonies as the weakest point in the armor of imperialism (India,

---

* Although Trotsky, in his manifesto prepared for the First Comintern Congress, had proclaimed to the "colonial slaves of Africa and Asia" that "the hour of proletarian dictatorship in Europe will strike for you as the hour of your own emancipation," he tended to regard colonial emancipation as a by-product of European revolution rather than as an essential condition for its success. (Leon Trotsky, *The First Five Years of the Communist International*, I [New York, 1945]: 25.)

for example, was widely regarded by Bolsheviks as "the Achilles heel" of British power),[5] but he felt strongly that Bolsheviks "would be very poor revolutionaries if in the great proletarian war for emancipation and socialism, [they] did not . . . utilize every popular movement against . . . imperialism in order to sharpen and extend the crisis [in the capitalist system]."[6] Insisting that "our policy must bring into being a close alliance of all national and colonial liberation movements with Soviet Russia," Lenin, in virtually the same breath, called upon communist parties affiliated with the Comintern to "give direct support to the revolutionary movements among the dependent nations . . . and in the colonies."[7] Primary responsibility for this task, he added, should be assigned to the communist parties within the respective European colonizing countries.[8]

In this way Lenin, at the Second Comintern Congress, succeeded in initiating active consideration of colonial issues. Interestingly enough, it was also at this Congress that he first sought to direct communist attention toward the problems of the Negro race. Calling upon the participants to "complete his theses" by drawing up brief reports on several important issues, Lenin selected the "Negroes of America" as one of the subjects upon which further study was to be conducted.[9]

In direct response to this request, the American delegate John Reed introduced discussion of the American Negro problem on the floor of the Congress. Agreeing with Lenin that Negroes in the United States were among those peoples of the world most sorely "deprived of their rights,"[10] Reed went on to assert that the Negro must be forced to recognize that only under communism could he find racial equality. In this spirit, he proposed that communists work for the elimination of racial prejudice and for the prompt inclusion of Negroes in all-white labor unions. In pursuing such objectives, he stated in conclusion, communists would be well advised to make use of Negro movements which were already in existence.[11]

Thus, communist concern for both the Negro and the colonial issue could be traced to the statements and discussions of the 1920 Comintern Congress. Yet it remained for two individuals—Pavlovich and David "Ivon" Jones of South Africa—to apply Comintern thinking specifically to Africa and to direct the international communist organization toward a more activist approach to African colonial questions.

At approximately the same time Lenin's "Theses" were being formulated Pavlovich was at work explaining the fundamental shift in Bolshevik thinking to an Eastern focus. The decision of the Comintern to actively "cooperate with every revolutionary movement in the East and in Africa" was, in his opinion, one of the most significant differences between the Second and the Third International.[12] Russians as well as their European communist comrades, he insisted, were realizing that given the brutal injustices of colonialism, it was their duty consistently and totally to repudiate colonial policies.[13] Moreover, Pavlovich observed, Comintern support of revolutionary movements in Asia and Africa was both necessary to the progress of these movements themselves and, as Lenin had suggested, essential to the success of communism in Europe. "While the yellow and black continents remain oppressed," he concluded, "the European worker cannot throw off his chains."[14]

If revolution in Europe was thus held to be conditional upon the downfall of colonialism in Africa and Asia, there was an obvious need for an energetic approach to colonial issues on the part of the Comintern. By involving himself personally in several efforts which the Comintern promptly undertook to carry its message to colonial peoples, Pavlovich was in a position to influence the international communist organization in the direction of an activist program. Not only did he teach "Eastern studies" to Soviet military officers, but he was active at the Communist University for the Toilers of the East (KUTV, also known as "Kutvu" and later as the "Stalin" University), established in Moscow in 1921 for the formation of a phalanx of communist agitators to carry the revolution into the Third World.[15]

Far more important than these academic responsibilities, however, was the role of Pavlovich in assisting Zinoviev to organize the Congress of the Peoples of the East held in Baku in 1920. This prototype of the more recent Soviet-inspired Afro-Asian Peoples' Solidarity Conferences was devoted primarily to the question of "liberating" Asia and the Moslem world. Although Pavlovich devoted considerable energy to exhorting Moslems present at Baku to declare a "holy war" against capitalism,[16] he confidently expected that the revolutionary influence of the Congress would extend to Negro Africa as well—that, as he put it, "even on African shores the mole of revolution would do his work and neatly burrow the soil from beneath the feet of capitalism."[17]

At the time of Baku the most promising African soil seemed to be in the Mahgreb, where the westernmost inhabitants of the Moslem world were showing signs of restiveness under French and Spanish domination. Although Pavlovich and other Comintern faithful tended to see in the Moroccan Rif War the first fruits of the campaign they had launched at Baku,* they were by no means disposed to regard revolution in North Africa as their ultimate objective. Instead, it was hoped that the inhabitants of the Mahgreb would serve as messengers for transmitting Comintern ideas southward across the Sahara into Negro Africa. In fact, it was believed that the Rif uprising was already producing repercussions in the adjacent Negro regions of West Africa.[18] Thus, in 1921–22 the Comintern held high expectations that communist contagion might sweep into sub-Saharan Africa from a North African point of departure.

Another possible way in which communists hoped to penetrate Black Africa was by extending northward the activity begun among Negroes in South Africa. This approach was suggested to the Comintern by David Jones, a founder of the Communist Party of South Africa (CPSA), and one of the individuals most responsible for promoting Comintern interest in sub-Saharan Africa.[19]

Jones had been active before World War I as a trade union organizer and apostle of Marxism in South Africa. This experience had convinced him of the necessity of bringing South Africa's black workers into the struggle against capitalism. In 1917 he therefore assisted Comrade S. P. Bunting (leader of the CPSA) in an effort to create a Bantu trade union organization, calling it "The Industrial Workers of Africa."[20] However, like Bunting, Jones recognized that South African capitalists regarded as a potential labor reservoir not just South African Negroes, but "the whole native population of the

---

* The Rif War received considerable attention both in *Novyi Vostok* and in *Zhizn Natsional'nostei*. (See, for example, Pavlovich, "Vosstanie v Ispanskom Marokko i ego Mezhdunarodnye Posledstviia" ["The Rebellion in Spanish Morocco and its International Consequences"], *Zhizn Natsional'nostei*, no. 16 [August 13, 1921]: 1. See also Pavlovich's introduction to P. V. Kitaigorodskii, *Ot Kolonial'nogo Rabstva k Natsional'noi Nezavisimosti* [Moscow, 1925]: 12.) Following the Baku Congress a "Council of Propaganda and Agitation for Eastern Peoples" was established in order to give support and direction to liberation movements in the Third World. It is possible that this council (one of whose members was Pavlovich) provided direct assistance to Abdel Karim's mountaineers in the Rif. At least it was claimed in the French press that Bolshevik agents had participated in the rebellion. (M. Pavlovich, *Bor'ba za Aziiu i Afriku*, [Moscow, 1923]: 209.)

African continent."[21] Hence, Jones decided to look beyond the confines of his own country and to think in terms of the problems of
Negro workers throughout sub-Saharan Africa.

The year 1920 brought not only the first large-scale participation
by Negroes in South African labor strikes, but also financial difficulties for the fledgling South African communist movement. It was
probably with such factors in mind that Jones decided to make the
long journey to Moscow to attend the Third Comintern Congress in
May, 1921.

In Moscow Jones made a direct appeal to the leadership of the
Comintern to "reinforce" the communist movement in South Africa.
It is interesting to note that among the arguments offered by Jones
to encourage support for the movement was his insistence upon the
importance of South Africa as a territorial base from which the
Comintern gospel might be disseminated into the rest of sub-Saharan
Africa. Arguing that "Africa's hundred and fifty million natives are
most easily accessible through the eight millions or so which comprise
the native populations of South Africa and Rhodesia," Jones further
explained that active efforts had already been made by the South
African party to penetrate the Negro heartland of the continent.[22]
Why not, he asked the Executive Committee of the Comintern
(ECCI), send us a few revolutionaries, for "primitive though they be,
the African natives are ripe for the message of the Communist International."[23]

Presumably, in response to such initiatives, the Third Comintern
Congress asked its newly established "Eastern Commission" to look
into the task of formulating a resolution on the Negro question.[24]
Thus the Third Congress, although it did not itself contribute directly
to the development of Comintern policy toward Africa, did through
these efforts establish a framework for consideration of the Negro
question at the Fourth Comintern Congress in 1922.

By no means, however, did the revolutionary efforts of Jones end
with the Third Comintern Congress. Instead, he remained in Moscow until the end of his career in 1924, writing extensively for the
Comintern on the politics of South Africa and on the plight of Negro
peoples.[25] Perhaps his most important contribution during his
Moscow sojourn was the study which he devoted to the tactical
problems which communists were likely to encounter in their efforts
to conduct organizational work among Negro Africans.[26] Like John

Reed, Jones was particularly concerned lest the white proletariat be beguiled by the capitalists into treating the Negro as a worthless inferior or as a rival in the labor market. In this context he, like Reed, insisted forcefully on the need to fuse white and Negro trade union bodies.[27]

As a Comintern publicist (writing in English) Jones undoubtedly did much to impress European communists, particularly in Britain, of the need to espouse the interests of Africa's colonial Negroes. By drawing attention to their sufferings, as well as to their potential for political development, he also played a central role in promoting interest in Africa at the Comintern headquarters itself. If indeed it was not as a direct response to his pressure at the Third Comintern Congress, it was in part an outgrowth of his agitational work in Moscow that the Comintern decided, at its Fourth Congress in 1922, to embark upon a campaign directed specifically toward the Negro race.

THE FOURTH COMINTERN CONGRESS AND THE EMERGENCE OF AN ACTIVE POLICY ON THE NEGRO QUESTION

The real beginning of an active Comintern policy toward the Negro question can be traced to the Fourth Comintern Congress, held in Moscow in November and December, 1922. At this gathering a resolution was adopted which dedicated the international communist movement to the task of promoting revolution among the world's black populations. As a result of the emergence of a well-defined policy at this Congress, the Negroes of Africa, in addition to those in America, became the special objects of communist concern. In short, not only did the Fourth Comintern Congress launch the first concrete program directed toward the Negro race, but in effect it initiated active Comintern interest in the politics of sub-Saharan Africa.

By examining the resolution on the "Negro Question" adopted in 1922, it is possible to discern the initial outlines of Comintern policy. The discussions which surrounded the enactment of this resolution, as well as the literature which appeared in the Comintern press at the time of the Congress, provide a further means of understanding the pattern of thought which underlay the communist approach. In general it can be stated that the Soviet leadership of the Comintern, motivated by the desire to safeguard the security of communism in Russia and encouraged by the belief that Negro peoples were receptive to Marxist thinking, set out in 1922 to apply Lenin's Theses on the National and Colonial Questions specifically to the Negro world. In so doing, Comintern leaders brought Africa clearly into the purview of revolutionary communist activity.

There is little doubt that considerations of Soviet security played a critical role in shaping the Comintern's approach toward the Negro question. The fear that black colonial troops would be used by European powers to fight aggressive wars—even against Russia itself—lent an air of immediacy to Comintern proceedings. Those individuals who, like Jones, were anxious for the Comintern to formulate an active African policy were not reluctant to remind communists that "the time is pressing, the Negro armies of Imperialism are already on the Rhine."[28]

Similarly, Comintern activists were quick to point out that Negro armies might be used to suppress proletarian revolt in Europe. I. Steklov, for example, in an article written for *Inprecorr*, in November, 1922, described the use of Negro troops in Europe as "part of a conscious effort" by European capitalism to create "a soulless [war] machine to help maintain its own working masses in [a state of] slavery."[29] In a similar vein, the American Negro Claude McKay, on the floor of the Fourth Comintern Congress, discussed the relationship between the use of Negro armies and the success of the communist movement in Europe. Although McKay observed that "it would seem at the present day that the international bourgeoisie would use the Negro race as their trump card in their fight against the world revolution," he expressed the hope that Negroes would awaken to their predicament and would "come to Moscow" so that they might "learn how to fight against their exploiters."[30] Continuing this line of thought, he even went so far as to suggest that Negroes should be encouraged to enlist in the Soviet armed forces so as to demonstrate their defiance of the international bourgeoisie and their solidarity with the international proletariat.[31]

In explaining the practical reasons for including Negroes in the revolutionary program of the Comintern, these communist thinkers made certain to emphasize that black colonial peoples were economically indispensable to the successful functioning of the capitalist system. Approached from this vantage point, Africa, in particular, seemed to assume a pivotal importance in the balance of forces between capitalism and communism. Steklov had Africa primarily in mind when he asserted that "it is self-evident that the adherence of the black race to the world communist movement would be a severe blow to international capitalism on the economic as well as the political front."[32] Jones was even more explicit when he raised the spectre of East-West confrontation in the colonial world. "Who is to get this great Africa," he demanded bluntly, "the capitalist class or the Comintern?"[33]

The impassioned arguments of McKay, Jones, and others might have carried less weight in Comintern circles had not Leon Trotsky, then Soviet Commissar of War, been himself party to similar beliefs.* In a letter to McKay, Trotsky made clear his agreement that "the use of colonial reserves for imperialist armies is closely related to the question of European revolution."[34] Expanding upon Steklov's thinking, he went on to argue that:

> The use of colored troops for imperialist war, and at the present time for the occupation of German territory, is a well thought out and carefully executed attempt of European capital . . . to raise armed forces . . . so that Capitalism may have mobilized, armed and disciplined African troops at its disposal against the revolutionary masses of Europe.[35]

It is quite possible that Trotsky shared the fear, then current among Bolshevik leaders that France's occupation of the Ruhr might serve as a prelude to another Allied attack against Russia.[36] If this was indeed true, then the air of immediate concern in his statement that "the education of black propagandists is an exceedingly urgent and important revolutionary task at the present juncture," is easily explicable.[37] Whatever the case, it is certain that Trotsky, like other Russian leaders of the Comintern, was influenced in his thinking on the Negro question by practical considerations of Soviet security.

In this light it is not surprising that the resolution of the Fourth Comintern Congress dealing with the Negro issue clearly appeared to reflect Soviet security concerns. This comprehensive resolution, officially entitled the "Thesis on the Negro Question," was drafted

---

* It should be pointed out that given Lenin's physical incapacitation, Trotsky was probably at this time the single most influential figure in the Soviet government.

by a "Negro Commission" established by the Comintern and was adopted unanimously by the Congress delegates.[38] Although it made no specific reference to the military use of colonial troops by European powers, the resolution did discuss in general terms the strategic importance of Negroes in the balance of forces between capitalism and communism.

In particular, the Comintern in this resolution left little doubt that it viewed the exploitation of Negroes as essential to the survival of the capitalist system. "The penetration and intensive colonization of regions inhabited by black races," declared the Negro Thesis, "is becoming the last great problem on the solution of which the further development of capitalism itself depends."[39] Stating even more explicitly that "the Negro problem has become a vital question of the world revolution," the Thesis went on to assert that "the cooperation of our oppressed black fellow-men is essential to the Proletarian Revolution and to the destruction of capitalist power."[40]

If Comintern interest in the Negro question was provoked in part by security-related considerations, this interest was further enhanced by the belief that Negro peoples, because of the injustices long perpetrated against them, would be receptive to the communist message. As was apparent in both the resolution adopted at the Fourth Comintern Congress and the contemporary articles appearing in the Comintern press, Comintern leaders in the early twenties were both aware of the emergence of political unrest among Negro peoples and were ready to utilize this new phenomenon to further their revolutionary objectives.

It was at the Fourth Congress that members of the Negro race first participated in Comintern proceedings. That two American Negroes, Claude McKay and Otto Huiswood, attended the meeting in Moscow was heralded in the Comintern press as symbolic that Negroes everywhere were crossing the threshold of revolutionary consciousness.[41] Although Stekov, in his article "The Awakening of a Race," acknowledged that Africans were not present at the Congress, he nonetheless interpreted the American Negro presence there as evidence that the Comintern would soon add Africa's black inhabitants to the ever expanding group of "Eastern peoples" supporting its cause.[42] In his opinion, Negro Africans, having experienced the worst effects of capitalist exploitation, were particularly ripe for the Comintern message. "A doctrine offering [them] the promise of a return to the common family of . . . white brothers and a glimpse of liberation from exploitation must find a warm welcome," he observed.[43] In short, Negro Africa, according to Steklov, constituted a "virgin field" for Comintern activity.[44]

Likewise, David Jones was thinking of Africa when he described the Comintern's preparations to welcome Negroes into "the one great proletarian family."[45] "Negro emancipation is not an American question," he declared, "it is a question of Africa."[46] In angry terms he went on to describe colonial exploitation on the continent:

> Every capitalist government is drenched in the blood of the Negro. British imperialism in South Africa, the French in the Cameroons, Belgium in the Congo and the German Empire in Damaraland—they all constitute the blackest record in human history.[47]

Singling out the Negro as "the greatest living accuser of capitalist civilization," Jones implored the Comintern not to turn its back upon African workers.[48] Nor did he believe that the communists should be discouraged by racial problems which might arise between Negroes and whites.

Although he recognized that the Comintern would be obliged to exercise extreme tact in order to win the loyalty of Negroes, he felt that race consciousness on the part of black peoples could, in certain ways, prove beneficial to the communist movement. In Africa, he observed, awareness of race might break down "tribal sectionalism" and thereby induce Negroes to transfer their loyalties to a larger cause. More important still, because theirs "is a race of laborers," race consciousness on the part of Negroes could constitute a significant "step towards class consciousness," Jones suggested.[49] Thus, while communist thinkers did recognize that racial issues might create problems of a tactical nature, they did not consider that in implementing Comintern policy these problems would be insurmountable.

The belief that Negroes, irrespective of their racial peculiarity, would be receptive to the Comintern appeal was reflected in the resolution adopted by the Comintern Congress. In particular, the authors of the Thesis seemed impressed with the extent to which Negroes had become politicized by their experiences during World War I. Although referring specifically to American black soldiers who had served in the war, the resolution seemed almost to echo Houénou's writings on the plight of Africa's Negro troops:*

> When America was inevitably dragged into the world war, the American Negro was declared the equal of the white man to kill and to be killed for "democracy." . . . Fresh from the sacrifices of war, the returned Negro soldier was met with persecutions . . . disfranchisement, [and] discrimination . . . [A] spirit of revolt engendered by post-war persecutions and brutalities has [been] roused . . . [and] flames into action when . . . [racial injustice] cries aloud for protest.[50]

Not only in America, however, was there evidence of a militant spirit of discontent among Negro peoples. "The war, the Russian Revolution, and the great movements of revolt against imperialism on the part of the Asiatic and Mussulman [sic.] nationalities," had, as the Comintern explained it, "roused the consciousness of millions of the Negro race whom capitalism has oppressed and degraded beyond all others for hundreds of years."[51] More important still, there had emerged a "movement of revolt, which is . . . making successful progress against the power of world capital."[52] In short, the postwar political awakening of the Negro race was interpreted by the Comintern as part of a widespread movement of revolt, the progress of which would serve to undermine the strength of the capitalist system.

Perhaps the most innovative of the provisions contained in the resolution on the Negro question were those relating specifically to the implementation of Comintern policy. Comintern leaders as well as members of the Negro Commission emphasized the need for communists to translate their revolutionary beliefs into operational measures which would effectively carry the communist message to the black race. Jones, for example, spoke of the importance of making an "imposing gesture" to convince the black man that "a new dawn is breaking . . . that an army of liberation is coming to aid him,"[53]

---

* The effect of war on the Negro mentality was well understood by Trotsky. In his letter to McKay, he included the following observation: "The Negroes, and indeed the natives of all the colonies, retain their conservatism and mental rigidity only insofar as they continue to live under their accustomed economic conditions. But when the hand of capitalism, or even sooner the hand of militarism, tears them mechanically from their customary environment and forces them to stake their lives for the sake of new and complicated questions and conflicts, then their spiritual conservatism gives way abruptly, and revolutionary ideas find rapid access to a consciousness thrown off its balance." ("Trotzky on the Negro Question [A Letter from Comrade Trotzky to Comrade McKay]," Inprecorr, III, no. 25 [March 13, 1928]: 197.)

while Trotsky discussed the urgent need to "educate black propagandists" for revolutionary work among Negro peoples.[54] Otto Huiswood, addressing the Congress on behalf of the Negro Commission, was even more specific. In order to "coordinate and centralize" work among black people, he recommended that a Negro Commission be established in Moscow as part of the ECCI.[55]

To a certain extent, demands for a concrete policy program also found expression in the Negro Thesis itself. Stressing the need to secure racial equality for blacks, the Thesis announced the inauguration of a "special campaign" to organize Negroes into unions of their own.[56] More important still, the resolution called for immediate action to be taken within the Comintern system to organize all Negroes into one single world Negro movement. Toward this end it declared the Comintern's intention of "taking immediate steps to hold a general Negro Conference or Congress in Moscow."* [57]

Perhaps in recognition of its own lack of influence among Negroes, the Comintern also made a pragmatic and potentially more significant decision to support "every form of Negro movement which tends to undermine or weaken capitalism or Imperialism or to impede its further penetration."[58] This decision seemed to represent a tactical move to economize resources by authorizing communists to utilize organizations already in existence. In particular, it reflected the growing awareness in Moscow of the potentialities of Negro Americans as promoters of revolution in Africa. "The history of the Negro in America," it was observed in the Negro resolution, "fits him for an important role in the liberation struggle of the entire African race."[59]

American Negroes had certain qualities which recommended them to the Comintern as potentially effective agents for Africa's political awakening. Of all Negroes, those in the United States were the best

---

* The only immediate result of this Congress proposal was the formation of a special committee to study the Negro question. Although this committee recommended to the ECCI (at its first session, held June 23, 1923) that a Negro Conference be held simultaneous with the Fifth Comintern Congress in 1924, this proposal was apparently not acted upon. (*Inprecorr*, III, no. 52: 548.) As will be discussed subsequently, however, a Negro bureau of the Comintern was formed some years later under the leadership of George Padmore and a "World Negro Conference" was convened by him in Hamburg. It is thus possible to conclude that the directives of the Fourth Congress, although they did not receive prompt implementation, did inspire subsequent activity in Moscow which was oriented toward the formation of a world-wide Negro movement under Comintern auspices.

educated and sociologically the most highly developed.* In addition, many, like McKay,** nourished a self-image of militancy and were alive to the political issues of the day.[60] Finally, American Negroes not only retained a cultural nostalgia for Africa,[61] but they possessed, as Steklov pointed out, a racial entrée to the continent which could never be shared by their white colleagues, towards whom African Negroes often behaved with suspicion.[62]

Such considerations influenced the authors of the Negro Thesis. Not only did this resolution reveal the Comintern's awareness of the revolutionary potential of American Negroes, more interesting still, it betrayed communist ambitions with regard to specific American Negro organizations. As Huiswood's remarks at the Fourth Congress indicate, the Comintern had a definite operational interest in Garveyism as an anti-imperialist force in Africa. Impressed by the apparent ability of that movement "to plant race consciousness far into the interior of Africa,"[63] it saw Garveyism's "back to Africa" crusade as a useful channel through which to disseminate its own revolutionary message. Whether it had in mind cells of Garveyism or direct offshoots of the American Communist Party (CPUSA), the Comintern derived considerable encouragement from the knowledge that:

> We have also in Africa certain small organizations which get their direct inspiration from America, the headquarters and centre of political thought among Negroes. These organizations are stretching out and developing as far as the Sudan. These can be utilized by communists if the means of propaganda are carefully, deliberately and intensively used to link up these movements.[64]

---

* It was accepted by American communists almost as an article of faith, and not without a twinge of pride that: "From American Negroes in industry must come the leadership of their race in the struggle for freedom in the colonial countries. In spite of the denial of equal opportunity to the Negro under American capitalism, his advantages are so far superior to those of the subject colonial Negroes in educational, political, and industrial fields that he alone is able to furnish the agitational and organizational ability that the situation demands." (William F. Dunne, "Negroes in American Industries," *Workers Monthly*, IV, no. 6 [April, 1925]: 260, cited in Wilson Record, *The Negro and the Communist Party* [Chapel Hill, N.C., 1951]: 24.)

**William Nolan (*Communism versus the Negro* [Chicago, 1951]: 27) refers to McKay as the first American Negro whom the Comintern attempted to press into its service. Upon his arrival in Moscow in 1922, Nolan reports, the Russian authorities grilled him for information on American Negroes and, when they learned that he was still technically a British subject, offered him a job as an agitator in the African colonies.

Of all the radical American organizations, however, far the most promising for the promotion of Comintern interests in Africa was a body of Negro communists known as the African Blood Brotherhood (ABB). The program of this organization, published in early 1922, made clear the ABB's determination to incite anti-imperialist revolt among African Negroes.[65] Equally apparent was its attitude toward the Soviet Union and the Comintern. While Russia was praised unreservedly for "opposing the imperialist robbers who have partitioned our motherland and subjugated our kindred," the Comintern was singled out as an organization with which immediate contacts should be established.[66] In brief, no platform could have been better calculated to win the Comintern seal of approval. As Jones put it:

> The growing band of Negro radicals who look to Soviet Russia for guidance and inspiration in the struggle . . . under the banner of the African Blood Brotherhood, and in close touch with the class-conscious white workers of America, are pointing the way to proletarian emancipation as the only hope for their opposed Negro brothers in Africa and America.[67]

By the time of the Fourth Comintern Congress, communists seemed to be thinking not only in terms of the most promising organizations to use in order to carry the revolutionary message to Africa, but also of the most effective tactics by which this important task could be implemented. Although the Thesis on the Negro Question made no mention of specific agitational techniques, Comintern literature contemporary with the Fourth Congress does provide some indication of Comintern views on this subject. Trotsky, for example, spoke of the importance of creating a small avant-garde of "enlightened, young, self-sacrificing Negroes . . . filled with enthusiasm for the raising of the material and moral level of the great mass of Negroes and at the same time mentally capable of grasping the identity of interests and destiny of the Negro masses with those of the masses of the whole world."[68] Steklov was even more specific. In addition to the creation of "a Negro communist literature and press," he recommended the establishment of "training centres for agitators and propagandists who will carry on their work not only in the United States of America but in Africa itself by means of correspondence, as well as by the dispatch of special emissaries to the various localities."[69]

These recommendations, like certain of the projects proposed in the Thesis on the Negro Question, were destined to retain, at least for the time being, only the status of policy proposals. Yet, despite the Comintern's failure to implement immediately its directives, communists did, at the Fourth Comintern Congress, formulate concrete revolutionary objectives involving Negro Africa. There can be no question that after this Congress communists did firmly believe that "Africa, the patrimony of the [world's] most exploited peoples, must join the fraternity of [revolutionary] soldiers."[70] In other words, after 1922, Africa was unquestionably on the docket of world revolution.

THE FIFTH COMINTERN CONGRESS: A NEW ACCENT ON WORK IN THE COLONIES

Sub-Saharan Africa entered the Comintern frame of reference not only as the fatherland of the Negro race, but as a conspicuous scene of colonial exploitation. If the Negro question attracted considerable attention from the Comintern at its gathering in 1922, the same can be said of the colonial issue at the Fifth Comintern Congress of June and July, 1924. Before discussing the debate at the Fifth Congress itself, it is useful to trace briefly the background to this issue as it took shape during the first few years of the 1920's.

It should be recalled that Lenin, at the Second Comintern Congress in 1920 and at the Third Comintern Congress in 1921, had enjoined all communists to dedicate themselves to the active support of colonial emancipation. In the years immediately following these Congresses, however, at least on the part of the Comintern's Russian leadership, emphasis on work within the colonies had been allowed to wane. Instead of actively promoting revolution within the colonial world, Soviet leaders, for both psychological and economic reasons, had in effect relegated this task to the communist parties of the European metropolitan countries. Bound to their revolutionary colleagues in Western Europe by a common tradition of proletarian struggle, most Bolsheviks had tended to retain the traditional concept of Europe as revolution's *primus locus* and had been inclined in practice to treat colonial agitation merely as an extension of European revolutionary activity. Moreover, the launching in 1921 of the Soviet policy of economic retrenchment known as NEP redirected to a certain extent Bolshevik attention to domestic economic matters and reinforced the proclivity to retreat from the position taken by Lenin on the importance of colonial revolution.

By 1924, however, several factors combined to induce the Soviet leadership of the Comintern to revive its earlier emphasis on colonial work. The level of native unrest in the colonies had mounted in the years following 1920 and demands for revolutionary activity voiced by communist leaders from the Third World itself had become increasingly insistent.[71] In particular, these individuals sought to inaugurate a Comintern policy which would rely not primarily upon the work of communist parties within Europe but rather upon revolutionary movements based in the colonies themselves. Although Soviet leaders were apparently not yet convinced of the advisability of such a radical reorientation of policy, they nonetheless recognized by the time of the Fifth Comintern Congress that a more diligent effort would have to be made by the European communist parties if the Comintern was to retain its revolutionary image in the Third World.

The Soviet suspicion that European communists had been negligent in fulfilling their revolutionary duties provided, in fact, the most important immediate stimulus for the consideration of the colonial question at the Fifth Comintern Congress. However, instead of reassigning responsibility for colonial work to Soviet agitators or to native communists within the colonies themselves, the leaders of the Comintern chose to retain their original approach and to demand greater performance on the part of European communist parties.

In a certain sense the Comintern was unduly critical of its European affiliates. As far as Africa was concerned, at least, some revolutionary efforts had actually been initiated by the British and French communist parties in the early years of the 1920's. That the French Communist Party (PCF) had made moves in the direction of an active colonial policy was even recognized by the ECCI itself as early as 1922. In a directive issued on May 4 of that year, the ECCI instructed the communist parties of Britain and Italy to follow the example of their French counterpart and establish colonial commissions within their organizations.[72] Its further request that all parties endeavor to publish communist literature in the native languages of the colonies in order "to establish a closer contact with the oppressed colonial masses"[73] seemed again to have been inspired by the model of the PCF, which had formed an overseas branch section in the French colony of Tunisia and was actively publishing its message in the local Arabic press.[74]

The efforts of the PCF in North Africa (although they created grave concern on the part of the French government that communist propaganda might spread throughout all of French-speaking Africa)[75] seemed to have been precisely what the Comintern was seeking at this juncture. Deciding that the moment was ripe for more direct confrontation with French colonialism, the ECCI issued, on May 20, 1922, a "Manifesto on the Liberation of Algiers and Tunis" which urged French workers to seek common cause with the indigenous peoples of the entire African continent.[76]

It is particularly interesting that this Manifesto, reflecting the thinking of Pavlovich and Trotsky, singled out for special discussion the subject of France's Negro army:

> The French slave holders are attempting to recruit a great native army which they wish to use as the main instrument of suppression of the proletarian revolution in France. It is a question of raising black troops in order to convert them into White Guards.[77]

Instead of granting a *carte blanche* for the support of rebellion in the colonies, however, the Manifesto's formulation for action remained a comparatively cautious exhortation: "Proletarians of France, to the aid of the African Proletariat."[78]

In theory at least, the PCF was, by 1924, committed to the principle of total emancipation for the French colonies. In its "Action Program" adopted in 1922, the party made unmistakably clear its adherence to this fundamental principle. In addition to dedicating French communists to "the struggle against native conscription," this program insisted that "the party must take up the cause of the colonial peoples, oppressed and exploited by French imperialism, and support their national claims—support without reserve their right to autonomy or independence."[79]

Similarly, the Communist Party of Great Britain (CPGB), on a number of occasions prior to the Fifth Comintern Congress,* professed

---

* British communists declared as early as 1920 that "the principle of self-determination is clearly contained in our communism. To all struggling subject peoples in the British Empire we owe support in no grudging fashion, seeing that the Imperialism which crushes them is but an extended expression of the capitalism which degrades us." ("British Imperialism in Egypt," *The Call* [an "organ of the Comintern," published in London by the CPGB], November 11, 1920: 2.)

sympathy for the aspirations of colonial nationalism. However, when it came to the point of advocating an abrupt severance of all imperial ties, the CPGB appeared to have second thoughts. Of course it condemned the oppressive colonial policies of the British Empire,[80] but it also spoke in paternalistic terms of the need to cultivate "a sense of responsibility towards the peoples of Africa."[81] In short, what British communists appeared to have in mind in the early twenties was not the total breakup of the Empire, but instead the establishment of a series of free workers' republics associated with England in a form of commonwealth relationship. The CPGB's hesitancy to make a categorical endorsement of colonial independence was most conspicuous immediately prior to the Fifth Comintern Congress, when the party submitted a draft program to the ECCI calling for "the full political and industrial freedom of India, Egypt and the 'protectorates' within the confines of the Empire."[82] To the Comintern's Soviet leadership, now under increasing pressure to establish a reputation for unwavering militancy in the colonies, this was clearly "not enough."[83]

The Comintern was confronted by a real dilemma in desiring both to rely upon European communist parties for colonial work and at the same time to enhance the scope and effectiveness of revolutionary agitation. Perhaps the principal difficulty was the simple fact that British and French communists were in most cases subject to the same economic pressures which led to what Lenin had denounced as "social chauvinism" among other European workers. Indeed, even when their declared policies embraced unreservedly complete colonial independence, European communists were never able, in the eyes of colonial nationalists, to escape altogether the stigma of identification with metropolitan interests. In sub-Saharan Africa, moreover, racial differences made it all the easier for Negroes to identify communists with their white European oppressors.[84]

One possible solution of course was that offered at the Fourth Comintern Congress—namely to rely upon the services of American Negroes for African revolutionary work. However, given the small number of qualified cadres in that quarter, Comintern leaders recognized the need to resort to the additional expedient of expressing their dissatisfaction with the pace of colonial work on the part of the European communist parties and of prodding them on to greater efforts.

Soviet frustration over the progress made by the British communists, in particular, came to the surface as early as 1923. At that time Alexander Lozovsky, Chairman of the recently formed Profintern (the trade union wing of the Comintern, otherwise known as the Red International of Labor Unions, RILU), complained that whereas "a wide field of activity" was open for communist and revolutionary trade unions to organize labor in the colonies, British communists had done "almost nothing" in this sphere.[85]

The most comprehensive and penetrating castigation of British communists, however, came in the course of proceedings at the Fifth Comintern Congress. There, D. Z. Manuilsky, President of the ECCI Commission on National and Colonial Questions, took British communists to task for their "passive" attitude on the colonial question. In particular, he condemned the CPGB policy on the issue of colonial independence. "Not one of the [CPGB] documents that we have examined," he charged, "contains a single word by which the English party declares itself unequivocally for the separation of the colonies from the British Empire."[86]

Manuilsky was hardly less severe with the PCF. Referring to the "800,000 natives" resident in France, he demanded of French communists:

> what have you done to organize them, to form among them cadres of revolutionary agitators for the colonies? The French army includes 250,000 blacks. Do you think you will be able to create social revolution if tomorrow these 250,000 are on the other side of the barricade against you? Can your working class win a single strike if the bourgeoisie has at its disposal black reserves which can be thrown against it at any moment? Have you conducted anti-military propaganda among the black soldiers?[87]

Clearly the intention of the Fifth Congress leadership was to put the PCF on the spot regarding its performance in the colonial world. Maintaining that the numerical superiority of French communists as compared with their British counterparts had imposed upon the former greater responsibilities in the colonial sphere, Comintern delegates repeatedly pressured the PCF to give evidence of achievement in colonial work. In this atmosphere of criticism, the essentially unfair allegation was even made that the PCF had "refused to demand the liberation of the colonies," and was instead promoting no more than autonomy for France's subject peoples.[88]

In an attempt to defend themselves, the French representatives at the Congress reminded the Comintern of the PCF commitment to the principle of colonial liberation and of the work which had already been carried out by the party in North Africa and within the French army and urban proletariat.[89] Moreover, one French communist, Louis Sellier, pointed out to the Congress the enormity of the colonial task. "Has anyone here a clear notion of the magnitude of an apparatus capable of reaching a population of fifty-nine and one half millions scattered through Madagascar, West Africa (and Dahomey), Senegal, the Soudan, part of the Congo, the West Indes, Asia, Indo-China, [and] North Africa?" he demanded.[90]

More important than these arguments in justification of PCF action, however, were the suggestions for Comintern policy which French representatives presented at the Fifth Congress. If a large-scale campaign in the colonies was what Comintern officials had in mind, then why, French communists wondered, did not the ECCI offer some of its own resources to the colonial task and encourage a joint effort to spread the burden among all the communist parties of European colonial countries. With such an objective in mind, Sellier proposed that "we unite our efforts with those of our brother parties in Great Britain and Belgium and build up an apparatus for agitation and propaganda on the model of the apparatus which the International set up for the East."[91] According to the French scheme, the principal target of Comintern activity would be Negro Africa. Indeed, Sellier even had in mind a particular geographic strategy according to which penetration of East Africa would be launched from Madagascar, while penetration of West Africa would begin in Dakar and spread eastward to the interior of the continent.[92]

It is interesting that the French proposal for a concerted Comintern effort in colonial Africa received encouragement from the American delegate, Israel Amter, who spoke at some length on the Negro question at the Fifth Congress.* Invoking the familiar spectre of the French trans-Saharan railroad project and the use of Negro armies

---

* In the spirit of the preceding Comintern Congress, Amter renewed the call for a general Negro Conference and emphasized the role of American Negroes in revolutionizing Africa. (*Piatyi Vsemirnyi Kongress Kommunisticheskogo Internatsionala: Stenograficheskii Otchet* [2 vols; Moscow, 1925], I: 675.) An even fuller exposé of Amter's views on the importance of "the liberation of Africa" and the role to be played in this process by the Comintern was published in Moscow in 1925 under a separate title: *Mirovoe Osvoboditel'noe Dvizhenie Negrov* ("The World Liberation

in the occupation of the Ruhr, Amter emphasized the importance of conducting a "determined campaign" to prevent the deployment of Negro troops beyond their own colonial borders.[93] Most important, however, was the tactical proposal which Amter made as an elaboration upon Sellier's plan for Africa. "We must," he declared, "distribute via sailors sailing to various parts of the world small brochures and leaflets in the languages of African natives. They will find their way into African harbors and from there penetrate into the interior of the continent."[94]

These recommendations of the French and American delegates at the Fifth Congress ultimately found their way into Comintern policy. Immediately following the Congress, in fact, the ECCI adopted a resolution calling for the establishment of a "Negro Propaganda Commission," composed of representatives of the PCF, the CPGB, the Belgian Communist Party, and the ECCI.[95] Moreover, according to one source, this organization (which was to have its headquarters in Geneva) received ten million gold francs from the Soviet government in order to assist it in the task of promoting revolution in Africa.[96]

Although this particular commission was not itself successful in launching an effective campaign in Negro Africa, its formation nonetheless served as an important precedent for subsequent Comintern efforts. In the early development of Comintern policy, the establishment of the Negro Propaganda Commission in 1924, like the adoption of the Negro Thesis at the Fourth Comintern Congress in 1922, represented a significant move in the direction of an activist approach. The decision to set up this commission provided, in short, unmistakable evidence of the extent to which the Soviet leadership of the international communist organization had, as early as 1924, formulated it plans to carry revolution into sub-Saharan Africa.

Movement of Negroes"). This text is a Russian translation of a manuscript by Amter dated Moscow, July 20, 1924—undoubtedly prepared by him for delivery at the Fifth Comintern Congress.

6

Some Experiments in Political Activism

THE ORGANIZATION OF COLONIAL LABOR

It was the Fifth Comintern Congress which produced the first identifiable results in terms of concrete agitational efforts by communists among colonial workers. Unlike the directives embodied in Lenin's Thesis on the National and Colonial Questions delivered in 1920, the new accent on colonial activism emerging from the Fifth Comintern Congress appears to have been immediately passed down the Comintern chain of command and translated into specific activities which involved Negro Africans.

No sooner had the Congress ceased deliberations than the Profintern began to exhort its followers to use "all the means at their disposal" to aid African workers and, in particular, "to associate with them, assisting them with literature, organizers and agitators, and . . . sympathetic strikes."[1] Not only did the Profintern direct the members of its affiliated trade union bodies to undertake concerted efforts in colonies themselves, but it also instructed them to seek ways of reaching the numerous members of Africa's colonial proletariat who were working in Europe. In view of the restrictions placed by colonial governments on the organization of indigenous labor, the greatest practical emphasis was given to the task of forming trade unions among Africans living in the metropoles.[2]

It was in response to this Profintern directive that the PCF, acting in conjunction with the *Confédération Générale du Travail Unitaire* (CGTU, the Profintern's French affiliate), called late in 1924, the first organizational conference of French North Africans working in the vicinity of Paris.[3] At approximately the same time, the PCF, probably at the initiative of the head of its colonial commission, the *Deputé* Jacques Doriot, established a school for colonial workers, patterned after KUTV University in Moscow.[4]

In its 1924 policy formulation the Profintern had singled out one group of workers in particular—colonial sailors—as meriting the highest priority for communist agitational efforts.[5] There were certainly important reasons for a tactical focus on this segment of the European based colonial proletariat. Indeed Russian communists, while carrying out their own revolution, had recognized the value of seamen in transmitting the revolutionary message and in maintaining contact between the Russian underground and its European sources of support.* Why then could not the same channel of communications be used in the opposite direction, so that literature and agitational instructions flowing from Russia to European ports could be transmitted to colonial sailors and from them to the colonial world beyond? In other words, by concentrating its limited resources on revolutionary work among seamen, the international communist movement would be able to maximize the geographical impact of its initial effort.

This special interest in colonial sailors expressed in the higher councils of the Comintern in 1924 was translated directly into action by European communist parties. During the mid-twenties, seamen's clubs began to appear in key European ports. In 1925, for example, the PCF opened a "Cercle Internationale des Marins" in Bordeaux, the gateway to France's West African colonies. Not only did this organization provide a fixed meeting place for its members, but its facilities included a library and study hall where colonial sailors could be "assisted with literature."[6] Since Soviet commercial vessels were currently visiting the same ports where sailors' clubs were being established, notably Bordeaux and Hamburg, these organizations were able to enjoy the advantages of a direct link with the home base of the revolution (and perhaps the more questionable benefit of Russian supervision).

By 1925, therefore, it could be said that Comintern policy on the colonial question had begun to filter down to the operational level.

---

* Both Chicherin and Pavlovich were aware from personal experience of the practical utility of revolutionary work among sailors. Together they had published in France, prior to 1917, a revolutionary journal, *Moriak* ("Sailor"), which was distributed to Russian sailors visiting French ports and was then carried by the latter into Russia. In a similar context, it is interesting to note that Pavlovich in 1913 was asked by the Foreign Bureau of the Russian Social Democratic Party in Paris to address sailors in Marseilles on the subject of French imperialism. Since his audience reportedly included French colonial sailors, it is quite possible that Pavlovich gained from this experience firsthand knowledge of the problems of revolutionary work among France's African Negroes. (See N. Gik, "M. P. Pavlovich sredi Moriakov," *Novyi Vostok*, no. 18, 1927: 73–74.)

Interestingly, the same appears to have been true with regard to the Comintern's formulations on the Negro Question. Taking its cue directly from the Fifth Comintern Congress, the Profintern in 1924 directed its attention to the problem of labor organization among the world's Negroes.

Observing that "from the point of view of the labor union movement the Negro question has its own peculiarities demanding special study," the Profintern directed that a study commission be set up, and on the basis of a "detailed acquaintance with the [Negro] question," that it "put forward concrete proposals at the next congress of the RILU."[7] In the meantime, however, Profintern affiliates were not to remain inactive. In forceful terms the RILU charged its adherents in "America, South Africa, and in other countries where there are Negro workers" to "immediately commence work among the Negro worker masses, endeavoring to secure the fusion of parallel organizations of whites and Negroes wherever such exist."[8] Thus, it appears that the Comintern's special interest in the black race, like its emphasis on revolutionary work among colonial peoples, was first translated into specific operational programs by means of RILU directives.

TENTATIVE COMINTERN EFFORTS TO USE AMERICAN NEGROES FOR AGITATION IN AFRICA

Certainly by 1925 communists in America had become manifestly aware of the special responsibilities bestowed upon them by the Comintern. In October of that year Otto Huiswood and other American communists promoted a gathering of black labor leaders in Chicago for the purpose of founding an organization known as the American Negro Labor Congress (ANLC).[9] This initiative represented a conscious effort on the part of the American Communist Party to respond to the Profintern's plea for agitation among Negro workers. It constituted, moreover, a definite move designed to comply with the Comintern's emphasis on creating a worldwide Negro movement as well as with its insistence on the special importance of American Negroes in promoting African revolution.

The program adopted by the ANLC left little doubt of the coincidence in objectives between this new organization and the

Comintern. At its gathering in Chicago the ANLC enacted a resolution which, after hailing the Soviet government as "the first to have achieved complete social, economic, and political equality of all peoples without distinction of race,"[10] called upon its own executive committee to:

> lay the foundation for a world organization of the workers and farmers of our race and to make this organization a leader and fighter in the liberation movements of all darker-skinned peoples in the colonies of imperialism everywhere.[11]

Although it is difficult to see how the ANLC ever achieved, as one Comintern source put it, "ideological influence over large numbers of Negroes in America and to some extent abroad,"[12] the formation of this organization was nonetheless significant in that it provided a forum for launching the Comintern's appeal to Negro workers and furnished training for Negro activists who would later play critical roles in promoting African revolution.

The ANLC was not the only specific organization through which communists sought to mobilize American Negroes for revolutionary work in Africa. For example, the International Labor Defense (ILD), a body spawned by the Comintern in 1922 to give assistance to indicted workers, devoted considerable attention to the legal problems of Negroes in both America and Africa.[13] According to Wilson Record, the CPUSA "viewed the ILD as an instrument for providing helpful experience for American Negro communists in preparing them for revolutionary leadership in the colonial areas as well as in the United States."[14]

However, in Comintern eyes, perhaps the most important spawning ground for black revolutionaries was the radical Garveyite movement. Although Garveyism itself was not communist inspired, there is evidence that communists did try to infiltrate the movement with the aim of training its members for revolutionary work.[15] George Padmore (subsequently Secretary of the Comintern's Negro directorate) singled out perhaps the most pressing objective of the Comintern vis-à-vis Garveyism:

> Had the Communists succeeded in capturing the Garvey Movement and in gaining control of other black nationalist groups, specially selected Negro militants would have been recruited and trained in Moscow as cadres for colonial work in Africa.[16]

Although communists were not successful in effectively taking control of Garvey's organization, it is nonetheless significant that they were able to persuade a small group of Negro youths (including a "Gold Coast African" and at least one member of Garvey's UNIA) to leave the U.S. in 1925 to come to study at KUTV University.[17] In 1926 this group was followed by yet another American Negro visitor to Russia, W. E. B. DuBois, who had attracted Soviet attention by his militant role in the Pan-Africanist movement and who allegedly had been cooperating with Soviet agents in the U.S. to form an activist organization for work among Negro Africans.[18]

Undoubtedly the warm hospitality bestowed upon him by the Soviets influenced DuBois' thinking. Yet it is indicative of the enthusiasm which the Soviet experiment was capable of kindling among American Negroes that DuBois, upon his return, declared with conviction: "If what I have seen with my eyes and heard with my ears in Russia is Bolshevism, I am a Bolshevik."[19]

COMINTERN ASSOCIATIONS WITH AFRICAN NATIONALISTS

For all its faith in their revolutionary potential, the Comintern was never prepared to rely solely upon American Negroes to promote communist rebellion in Black Africa. In fact, there is good reason to believe that during the mid-twenties the international communist movement not only courted the favor of American Negroes, but actually experimented with the idea of lending direct assistance to Negro nationalists of Africa itself.

The activities of Kojo Tovalou Houénou are a good case in point. Certain evidence leads to the supposition that Houénou and his *Ligue* might well have received direct support from the communist movement. Several contemporary observers, at least, believed this to have been the case. Blaise Diagne, the Negro parliamentary deputy from French West Africa, was, for example, convinced that Houénou and his associates in the LDRN were part of a communist conspiracy to end the recruitment of Negroes in French African colonies.[20] In addition, François Coty, the well-known French journalist and author, made more specific accusations regarding the LDRN's communist associations, charging that the *Ligue* had actually been sponsored by the Colonial Commission of the French Communist Party.[21]

Even French government agents conducting surveillance on the LDRN for the French Ministry of Colonies, although they doubted that the editors of the *Ligue*'s publication, *Les Continents*, were faithful to orthodox communism, nonetheless supplied corroborative information for Coty's allegations.* [22]

It is possible that communists first became attracted to Houénou as a result of his Garveyite sympathies. Whatever the case, the Comintern reportedly financed a trip by Houénou to the United States in the fall of 1924, probably with the aim of bringing him into contact with radical Negro leaders of the U.S.[23] During his American visit, not only did Houénou address a congress of Garvey's UNIA held in New York City, but he spent several weeks in Chicago, giving a series of speeches in order to acquire membership and funds for his LDRN.[24]

In addition to subsidizing his trip to America, it is possible that the Comintern had some share in supporting Houénou's West African mission following his visit to the U.S. Reportedly charged by Garvey with the task of promoting an uprising against French power in West Africa, Houénou, in the company of five other agitators, set off, probably in early 1925, to foment revolution in Dahomey.[25] Unfortunately for the future of the revolutionary cause, however, Houénou's African enterprise ended rather ignominiously—he was arrested in Togo for doing nothing more momentous than passing bad checks.[26]

However limited may have been Houénou's influence on the political life of West Africa, his work in Paris made a real contribution to the subsequent development of militant nationalist sentiment among Negro Africans. Just as the activities of his LDRN had corresponded in principle to the colonial objectives of the Comintern, so did the

---

* Despite the need to maintain secrecy concerning its true beliefs, the LDRN itself, through various articles in *Les Continents*, hinted of possible communist sympathies. At one point, for example, it was openly avowed that some of *Les Continents'* collaborators were "interested in Socialism." (See René Maran, "Les Continents," *Les Continents*, I, no. 4, July 1, 1924: 1.) At another time it was unblushingly suggested that communism might indeed have a future in France's colonies. "Every day the Ministry of Colonies is gnawed by Bolshevik propaganda" it observed; "[this propaganda] is gaining ground in Indo-China, in Madagascar—virtually everywhere that the native is becoming conscious of his own dignity . . . If it continues to procrastinate this way, if it continues to be imperialist—slaving or anti-liberal, France, through no fault but its own, will lose all its colonies." (See René Maran, "Au Pied du Mur," *Les Continents*, I, no. 5, July 15, 1924: 1.)

beliefs which he helped to promote predispose his followers to become active partners in the communist effort to bring revolution to Africa. Indeed, no sooner had Houénou's *Ligue* ceased operations, than leadership of his revolutionary cause was assumed by another West African veteran of World War I, Lamine Senghor.[27]

Unlike Houénou, Senghor was an avowed communist. First drawn into politics by the controversy between Diagne and *Les Continents*, Senghor became an active member of the PCF in 1924.[28] Together with several former adherents of the LDRN, he decided in March, 1926, to revive Houénou's enterprise. Rebaptized *Le Comité de Défense de la Race Nègre*, the new organization proceeded to name Lenin its "perpetual honorary chairman" and to alarm the French Right with assertions that in the interests of liberating Negro colonies from French domination, members had decided "it is our right to be communist if we want to."[29]

If it cannot be proven that the *Comité* under the presidency of Senghor was "monopolized by the communists,"[30] it is nonetheless quite certain that the activities of the organization conformed well with Comintern designs. By the fall of 1926, for example, the *Comité* was actively establishing branches in the principal port cities of France and was boasting a membership of "several hundreds" of Negroes, notably African sailors.[31] At the beginning of 1927, moreover, the organization commenced publication of a monthly journal, *La Voix des Nègres*, made possible, in all likelihood, by financial support from the PCF.[32] The clear statement of *Comité* objectives set forth by Senghor in the first issue of this journal left little doubt of the effect of communist thinking on the new organization. Declaring that Negroes would no longer tolerate being used as "strike breakers, stool pidgeons, agents of colonialism in the colonies, or counter-revolutionary soldiers," Senghor went on to assert militantly that the black race would "make an about-face, and turn upon the only author of universal misery: international imperialism."[33]

Equally compatible with Comintern interests were the *Comité*'s efforts—in keeping with a goal of achieving "total liberation and emancipation of Negroes"—to disseminate *La Voix des Nègres* and other publications in Africa itself. It is significant that these activities, which began in early 1927, caused considerable concern on the part of the French Ministry of Colonies as well as on the part of the governors of French West African territories, who were anxious lest indigenous political opposition "surpass the bounds of nationalism and spill over into communism."* [34]

Thus the efforts of Senghor and other French communists to give leadership to a militant nationalist movement in French colonial Africa could be viewed as an expression of the Comintern's growing desire to forge a working alliance with the forces of colonial nationalism throughout the Third World. Even more indicative of this desire, however, was the Comintern's policy with regard to the Brussels Conference of 1927. Its enthusiasm concerning this conference, and particularly its support of the ongoing organization to which the conference gave birth, can be regarded as the strongest possible evidence of the Comintern's ambition to assert its influence among Third World nationalists.

The origins of the Brussels Conference can be traced to an organization founded by German communists in 1926. This body, known as the "League Against Colonial Oppression," had been formed in order to combat the rising tide of colonial revanchist sentiment in Germany during the mid-twenties.[35] Shortly after its establishment, however, it was decided (possibly with the benefit of Comintern advice and financing)[36] that the scope of the League's campaign should be expanded to include the entire colonial world. Toward this end, the League issued a call to nationalist groups throughout the Third World, inviting them to send representatives to a "World Anti-Colonial Conference" to be held in Brussels in February, 1927. This conference, it was anticipated, would facilitate both the interchange of ideas and the coordination of efforts among various liberation movements.[37] More important still, as the statements of Willy Munzenberg, head of the German Communist Party (KPD) and chief organizing spirit behind the conference, reveal, such a meeting would help to establish valuable links between the nationalist and the communist movements. According to Munzenberg, in fact, the real purpose of the undertaking, at least in the eyes of the Comintern,

---

* Recipients of La Voix des Nègres were placed under surveillance by colonial authorities and, at least in one territory—Togo—circulation of the paper was outlawed. (Arrêté du Cabinet, Lomé, March 16, 1927, in SLOTFOM, V, Box 3, File 73, subfile 51.) The French government's concern lest Senghor's own activities result in the spread of the communist toxin in West Africa was so great that after 1923 it refused to allow him to travel to Senegal. (See "La Ligue est en Deuil: Lamine Senghor est Mort," La Race Nègre, I, no. 5 [May, 1928]: 1.)

was to "establish an effective liaison between the socialist organizations of the different countries and the national liberation movement."[38]

The promoters of the Brussels Conference received an unexpectedly large and enthusiastic response from the Third World. Not only in initial declarations of support (reportedly including responses from Negro organizations in both East and West Africa),[39] but in actual attendance at the conference, the affair was unmistakably a success. With considerable justification the Brussels gathering has in fact been referred to as a "first Bandung," since it brought together for the first time such key nationalist leaders of the Third World as Nehru, Madame Sun Yat Sen, and Ho Chi Minh—to name but a few.[40]

Also included in this august assemblage was Lamine Senghor, who, as delegate of Le Comité de Défense de la Race Nègre, took the responsibility of representing all of French West Africa and French Equatorial Africa at Brussels.[41] Although J. T. Gumede, President of the African National Congress of South Africa, spoke to the conference on the plight of African Negroes, it was Senghor, in a speech before the third session on February 11, 1927, who delivered the most ringing denunciation of imperialism in Africa.[42] So virulent were his attacks on French colonial policy that Senghor, upon his return from Brussels, was incarcerated by the French government.*

Although not all the conference participants shared the communist faith, it is nonetheless true that the communist point of view was heavily represented at Brussels. Conspicuous in this representation was a Comintern delegation under the leadership of B. Lominadze and a large mission of Russian trade unionists led by G. N. Melnichansky.[43] It is difficult to substantiate accusations made by contemporary observers that these Russians manipulated the proceedings at Brussels;[44] yet it is possible to conclude that through its support of this conference the Soviet leadership of the Comintern was able to gain valuable publicity among Third World nationalists.

---

* Although Senghor was soon released by the French authorities (probably as a result of protests voiced by the League Against Imperialism), he died in November, 1927—according to Comintern sources, as a result of illness contracted in prison. (See "La Deuxième Conférence de Bruxelles de la Ligue Anti-Impérialiste," Correspondance Internationale, VII, no. 127 [December 21, 1927]: 1952.) The Comintern charge was probably an exaggeration, for Senghor's tubercular condition appears to have been equally attributable to his service in World War I. (See also "La Ligue est en Deuil," op. cit.: 1.)

Nowhere was the Comintern influence more apparent than in the manifesto ("Against Imperialism: For National Liberation!") issued by the conference. In this widely circulated document the Soviet Union was referred to both as an "historical example of the free union of nations and races constructed on the ruins of imperialism," and as "the guiding star" of the national liberation movement.[45] In addition, the manifesto spoke of such subjects as the wartime sacrifices of colonial troops and the unjust political practices of colonial government in terms that appeared to have been drawn directly from Comintern statements.[46] Following the Comintern precedent, moreover, the Brussels Conference issued a special "Resolution on the Negro Question" which was presented to the gathering by Richard Moore, delegate from the ANLC.[47] Speaking in Leninist terms, this resolution directed specific attention to the economic plight of Negroes in Africa. Charging that Africa's black population had long been exploited in the interests of European prosperity, the resolution demanded unequivocally "complete political and economic independence for all the Negro peoples of Africa," as well as the Africanization of administration and land ownership throughout the continent.[48] By including a recommendation that measures be taken to "organize movements for Negro liberation,"[49] the resolution of the conference came even closer to echoing contemporary Comintern pronouncements on the Negro question.

However, the lasting significance of Brussels was to be found not in the manifestos or resolutions adopted, but in the organization founded to carry on the work of the conference. The establishment of an organization "to support the liberation movement in the colonies" had in fact been one of the original objectives of the conference organizers.[50] Hence, before the close of deliberations, the Brussels "Presidium" (presumably under the direction of Munzenberg) presented participants with a pre-drafted proposal for a permanent organization, complete with program and constitution, which they approved unanimously.[51] Christened the "League Against Imperialism and for Colonial Independence (LAI)," this organization soon developed an extensive apparatus and began to engage in a wide range of activities to promote the political interests of the Third World—and, one suspects, those of the Comintern as well.

Although the Executive Committee of the LAI was based in Germany where it held meetings and issued a quarterly journal,

The Anti-Imperialist Review, the organization succeeded in establishing a number of active national branches, notably in Latin America, India, and North Africa.[52] Its principal European offshoots were a branch in Paris, founded with the help of Lamine Senghor, and one in London, which grew into an active body largely through the efforts of the British communist Reginald Bridgeman.[53] These two LAI branches, together with the Executive Committee in Berlin, were to play a conspicuous role in promoting Comintern relations with Negro Africa throughout the decade after 1927.

With respect to colonial Africa, however, the significance of the Brussels Conference extended beyond formal declarations or policy decisions. By the simple act of attending this gathering, Negro Africans were exposed, through their meetings with other colonial leaders, to the main currents of nationalist thinking in the Third World. More important still, from the communist point of view, the Brussels Conference made possible some of the first personal contacts between African nationalists and Soviet Russians. In the course of their meetings at Brussels, Russian representatives found an opportunity to invite the South Africans Gumede and La Guma to visit the U.S.S.R. Accordingly, in the fall of 1927, these Africans, together with the Chairman of the Sierra Leone Railroad Workers Union, E. A. Richards (who had been invited to the Soviet Union in the name of the LAI), toured Russia and attended the celebrations in Moscow of the tenth anniversary of the Bolshevik Revolution.[54]

Thus, not only from the point of view of the Third World delegates themselves, but from the vantage point of the Comintern, the Brussels Conference was a distinct success. According to Munzenberg, who was presumably voicing the sentiments of the Comintern leadership, this conference provided the first real opportunity for the Comintern to make a significant impact upon the colonial world. "The Congress of Brussels," he concluded, "has had a powerful echo in the colonial and semi-colonial countries—a repercussion which no other movement has ever had since the founding of the Communist International."[55]

Certainly an important factor in the success of the conference was the participation not just of convinced African and Asian communists, but of representatives from large noncommunist nationalist movements such as that of India. In the period leading up to Brussels, Soviet, and hence Comintern policy had been essentially favorable to the concept of cooperation with communist and noncommunist leaders alike. Shortly after the conference, however, events took place in China which profoundly altered the willingness of Stalin and other Soviet leaders to seek a working relationship with a broad spectrum of Third World nationalists. Indeed, it was not until after the "second" Bandung Conference in 1955 that Soviet confidence in the revolutionary value of African and Asian nationalists was fully restored. Thus, in a sense, the Brussels Conference can be regarded as having marked a highpoint in the Soviet relationship with Third World nationalism before World War II.

Curious as it may seem, Soviet Russia developed an early and definable interest in sub-Saharan Africa. Indeed, concern for the people and the politics of this region was reflected in Bolshevik writings both at the time of the Russian Revolution and during the early twenties. Through the agency of the Communist International, moreover, this concern was expanded during the first decade of Soviet power, becoming in the following decade a conspicuous feature of the Comintern's revolutionary work in the colonial world.

Whether it was expressed in Bolshevik writing or in the policies of the Russian-dominated Comintern, Soviet interest in Africa was distinguished by one salient characteristic—it was, above all, a product of the national security calculations of the Russian state. To a significant extent, therefore, early Soviet concern for Africa should be viewed as an outgrowth of the same pragmatic political considerations which had led to Russian involvement in Africa during the Czarist era. In fact, the new postwar political situation created by the establishment of the Soviet regime served only to intensify the traditional security rationale for Russian interest in Africa. Faced with the prospect of direct military confrontation with capitalist Europe, Bolshevik leaders were quick to recognize the strategic importance of depriving the imperialist powers of their African economic resources and, in particular, of denying them their reservoir of Negro military manpower.

During the early postwar years not only did Bolshevik leaders believe that Negro armies might be employed directly against the Soviet Union itself, but they were convinced that the capitalist use of African resources could sabotage the progress of communist revolution in Western Europe. Carrying this line of reasoning one step further, however, communist thinkers concluded that revolution in Africa could, conversely, serve as an important means of destroying the economic and military foundations of the capitalist system. Such strategic thinking found its expression not just in the writings of Pavlovich, Trotsky, and other Bolshevik leaders, but in the official pronouncements and policy initiatives of the international communist movement.

Although Soviet self-interest appears to have played the primary role in directing communist attention to sub-Saharan Africa, it should nonetheless be observed that this attention produced, on the part of communist observers, surprisingly accurate insights into the political sentiments of Negro Africans. In contrast to their capitalist contemporaries in Western Europe, communists were aware of the grievances of Africans who had fought in World War I and supported sympathetically their mounting political demands. More important still, communist observers were conscious of the extent to which indigenous unrest in Africa had become mobilized in the early post-war period and grasped with comparative alacrity the significance of nationalism as a revolutionary force in the colonial world.

Not only did communists recognize the importance of the first organized expressions of Negro nationalist sentiment, but, through the instrumentality of the Comintern, they decided to lend whatever support they could to nationalist revolt in sub-Saharan Africa. Although by 1927 no concerted communist penetration of Africa had occurred, the beginnings of an active Comintern policy could already be discerned. The French Communist Party had begun its proselytizing work among African Negro troops; sailors and other African laborers in Europe were coming into initial contact with communist literature; and, for the first time, the Soviet government was welcoming to Russia Negro students and visitors. Even with respect to sub-Saharan Africa itself, plans were afoot for subversive activity among newly politicized elements of the indigenous population.

Even if one questions the realism of the Comintern's African ambitions, the efficacy of the methods proposed for achieving them, or the significance of the efforts actually undertaken, it must be recognized that by 1927 communists were clearly committed to carrying revolution into sub-Saharan Africa. As will become apparent in the discussion which follows, this commitment to African revolution was to prove responsible for a series of remarkable Comintern efforts in the period from 1928 to 1934—efforts which served, in turn, to prepare the ground for subsequent Soviet relations with the independent nations of Black Africa.

PART III

THE COMINTERN AND BLACK AFRICA: FROM THE SIXTH CONGRESS TO THE REALIGNMENT OF SOVIET FOREIGN POLICY IN THE FACE OF FASCISM

The changes in Comintern policy toward the colonial world which occurred in 1927 and which were formalized in the pronouncements of the Sixth Comintern Congress in 1928 were both broad in scope and profound in character. On the surface at least, they seemed to signify not only an abrupt reversal in the Comintern's desire to court the friendship of colonial nationalists, but a reappraisal of the communist ambition to promote separatist forces in the dependent territories of world capitalism. So striking in fact were the apparent shifts in policy emanating from the Sixth Congress that many observers have been tempted to conclude that the colonial world as a whole—together with its bourgeois nationalist leaders—was abandoned by the Comintern after 1928.

In a real sense, however, the years immediately following 1928 marked a highpoint in the Comintern's concern for colonial Africa. Particularly in the wake of the depression, communist revolutionary activity took on new momentum as Africa assumed heightened importance in Comintern eyes both as a last base of support for the capitalist system and as a likely prospect for anti-colonial upheaval. It was not until after 1933, when the rise of German fascism wrought profound changes in the international political scene, that the Comintern relaxed its campaign to promote revolution in Africa and realigned its policy to conform to the changed interests of the Soviet state.

7

The Sixth Comintern Congress and the Beginning of a New Era in Relations with Black Africa

Clear evidence that the Comintern did not abandon its concern for colonial questions after 1927 can be found in the deliberations and resolutions of the Sixth Comintern Congress. This Congress, held in Moscow from July through September, 1928, devoted greater attention to revolutionary work in the colonies than had any previous Comintern gathering. Best remembered for its adoption of the ideologically orthodox revolutionary strategy known as the "United Front from Below," the Sixth Comintern Congress marked the beginning of a new activist era in the relationship between communism and the Third World.

The revolutionary approach embodied in the "United Front from Below" represented a clear departure from earlier Comintern policy. Essentially it involved a shift away from reliance upon bourgeois nationalists for revolutionary leadership in favor of a "fighting front" led by the proletariat with the peasantry at its side. Before discussing either the nature of this new strategy or the policies of the Sixth Congress relating to colonial work, it is important to describe some of the basic motivations which led the Comintern to focus its attention on the colonial world and to alter so fundamentally the earlier communist policy of comparatively indiscriminate cooperation with nationalist leaders.

One of the most obvious and immediate reasons for the shift in revolutionary strategy was the disillusionment over the Comintern experience in China. In both the spring and the fall of 1927 the bourgeois nationalist Kuomintang Party, after having combined forces with the Communist Party of China, turned upon its revolutionary allies, sparking the famous blood baths at Shanghai, Peking, and Canton. Such unsettling evidence of the failure of a cooperative approach had a profound impact upon Comintern leaders. In particular, the betrayal of communists at the hands of the Kuomintang made an indelible impression upon the one individual who more than any other was to determine the shape of communist policy in the decades ahead.

Stalin, who in 1927 was in the final stages of his rise to unlimited power in the Kremlin, was himself widely regarded as the principal author of the unsuccessful Comintern approach to the Chinese revolution. Sensitive to political criticism, he was undoubtedly embarrassed that his own tactical prescriptions should have failed so dramatically in China. Above all, he was anxious to establish his own image as Moscow's foremost practitioner of revolution and to eliminate once and for all left-wing opposition to his bid for power—particularly the critical voice of Trotsky.[1] Thus, concern for his political position provided Stalin with an irresistible incentive to promote the decisive return to orthodoxy embodied in the "United Front from Below" policy.*

In addition, the inauguration of a new strategy for colonial revolution appeared to have been sparked by the belief, entertained by Stalin and other Comintern leaders, that new revolutionary opportunities were rapidly developing in colonial territories[2] and that it would be necessary for the Sixth Congress to "take an energetic stand

---

* It is interesting to note in this context that for Stalin the revised revolutionary strategy did not represent an altogether new theoretical stand, but instead reflected an outgrowth of earlier thinking. Despite his insistence upon cooperation with Chiang Kai-shek, Stalin had long harbored misgivings concerning both the reliability of the Third World bourgeoisie and the extent to which this group could be trusted to promote the progress of revolution. In May, 1925, he had emphasized to the students of KUTV University that the upper strata of the bourgeois class would eventually defect to the camp of the imperialists. "Progress for the colonial revolutionary movement," he declared, "is only possible through isolating the nationalist bourgeoisie inclined to come to terms with imperialism, through detaching the middle classes of this bourgeoisie, and through the hegemony of the proletariat and the organization of the advanced elements of the working class into communist parties." ("Pour l'Emancipation des Peuples Opprimés des Colonies: Extrait d'une Conférence de Staline aux Etudiants de l'Université des Peuples de l'Orient," Moscow, May 18, 1925, *Correspondance Internationale*, V, no. 56 [May 30, 1925]: 455.) As early as the Tenth Communist Party Congress in 1921, Stalin had chided indigenous communists in the Third World for stressing the nationalist character of their struggle and not sufficiently emphasizing its class basis. (*Protokoly i Stenograficheskie Otchety S'ezdov i Konferentsii Kommunisticheskogo Partii Sovetskogo Soiuza: Desiatyi Sezd* ["Protocols and Stenographic Accounts of the Congresses and Conferences of the Communist Party of the Soviet Union: Tenth Congress"] [Moscow, 1963]: 703.)

on the question of support of colonial movements by the proletariat of imperialist countries."[3] This position, which might otherwise have seemed incompatible with the prevalent ideological emphasis upon "socialism in one country," could be understood in light of the Comintern's fear of a challenge to its leadership over the world revolutionary movement. Not only was it anticipated that the new approach would offer an orthodox alternative to Trotskyism, but it was hoped that the strategy would succeed in thwarting the efforts already begun in the colonies by the Comintern's arch rivals, the Social Democrats.[4] In short, by the late 1920's an element of immediate competitive pressure had been introduced into the world revolutionary equation.

Finally, the new emphasis on colonial issues which emerged from the Sixth Comintern Congress was directly related to Stalin's attempt to rekindle within Russia the familiar fear that imperialist powers would again invade the Soviet Union and rely in part upon colonial troops for the project. Wise in such matters, Stalin must have realized that public anxiety over an impending foreign invasion would be of political value to him. By recreating the mood of 1918 he may have consciously sought to achieve a domestic closing of the ranks similar to that which had taken place in Russia following the Allied intervention and which had greatly strengthened the hand of his predecessor in the Kremlin. Stalin may have recognized that widespread apprehension concerning the prospects of an imperialist attack would help to set the stage for his own enthronement as supreme guardian of Russia's security interests. Certainly he must have calculated that a government-inspired war alarm would both drown out the voices of internal criticism and help to mobilize the domestic energies necessary for the implementation of the First Five Year Plan.

Thus there were good reasons for the Soviet government to cultivate popular fears of an imperialist-inspired war against Russia. Although the Kremlin did exploit the war issue to its fullest extent, it would be a mistake to assume that the atmosphere of insecurity which prevailed in the Soviet Union during the late 1920's was entirely a product of government contrivance. Indeed, the period immediately preceding the Sixth Congress was one of genuine uncertainty in Russia. Not only did the year of the Congress witness widespread famine, but the preceding year had seen the beginning of a real trend toward Soviet isolationism. Accompanying a breakdown in the Soviet entente with the English trade union movement and a cessation of diplomatic relations with Great Britain in 1927, came a recurrence of the historic Russian strategic anxiety over British power in the Middle East. Similarly, a reemergence of the familiar Russian concern over France's colonially based military strength was apparent in the period immediately preceding the Sixth Congress, contributing a further element of realpolitik to the Comintern's deliberations.[5]

In sum, it can be said that the Sixth Comintern Congress took place in an atmosphere characterized by increasing Russian estrangement from the Western world. Indeed, the exhumation of the spectre of imperialist war in the late twenties was partially explicable in terms of this revived isolationist attitude toward Western powers. The possibility of a foreign attack against the Soviet Union served, in turn, as a factor in shaping the Comintern's approach to the colonial world. Whether it was in some measure justified or altogether imaginary, communist fear of an imperialist war formed an important backdrop for the Comintern's reconsideration of its revolutionary strategy.

PROCEEDINGS OF THE CONGRESS

Given the alarmist climate of thought which had descended upon Moscow prior to the summer of 1928, it is not surprising that the Sixth Congress in both its deliberations and its policy formulations dwelt at considerable length on the possibility of a foreign attack on the Soviet Union. As far as the Comintern's relationship with Negro Africa was concerned, communist anxiety over the war issue fulfilled several functions. Not only did it act as a catalyst in directing Comintern attention to the colonial world, but it contributed significantly to the Comintern's belief that both the colonial and the Negro questions were directly related to the security of the Soviet state. Indeed, because of the Comintern's preoccupation with the threat of imperialist attack, the Sixth Congress chose to use discussion of the "war danger" as a context in which to issue its emphatic call for revolutionary work in the colonies.

It was apparent from the proceedings of the Sixth Congress that communists viewed colonial revolution as integrally linked to Soviet national security. Although Comintern literature appearing at the time of the Congress suggests that Soviet strategists were contemplating a variety of means to thwart the colonial initiatives of imperialist powers,* it seems that the Comintern in 1928 considered the promotion of separatist and insurrectionary forces within dependent territories to be the principal means of undermining the imperial position of European capitalist states.

In both the "Program of the Communist International" and the "Theses on the Struggle against the War Danger" adopted by the Sixth Congress, reference was made to the strategic importance of insurrectionary work in the colonies. Declaring that "at the world level, the most important strategic tasks of the Comintern . . . are concerned with the revolutionary battle in the colonies and semi-colonies, and dependent countries,"[6] the Program of the Communist International further specified that:

> In case of attack on the USSR by imperialist powers, it is imperative that in the colonies—especially in the colonies of imperialist countries attacking Russia—communists seek to use the distraction of the military forces of imperialism with a view to exerting maximum efforts to develop anti-imperialist struggles and to organize revolutionary demonstrations which will have the purpose of overthrowing the yoke of imperialism and winning the battle for full independence.[7]

Toward the same end, the Theses on the War Danger went on to issue a strong call to communists to work vigorously for the "withdrawal of imperialist armed forces from the colonies," and to insist upon the "removal of imperialist cadres and officers detachments from native armies."[8]

The Comintern's fear that non-European troops would be used for an aggressive war against the Soviet Union was reflected not only in Congress pronouncements relating to the colonial world, but

---

* It is interesting that some of the means contemplated for dealing with the supposed intensification of anti-Soviet military moves on the part of imperialist powers were not significantly different from the policies put forward during the late nineteenth century. It was apparently felt, for example, that British power could be seriously weakened by separating Great Britain from its colonial empire. This, in turn, was to be accomplished by the interruption of British maritime communications, as proposed by Mashkov. Similar strategic thinking, moreover, seems to have been applied to the French, who in the late twenties were building up their naval power in the western Mediterranean in order to secure their maritime supply lines from North Africa. (See E. Paul, "Les Blocus et les Problèmes de la Marine dans la Guerre Future," *Internationale Communiste*, no. 12 [June 1, 1928]: 949; and Pavlovich, ed., *Sredizemnoe More: Politiko-Strategicheskii Ocherk* [Moscow, 1927]: 18f.)

in Congress discussions surrounding the Negro question. Although several speakers, including Bukharin, alluded to the importance of winning the allegiance of the world's Negroes—particularly in the event of an imperialist-inspired international conflict[9]—it was the black American communist, James W. Ford,* who pointed out most clearly to the Congress the relevance of Negroes to the security of the U.S.S.R.

One of four American Negroes invited to attend the 1928 convocation, Ford distinguished himself by delivering at the 34th Session an extensive speech on the role of black people in what he ominously termed "the coming war."[10] In the course of his remarks, Ford not only invoked the memory of Negro participation in the Allied intervention in Russia, but, citing the "feverish" war plans of British, French, and American imperialists, he emphasized the likelihood that members of his race might again be forced to draw the sword against their Soviet brothers. Calling upon Negroes to rise up against their imperialist overlords in the event of future hostilities, he exhorted his people to be prepared to join the Soviets in their attempts to convert such hostilities into international class warfare. Declaring adamantly that "we must not be pacifists on the question of the preparation of black armies by the imperialists," Ford then summed up his program for communist action:

> We must penetrate the colonies and prepare the colonial armies in order that they turn their weapons against their oppressors. . . . The fraternal communist parties of France, England, the United States, Belgium, South Africa must immediately begin work in this direction in order that the Negro armies . . . should come forward hand in hand with the workers in defense of the USSR.[11]

Thus the movement for Negro emancipation, like the drive for colonial liberation, was viewed in Comintern eyes as a principal component in the great constellation of international forces surrounding and protecting the Soviet Revolution.

Not satisfied alone with describing the importance of revolutionary work among the world's subject peoples, the Sixth Comintern

---

* Ford, like many of his Negro communist contemporaries, was himself a disgruntled veteran of World War I, having fought in the American army on the battlefields of France. Perhaps the most prominent of the CPUSA's early Negro members, Ford ran for the office of Vice President of the U.S. on the communist party ticket in 1932. ("Negro Worker Nominated for Vice President," *Negro Worker* [new series] II, no. 6 [June, 1932]: 25–27.)

Congress dedicated itself to the task of delineating a new strategy by which world revolution was to be accomplished. As mentioned previously, the basic approach decided upon by the Comintern was that known as the "United Front from Below." As Bukharin explained it, this strategy was not intended to be a renunciation of the previous policy of cooperating with noncommunists, but instead simply a joining of forces with the rank and file of noncommunist movements and a rejection only of their bourgeois leadership.[12] Applied to the colonial world, this new approach in no way meant an abandonment by communists of the nationalist-independence movement. Indeed, the Sixth Congress, in its far-reaching "Theses on the Revolutionary Movement in Colonial and Semi-Colonial Countries,"* made unmistakably clear its belief that all "colonial peoples" should be granted "unconditionally and without reservation, complete state independence and sovereignty."[13] What the new revolutionary approach did involve for the colonial world, however, was a definite parting of the ways between communists and the nationalist bourgeoisie and a return to the relatively purist Marxist-Leninist practice of relying primarily upon the energies of the proletariat.

The primacy of the proletarian class in the revolutionary process was indeed the principal tenet of the new Comintern approach.[14] Although precedents for applying this approach to the colonial world could be detected in both the Comintern's attitude toward the Brussels Conference of 1927** and the ECCI's 1928 directives to the

---

* This extensive document, which contained the bulk of the Congress pronouncements on colonial issues, was prepared almost single-handedly by the Finnish Comintern official, Otto Kuusinen—possibly at the request of Stalin himself. Presented by Kuusinen at the 46th Session of the Congress on September 1, 1928, the Theses on the Revolutionary Movement were adopted by the Comintern virtually without change. That such a document would have comprised so fundamental a part of the Comintern's official policy pronouncements serves as testimony to the extent of communist interest in the colonial world at the time of the Sixth Congress. (See O. V. Kuusinen, speech at 46th Session of the Congress, "O Revoliutsionnom Dvizhenii v Kolonialnykh i Polvkolonialnykh Stranakh," *Stenograficheskii Otchet VI Kongressa*, Kominterna [6 vols.; Moscow, 1929]: IV: 122–26, compared with text of the Theses appearing in Bela Kun, ed., *Kommunisticheskii Internatsional v Dokumentakh* [Moscow, 1933]: 832–70. See also remarks of Lominadze at Congress, *Stenograficheskii Otchet VI Kongressa*, IV, *op. cit.*: 439.)

**No sooner had Nehru and representatives of the Kuomintang concluded their sessions at Brussels, than Comintern analysts began speaking of the "task [which lay] before the most conscious, class-organized part of the conference to induce

Communist Party of China,[15] it was in the pronouncements of the Sixth Congress that the insistence on a proletarian-led revolution in the colonies became established Comintern policy. Just as the first task of every communist party was "to win over to its side the majority of its own class,"[16] so, according to the Congress, communist parties in colonial and semi-colonial countries were to concentrate their efforts on recruiting leadership from "the working class itself."[17]

But in executing its revolutionary function, the proletariat was not to act alone. Indeed, the need to mobilize the strength of the peasantry as the most important class ally of the proletariat was a second axiom of the "United Front from Below" approach. Particularly with respect to the colonial world, the importance of winning the allegiance of the peasant class was underscored. Not only did the Comintern recognize that "the immense many-millioned peasant mass constitutes the overwhelming majority of the population even in the most developed countries,"[18] but it noted that peasant discontent was rising throughout the Third World and that opportunities were rapidly emerging for "the unleashing of a mass peasant agrarian revolution."[19] Communists were thus exhorted at the Sixth Congress to intensify their work among colonial peasants in order both to "emancipate [this group] from the influence of the nationalist bourgeoisie"[20] and to forge "a fighting bloc of the proletariat and the peasantry."[21] If in colonial areas the proletariat were able to win the peasantry to its side, concluded the Comintern, it could expect to assume leadership not just over the second or "proletarian" phase of the communist revolution, but over the first or "bourgeois democratic" phase of the struggle as well.[22]

The repudiation of the nationalist bourgeoisie embodied in the "United Front from Below" strategy was to find its reflection in the Comintern approach to both the Negro and the colonial questions. Some of the more immediate implications of the new communist policy were spelled out in the pronouncements of the Sixth Congress itself. With regard to the Negro question, the new policy shift involved a thorough-going repudiation of Garveyism. With respect

these wavering and not always reliable elements onto the path of actual struggle." ("Pod Kontrol Boriushchikhsia Mass" ["Under the Control of the Struggling Masses"], *Kommunisticheskii Internatsional*, IX, no. 8 [February 25, 1927]: 5.) What seemed of greatest importance to these Comintern strategists was that the revolutionary movement in the colonial world be led by the increasingly "leftist-oriented proletarian masses." (See *ibid.*: 1–8.)

to colonial issues, it prompted the formulation of a whole new series of directives for the conduct of revolutionary work in the less-developed world.

The Theses on the Revolutionary Movement in Colonial and Semi-Colonial Countries (or the "Colonial Theses," as they were more widely known) contained a separate section dealing with "The Negro Question."[23] In its discussion of such general issues as racial discrimination and Negro exploitation this statement did not differ noticeably from the pronouncements of the Fourth Comintern Congress six years before. Similarly, the call for communist agitational work and trade union organization among Negroes contained in this statement was substantially a repetition of the policy directives issued in 1922. In two important respects, however, the Sixth Comintern Congress departed significantly from previous treatment of the Negro question. On one hand, Comintern pronouncements of 1928 incorporated a totally different approach toward the Negro bourgeoisie; and on the other hand, they advanced a radical new scheme for promoting self-determination in certain specific regions of the Negro world.

Perhaps the clearest indication of the change in Comintern attitude toward the Negro bourgeoisie was the policy adopted by the Sixth Congress vis-à-vis the Garveyite movement. Once looked to as a vehicle for carrying the communist revolutionary message to Africa, Garveyism was by 1928 regarded as a reactionary force no longer fit to be the object of Comintern support.

This reversal in the Comintern's attitude toward Garveyism, though dramatic in nature, was not without antecedents—both in the statements of David Ivon Jones, and in Comintern literature published immediately prior to the Sixth Congress. Angered by the Garveyites' refusal to coordinate efforts with the pro-communist American Blood Brotherhood and by their competition with Bolshevik propaganda efforts in South Africa, Jones, even in the early twenties, began to condemn Garveyism as a strictly "bourgeois" movement and to describe its leader as "a religious fanatic who carries hatred of whites to an extreme and exalts the cult of his own race."[24] Similarly, Comintern literature published in 1928 reflected considerable suspicion of the American Negro bourgeoisie. The latter's peculiar sense of racial identity was regarded as a device used by black capitalists to develop their own clientele without the interference of white competitors. In this context, Garveyism's "Back to Africa" campaign became just another exploitative capitalist scheme to dispossess African Negroes.[25]

Although by the time of the Sixth Congress Garveyism posed no serious threat to communist activity among the world's Negroes, as an organ of the black American bourgeoisie it clearly had no place in the Comintern's new scheme of proletarian orthodoxy. For those who followed the shifts in Comintern thinking, it was therefore not surprising to find among the official pronouncements of the Sixth Congress the following unequivocal declaration:

> Garveyism, at one time the ideology of the American Negro petty bourgeoisie and workers, and still with a certain influence over Negro masses, today impedes the movement of these masses towards a revolutionary position. While at first advocating complete social equality for Negroes, it turned into a kind of "Negro Zionism" which instead of fighting American imperialism advanced the slogan "Back to Africa." This dangerous ideology, without a single genuinely democratic feature, which toys with the attributes of a nonexistent "Negro Kingdom," must be vigorously resisted, for it does not promote but hampers the struggle of the Negro masses for liberation from American imperialism.[26]

It is important to note that this resolute condemnation of Garveyism, while sparked by communist mistrust of black bourgeois nationalists, was in no way intended as a repudiation by the Comintern of Negro nationalism in all its forms. In fact, even as it denounced certain aspects of the Garveyite program, the Comintern seemed to be adopting for itself one element of Garvey's platform—the creation of an independent Negro republic in the "Black Belt" of the United States.

In this maneuver it may be possible to detect the hand of Stalin himself who, it should be remembered, had already acquired considerably notoriety for eliminating his enemies while at the same time adopting their ideas. Reportedly the Soviet leader took a personal part in outlining some of the points to be dealt with by the Sixth Congress with respect to the Negro question.[27] Whether or not this was the case, Stalin did at least have an opportunity to acquaint himself personally with the problems of American Negroes (and presumably also with certain Garveyite programs) when, in 1925, he received in the Kremlin the five Negroes who had come to study at KUTV University.[28]

Whatever may have been the extent of the Soviet leader's involvement, it is clear that the Sixth Comintern Congress deliberately chose to apply Stalin's definition of nationhood to the Negro question. In demanding that independent Negro republics be established "in those areas of the South [of the U.S.] inhabited by compact Negro masses and in South Africa,"[29] the Comintern demonstrated both its lack of understanding of the Negro problem in these two societies and its insensitivity to the opinions of communist party representatives from the countries involved.* Although in the end the Negro republic scheme proved both unrealistic and counter-productive, its adoption nonetheless served as an important indication of the extent of active communist interest in the Negro question at the time of the Sixth Congress. Perhaps even more significant, the fact that the Comintern embraced this scheme in 1928 provides clear evidence that the world communist movement—though preoccupied with the application of the "United Front from Below" strategy—placed continued if not heightened faith in the revolutionary power of Negro nationalism.

The Comintern was undoubtedly aware that its new emphasis on a proletarian-led revolution would raise certain practical problems vis-à-vis communist policy toward the colonial world. In particular, Comintern leaders must have realized the difficulties which would arise in trying to apply proletarian orthodoxy to the specific group of "backward colonies" little touched by industrialization. Essentially the issue could be reduced to the following: how could communist uprisings be brought about in those underdeveloped areas—such as the majority of the territories of sub-Saharan Africa—which were basically deficient in the strata of the population necessary for revolutionary leadership.

---

* In a vain attempt to oppose the black republic scheme at the Congress, Sidney Bunting, leader of the CPSA, argued that such an approach would be unwise not only in South Africa but throughout colonial Africa since it overemphasized the nationalist features of revolutionary struggle and unduly subordinated its class characteristics. (See Bunting remarks at the 38th Session of the Congress, August 20, 1928, *Correspondance Internationale*, VIII, no. 139 [November 20, 1928]: 1569–70.) Shortly after the Congress Bunting and the entire leadership of the CPSA was purged and the party lost a substantial portion of its membership. The fear that the party would fall under a dictatorship of the black race was no doubt responsible for alienating many white supporters. In addition, concern that the new communist scheme, with its support of separate development for blacks, would be no better than apartheid was an important factor in destroying the allegiance of more idealistically-motivated CPSA members. (See Edward Roux, *Time Longer Than Rope* [London, 1948]: 263ff.)

Basically the strategy decided upon was that first suggested by Lenin at the Second Comintern Congress in 1920. If the proletariat of advanced countries was used to fill the gap in the class structure of non-industrialized societies, then the latter could hope to achieve a non-capitalist path to revolution. Adopting this important concept of Leninist theory, the Sixth Congress declared that in "backward countries (for example in parts of Africa) . . . victorious national uprisings may open the road to socialism while by-passing the capitalist stage, if sufficiently powerful help is given by the countries with a proletarian dictatorship."[30] In practical terms this meant that the Soviet Union was reserving an option to intervene directly in the colonial revolution.

But in addition to highlighting the importance of Russia's role in the underdeveloped world, the reapplication of Lenin's formula served to underscore the need for increased revolutionary activity on the part of another segment of the world's more advanced proletariat —the members of Western European communist parties. Although they did not technically belong to "countries with a proletarian dictatorship," European communists were given an added prod by the Sixth Congress to increase their revolutionary work in the colonial world.

In phrases reminiscent of the Fifth Comintern Congress, European communists were criticized for the inadequacy of their previous efforts. Indeed, there was little doubt who the Comintern had in mind when it included in the Colonial Theses the following observation:

> So far not all the Parties in the Communist International have fully understood the decisive significance of the establishment of close, regular and constant relations with the revolutionary movements in the colonies for the purpose of affording these movements active support and immediate practical help.[31]

So important was this task considered that the Comintern in effect warned that henceforth the conduct of colonial work would be used as the principal basis for evaluating the overall revolutionary performance of European communist parties—if not their standing in the world communist movement.[32]

According to the directives contained in the Colonial Theses, there were three types of organizational efforts which communists from advanced countries were to conduct among colonial peoples. The first of these was party organization. Recognizing the need to develop a cadre of colonial communists, the Sixth Congress called upon communist parties in the metropolitan countries to expand their membership to include resident natives from the colonies.[33] Yet, cognizant of the extent of indigenous colonial mistrust of metropolitan workers, the Congress accompanied this call with the suggestion that communist parties be organized within the colonies themselves and that these parties be allowed both to develop independently of their European counterparts and to maintain direct relations with Comintern headquarters.[34] In so departing from earlier policy, it might be noted, the Comintern was in effect complying with Stalin's desire for centralized organizational control—something which inspired more than one policy innovation introduced by the Soviets at the Sixth Congress.

In addition to party organization, a second equally important communist effort was to be the formation of colonial centers of trade union activity. Singled out in the Colonial Theses as "the most important of the immediate general tasks in the colonies," trade union work was to be conducted either from within existing mass trade union organizations or through the establishment of new revolutionary unions.[35] Directing its remarks specifically to communist parties in colonial countries, the Comintern went on to demand that communists assist the fledgling trade union movement in the colonies "by advice and by the dispatch of permanent instructors."[36]

Finally, in conformity with the "United Front from Below" strategy, the Colonial Theses underscored the importance of communist organizational efforts designed to bring revolution to the immense agricultural population of the colonial world. In order to "give a revolutionary character to the existing peasant movement," communists were to penetrate mass peasant organizations—regardless of their political complexion.[37] Moreover, in conducting their activities, communists were to make a special effort to win the allegiance of women and youth.[38]

In this way, by concentrating efforts on the peasant masses, as well as by conducting trade union and party work among colonial peoples, communists could hope to carry the proletarian class struggle even to the most sociologically primitive of dependent territories. Thus no region, not even colonial Africa—classed by the Comintern as among the most "economically backward" of areas[39]—was to be excluded from world communism's grand revolutionary design.

Not only did the Sixth Comintern Congress devote its energies to the elaboration of operational guidelines for agitational work in the colonial world as a whole, but more significantly it evinced specific concern over the question of revolutionary activism in the colonies of Negro Africa. In both the deliberations and the resolutions of the Sixth Congress, colonial Africa was singled out as a region worthy of concerted communist efforts.

In the course of the Congress proceedings a number of voices were raised decrying the paucity of previous revolutionary activity oriented toward Negro Africa. Among these none was more critical than that of the American communist Otto Hall (pseudonym Jones), who assigned responsibility for this failure to Comintern headquarters itself. Reminding the Congress that communist-led revolutionary forces in Mozambique had recently attempted without success to establish contact with the Comintern, Hall questioned why more had not been done at the Moscow headquarters to forge ties with this and similar African movements.[40] Insofar as he was able to determine, the "Negro Propaganda Commission" which had been charged by the preceding Comintern Congress with the task of promoting revolution in Negro Africa had "in effect done little work."[41] What was needed, Hall concluded, was not so much the elaboration of new policies, as simply the effective implementation of decisions of preceding congresses. In this context, he seemed particularly eager for the establishment of a central Comintern bureau which could accurately determine the revolutionary situation in countries inhabited by Negroes.[42]

In explaining the reasons for according Africa revolutionary priority, Congress participants repeated such familiar arguments as the need to prevent imperialist use of African military resources. In addition to these traditional themes, however, several new considerations were brought to the attention of the Sixth Congress. Heller, a delegate of the RILU, argued, for example, that revolutionary pressure in Asia was inducing the world's imperialists to look upon Africa as a "second line of entrenchment," behind which they could defend their system and from which they could extract the profits which were increasingly difficult to obtain in China and India.[43] Moreover, he maintained, rising American economic involvement in Africa (specifically in Liberia, Abyssinia, and the Portuguese colonies) added even further to the increase in capitalist penetration of the continent. In short, Heller concluded, Negro Africa was a region of growing economic significance to the capitalist world and as such it was not to be underestimated in Comintern policy formulations.[44]

On a related tack, Edward Roux, representative of the CPSA, complained that "the enormous development of colonial revolution in Asia" had not only redirected capitalist energies toward Negro Africa, but had "diverted the attention" of the world communist movement away from this region.[45] Echoing sentiments expressed by several preceding speakers, Roux heralded the recent appearance of a wage-earning class among African Negroes, seeing in this an indication that Africa too was beginning to develop the sociological bases for a successful revolution.[46]

In short, a considerable number of Congress delegates had reached the conclusion that regardless of the backwardness of Africa's Negro colonies these areas presented the Comintern with distinct revolutionary opportunities. This belief, most fully expressed by Lozovsky, Chairman of the Profintern, at the 37th Session of the Sixth Congress, had important implications for Comintern strategy. Referring to those "countries" (East and West Africa, the Congo, and Portuguese colonial Africa were specified) where labor organizations had not yet commenced agitation but where spontaneous opposition to capitalist exploitation had already begun to surface, Lozovsky declared:

> Our tactics must be adapted to the different colonial countries in order that we can "lead simultaneously the advanced proletariat of Shanghai and Bombay and the black slave of the rubber plantations." That is why we must have precise directives and specific action programs for each of these countries.[47]

In conformity with this demand, Otto Kuusinen, head of the Colonial Commission, announced to the Sixth Congress that his group had included in the Colonial Theses an entire section "on the question of Negroes as it is posed in the United States as well as the Negro colonies of Africa."[48] In this manner, the following statement devoted specifically to Black Africa found its way into the official pronouncements of the Comintern Congress:

> In the Central African colonies of Imperialism colonial exploitation takes on its worst forms, combining slaveholding, feudal and capitalist

methods of exploitation. In the postwar period capital from the imperialist metropoles in ever greater strength swoops down upon the African colonies, creating a concentration of a significant mass of expropriated and proletarianized population on plantations, in mining and industrial enterprises, et cetera. The Congress imposes upon the Communist Parties of the corresponding metropoles the obligation to end the indifference which they have shown with regard to the mass movements in these colonies and instead furnish energetic assistance to these movements, both in the metropoles and in the colonies themselves. At the same time they must carefully study the situation in these countries for the purpose of disclosing the bloody exploits of imperialism and creating the opportunities for organizational connections with the growing proletarian elements of these most mercilessly exploited colonies of imperialism.[49]

Thus, for the first time in a major pronouncement, the Comintern formally declared its intention to embark upon active measures to ensure that black Africa's "victims of imperialism" would one day join the legions of world revolution.

THE IMMEDIATE RESPONSE TO THE CONGRESS: THE INSTITUTIONALIZATION OF COMINTERN INTEREST IN NEGRO AFRICA

During the period from 1928 to 1930 the new accent on colonial and Negro questions which emerged from the Sixth Congress provoked a definite operational response within the Comintern system. The most significant aspect of this response was the institutionalization of world communism's special interest in Negro Africa. In the first place, this institutionalization was expressed in the establishment at Comintern headquarters of a central Negro revolutionary directorate —the International Trade Union Committee of Negro Workers (ITUC-NW). In the second place, it was reflected in the formal inauguration in Moscow of a special program of Soviet academic studies devoted exclusively to Negro Africa.

The formation of the permanent ITUC-NW represented the Comintern's most serious move toward organizing a communist revolutionary movement among the world's Negroes. The series of steps which culminated in the establishment of this agency at the Hamburg Conference of 1930 was undertaken through the offices of two rather disparate organizations: the Red International of Labor Unions

(RILU)—the Comintern's trade union affiliate; and the League Against Imperialism (LAI)—the Third World nationalist body formed at the Brussels Conference of 1927.

It is interesting that the Comintern's decision to elevate Black Africa's priority as a revolutionary target was communicated to the RILU even before discussions on the subject at the Sixth Congress were fully under way. As early as March, 1928, the RILU at its Fourth Congress had placed special emphasis on the need for revolutionary work among African Negroes. Not only did it observe that Africa as a whole was "acquiring ever larger importance as the object of capitalist exploitation," but it went on to specify that "the imperialist powers are betraying more and more interest in Equatorial Africa . . . the British [by] devoting attention to the Gold Coast, the Elephantine Coast, and Nigeria . . . the USA [by] developing plans for the 'peaceable' capture of definite territories such as Liberia."[50] Observing that previous communist agitational work among Negroes in Black Africa and elsewhere had been sorely inadequate, the RILU concluded that a meeting to decide upon "measures for strengthening this work" was urgently required.[51]

This meeting took place on July 31, 1928—concurrent with the Sixth Comintern Congress. Although it was technically a session of the RILU Executive Committee, included in those asked to participate were all Negroes attending the Congress and Congress delegates "from imperialist countries with colonies having a Negro population."[52]

Following a "detailed discussion" of the Negro question by the representative group, the RILU Executive Committee issued an important resolution calling for the establishment of a special "Committee of Negro Workers."[53] Apparently modeled after the Pacific and Latin American trade union secretariats which had been set up by the RILU the preceding year, this "Pan-Negro" trade union secretariat was assigned the responsibility of drawing Negroes into existing trade unions and, where necessary, of promoting the establishment of new unions specifically for black workers.[54]

Judging from the provisions specifying Committee membership, the planners of this project no doubt felt that America and South Africa would at the outset be the principal geographical foci of the new organization's activity. However, while these provisions stated that original membership would comprise Negroes from the Western

Hemisphere and South Africa, they stipulated that future member-ship should embrace representatives from East Africa, Portuguese Africa, the Belgian Congo, Liberia, and French Equatorial Africa[55] —an unmistakable indication that the field of action anticipated for the new body would include most of Negro Africa. In fact, like other broad Comintern schemes, the plan for the Negro Committee was designed to include all regions of the world containing black inhabi-tants and to place a new organ of the Comintern at the head of a global movement of black revolutionary workers. As the RILU reso-lution explained it:

> The principal task of the committee is to work for the establishment of liaison among all the Negro workers of the entire world and for the organization of the world masses of the Negro proletariat on the basis of the class struggle.[56]

In the interests of such "liaison" it was stipulated that the Committee prepare and convene "towards the end of 1929" the conference of Negro workers which had been called for in earlier Comintern pro-nouncements. To the same end, the Committee was also charged with the responsibility of publishing "a special bulletin" to be distri-buted among black workers.[57]

Curiously, the July 31 resolution of the RILU was actually calling for the establishment of an organization which, for all practical pur-poses, was already in existence. On July 15, 1928, a bulletin entitled the *Negro Worker* had appeared in Moscow under the auspices of an "International Negro Workers Information Bureau," affiliated with the RILU and led by the Negro communist James Ford.[58] This "Negro Bureau" together with its specialized bulletin were, in effect, the operating nucleus first of the RILU Negro Committee and subse-quently of the permanent ITUC-NW. Not only did Ford become the original chairman of this organization, but the *Negro Worker* became its regular mouthpiece. One suspects, in fact, that Soviet leaders of the Comintern had made the basic decision to form a permanent Negro Trade Union Committee even prior to the time of the Sixth Congress and had then simply stage-managed the steps taken in various Comintern-sponsored gatherings which in 1930 resulted in the establishment of the permanent ITUC-NW.

It is particularly interesting to note in this context that the forma-tion of a special Negro Committee by the RILU in 1928 was clearly in line with Soviet strategic policy. Indeed, by examining the stated objectives of this organization, one can easily see the effects of Russia's security-oriented thinking. As James Ford explained it to the Sixth Congress, the purpose of the Negro Committee was to "publish bulletins and brochures and other literature in the interests of propagating the idea of unifying the proletariat of the entire world for the struggle against imperialist oppression, against world war, and for the defense of the USSR."[59] Similarly, judging from its early editorial statements, the *Negro Worker* was formed not just to strengthen class consciousness and intercommunication among Negroes, but also "to provide them with information on the successful building of socialism in the USSR"[60] and to instruct them as to their proper role in the event of an imperialist war against the Soviet Union.[61] Finally, the notion that the Negro Committee was a body whose inspiration owed something to the communist desire to promote the foreign policy interests of the Soviet state was confirmed in the action program of the new organization, published in the first part of 1929.[62] A comprehensive political platform (which included Negro demands for civil rights, better working conditions, and self-determination), the action program consecrated its final paragraphs to a discussion of the war danger against the U.S.S.R. and concluded with the firm declaration: "We must defend the Soviet Union."[63]

Whatever the underlying reasons for its formation, the Negro Committee was, by the beginning of 1929, a fully functioning organization, complete with Negro leadership, press, and detailed program. There yet remained, however, the task of convening an international conference of Negro workers and thus launching the Comintern's appeal to a wider Negro audience than that which could be reached directly through the CPUSA or through the existing instrumentalities of the RILU. It was probably with these thoughts in mind that those responsible for the destiny of the ITUC-NW turned to an additional forum in which to conduct their efforts —the League Against Imperialism.

From its very inception at Brussels, the LAI was regarded by the Comintern as an important channel through which to forge ties between the colonial nationalist movement and the advanced proletariat of Western Europe and Russia.[64] Despite the changes in communist strategy toward the colonial world which occurred at the time of the Sixth Congress, this fundamental conception of the LAI was retained by the Comintern in the years following 1928. In fact, even at the Sixth Congress itself voices were raised in behalf of supporting the League, urging communists to place renewed faith in the organization and to recognize its anti-imperialist objectives.[65] Thus, rather than repudiate the efforts already undertaken to promote and guide the work of the LAI, the Sixth Congress declared that henceforth it was "imperative" for the Comintern "to strengthen and improve the work of communists in such organizations as the League Against Imperialism."[66]

This sympathetic attitude toward the LAI can be more easily understood in light of the increasing communist domination of the organization in the years following its establishment in 1927. Within months after the Brussels Conference, European socialists began to accuse the LAI of having fallen under communist—and even Russian domination.[67] Although there was some question regarding the truth of such charges at the time they were made,[68] after the Cologne meeting of the LAI Executive Committee in January, 1929, there was little doubt that the organization had indeed come under the control of the Comintern and its Soviet leadership. Not only did the Russian trade union leader Melnichansky play a dominant role in the proceedings at Cologne,[69] but Comintern observers themselves regarded this meeting as having constituted "a sharp turning point in the League's program of activity"—a turning point which brought League policies into direct conformity with the Comintern's left-wing revolutionary orthodoxy.[70] Although after the Cologne meeting the LAI continued to be officially viewed as a "non-party mass organization," for all intents and purposes it had become the first in a series of "front organizations" through which international communism sought to promote its revolutionary objectives in the colonial world.

Nowhere was the League's new orientation more apparent than in the proceedings of its second world congress, held in Frankfurt, July, 1929. In contrast to the first League conference at Brussels, the attendance at this second LAI gathering reflected a shift in gravity away from colonial bourgeois nationalists in favor of colonial workers and peasant organizations.[71] In place of the many well-known Third World leaders who had attended the Brussels Conference (many, like Nehru, had terminated their association with the League), there appeared at Frankfurt a "revolutionary wing" composed of individuals whose allegiance to the Comintern seemed beyond question.[72]

Prominent among these were two Negroes, James Ford, representing the RILU's Negro Committee, and Garan Kouyaté, a native of the French Soudan who had succeeded Lamine Sanghor as leader of the communist-supported LDRN. Both delivered anti-imperialist diatribes which surpassed in militancy anything previously heard—even at Comintern gatherings. Invoking the memory of the fallen Senghor, Kouyaté, for example, warned that all past rebellions of black Africans against European rule were but a "prelude" to the real conflagration yet to come.[73] Similarly, Ford displayed his anti-colonial mettle when, in describing imperialist plans to "lead hordes of black troops against the USSR," he exhorted "Negro working men and women in the colonies to organize against imperialist war" and to work diligently for the achievement of "complete national independence for all the colonies of West Africa."[74]

As these statements of Ford and Kouyaté indicate, the LAI was clearly in step with the Comintern's new emphasis on Black Africa as a promising terrain for nationalist insurrection. In fact, in its concluding manifesto the Frankfurt Congress affirmed with confidence that:

> The revolt of the African peasantry and the struggle against the inhuman oppression of English, French, Belgian, Italian and Portuguese imperialism and its agents, as well as the recent peasant insurrection in French Equatorial Africa, are only the beginning of new more extensive struggles against imperialist domination in Africa.[75]

Based on such beliefs, the League resolved to devote special effort to the task of forming sections in Africa and establishing ties with revolutionary African organizations already in existence.[76] Thus, to the obvious satisfaction of Comintern observers, the LAI's second general meeting at Frankfurt provided not only an arena in which to combat the "reformist" currents of colonial nationalist thought, but a platform from which to trumpet the Comintern strain of militant nationalism and to launch communist agitational work in the colonies of Negro Africa.

In the final analysis, however, perhaps the most important way in which the Frankfurt Congress contributed to the Comintern's plan for Black African revolution was by providing Ford with a unique opportunity to make contacts among revolutionary-minded Negroes and so to carry forward the plans of his RILU Committee to organize a world movement of Negro workers. As a result of Ford's efforts,

THE SIXTH COMINTERN CONGRESS

Negro delegates to the Congress were persuaded to remain in Frankfurt to discuss the problems confronting their race.[77] At one of their post-conference meetings these delegates elected a "Provisional Executive Committee" which was reportedly supplied with Comintern funds[78] and charged with the responsibility of organizing the long-awaited international conference of Negro workers—set to be held in London the following July.[79] Although the Provisional Committee was nominally responsible for the conference preparatory work, it was primarily through the energies of Ford, its Chairman, and a young Trinidadian Negro, George Padmore, whom Ford had brought with him from the United States,* that the conference of Negro workers ultimately became a reality.

That London was originally chosen as the site of the Negro conference was in part a product of the communist belief that Great Britain occupied a central position among imperialist powers in the exploitation of the world's Negroes. In addition, however, it reflected a desire on the part of the conference organizers to draw out the British Labor Government on questions of colonial policy.[80] Although the request for permission to hold the conference in London did stimulate some debate within the Ramsay MacDonald Government, this request was firmly denied.** [81] Not only were British port authorities ordered to obstruct entry into England of Negro delegates arriving to attend the conference, but the governors of Britain's Negro colonies were reportedly instructed to prevent the departure of these delegates in the first place.[82]

Given the probable character of the Negro conference, it was understandable that the British government would have taken this negative stand. Certainly Ford, in his militant statements prior to

---

* Active in the CPUSA in the period immediately prior to the Frankfurt Congress, Padmore was destined to figure prominently in subsequent communist work among Negroes. (See J. R. Hooker, *Black Revolutionary: George Padmore's Path from Communism to Pan-Africanism* [New York, 1967]: 12f.) It is interesting that both he, as well as another member of the Provisional Executive Committee, Johnstone (Jomo) Kenyatta, were later to become dominant figures in the movement for Black African independence.

** According to one source, this negative attitude on the part of the British government was strongly influenced by its desire to enlist South African support at the forthcoming Dominion Conference in London. (François Coty, "Le Péril, Rouge en Pays Noir," *L'Ami du Peuple* [December 15, 1930].) South African separatist proclivities had reportedly been stimulated by the failure of the British imperial system to provide adequate protection against agitation already begun by the Comintern among South African Negroes. (*Loc. cit.*)

the conference, did little to allay Britain's fear that the gathering would constitute a platform from which to attack British colonial policy.[83] Indeed, the MacDonald Government, beset by serious problems in India and the Far East, had every reason to believe that the proposed Negro conference would both intensify colonial unrest throughout the empire and stimulate direct opposition to British rule in Africa.

But if Britain was thus concerned lest Ford's project threaten the integrity of its African possessions, this was hardly true of Britain's former World War I enemy—Germany. A nation recently dispossessed of its territories in Africa, Germany could be expected to look with favor on communist revolutionary activity in the colonies of its former adversaries. Moreover, a tolerant attitude toward Ford and his project would clearly fall in line with the postwar German policy of cooperation with the Soviet Union.[84] Such thinking was no doubt instrumental in the final decision to make Hamburg the site of the International Conference of Negro Workers. Already this city was the location of a Comintern-sponsored Seamen's Club and a strong local communist party. In addition, as a well-located maritime port, it offered comparatively easy access from both the U.S.S.R. and the colonies of Africa.

On July 7, 1930, the Hamburg Conference of Negro Workers was formally convened. Although possibly as a result of restrictive measures imposed by Britain and France the colonial attendance was not as great as had been expected, the Conference could boast not only of representatives from America and the West Indies, but of Negro delegates from British and French colonial Africa as well.* [85] What these individuals lacked in numbers, moreover, they made up in revolutionary stature. E. F. Small of Gambia, I. T. A. Wallace-Johnson of Sierra Leone, and Jomo Kenyatta of Kenya, for example,

---

* Whereas delegates came from all four colonies of British West Africa, only one representative of the continent's French colonial regions was present. The latter, listed as W. Bile of the Cameroon, was apparently in charge of a Berlin branch of the LDRN. (ITUC-NW, *Report of Proceedings and Decisions of the First Conference of Negro Workers* [Hamburg, 1930]: 1.) Kouyaté, leader of the LDRN, was himself unable to attend. Since the organization's headquarters in Paris had made known its intention of sending delegates to Hamburg and the PCF had even offered to pay their expenses, it seems likely that the LDRN representatives were prevented by French authorities from participating in the Conference proceedings. (Report of Agent Paul, June 28, 1930, SLOTFOM, V, Box 3, File 73, Subfile 51.)

THE SIXTH COMINTERN CONGRESS 183

figured prominently not only in the conduct of Comintern agitational activity but in the promotion of the independence movement in Africa's English-speaking colonies.[86] By establishing contact with these and other Negro activists at Hamburg, the Comintern made an important step toward transforming its provisional Negro Committee into a permanent organ for the promotion of revolution in Africa.

The proceedings and resolutions of the Hamburg Conference were interesting primarily because they shed light on the nature of subsequent Comintern policy toward the Negro world. For example, it was apparent even at the beginning of the Conference that future Comintern operational efforts among Negroes would be directed principally toward sub-Saharan Africa. This shift in the "center of gravity" of Comintern activity was predetermined in a special program drafted by the Hamburg Preparatory Committee prior to the Conference. Concomitantly this program seemed to suggest a modification of the earlier Comintern policy of relying upon American Negroes as the authorized agents of revolution in Africa.[87] That such a change in approach had taken place was confirmed in a Comintern account of the Hamburg proceedings. Although continuing to recognize that Africans could benefit from their association with the more advanced Negroes of the United States, this account nonetheless stressed the distinctive characteristics of the Negro problem in Africa and pointed out the possibility that the "American Negro workers might have a certain tendency to consider the question of Negro Africans too much from the American point of view."* [88]

In addition to indicating a basic change in the direction of the Comintern's revolutionary efforts, the Hamburg Conference also revealed certain fundamental characteristics of the organization's future operational strategy. Perhaps most significant in this respect was the communist emphasis upon the use of trade union agitation as a means to achieve the more basic political objective of colonial emancipation. Just as delegates had been advised to use trade union

---

* This new emphasis on a direct approach to African revolution made the representational deficiency at Hamburg seem all the more disappointing. Since opinion in Moscow had begun to stress the importance of firsthand information on local conditions as a basis for organizing future revolutionary struggles, the organizers of the Negro Conference had no doubt been under considerable pressure from Comintern headquarters to secure as wide an attendance from the colonies as possible. (See A. Z. Zusmanovich, ed., *Prinuditnel'nyi Trud i Profdvizhenie v Negritianskoi Afrike* [Moscow, 1933]: 743.)

labels for obtaining passports for travel to Hamburg,* so upon returning to the politically restricted climate of colonial Africa they were
instructed to conceal their more fundamental objectives by confining
their initial demands to questions of labor relations.[89] Thus, by beginning with requests for the most elementary privileges such as the
right to organize trade unions, African workers could lay a solid
foundation for the subsequent struggle to improve their economic
and political existence. As Ford put it: "the economic organizations
of the Negro workers will have the most to do with the liberation
struggle of the whole Negro population."[90]

Although Hamburg thus reflected a shift toward a more syndicalist approach, it is important to emphasize that in its basic position
on Negro revolution the Conference departed in no way from the
strictest dictates of post-1928 Comintern policy. The condemnation
of Garveyism and the insistence on a proletarian-led struggle in the
Negro world, for example, found their way into a pre-prepared
resolution on "The Economic Struggles and Tasks of Negro Workers," delivered by George Padmore.[91] Similarly, the standard sermon
on "The Negro Workers and the War Danger" was pronounced at
the Conference by Frank Macauley, representative of the Nigerian
National Democratic Party.[92] In fact, the triumph of Comintern
orthodoxy was so complete that Soviet observers could not detect the
least indication of a "narrow sectarian spirit" at Hamburg.[93] This
success was primarily the result of the efforts of Ford and Padmore
who as members of both the RILU Negro Committee and the Provisional Executive Committee had worked out in advance not only
the Conference agenda but also the resolutions which were later
adopted by the delegates.[94] In short, the preparation for the Conference had been so efficient that when the delegates convened there
was simply "no room for wavering" or for "the capitulationist policy
of a 'united front from above.' "[95]

Most important of all, there was no question that the delegates at

---

* A similar problem confronted the Comintern in its desire to see Africans visit
the U.S.S.R. Complaining that "the British, French and other colonial governments don't want the Negro masses in the colonies to know the truth about the
Soviet Union, so they will not grant the natives passports," the editors of the
Negro Worker urged that "the workers must first of all organize labor unions and
demand the right to travel wherever they want as free human beings." (*Negro
Worker*, I, no. 10/11 [October/November, 1931]: 29.)

Hamburg would fulfill what the Comintern regarded as the fundamental task of the world Negro Conference—the establishment of a permanent ITUC-NW. Well in advance of the Conference, literature in the Comintern press had spelled out the theoretical case for establishing an international headquarters for Negro revolution.* Similarly, in drawing up plans for the Conference, the Hamburg Preparatory Committee had resolved that the most important order of business at the meeting would be "the creation of a permanent central organization which would bring together the Negroes of the entire world."[96] Finally, lest there remain any doubt among delegates concerning the course of action they were to follow, a confidential memorandum emphasizing the need to give organized leadership to a world Negro movement was circulated among the Conference participants prior to the formal opening of the sessions at Hamburg.[97]

Thus the delegates were led to approve the establishment of a permanent Negro body which succeeded both the RILU Negro Trade Union Committee and the Provisional Executive Committee formed at the Frankfurt Congress of the LAI.[98] In addition to Ford and Padmore, three West Africans—Kouyaté, Small, and Macauley —were "elected" to this new International Trade Union Committee of Negro Workers.[99] No sooner had these formalities been completed than the Conference delegates were invited to come to Moscow to attend the Fifth Congress of the RILU.[100] Accordingly, Padmore, joined by Kouyaté, several Africans of the LDRN, and more than a dozen Conference delegates, made the pilgrimage to Moscow to receive the Comintern's blessing upon their accomplishment.[101]

Although the details remain obscure, it appears that this blessing involved more than simple approbation. Indeed, it seems that the Comintern went so far as to invite the new ITUC-NW to establish

---

* Ford, for example, emphasized the plight of African workers, pointing to their comparative isolation from the more activist and experienced revolutionary proletariat in Europe and America. (Ford, "Conférence Syndicale Internationale des Ouvriers Nègres à Londres," Correspondance Internationale, X, no. 46 [May 31, 1930]: 543.) Chattopadhyaya, on the other hand, noted that various spontaneous outbreaks had occurred among African workers, yet nothing had been done to coordinate the energies of these "victims of colonialism" or to facilitate contact between African revolutionaries across colonial boundaries. (V. Chattopadhyaya, "La Première Conférence Internationale des Ouvriers Nègres," Correspondance Internationale, X, no. 62 [July 23, 1930]: 742.) A centralized revolutionary headquarters, both concluded, would be of value not only in promoting intercommunication among colonial activists, but in providing overall direction to African revolution.

offices in the Kremlin itself. As a result, George Padmore (who assumed the post of Secretary of the ITUC-NW) was installed at the seat of world communism and charged with the responsibility of guiding the progress of revolution among Negroes.[102] Thus, from the Comintern point of view, the Hamburg Conference made possible not only the establishment of new contacts with Negro activists, but the formation in Moscow of a specific operational division for the pursuit of revolution in the Negro world. Indeed, it was not without a certain tinge of revolutionary optimism that communists viewed the Hamburg Conference as having represented "a landmark in the struggle of the toiling Negro masses for their liberation."[103]

Soviet academic concern for sub-Saharan Africa, which had been initiated by Pavlovich, was by no means discontinued after his death in 1927. In fact, that very year a journal appeared entitled *Revoliutsionnyi Vostok* (Revolutionary East) which represented essentially a continuation of his *Novyi Vostok*. This journal, during the ensuing decade of its existence, devoted even more attention to the problems of Black Africa than had its predecessor. Similarly, after Pavlovich's death, Soviet readers were able to follow, as they had in the early twenties, the machinations of European imperialism among black Africans. In 1928 the *Moskovskii Rabochii* (Moscow Worker) Press published a Russian translation of M. E. Burns' critical account of *British Imperialism in West Africa* ("Angliiskii Imperializm v Zapadnoi Afrike").[104] The following year it released a series of pamphlets edited by E. Pashukanis and B. Vinogradov entitled *Mirovaia Politika* (World Politics) dealing with such subjects as the exploits of "Imperialism on the Dark Continent."[105]

However, it remained for the Sixth Comintern Congress with its accent on colonial affairs, to stimulate a real expansion of Soviet academic interest in Negro Africa. Although the new focus on Africa was a logical outgrowth of the generally heightened concern for colonial regions which prevailed within Soviet scholarly institutions in the wake of the Sixth Congress, this emphasis was more than simply an academic by-product of the Comintern's increased interest in the colonial world. Indeed it appears that this emphasis represented a direct and deliberate response to the Soviet decision, revealed at the Sixth Congress, to accord greater revolutionary priority to Negro Africa. Certainly it would be difficult to interpret otherwise the proceedings of a meeting called on April 13, 1929, by the Scientific Research Association for the Study of National and Colonial Problems (NIANKP).* Convened to establish "a special scientific-research group for the study of the socio-economic problems of Negro Africa," this meeting served as the forum in which Soviet scholar, A. A. Shiik, presented the first detailed plan for a Soviet program of Black African studies.[106] Because his proposals appear to have formed the basis for Russia's Africa-oriented academic pursuits in the years after 1929, Shiik's plan merits more than passing reference.

Arguing that Negro Africa was of "enormous importance" not only to imperialist powers but to the forces of world revolution, Shiik made a convincing case at the NIANKP meeting for the establishment of a distinct new discipline of Soviet African Studies.[107] The creation of this "completely new Marxist science of Black Africa," he argued, would involve essentially two tasks.[108] In the first place, it would require a total rejection of all "mendacious bourgeois" literature on Africa and its replacement by communist analyses which would reveal both the " 'truth' of hundreds of millions of oppressed black toilers," and the " 'truth' of the international proletariat."[109] Secondly, it would necessitate an amplification of communist theory. If, as the Sixth Congress had maintained, such economically "backward" regions as colonial Africa could achieve a noncapitalist path to revolution, then, Shiik recognized, it was necessary for communists to specify more thoroughly the ways in which the advanced proletariat of Western Europe and Russia could be substituted for the deficiencies in the class structure of largely nonindustrialized regions.[110]

Prefacing his discussion with these more general observations, Shiik went on to outline his specific plan for African studies. First

* Originally formed in 1927 as the "Scientific Research Association attached to KUTV University," this organization was reconstituted in 1929 in order to give more emphasis to work on national and colonial problems. From its inception the organization sponsored a number of academic activities relating to "the East," including publication of *Revoliutsionnyi Vostok* and a special series of book-length studies (*Trudy*). Like other Soviet research organizations, the NIANKP evidently maintained its own institute and library in Moscow. (See "Iz Deiatel'nosti Nauchno-Issledovatel'skoi Assotsiatsii pri Kom. Universitete im. Stalina," *Revoliutsionnyi Vostok*, no. 6, 1929: 258–61 and F. T. "O Rabote NIANKP," *Revoliutsionnyi Vostok*, no. 8, 1930: 339–43.)

emphasizing the need to examine the history of Black Africa from precolonial times to the postwar period, Shiik stressed (as Pavlovich had done before him) the importance of approaching this subject from the perspective of Africa's black inhabitants.[111] The historical knowledge thus acquired would serve as a basis for the more significant task of analyzing the existing socio-economic problems of the region. In this connection, Shiik observed, such factors as the economic wealth and potential of Africa, its importance to both the capitalist and the socialist systems, and its comparative sociological development (i.e. the degree of class formation by tribe and region) would be of primary interest.[112] Finally, according to Shiik's plan, the historical and socio-economic information resulting from the successful completion of the first two phases of research would enable Soviet students of Black Africa to look to the future and to estimate the prospects for "noncapitalist development" in the region.[113] Unable to suppress his own thoughts on this subject, Shiik concluded by observing that Africa, because of the rudimentary nature of its class structure, would require "an enormous amount of instructional and organizational activity and support on the part of the leading ranks of the world proletariat" if it were "even to begin" the struggle for liberation.[114] Thus, not only did he condemn the Comintern for its failure to develop more "concrete programs for practical work" in this regard, but he emphasized that among the primary objectives of his plan would be the facilitation of "future revolutionary activity" in Negro Africa.[115]

Viewed in its entirety, Shiik's plan for African studies represented no hasty scheme devised solely in the interests of applying Stalinist dogma to a hitherto unreformed branch of political research. Rather, it had every appearance of being a carefully considered blueprint for undertaking comparatively long-range research projects directed toward a newly appreciated portion of the globe. The general and specific subjects which were suggested for further investigation sounded altogether appropriate for serious seminar papers, lectures, and books. The importance of future detailed study of Africa was propounded as an object in itself. The complexity of the subject was emphasized and the diversity of African life was stressed. The relevance of Black African studies to other fields was not overlooked. Notably as a basis for understanding Negro and colonial problems elsewhere in the world, a specialized knowledge of sub-Saharan

Africa was recognized as invaluable. In short, Shiik's plan could well be regarded as the first detailed and intellectually sophisticated attempt to direct Soviet scholarly concern specifically to Negro Africa. As such it provided a basis for all subsequent Soviet African studies.[116]

Shiik's proposals for an independent program of African studies apparently provoked a direct response, for following the meeting of April 13, 1929, a permanent "African Bureau" was established under the auspices of the NIANKP. During the early 1930's this body produced, on a regular basis, studies dealing with Africa and published them in the NIANKP's *Materialy po Natsional'no-Kolonial'nym Problemam* (Materials on National-Colonial Problems). Not only did the African Bureau treat such general subjects as "Colonial Armies in Africa" and "Emigration and Immigration in Africa," but it included in the NIANKP publication descriptions of individual Black African colonies such as the Gold Coast and the Belgian Congo, and on occasion even reproduced detailed bibliographies of foreign literature on various territories and problems of the region.[117]

Associated with the Bureau's work in these years were a number of scholars who came increasingly to devote their attention to Negro Africa. Among this emerging group of African specialists, one name in particular stands out—that of I. I. Potekhin. Drawn into the study of Black Africa in the wake of the Sixth Congress and the CPSU's consequent "need for active members with some knowledge of Africa," Potekhin subsequently rose to become the dean of Soviet African studies, presiding over their renaissance in the mid-1950's.[118]

While serving in the Soviet Secretariat of the Comintern in the early 1930's, Potekhin, together with A. Z. Zusmanovich (who also became a prominent Soviet authority on Negro Africa in the fifties), succeeded in forming personal associations with Negro Africans.[119] At the same time, the two men were able to pursue more academic interest in Negro Africa as well. In 1933 they collaborated in publishing *Forced Labor and the Trade Union Movement in Negro Africa*,[120] a book which was remarkable not only for the depth in which it investigated some of the questions posed by Shiik,[121] but for the extent to which it utilized indigenous African publications as source materials. By quoting West African nationalist newspapers, as well as by citing ITUC-NW correspondence with Africans,[122] the study by Potekhin and Zusmanovich revealed that Soviet Africanists—even in the early thirties—were endeavoring to base their findings upon direct sources of information from the field.

This accent on acquiring firsthand information on Negro Africa was reflected in the Soviet attitude toward the study of native languages. At a meeting held in January, 1934, the African Bureau, after listening to reports by Potekhin, Zusmanovich, and Shiik, added a further dimension to Soviet African studies by establishing a special center for the study of African languages.[123] This move, it was emphasized, was intended to have more than a purely academic function—in fact, it was designed "to raise native languages to the level of powerful weapons in the political struggle."[124] In other words, the Soviets recognized that in addition to specialists on Africa, they would need to have native language speakers if their plans to foment revolution were to make significant headway among the majority of the African population.

Thus the Soviet program of African studies progressively expanded during the early 1930's. In so doing it increasingly revealed a basic orientation toward the practical needs of propagating revolution, rather than toward the theoretical requirements of pure academic research. In sum, by the time of the depression, Moscow could boast of two institutions which, though very different in nature, were specifically designed to facilitate communist activity in Africa. With a specialized bureau to gather information on the region, and a permanent Negro committee to guide and promote agitational work, Moscow possessed the institutional framework necessary to conduct the most active phase in its pre-World War II plans to bring revolution to Africa.

8

The World Economic Crisis and its Effect upon Comintern Attitudes and Policy

The events of October, 1929, shook the capitalist world to its very foundations. The international financial collapse and the ensuing depression indeed seemed to foreshadow the downfall of the capitalist system. To communists, the "world economic crisis" (as the depression came to be known in Comintern parlance) appeared to represent both a fulfilment of their prophesies and a dramatic opportunity for increased revolutionary effort. Not only did it promise to open broad new fields for communist activity, but it seemed to confirm beyond doubt the superiority of the Marxist world view. In short, the years immediately following 1929 gave rise to a new burst of revolutionary optimism emanating from Moscow—an optimism which was given added stimulus by the international popularity of the Soviet model of development as a valid alternative to capitalism.

THE REVOLUTIONARY IMPACT OF THE DEPRESSION ON BLACK AFRICA

World communism's optimistic expectations concerning the revolutionary impact of the depression were perhaps most clearly revealed in Comintern literature. While communist observers recognized that the most immediate impact of the economic collapse would be felt in Western Europe and the United States, they did not fail to note that the crisis would have profound repercussions in such colonial regions as Negro Africa. Indeed, the proliferation of communist literature on Africa in the early 1930's was testimony to the Comintern's belief that the depression had created unparalleled revolutionary opportunities not only in the economically advanced countries of Europe and America, but also in the most distant colonial outposts of the capitalist world. By examining the basic themes which appeared in this literature, one is able to understand more clearly the thinking which underlay communist revolutionary activity in Africa during the period of capitalist economic crisis.

One aspect of Comintern writing during this period was the emphasis on world capitalism's penetration of sub-Saharan Africa and the consequent susceptibility of this region to the effects of the world economic collapse. For several years prior to the depression communist observers had been noting with concern the increase in American and European involvement in Africa.[1] According to the Comintern interpretation, capitalist powers, discouraged by labor and political difficulties elsewhere in the world, had settled upon Africa as the last remaining labor market from which to draw sizable "super profits."[2] In search of minerals and other raw materials increasingly needed by the technology of mass production, they had, by the late 1920's, carried their exploitative system into even the most remote and hitherto untouched portions of the continent. In short, by the time of the depression Africa had become a major "appendage" of the capitalist economic system.[3]

Given its role as a supplier of raw materials, it was logical to expect that Africa would suffer some of the worst effects of the dramatic fall in capitalist production which accompanied the depression. Comintern writers, even at the outset of the crisis, were quick to point out that Africa would be subject to severe economic dislocations in this regard. If "the smash of the motor 'prosperity' in America has first and foremost been a blow to rubber," observed one Comintern writer in 1930, then was it not appropriate to expect corresponding injury to African producers of that commodity?[4] By the same token, African economies which were essentially exporters of agricultural products, the demand for which had plummeted, could these not be expected to suffer acutely from the depression?[5] Preconditioned by their previous study of capitalism, Comintern observers were clearly prepared to expect the worst.

In particular, they were predisposed to see in capitalist behavior signs of conscious discrimination against colonial peoples. As early as February, 1930, the Comintern writers had warned that "Imperialism will seek its way out of the economic crisis . . . along the line of least resistance, i.e. at the cost of the colonies and semi-colonies."[6] According to the communist view, the unfortunate inhabitants of the less developed world stood to suffer not only from the spontaneous economic repercussions of the crisis, but from world capitalism's conscious attempt to transfer to their shoulders the principal burdens of the depression. Particularly in Negro Africa, communist observers found increasing evidence to confirm this belief.

Maintaining that of all the regions of the underdeveloped world Black Africa was the most directly and severely affected by the depression, Comintern writers noted three basic methods used by colonial powers to transfer the effects of the crisis "onto the backs of the millions of black slaves."[7] These involved the intensified application of techniques developed earlier for exploiting the African population —taxation, the recruitment of forced labor, and land expropriation. Although they were applied in different fashions depending on the African colony involved,* these three techniques, in the Comintern view, had basically the same objective—to sap the meager economic resources of the indigenous population. Whatever their differences in application, moreover, they all had basically the same result—the progressive pauperization of African Negroes.[8] Certainly, Comintern analysts concluded, the intensification of colonial oppression in the wake of the economic collapse could not but affect the revolutionary sentiments of Black Africa's colonial population.

Indeed, nowhere were Comintern accounts more optimistic than in their descriptions of the African reaction to the depression. Even as they deplored Africa's predicament, communist writers noted with undisguised satisfaction that the continent's colonial population was openly expressing its discontent with the current economic and political order. As was the case elsewhere in the world, thoughtful Africans were beginning to raise fundamental doubts about the workability of capitalism as an economic system and were voicing their disenchantment with any regime which was not totally committed to redressing economic and political injustices.[9] In more active ways,

---

* Zusmanovich and Potekhin, for example, described in some detail the differences in application of the three types of exploitation. The expropriation of native land, they found, occurred more frequently in East Africa where a greater number of Europeans had preferred to settle. In West Africa, on the other hand, colonial governments apparently found it more necessary to resort to forced methods of labor recruitment. Variations were also observed in the application of a single basic type of exploitation. Depending on the colony concerned, "hut" taxes or "head" taxes might be used, assessments might be paid in different ways, and different systems might be employed for their collection. (Zusmanovich, ed., *Prinuditnel'nyi Trud i Profdvizhenie v Negritianskoi Afrike* [Moscow, 1933]: 58ff.)

moreover, Africans were beginning to react specifically to the stringent measures imposed by colonial powers in the wake of the depression. Each form of exploitation was accompanied by a corresponding outburst of militant opposition. Each manifestation of opposition, in turn, was observed and analyzed in the Comintern press.

The reaction to colonial taxation was a case in point. In December, 1929, market women in Nigeria objected to new government per capita taxes. This sparked a general strike in the colony, accompanied by government military countermeasures which resulted in a number of fatalities. Referred to repeatedly in Comintern publications, this confrontation was viewed as an unmistakable indication that popular discontent was rising in West Africa and that it could easily be provoked into open rebellion by the imposition of new tax measures by colonial governments.[10] As Shiik put it, "this first manifestation of revolutionary resistance of the oppressed masses of Negroes appears to be only a prelude to great battles . . . for full and final liberation."[11] In a similar vein, George Padmore, perhaps the keenest Comintern observer of the African scene, described the situation in Kenya where British tax collectors were being attacked by natives in various parts of the colony. Like events in West Africa, the situation in Kenya was interpreted as evidence of what Padmore termed "the growing anti-British movement which is taking place throughout the . . . African colonies."[12]

If taxation was thus recognized by the Comintern as a primary cause for revolutionary unrest, the forced recruitment of African labor by colonial governments was regarded as an equally promising abrasive for igniting African rebellion. Although labor disturbances —particularly in West Africa—attracted the attention of Padmore and other communist observers during the early 1930's,[13] the single episode which most thoroughly captured their imagination was the construction of the Congo-Ocean Railroad in French Equatorial Africa.

First made aware of the plight of Congolese workers on this project by the accounts of Ho Chi Minh in the mid-1920's,[14] Comintern writers made a cause célèbre of the fate of the nearly 20,000 black Africans who reportedly perished on the railroad under conditions of forced labor. The death of these workers, together with the "annihilation" of millions of other French Negro subjects in the Congo, was offered by the Comintern as material evidence of the effects of

"French civilization."[15] The "great Equatorial African uprising" which broke out in the Congo during 1928 was regarded in this context as a direct and legitimate response to the injustices of French labor policy. Not only did communists take satisfaction in the knowledge that this rebellion had slowed the pace of construction on the railroad and caused the French government to go to considerable lengths to reestablish order, but they found in it encouraging signs that "class consciousness" and the "nucleus of a workers' movement" were developing even in this primitive heartland of the African continent.[16]

Finally, Comintern writers were aware that in the predominantly agrarian colonies of Black Africa the colonial policy of land expropriation was apt to arouse fierce opposition on the part of the indigenous population.[17] In East Africa, for example, where European settlers had become directly involved in exploiting the land and were continually pressuring the colonial governments to expropriate ever greater amounts of property from the natives, "land hunger" was recognized as the principal catalyst for indigenous political organization. The repeated protests of the Kikuyu Central Association (KCA) against the British government's land policy in Kenya were followed with particular interest in the Comintern press.[18] Examining the plight of the growing mass of landless peasants, communist writers were led to conclude that a revolutionary movement was indeed taking shape in Kenya and that this movement would pose a "great danger to the solidarity of British hegemony" throughout East Africa.[19] In the angry statements of the Secretary of the KCA, Jomo Kenyatta, Comintern observers were able to find further indication of an impending confrontation between British imperial rule and the forces of Black African nationalism. Not only did Kenyatta insist that the land of Kenya belonged by right to the natives and was therefore to be "unconditionally returned," but he ominously warned the British government "that any nation that is built up by force of arms may one day be destroyed by the same force itself."[20] "Regardless of the number of soldiers sent against us," he declared, "we will not cease our agitation until we achieve freedom."[21]

In sum, it was becoming increasingly clear to those who followed African affairs at Comintern headquarters that patience was wearing thin on the part of Africa's colonial subjects. No longer did they seem prepared to tolerate on a continuing basis the type of economic exploitation they had known in the past. Even if readiness to reject the current system had not yet extended to the majority of the indigenous population, at least there were "revolutionary leaders" of the Kenyatta mold who would carry popular economic demands to their logical conclusion and insist upon nothing less than total independence. Thus, as Comintern observers were eager to detect, widespread dissatisfaction with the economic situation was indeed adding fuel to the revolutionary flames of African nationalism.

Yet in still another less obvious way the world economic crisis was producing an equally profound revolutionary impact upon Negro Africa. In addition to its catalytic effect upon the anti-colonial sentiments of the indigenous population, the depression was, according to the Comintern, contributing to Black Africa's revolutionary future by accelerating the "sociological development" of the region and thereby enhancing its prospects for proletarian class struggle. Indeed one of the most interesting aspects of communist writing on Black Africa during the early thirties was its relatively insightful analysis of the effects of capitalist exploitation upon the native society of the region and particularly upon its indigenous class structure.

As communists saw it, the increase in capitalist exploitation of Negro Africa during the late twenties and early thirties served to accelerate the formation of a Negro African proletariat. Although it was recognized that the primary crucible for the proletarianization process was South Africa where the capitalist economy was well ensconced and highly dependent upon black labor,[22] Comintern observers were able to note with satisfaction that by the early 1930's other regions of Negro Africa were developing a solid class basis for revolution.

In particular, they noted that the extractive industries of the Congo and West Africa were drawing increasing numbers of black laborers into the capitalist system. Statistics for gold mining were considered particularly relevant. By 1931 the mines of the Belgian Congo alone were employing over 40,000 natives.[23] By 1933 approximately 30,000 black Africans were at work in the mines of the Gold Coast and equally large gold mining operations were being opened in Nigeria.[24] As far as the Comintern was concerned, the rapid expansion in the African labor force suggested by these figures was cause for considerable optimism. As George Padmore put it:

Since the beginning of 1930, new events of tremendous significance for the revolutionary movement [in Black Africa] have taken place. . . . With the rapid proletarisation of large sections of the Negro population thanks to the exploitation of the mining resources of the colonies, class differences are beginning to manifest themselves more sharply.[25]

In addition to mining, communists noted that the maritime industry was making an important contribution to the expansion of the native work force. Particularly in the port cities of West Africa, increasing numbers of Negro laborers were being drawn into numerous port enterprises such as shipping. As in the case of the Kru tribe (originally natives of Liberia), many were hired as sailors by European maritime lines. Finding their way to such ports as Liverpool, Hamburg, and Marseilles, many either became transient dock workers or joined the ranks of the unemployed. Whether aboard European ships or in European ports, the experience of these black Africans was an unsettling one. As Comintern writers were eager to point out, Negro workers were discriminated against racially; their working and living conditions were markedly inferior to those of whites; and, to make matters even worse, they were socially rejected for taking jobs away from higher paid white workers.[26] Though their condition was deplorable, these black maritime workers, like their compatriots in African mining and construction industries, were undergoing what communists viewed as an essentially progressive experience. Not only would the dramatic change in their way of life "educate them technically," but far more important in Comintern eyes, it would "at the same time lead them from tribal seclusion to class consolidation."[27]

As these statements suggest, the Comintern's analysis of the sociological impact of the depression was not confined solely to a discussion of Africa's class structure. Indeed, according to communists, Africa's revolutionary potential was enhanced not just by the increase in the size of its proletariat, but by other equally fundamental transformations in African society which occurred when indigenous workers were thrown into the service of the capitalist machine. The urbanization process, for example, was recognized as a force of profound sociological impact. Provoked in part by colonial taxation and forced labor policies, this migration to the cities was often abrupt and dramatic in character, creating severe changes in the Africans' former way of life. The disruption of traditional family ties and the weakening of tribal loyalties which accompanied the urbanization process were developments welcomed by the Comintern. Articles in the communist press devoted special attention to the psychological effects of detribalization and forced labor migration, concluding that such experiences had a definite revolutionizing influence upon Africans.[28] Even the comparatively brief exposure of many rural inhabitants to the capitalist system in mines was recognized as an experience likely to create radical attitudes which would be carried back to the hinterland.[29] In short, "the disorganization of the entire former life of the indigenous population" which was occurring in Black Africa in the early thirties was regarded as a progressive development and one which would further enhance communist opportunities for shaping the future of the region.[30]

Finally, in addition to accelerating the proletarianization and urbanization process, the depression served to bring a further disruptive element into the social and economic life of Negro Africans—unemployment. Realizing that wide-spread loss of work would undoubtedly stir anti-colonial sentiments among the native population, Comintern writers were quick to note that Africans were being dismissed in large numbers from capitalist enterprises—often without prior notice and without alternative means of livelihood.[31] In the Belgian Congo in 1933, for example, an estimated 150,000 natives were left without their former employment.[32] Although statistics regarding West Africa were more difficult to obtain in Moscow, Comintern observers could report that unemployment there was "increasing in astonishing proportions" and that its effects were particularly acute in the Gold Coast.[33] Thus they were able to conclude that in Negro Africa, as elsewhere throughout the capitalist world, the forces of revolutionary discontent were being strengthened daily by an "ever-growing army of unemployed."[34]

Given this unprecedented combination of favorable revolutionary conditions, Comintern analysts could not fail to conclude that "the contemporary situation in the colonies [of Black Africa] . . . opens before us brilliant perspectives in the task of bringing the Negro workers into the ranks of our movement, of bringing them into participation in the concurrent struggle against imperialist powers."[35] Indeed, it was the general conviction in Moscow at the outset of the 1930's that the Comintern was confronted with a unique opportunity to promote revolution in Black Africa. Failure to act immediately, it was felt, risked the possibility that rival pro-capitalist organizations would win the allegiance of Negro Africans, or even worse, that world capitalism would somehow revive by using Africa as a basis for its recovery. In brief, the depression had injected a note of urgency as well as a note of revolutionary optimism into the Comintern demand for agitational work among Negro Africans.

There is good reason to believe that communists, at the same time they sought to assess the effect of the depression upon Black Africa, also made a deliberate effort to adapt Comintern operational strategies to the improved revolutionary situation which they found in the region. Although in the years immediately following 1930 there were no such authoritative policy pronouncements as those emanating from the Sixth Comintern Congress, it is nonetheless possible to determine with some accuracy the direction of world communism's African policy during this period by a close reading of statements made at other less exalted Comintern gatherings, as well as by extrapolation from material appearing in Comintern periodicals.

Perhaps the forum which manifested most clearly the nature of communist policy in the depression years was the Fifth Congress of the RILU, held in Moscow in August, 1930. Lozovsky set the tone for this meeting when he declared:

> The revolt of the Black Continent against imperialism is only beginning ... Our job is to make use of this huge amount of combustible material, to make allies for ourselves of these vast masses seething with hatred against their oppressors, to draw them closer to ourselves, and to assist them with the vast amount of experience we have accumulated.[36]

In this context the RILU made a pointed effort to welcome African and other Negro participants who had come to Moscow directly from the Hamburg Conference of the preceding month.* [37] In particular, it sought to endorse the organizational efforts initiated at Hamburg and to marshall the resources of RILU affiliates behind

---

* At the RILU Congress, delegates heard a lengthy report on the Hamburg Conference delivered by Ford. (See "Summary of the Report of Comrade Ford to the Fifth World Congress of the RILU on Work amongst Negroes," *Negro Worker*, I, no. 3 [March, 1931]: 18–22.) For the first time at a Comintern gathering West Africans were given the floor to discuss the subject of African revolution and reportedly Garan Kouyaté was chosen to preside over a special Negro commission set up by the Congress. (See "Un Discours Nègre au Congrès de L'I. S. R.," *La Race Nègre*, IV, no. 1 [July, 1930]: 2; also Report of Joe [November 20, 1930]: 2, SLOTFOM, V, Box 3, File 73, subfile 51. This report stated that twenty-five Negroes were present at the RILU Congress and that most of Africa except Madagascar and Ethiopia was represented.)

the projected work of the ITUC-NW. Again it was Lozovsky who explained most succinctly the task of his organization. "The RILU," he declared, "must do everything possible to develop the labors of the conference which was held in Hamburg and to transform the ITUC-NW into an organization with a backing throughout the whole Black Continent."[38]

To this end the RILU issued the standard directive to European communists to recognize "the political significance of organizational efforts among Negro workers" and to establish the "closest ties" with these workers in the African colonies of their respective countries.[39] In addition, according to one account, the RILU decided to establish in Brussels an additional operational headquarters for revolutionary work among Negroes. Reportedly this organization was to be under the chairmanship of Ford and was to be responsible for directing a "violent and energetic" campaign against colonial domination using mass propaganda and labor strikes.[40] Although there is no evidence that this organization was ever established in Brussels, an operational headquarters along the lines described was set up in Hamburg not long after the Fifth RILU Congress. Under the direction of Padmore, this branch of the ITUC-NW maintained offices in Germany, notably for the publication of the *Negro Worker*.

Of the policies emerging from the Fifth RILU Congress perhaps the most significant was that emphasizing a syndicalist approach. In effect the RILU gave its official endorsement to the operational strategy advocated at Hamburg—namely, that economic demands of Negro workers should serve as the principal means for obtaining political objectives—or, as Garan Kouyaté termed it, that "the political should give precedence to the economic."[41] Although it was recognized that indigenous economic organizations in Negro Africa were only in the initial stages of development, the resolutions of the RILU Congress nonetheless referred to "embryos of a trade union movement in Sierra Leone, the Congo, and Mozambique" and suggested that these be regarded as the cornerstones for future Comintern work in the region.[42]

This accent on the formation and use of trade union organizations in Africa was in actuality a strict application of the "United Front from Below" strategy. So faithfully did the RILU follow the policy of proletarian orthodoxy that it was even suggested that non-proletarian elements be "weeded out" from trade union organizations already in existence.[43] Regardless of its limited numerical size, "the industrial proletariat" even in Africa was regarded as "the fundamental basis of the revolutionary anti-imperialist movement" and as such was to be the principal target for communist organizational efforts.[44]

Although the emerging African proletariat as a whole was thus selected as the primary object of Comintern activity, certain important subgroups within this proletariat were singled out as worthy of the most concentrated organizational attention. Conspicuous among these was the expanding group of African sailors. Recognized by the Comintern as important agents for transmitting "the lessons of struggle to other workers,"[45] these discontented victims of particularly severe capitalist exploitation had long been regarded as prime subjects for communist energies. By sponsoring the establishment of an International of Seamen and Harbor Workers (ISH) in 1931 and by actively cooperating with this trade union organization in its efforts to enlist an African following, the Comintern gave continued evidence of its belief that "Negro seamen have a very important role to play in the development of the workers' revolutionary liberation movement in Africa."[46]

Organizational work among African sailors and other maritime laborers served to enhance Comintern interest in another, sometimes overlapping sub-group of the colonial proletariat—the growing mass of African workers based in the metropoles. Like many of their fellow countrymen living in the port cities of Africa, a large number of these African emigrés were either altogether unemployed or had great difficulty finding work during the depression years. Recently exposed to the proletarianizing experience of working in the capitalist enterprises of huge European cities, this group formed perhaps the most dissatisfied element of the new African proletariat. As such it could not be excluded from the revolutionary plans of the Comintern. Indeed, the path to salvation for unemployed Africans was spelled out clearly by the ITUC-NW: it lay in combining forces with the trade unions of employed workers or in establishing independent "Action Committees" to extort economic relief from the capitalist exploiters.[47]

Although organizational efforts were to be directed primarily to Negro workers in the urban areas of Africa and Western Europe, communists after 1930 by no means overlooked the importance of activity among Black Africa's vast peasant masses. Whereas the agrarian population did not represent part of the newly emerging African proletariat, communists recognized that the very enormity of this group rendered imperative major efforts to bring about its organization.[48] Discussing West Africa specifically, Padmore went so far as to contend that:

> The basic force in the revolutionary liberation movement in West Africa lies in the agrarian masses, who form the overwhelming majority of the toiling population under the leadership of the proletariat; and because of this, the question of the organization of the agrarian workers as well as the peasantry must be made one of the central tasks of the trade unions.[49]

As a matter of first priority, according to the decisions of the Fifth RILU Congress, communists were to organize agrarian laborers on the large capitalist plantations of Africa.[50] After this work had been initiated, they were to undertake in other agrarian situations the establishment of "Peasant Committees" linked by "voluntary and fraternal" ties to workers' associations.[51] Whatever the conditions, however, the organization of African peasants was to be pursued in close conjunction with proletarian activity in order to "raise the ideological level [of the peasants] and give them more conscious leadership."[52] By applying such an approach, concluded the RILU, "the successful organization of the most backward [Negro African] agricultural workers is altogether possible."* [53]

In addition to singling out for communist attention specific subgroups of the African population, Comintern policy formulations during the depression years were noteworthy in that they revealed for the first time a pattern of geographical emphasis in world communism's concern for Black Africa. In this context, probably the most interesting development was the emergence of West Africa as a priority target for Comintern energies.

---

* It should be noted that two other major subdivisions of the African population were considered worthy of special operational emphasis—women and youth. Although these groups did not receive extensive attention in communist policy formulations, Padmore, for one, did discuss their significance in the revolutionary process. In examining the role of women, for example, he explained: 'Because of the peculiar African social system which imposes upon the women the financial burdens of family life, the women are among the vanguard in the struggle." (Padmore, "Africans Massacred by British Imperialists," *Negro Worker*, II, no. 5 [May, 1929]: 3.)

The choice of this region as an important center for communist activity was in no sense fortuitous. In the first place, the Comintern tended to direct its attention almost automatically to those areas where the appearance of a comparatively "well crystalized proletariat" could be detected. This, as Padmore reminded the Comintern, was clearly the case in West Africa.[54] Secondly, and perhaps more important, it was the general belief among communists in the early 1930's that this part of the continent was undergoing most dramatically the revolutionizing effects of the depression.

Liberia, for example, given its binding economic ties with the United States, could not fail to escape the most severe repercussions of the capitalist crisis. In fact, so acute was the economic malaise in this African country that Padmore was inclined to regard it as a potential base both for spreading revolution throughout the rest of Black Africa and for "delivering the final blow to the whole system of imperialism."[55] Similarly, the colonies of British West Africa were accorded unusual revolutionary significance by Padmore and other Comintern strategists. Not only was it observed that these colonies were of "tremendous economic importance" to Britain, but it was recognized that they were responding in a particularly rebellious manner to the hardships of the depression.[56] Of the four, the Gold Coast, long the scene of nationalist stirrings, and Nigeria, the largest of Britain's African colonies, drew the greatest share of Comintern attention.

It should be noted that communist policy makers, though they had begun by 1930 to display a marked interest in West Africa, continued to regard the Communist Party of South Africa as "the ideological and organizational leader of the revolutionary communist movement in other parts of Black Africa."[57] While the CPSA was almost certainly not meant to have a monopoly over operational initiatives undertaken in the Negro regions of the continent, it was expected to provide a kind of field headquarters for the preparation of Black African revolution. In 1928, for example, the RILU Negro Committee announced:

> The tasks and programs of a trade union center [in South Africa] should be worked out and contact made with east, west, central Africa for the purpose of linking up the workers there with the South African center.[58]

It is not known whether this center ever came into existence or whether West Africa in fact superseded South Africa as the major launching ground for communist-sponsored agitational activities. What is clear, however, is that both areas, possibly at different times, were looked to by the Comintern as points of departure from which the waves of upheaval would sweep across the entire expanse of Black Africa.

Finally, in tracing the contours of Comintern policy during the early 1930's one further characteristic emerges. In this period, even more than in the years immediately following the Sixth Congress, communists appeared determined to combat in every way possible the black bourgeoisie. In calling for a "concerted struggle to draw the Negro masses away from the influence of national reformism," communists had in mind not only the need to oppose tribal leaders and other "comprador" elements within African society,[59] but more pointedly the necessity to eliminate once and for all the influence of American bourgeois nationalism. In this context, the inveterate opposition to Garveyism was the most striking case in point.

Although communist operational interest in Garveyism had been firmly laid to rest at the time of the Sixth Congress, it was deemed appropriate in the early thirties to go one step further and launch a concerted attack on Garvey and his movement. George Padmore led the way in the Comintern's vilification of the already excommunicated Negro leader, devoting considerable effort to denouncing him as a "fraud" and a "dishonest demagogue."[60] Least pardonable of all his sins, Garvey had in 1931 established offices in London and made approaches concerning his "Back to Africa" scheme to the League of Nations. To Padmore (and undoubtedly to the Comintern at large) this was conclusive evidence that Garvey had made an irrevocable defection to the camp of the imperialists.[61] Accordingly, the communist position came full circle—instead of supporting Garvey's "Back to Africa" campaign as a means for transmitting revolution to Africa, the Comintern chose to instruct American Negroes to forget about returning to their native continent and to "remain where they are."[62] At the same time, their black brothers in the African colonies were informed that "the struggle against Garveyism represents one of the major tasks of the Negro toilers."[63] Indeed, world communism's resolute antipathy toward Garveyism, as well as its opposition to other currents of bourgeois Negro nationalism (such as that represented by W. E. DuBois' Pan-African Congress movement*) represented central and recurrent themes both in Comintern literature and in Comintern policy formulations during the depression years.

THE MILITARY AND STRATEGIC IMPACT OF THE DEPRESSION ON IMPERIALIST POWERS

The advent of the depression caused the Comintern to alter significantly not only its expectations concerning revolutionary prospects in Negro Africa, but its fundamental conception of world politics and its calculations regarding the behavior of imperialist states. With "inner antagonisms . . . shaking the world system of capitalism at its foundations" and with Russia's socialist economic system enjoying its first relative success, the "two camp" view of world affairs so familiar in the Cold War period emerged for the first time as a basic characteristic of the Comintern analysis of international relations.[64]

Indeed, antagonism between the capitalist and socialist economic systems came to be regarded by the Comintern as the central feature of international politics, supplanting in importance even the internal "contradictions" of capitalism.[65] The intensity of the economic crisis, communists maintained, had served to convince the capitalist powers that they could no longer tolerate coexistence with a rival economic system which offered a successful alternative to their own way of life. By the same token, the depression had demonstrated conclusively to the capitalist world the need to extend its system of exploitation to new territories such as the vast expanses of the U.S.S.R. in order to guarantee its very survival.[66] In short, the Comintern believed that as a result of the capitalist economic crisis "the danger of imperialist intervention and war against the Soviet Union organized by the great powers has entered a new, extremely intensified and more serious phase . . . Imperialism sees no other way out than an imperialist war against the Soviet Union in order to overcome its own inner difficulties."[67]

---

* At the time of the depression DuBois' movement which had earlier attracted favorable interest in Moscow, was emphatically condemned for the support it was allegedly giving "imperialist colonial administrations in their work of domination over African colonies." (See Ford, "Le V Congrès Panafricain au Service de l'Impérialisme, *Correspondance Internationale*, IX, no. 124 [December 18, 1929]: 1654.)

Although it should be noted that communist strategies in the early thirties continued to express the fear that conflicts between imperialist powers would spark the outbreak of new international hostilities,* the emphasis in Comintern thinking during this period was more often upon "imperialist collusion" as the principal threat to peace. Everywhere evidence was uncovered to show that imperialist powers were indeed developing a concerted plot against the U.S.S.R. The world disarmament regulations, for example, were denounced as deliberate hypocrisy; the Ottawa Empire Conference of 1932 became in Comintern eyes "a war preparations conference;" and, prior to the Moscow trials of December, 1930, and March, 1931, "foreign saboteurs" were even discovered conducting underground activities within the U.S.S.R. itself.[68]

The nature of the newly intensified anti-Soviet threat was explained in perhaps greatest depth by the French communist Marcel Cachin in his remarks (April 8, 1931) at the Eleventh Plenum of the ECCI.[69] Asserting that the danger of war was more immediate than at any time in the past, he pointed out that whereas the imperialist powers had been at loggerheads on other issues, when it came to plans for an attack on the U.S.S.R. they were now remarkably united. Notably Britain and France, whose colonial rivalry was legendary, were drawn together by a common desire to retain their colonial possessions and to combat the mounting international influence of the Soviet state.[70] Nowhere was the conspiratorial intent of these powers more dramatically revealed than in the Anglo-French Pact of 1932. The Comintern viewed this agreement both as an attempt by the imperialists to promote cooperation in the colonies against "revolutionary and communist activity" and as an effort to pursue preparations for an anti-Soviet war.[71]

---

* In Africa, for example, Comintern observers noted the continued existence of Anglo-French rivalry in the region of Ethiopia and the valley of the Upper Nile. (See Yobe, "Le Pacte Franco-Britannique et l'Oppression Coloniale," *Correspondance Internationale*, XII, no. 64 [August 3, 1932]: 711.) At the same time they pointed out that new conflicts, such as that between Britain and the U.S., had emerged in Africa, promising to involve the continent's Negro inhabitants in an imperialist war. Ford, for one, speculated that future hostilities between Britain and the U.S. might witness Negro troops fighting one another for "their" respective patrimonies. Moreover, he stressed the possibility that such international conflicts would transform Africa into a major war theater. (See Ford, "Les Nègres dans la Prochaine Guerre," *Correspondance Internationale*, VII, no. 103 [September 15, 1928]: 1097.)

No vague or spontaneous imperialist scheme, the project for "fresh military intervention in the U.S.S.R." was in effect regarded by Moscow as a consciously organized conspiracy in which the role of ringleader had been assumed by France—in Stalin's words, "the most aggressive and militarist country of all aggressive and militarist countries of the world."[72] As the Comintern saw it, a conspicuous characteristic of the French-inspired war plans was a massive reliance upon Negro colonial troops. Since regular French armies were expected to disobey orders to attack the U.S.S.R., communists concluded that France, fearing this, was actively grooming its Negro army for the task.[73]

A variety of indicators were cited in support of this belief. Cachin, for example, noted the extent of Negro troop maneuvers in France.[74] Padmore, in turn, discussed the "phenomenal rapidity" of railroad development in French West and Equatorial Africa, citing it as evidence of "the imminence of another imperialist war, and a war against the Soviet Union."[75] It is interesting that in this context the perennial question of France's Trans-Saharan Railroad was raised once again. On the basis of French press reports Padmore contended that resumption of work on the railroad was imminent[76] and that Belgium, moreover, planned to construct a spur of the Trans-Saharan into the Congo in order to furnish its French ally with additional facilities for black troop mobilization.[77]

In addition to citing measures taken by the imperialists to enhance the potential mobility of their African military reserves, Comintern strategists were equally quick to point out recent increases in the size of Negro colonial contingents. Black troops, it was argued, would play a quantitatively greater role in the "coming conflict" than they had in 1914.[78] In 1933 alone, reported one Russian survey of "Colonial Armies in Africa," France added some 86,000 African troops to its already sizable Negro contingents.[79] Similarly Britain, pursuing a strict system of white officer control, was increasing its reliance upon African and other colonial forces.[80] In the event of an anti-Soviet war, communists concluded, such forces would be of critical importance to the imperialists not only in an offensive capacity but in the defensive role of "securing the colonial rear" of the British and French empires.[81]

But from the communist vantage point there was also a bright side to the African scene. Military conscription policies, it was recognized, were creating strategic problems for imperialists in this increasingly volatile region of the colonial world. French West Africa, for example, was being drained of manpower by mass native emigration sparked by government recruitment programs. Moreover, those natives who did become members of the armed forces of imperialism were acquiring familiarity with the use of modern weapons—"a serious danger for all whites in Africa."[82] Finally, and perhaps most impressive of all, conscription and military service were, in certain instances, provoking black Africans to initiate direct armed confrontation with the imperialists.[83] With expanded recruitment in a wartime setting such opposition to colonial military policies could be expected to intensify, adding substantially to the reservoir of indigenous resentment against European rule already aroused by social and economic injustices. This development, argued communists, would be enough to tip the scales against imperialism. In short, the Comintern was led to the easy conclusion that any attempt on the part of the imperialist nations to launch a military campaign against the U.S.S.R. would "detonate the colonial volcano" and thus bring an end to the imperial rule of the capitalist powers.[84]

However optimistic their expectations concerning the revolutionary effects of colonial military policies, Comintern leaders realized that it would do no harm to take certain steps to hasten their predictions along the way to fulfillment. At the Fifth RILU Congress in Moscow the Comintern reportedly decided to undertake with respect to Negroes "a vast anti-military campaign" employing illegal methods.[85] The advisability of such a campaign was also discussed in some detail the following April at the Eleventh Plenum of the ECC (April 9, 1931). The mood of this gathering was perhaps best reflected in the remarks of Otto Huiswood. Noting the important role assumed by African troops in anti-Soviet war preparations, Huiswood urged British and French communist parties to dedicate themselves more fully to the pursuit of anti-military work among these soldiers.[86] "In so far as the anti-Soviet interventionist campaign processes," he declared, "the task of bringing the Negro masses into the struggle against the imperialists and for the defense of the Soviet Union becomes a task of primary importance for the parties of the imperialist countries."[87]

Shortly after the Eleventh ECCI Plenum a general call went out to the Comintern faithful exorting them to form new communist "cells" within imperialist armies and to convert existing factory cells, especially in enterprises of military significance, into secret, illegal, party organizations.[88] Negroes, and particularly Negro Africans performing military duty in France, were singled out as critically important target groups in this broad program of anti-military agitation.*[89]

For the implementation of communist organizational and propaganda work among Negro soldiers, the Comintern looked to its special subsidiary, the ITUC-NW. Through the services of the *Negro Worker* and other ITUC-NW publications the Comintern was indeed able to launch a propaganda campaign of significant proportions aimed specifically at the black members of imperialist armies.[90] Responsibility for this propaganda campaign fell largely upon the shoulders of George Padmore, who published in 1931 a special pamphlet on *Negro Workers and the Imperialist War—Intervention in the Soviet Union* (the pamphlet was published concurrently in French under the title *Les Ouvriers Noirs et l'Intervention Armée Anti-Soviétique*),[91] together with numerous articles concerning imperialist war plans in the *Negro Worker*.

The essential objective of these ITUC-NW publications was to promote dissention among the black soldiers of imperialist armies and to convince them, as well as other Negro colonial subjects, that in the event of an imperialist-initiated war against Russia they should emulate the Soviet example of 1917 and turn the conflict to their own advantage. "We must let the imperialists know that if they dare to invade the land of socialist construction," declared Padmore, "we will refuse to fire one shot against our heroic comrades of the Soviet Union who are showing us the path to freedom and emancipation."[92] Speaking expressly on behalf of Negro Africans, Padmore summed up the central theme of the Comintern propaganda effort:

> We will not permit ourselves to be misled as in 1914. When the imperialists call upon us to shoot down our class brothers, we will turn our guns upon them. We shall utilize the imperialist war to raise the standard of revolt and strike a blow for the freedom of Africa.[93]

Whether the propaganda campaign was actually initiated by the

---

* A letter from the ITUC-NW to the Paris branch of the LAI (reproduced in *Negro Worker*, III, no. 3 [March 15, 1930]) claimed that communist cells had actually been established in eleven battalions of Senegalese troops in France.

Fifth RILU Congress or by the Eleventh Plenum of the ECCI, there is little doubt that by mid-1931 the Comintern was fully embarked upon a concerted effort to prevent imperialists from using Negro troops to jeopardize the security of the U.S.S.R. If the campaign was in part a product of Stalin's paranoic imagination, it was nonetheless tangible evidence that Moscow was attempting to adapt Comintern policy to its perception of the strategic consequences of the world economic crisis.

The new accent on Negro Africa which emerged in the wake of the depression was thus a product not only of the Comintern desire to undermine the economic strength of the capitalist system, but of Moscow's ambition to destroy the colonial foundations of imperialist military power. In effect, the depression served to highlight the extent of imperialist dependence upon Black Africa's economic resources and upon its military manpower. As such, the crisis enhanced significantly the importance of the region as a target for communist revolutionary activities. By analyzing Comintern attitudes and policy emphases during the period following 1929, one is led to the conclusion that communists were indeed resolved to "deny imperialism an exit from the world economic crisis on the backs of the colonial peoples."[94]

9

The Implementation of Comintern Policy
after 1928

ACTIVITIES OF THE RILU

During the years of most active Comintern interest in Negro Africa, the principal agency relied upon for the execution of world communism's African policy was the RILU. Both directly and through its specialized affiliate, the ITUC-NW, this organization presided over a remarkable number of efforts designed to bring Black Africa into the mainstream of world revolutionary struggle.

In general, three types of RILU activities could be distinguished. Perhaps the most conspicuous and quantitatively significant were operations of a general propaganda nature. Of equal political importance, however, were programs designed to supply Negro Africans with specific organizational advice. Finally, and perhaps most interesting, were activities among Negro Africans which could be described as essentially clandestine in character. Although these three varieties of RILU activism were conducted simultaneously and no clear lines separated them in communist thinking, each represented a distinct and significant element in the total revolutionary process.

In fulfilling its propaganda function the RILU relied extensively on the services of the ITUC-NW. However, independently of the latter agency, the RILU itself produced a considerable amount of literature relevant to work in Negro Africa. During the late twenties and early thirties communist followers both in the Soviet Union and abroad were kept informed of the progress of the labor movement in Negro Africa through regular RILU periodicals.[1] Presumably for the benefit of Soviet labor agitators, the RILU also published (under the editorship of its Secretary General, Lozovsky) handbooks which explained in a detailed fashion the political and economic background of the region.[2] Concurrently, material was prepared—some of it in native languages—which could be disseminated among Negro

Africans.[3] Through a special series of publications known as the "Little Red Library" (published simultaneously in French), Negro Africans were told of the achievements of trade unions in the U.S.S.R.[4] At the same time, by reading such RILU publications as *A.B.C. of Trade Unionism for Negro Workers*, they learned of specific revolutionary techniques to be used in their own colonies.[5]

Although significant in their contribution to the general agitational effort, the propaganda activities undertaken directly by RILU headquarters were of relatively minor importance compared with those channeled through the offices of the ITUC-NW. In conducting propaganda work among Negroes, as well as in issuing specific instructions for revolutionary activity in Africa, the role of this organization was paramount within the Comintern bureaucracy. Indeed, during the early 1930's the ITUC-NW, run by its professional Secretary, George Padmore, became the leading actor in the drama of Comintern activism in Africa.

During his stay in Moscow Padmore was granted the use of an office in the Kremlin and was accorded other privileges usually reserved for the upper echelons of Soviet bureaucracy.[6] No minor cog in the wheels of the Comintern system, Padmore was led to believe that he was, in fact, the annointed guardian of the destiny of Negroes everywhere.[7] In a sense, the elevated status he was accorded in the Kremlin was itself a propaganda device. It is almost certain that he owed his position at least in part to the desire of the Soviet government to publicize domestically and abroad its benevolent treatment of Negroes—a treatment which was designed to appear antithetical to that accorded members of the black race under capitalism. Moreover, concern for ensuring loyalty on the part of the U.S.S.R.'s large non-white Central Asian populations, together with communism's universalist pretensions, seemed to reinforce the need for concrete symbols of racial harmony in Russia. Thus, in order to demonstrate Russian "solidarity and internationalism with the toilers of all races and nationalities," Padmore was "elected" (along with Kaganovich and Stalin) to the Moscow Soviet—living proof that "we have Negroes in our government."[8] When the occasion arose for May Day parades in Red Square, he was duly displayed on the sacrosanct balcony of the Lenin Mausoleum—a black figure in the iconography of the Soviet socialist utopia.[9]

Padmore also supplied the Soviet state with public relations services of a more active nature, notably in facilitating the direct exposure of Negro Africans to Soviet society. He both lectured on colonial and African affairs at KUTV University and served as host and guide to a number of African students in Russia, some of whom, like Wallace-Johnson and Johnstone Kenyatta, were to figure prominently in the subsequent political development of Africa.[10] Perhaps even more significant than his function as teacher and guide was Padmore's role in encouraging Africans to come to the Soviet Union in the first place. Notably in the case of the Congress of the International Labor Defense, held in the Soviet capital in 1932, Padmore seems to have been responsible for attracting the sizable number of Negro Africans who participated.[11] Not only did he conduct personal correspondence with such West African political leaders as Kobina Sekyi, urging them to attend the Congress, but he even offered to assume the expenses of their journey to Moscow.[12]

In the final analysis, however, Padmore's primary propaganda function while in Moscow was journalistic. Not since the days of David Ivon Jones had the Comintern enjoyed the services of so prolific a writer on African affairs. Like his predecessor, Padmore made numerous contributions to the Comintern's English-language periodicals (principally the *Moscow Daily News* and the *Communist International*).[13] At the same time, he produced an impressive number of independent publications dealing largely, and in some cases exclusively, with the problems of Negro African labor. The most comprehensive of these works was his *Life and Struggles of Negro Toilers*, published in 1931 by the RILU. Padmore's proficiency as a publicist on behalf of Negro Africans also found ample demonstration in such contributions to the ITUC-NW pamphlet series as: *What Is the ITUC-NW?*, *Negro Workers and the Imperialist War*, *American Imperialism Enslaves Liberia*, *Forced Labor in Africa*, and *Labor Imperialism in East Africa*.* [14]

Of all Padmore's journalistic responsibilities during his career with the Comintern, probably most important was his job as editor of the *Negro Worker*. In the period from December, 1929, to August, 1933,

---

* Padmore was actively involved not only in the writing but in the dissemination of his works to Negroes. In some cases he dispatched copies directly to Black Africa. (For example, a letter from Padmore to Sekyi, March 23, 1932, cited in Samuel Rohdie, "The Gold Coast Aborigines Abroad," *Journal of African History*, VI, no. 3 [1965]: 392, refers to copes of *What is the ITUC-NW?* having been sent to the Gold Coast.)

this journal became, under Padmore's guidance, the principal organ through which the Comintern sought to win Negro Africans to its revolutionary cause. Although Padmore contributed a large quantity of articles and editorials to the publication during his years of editorship, it should be emphasized that the general themes of his writings were clearly prescribed by higher Comintern authority—particularly by the organization's Russian leadership. Potekhin (who apparently had come into contact with Padmore when both were at KUTV University[15] and who was himself a frequent contributor to the *Negro Worker*)[16] subsequently acknowledged this chain of authority. "Although others [i.e. Padmore] edited the paper," Potekhin explained, "we determined its direction from Moscow. After all," he added, "we in the [Comintern] Center had greater experience."[17]

An examination of the principal themes propounded in the *Negro Worker* provides further evidence that the journal was a creature of Soviet intentions. Prominent among these themes was the notion that African Negroes could do no better than to emulate the experience of the U.S.S.R. "Let these fifteen years of Soviet power be the greatest inspiration to us in our struggle for national freedom and social emancipation," proclaimed Padmore in 1932.[18] To this end, the *Negro Worker* included on a regular basis descriptions of life "In the Land of Socialism."[19]

Three basic features of the Soviet experience were singled out for special emphasis. In the first place, the Soviet economic system was held up as a model which Africans should adopt in order to abolish exploitation and achieve rapid economic and social progress. In tones befitting the rhetoric of the Cold War, African Negroes were continually reminded of the superiority of the socialist economic system as developed in the U.S.S.R. and were exhorted to choose it over the decadent system of capitalism.[20]

Secondly, the federally organized political structure of the Soviet Union was presented as the answer both to the general problem of obtaining political emancipation and to the more specific problem of securing full and equal rights for national minorities. Recommending that study circles of Negroes devote time to acquiring an understanding of Lenin's nationalities policy,[21] Russian contributors to the *Negro Worker* urged Africans to "follow us on the path of October, for that is the only way to your emancipation."[22]

Finally, in addition to rapid economic development and national self-determination, Africans were promised that by following the Soviet example they could achieve the goal of genuine racial equality. Whereas Negroes were the victims of racial bigotry under capitalism,[23] in Soviet society, it was stressed, they could enjoy the benefits of complete nondiscrimination.[24] It is interesting that a principal device used by the *Negro Worker* and the Comintern press to illustrate the alleged absence of racial prejudice in the Soviet Union was to publicize extensively an incident in Stalingrad involving two American "white labor aristocrats" who were accused of beating a fellow factory worker, a Negro named Robert Robinson.[25] After "mass meetings" of Soviet workers, an official inquiry, and a lengthy trial, the accused were deported from the U.S.S.R. on the grounds that "the workers of the Soviet Union will never tolerate race prejudice which is the chief weapon used by capitalists in poisoning the minds of workers against each other."[26] In brief, through the *Negro Worker* and other communist periodicals, a determined effort was made by the Soviets to appeal to the race consciousness of Negroes and to identify the U.S.S.R. in a meaningful way with their aspirations for equality.*

In addition to exhorting Africans to follow the Soviet model, the *Negro Worker* also sought to present to them the communist interpretation of world affairs. Whereas the U.S.S.R. was described as the only truly peace-loving country in the world, imperialist nations were portrayed as universally warmongering and exploitative.[27] These nations, it was maintained, were guilty of practicing the evils of imperialism no differently in Africa than elsewhere in the world. Like the workers of Indochina or Europe, Africans were inevitably the victims of maltreatment.[28] Nor was there any real difference between the imperialists of one nation and those of another. According to Padmore, it was simply an illusion to believe that the French, for example, were any less oppressive in their relations with Africans than were the British. Frenchmen may have assigned Negro subjects token positions within the colonial administration, but experience revealed that Africans under french rule fared no better than they

---

* In the process, it was apparently felt, no strand of cultural rapport between Negroes and Russia could be overlooked—as evidenced by the *Negro Worker's* popularization of the story of Pushkin's African heritage. (See William L. Patterson, "The Negro and the Centenary of Alexander Pushkin," *Negro Worker*, VII, no. 4 [April, 1937]: 7, 14, and Harold Acton, "Pushkin and Peter the Great's Negro," in Cunard, *Negro Anthology* [London, 1934]: 570ff.)

did under the hegemony of other imperial powers.[29] In other words, the image of imperialism which Padmore and others sought to convey in the *Negro Worker* was one of remarkably uniform tyranny.

But just as imperialism was immutable and universally evil, so too it was basically deceptive in its outward behavior. In the communist view, the grossest example of imperialist dissimulation in Africa was the hypocrisy of Christian missions. Under the protective guise of Christianity and benevolence, these missions robbed African lands of their wealth only to fill the pockets of European capitalists.[30] According to the *Negro Worker*, the Christian missionary in Africa was, in short, "A Friend of the Imperialists—an Enemy of the People."[31] His work represented nothing other than a conscious effort on the part of the imperialists to induce African Negroes to faithfully support the existing system of exploitation.

In conjunction with this harsh interpretation of the nature of imperialism, the editors of the *Negro Worker* thoughtfully supplied Africans with recommendations concerning optimal methods for overthrowing the imperial yoke. Indeed, not only was the *Negro Worker* used as an instrument for the dissemination of Soviet propaganda, but it was relied upon by the Comintern as an important channel for the communication of instructions and specific revolutionary advice.

The fundamental premise of the journal's didactic message was that Africans should place no faith in the promises of their colonial rulers, but instead should work for the overthrow of the imperialist system. All forms of compromise were condemned, and African organizations which devoted energy to promoting reform through legal processes were criticized for "wasting their time."[32] "Stop flirting with the enemies," Padmore warned unequivocally.[33] Moreover, Africans were admonished about the futility of attacking individual governors or administrators. "What you must hit at," Padmore advised straightforwardly, "is the *system* of imperialism."[34]

Eschewing a reformist approach, ITUC-NW writers insisted that the only positive solution was for African workers to organize themselves in such a way that they could force colonial governments to comply with their demands. Accordingly, the *Negro Worker* made available on a regular basis advice concerning practical organizational techniques. A special section entitled "Our Study Corner," for example, offered lessons on a broad spectrum of subjects from

"How to Organize for Mass Action (The Example of Russian Workers)" to "The Organization and Functions of a Strike Committee."[35]
In addition to emphasizing the importance of the strike weapon,
these lessons made a special point of encouraging Negro workers to
engage in intensive preparatory study for the revolution—either by
forming "study circles" among themselves, or by taking correspondence courses offered by the RILU.[36]

Although many of the "Study Corner" directives were phrased in
general terms, their wording often betrayed a basically African
orientation. On numerous occasions, for example, reference was made
to the importance of combatting the influence of tribal authorities—
even if it meant following the example of French Equatorial Africans
who had systematically killed all of their chiefs who acted as recruit-
ers of manpower for the imperialists.[37] Elsewhere in the pages of the
Negro Worker instructions regarding revolutionary tactics were addressed specifically, or even exclusively, to Negro Africans. Advice
issued to the KCA in Kenya was typical in this regard. Stressing "the
futility of isolated and spontaneous actions,"[38] the *Negro Worker*
counseled the KCA to conduct its organizational activity on a wider
regional scale and to concentrate its energies on such "burning,
immediate questions" as promoting peasant revolts against colonial
taxation and forming trade union groups which would exclude tribal
chiefs and "other government agents."[39]

In situations where the organizational development of Africans
was less advanced, Padmore and other ITUC-NW writers felt obliged
to issue more precise and comprehensive instructions. Sometimes on
the basis of surprisingly detailed information from the field, action
programs were devised—particularly for workers in the principal
ports of Nigeria, Senegal, and other colonies of West Africa.[40] Although not all such directives were communicated in the pages of the
Negro Worker, a striking example appeared there in 1932 under the
title "What the Workers of Sierra Leone Should Do."[41] In many
respects, the content of this action program was exemplary of the
type of comprehensive advice issued to African workers through the
pages of ITUC-NW publications.

Presumably authored by Wallace-Johnson (a member of the ITUC-
NW and organizer of the Sierra Leone Railroad Workers Union),
this program described at length the exact steps to be taken to promote revolution in Sierra Leone. Following a recruitment campaign

for increased membership in the Railroad Union, Freetown seamen and dockers were to be organized using the example of the rail workers as a model. Subsequently members of other professions were to be unionized and drawn into the struggle—a struggle seeking primarily the right to organize and to strike, improvement in labor conditions, and freedom of assembly, speech and press.[42] At the same time that organizational work was being conducted among the working population, a special meeting of the unemployed workers of Freetown was to be planned. At this well-publicized gathering a "Committee of Action" was to be elected. Aware of the British practice of setting Africans of one tribe against those of another in order to weaken their bargaining power, the ITUC-NW program made a special point of stipulating that this Committee include members of different tribes. Also in deference in local conditions it was suggested that the Committee conduct organizational work among peasants particularly on market days, when the rural inhabitants of the Sierra Leone Protectorate came down into the colony itself.[43]

Perhaps the central feature of the ITUC-NW program for Sierra Leone was the stress placed upon class unity among both employed and unemployed workers. Despite the attention devoted to peasant work, the emphasis was clearly on a militant proletarian-led struggle designed to achieve "national and social independence."[44] Possibly the most interesting aspect of the program was the extent to which it reflected the Comintern's awareness of political realities in Sierra Leone. Essentially it represented a serious attempt on the part of communists to apply the "United Front from Below" formula to the African situation on a grass roots level. It constituted, in effect, a complete recipe for revolution in a specific colony of Negro Africa.

If advisory and propaganda efforts of this kind were to make a significant contribution to fulfilling the Comintern's revolutionary ambition in Black Africa, then it was obviously necessary that the *Negro Worker*, as the mouthpiece for these Comintern communications, acquire as large a circulation as possible among the indigenous population of the continent. At the beginning of 1932, a time when the Comintern's operational interest in Africa was at a highpoint, the *Negro Worker* launched a concerted campaign to transform itself into an organ of "mass" readership—to become, in effect, the "organizer and leader" of political struggle in Africa.[45] Toward this end,

Africans were called upon to work for the journal's widest possible distribution, "as one of the duties you owe your class and oppressed race."[46] In addition, groups known as "friends of the *Negro Worker*" were to be formed in order to promote the journal's circulation and, most ambitious of all, an entire "network of workers' correspondents" was to be set up apparently with the aim of establishing ITUC-NW branch organizations on African soil.[47]

The extent to which the *Negro Worker* actually succeeded in penetrating Negro Africa and influencing the political opinions of its inhabitants is difficult to determine. Certainly the drive to make the *Negro Worker* a "mass organ" in Africa fell short of its mark. Although the LDRN made a concerted effort to distribute the periodical among Africans in France,[48] and there is evidence that in certain places such as Liberia copies did reach the African hinterland,[49] probably no more than several thousand Africans could ever have been counted among the journal's regular readers.[50] Despite its limited circulation, however, the *Negro Worker* could be credited with certain real achievements. It was, after all, the first journal of its kind ever to circulate among Negro Africans. Given the adverse conditions under which it was forced to operate, it was remarkable that the *Negro Worker* was able to boast even a limited readership. Moreover, the journal was able to maintain on a regular basis at least one correspondent in East Africa (Jomo Kenyatta) and two in West Africa (Wallace-Johnson and E. F. Small). Whether or not there was any justification for the claims of its editors that the *Negro Worker* had made contacts "with and between wide sections of the native African people,"[51] it can with certainty be said that the journal took some important first steps toward bringing Africans into touch with communist thinking.

Perhaps the best indication of the *Negro Worker*'s overall significance as a molder of African opinion were the pains taken by colonial authorities to confiscate the journal and to prevent it from reaching African readers. Notably in British West Africa, vessels arriving from Europe were searched regularly for copies of the publication[52] and the British colonial government reportedly imposed lengthy prison terms on natives in whose possession it was found.[53] In June, 1930, the Governor of Nigeria, Sir Frank Baddeley, went so far as to accuse the *Negro Worker* of having contributed to recent popular disturbances in that colony. In a statement made in London—and reported with barely disguised satisfaction by Padmore—the Governor announced that he had "discovered the circulation of the *Negro Worker*, a trade union bulletin published by the Profintern in Moscow, among the workers of Lagos" and that the government "was adopting precautionary measures to combat the spread of Bolshevism among the natives."[54]

Although such reactions on the part of colonial governments cannot be cited as irrefutable evidence of the success of ITUC-NW efforts, they do suggest that the revolutionary ideas propounded in the *Negro Worker* held real promise of radicalizing indigenous political attitudes in Africa. Through the pages of this journal the more educated strata of the African population were presented with a systematic exposé of the deplorable working conditions in their colonies. Through the *Negro Worker*'s polemics, moreover, they were encouraged—some perhaps for the first time—to promote the cause of colonial independence. Under such regular sections as "The Crisis in Africa" and "Africa in Revolt," potential revolutionaries were able to learn of indigenous opposition to colonial rule outside their own political boundaries and were able to derive encouragement from the example of revolutionary struggle elsewhere in Africa.[55] In short, beyond its immediate utility to the Comintern as an instrument for spreading propaganda and revolutionary advice, the *Negro Worker* provided one of the first channels for political communication among Africans. In fact, by helping to cross-pollinate some of the earliest blossoms of nationalist sentiment, the *Negro Worker* made perhaps its most lasting contribution to Africa's political development.

In addition to propaganda and instructional work, the ITUC-NW engaged in another type of activity designed to guide and accelerate the pace of revolution in Negro Africa—activity of a clandestine character. It is possible to distinguish at least two categories of clandestine effort. The first involved the use of ITUC-NW members for recruitment and agitational work among black Africans. The second involved the use of hired African agents for subversion in Negro African colonies.

Like other ITUC-NW projects, the task of surreptitiously recruiting African students for revolutionary instruction in Moscow appears to have fallen largely upon the shoulders of George Padmore. The search for promising candidates for RILU training was reportedly one of the principal motives for a visit which Padmore made to London in May, 1932.[56] Similarly, this search led Padmore the same year to correspond with Kobina Sekyi requesting him "to collaborate with us when you get back to the Gold Coast in selecting one or two young workers to come to Europe and study for about one year at our expense . . . in order to prepare them to organize the masses to carry on the struggle for the freedom of our motherland Africa."[57] Although repeated requests to Sekyi apparently elicited no effective response, the ITUC-NW was able to pursue the recruitment of African students through other channels (notably through the LDRN) and did succeed in attracting a number of Africans to Moscow for study.[58]

The conduct of covert agitational work among Negro Africans was likewise a task which fell under Padmore's jurisdiction. Given the extreme secrecy which surrounded his work, it is difficult to determine either the nature of Padmore's clandestine activity or the extent to which he obtained assistance from other ITUC-NW personnel. One account of his Comintern career goes so far as to assert that Padmore presided over a staff of "several hundred in Moscow and abroad" and was made a colonel in the Red Army "in order to have the needed authority over his secret agents."[59] Whether or not this was the case, there is convincing evidence that Padmore did in fact engage in clandestine work and that this work took him as far as Negro Africa itself.

Although no mention appears to have been made of Padmore's African mission either in his own or in other Comintern writings, according to records of the British officials in West Africa, he definitely traveled to Gambia in April, 1930, presumably in connection with the Comintern's interest in the Bathurst Trade Union and in the strike which this union had conducted the preceding year.[60] That Gambia was not the only stop on Padmore's African itinerary is suggested by C. L. R. James, an intimate friend of Padmore, who writes of a clandestine appearance in Johannesburg as well as of a "gunrunning expedition" to the Belgian Congo.[61] Even Padmore himself acknowledged on one occasion, "I know Dakar and environs quite well."[62] According to an account which he gave the American Negro journalist Roi Ottley, Padmore utilized his visit to Africa to "make strategic contacts" and to recruit Africans for training in Moscow. Posing sometimes as an "anthropologist," sometimes as a chauffeur, he reportedly succeeded in smuggling a sizable number of potential African revolutionaries out of the continent.[63]

This was a very different side of Padmore's Comintern career as conference organizer, teacher, and publicist. As Ottley describes him, Padmore was indeed a "first-class conspirator, a specialist in decoys, codes, and stratagems."[64] Equipped with an alias and disguise,[65] Padmore was a genuine revolutionary in the Bolshevik mold—a man who, perhaps even consciously, cast himself as a kind of Lenin for Black Africa.

If British official documents indicate that Padmore engaged in direct communist activity in Africa, they also suggest that the Comintern was not averse to hiring indirect agents to conduct acts of violent subversion against British and French rule on the continent. In 1927 a French official was murdered in Nigeria by a small group of Arab terrorists who had come across the Sahara from North Africa. The following year a similar fate befell a British official in Northern Nigeria.[66] After extensive inquiries British intelligence learned that the agents responsible for these acts had been sent to Nigeria by a Tunisian who had reportedly entered into an agreement with Moscow.[67] The object of this agreement—at least insofar as it concerned Nigeria—had apparently been to bribe powerful Muslim rulers in the Northern provinces into open opposition to the British government.[68] Since they were unable to execute the plot as planned, however, the five terrorists undertook to assassinate British officials in the region and to fix blame for the acts upon the native Muslim rulers.[69]

Given the tenuous relationship between the British government and the Northern Nigerian emirs, it was understandable that Britain should have regarded the entire affair with considerable concern. A number of precautionary measures were undertaken which included the establishment of an intelligence bureau for Northern Nigerian police forces, the negotiation of an agreement with the Governor General of French West Africa to exchange intelligence relating to the political security of the respective territories, and even the execution of joint Anglo-French military moves along the Northern Nigerian border.[70] By March, 1930, the Nigerian government had definitely reached the conclusion that "certain outside influences were at work . . . endeavoring to persuade the Sultan of Sokoto and the Emir of Katsina to reject British rule and support a general conflict against European power in Africa."[71] Although two such influences were identified—anti-British sentiment of the Mahdist variety and international communism based in North Africa—the latter appeared to be the source of greater apprehension to the British government.[72] On the basis of reports submitted by authorities in Nigeria, it was felt by members of the Colonial Office in London that there was "good reason" to believe that "Bolshevik cells in Tunis or elsewhere in North Africa" were indeed casting their eyes in the direction of Nigeria.[73]

In the final analysis, one of the most interesting results of the Nigerian episode was that it produced, on the part of the British government, a genuine respect for the political astuteness of the plot organizers—individuals who, in the words of the Lieutenant Governor of Northern Nigeria, were obviously "well posted in the internal history and affairs of Northern Nigeria."[74] If these individuals were in fact in the employ of the Comintern, as the British government suspected, then it must be concluded that world communism had come a considerable distance in learning to exploit local African conditions for the benefit of its revolutionary cause.

Whether or not the Comintern's clandestine efforts actually accelerated the pace of revolution in Africa, they unquestionably resulted in a better operational understanding of the actual conditions in the field.[75] Indeed, the information obtained surreptitiously by communist agents, as well as the personal contacts made with potential African revolutionaries, was of undoubted value to the Comintern in conducting its overall agitational campaign among Negro Africans. In this way, the clandestine work of the ITUC-NW, like the more conspicuous propaganda and advisory activities of the RILU, constituted an essential part of the Comintern's effort to transform the idea of African revolution from an abstract ambition into a practical enterprise.

WORK OF OTHER COMINTERN ORGANIZATIONS

Although the principal channel for Comintern activities among Negro Africans was the Profintern's ITUC-NW, other Comintern-sponsored international organizations made a point of directing their activities toward this segment of the world's colonial population.

Within the developing infra-structure of communist "front" organizations, several bodies can be singled out.

The youngest of these, the International of Seamen and Harbor Workers, came into existence in 1931. Like other communist organizations formed after the Sixth Congress, the ISH was created primarily in the interests of supplying the Soviet Union with fifth column support in the event of an imperialist attack.[76] Given the important role of African sailors and harbor workers in the maritime trade of both Britain and France, it was logical that communists would regard these workers as critical links in the imperialist war machine and hence as principal targets for ISH efforts. In case of hostilities, it was reasoned, not only would African maritime workers be able to disrupt the flow of vital European imports, but even more important, they would be in a position to sabotage the transfer of war materiel and troops.[77] The extent of communist propaganda already directed toward Negro sailors as well as the specialized work among Africans previously conducted by the International Seamen's Clubs in various European ports were testimony to the Comintern's belief that African seamen should be the object of particularly energetic organizational activity.

Given such thinking, it was understandable that one of the first efforts of the ISH was to conduct a determined drive to recruit African followers. Principal responsibility for this endeavor appears to have been assigned to Garan Kouyaté, who not only contributed articles on ISH organizational work to the *Negro Worker*, but undertook a dockside campaign among African seamen in France.[78] The ISH Executive Committee (which like the ITUC-NW had established offices in Hamburg) gave even clearer indication of the organization's African objectives when, in the fall of 1931, it resolved to open Seamen's Clubs in Africa itself and announced that Dakar and Freetown would be the initial locations for such establishments.[79] Action committees in the port cities, unified ship committees at sea, and ultimately, strong revolutionary trade unions among Negro maritime workers were to be the primary organizational goals.[80]

Perhaps the most striking evidence that agitational work among Negro sailors was a continuing objective of the ISH came to light in early 1932. At this time the organization prepared a detailed ten-point program of basic demands designed especially for the benefit of black sailors and issued an "Appeal to Negro Seamen and

Dockers" urging them to mobilize against the threat of an imperialist war.[81] In addition, the ISH, utilizing the model of the Hamburg Negro Workers' Conference, decided to hold the "First World Congress of Seamen" in Hamburg in May, 1932, and made a particular point of urging Negroes to attend.[82] At this Congress both Kouyaté and Padmore played prominent roles—the former presenting a report on his work among African seamen in European ports, the latter urging the ISH to redouble its efforts to organize African sailors, not just in the metropoles, but in the colonies themselves.[83]

In addition to the International of Seamen and Harbor Workers, another organization within the Comintern system—the International Labor Defense—merits special attention for the work which it conducted among Africans during the years following the Sixth Congress. Although the ILD was established in the early twenties primarily with the aim of providing legal assistance to workers in capitalist countries, by the time of the ILD Congress in Moscow in 1932 the organization had displayed a colonial orientation as well.

With regard to Africa the ILD could, by 1932, claim "certain successes" among the indigenous population.[84] In 1928, for example, it had dispatched representatives to Madagascar to give legal aid to Madagascans accused of leading separatist disturbances and with the help of the ITUC-NW it had established branch organizations both there and in South Africa.[85] Although by the time of the Moscow Congress the vast majority of the organization's claimed 11·5 million members was still composed of Soviet citizens, conference participants were nonetheless able to point with pride to the 500 new members which the organization claimed to have acquired among black Africans in the course of the first half of 1931 alone.[86] Not only were adherents to be found in Madagascar and South Africa, but committees and individual contacts had reportedly been established in Kenya, Nigeria, Sierra Leone, and Senegal.[87] By 1932, in short, Black Africa appeared to be an unusually promising field for ILD activity—activity which, like that of other communist organizations, sought to win the strategic support of colonial peoples and to promote their struggle for national liberation.

It should be noted that at the Moscow Congress the leadership of the ILD, after remarking upon the efforts already initiated among Africans, turned its attention even further in the direction of the colonies by exhorting all national ILD sections to intensify their colonial work, utilizing both legal and illegal means.[88] This directive was apparently heeded by one of the largest of the ILD national branches, that in France, for shortly after the Congress this organization began a concerted campaign to expand its influence among colonial subjects.

Under the auspices of a newly activated Colonial Commission the French ILD began publication of a monthly periodical, *Bulletin Colonial*,[89] which supplied regular information concerning the crimes of colonial administrators and the progress of the colonial revolutionary movement. In addition to these discussions, the *Bulletin* offered practical advice concerning agitational methods to be used in the colonial struggle and conducted a determined drive both to raise colonial issues to the forefront of ILD activity and to convince French supporters of the need to recruit membership among Africans and other colored residents of the metropole.[90] In keeping with its legal orientation, moreover, the French ILD championed the cause of Negro African political prisoners, publicizing, for example, the plight of such individuals as Cheikou-Cissé, a West African veteran of World War I who had been imprisoned for fifteen years for sedition against the French Republic.[91] Similarly, in the period following the Moscow Congress the ILD continued to support the cause of Madagascan independence, launching an energetic campaign in 1933 to raise funds to send yet another agitator and lawyer to the colony.[92]

As this description suggests, the ILD was more active with regard to the colonial territories of France than it was with regard to those of Britain. Even within the French Empire, it should be pointed out, Indochina probably received the greatest share of ILD attention. Nonetheless, as apparent from the pages of the *Bulletin Colonial* and other ILD publications,[93] the organization did make a determined effort to carry its message into Negro Africa and to convince the French public to endorse the cause of African independence.

A final organization which should be mentioned in connection with Comintern work among Africans is the League Against Imperialism. Throughout the 1930's this communist-dominated body served both as an instrument for supplying support to African nationalists and as an agency for the harassment of colonial governments. More than the efforts of the ISH or the ILD, the activities of the LAI produced a traceable effect upon the subsequent political development of Negro Africa.

A principal means used by the LAI to promote revolutionary discontent among Africans was the dissemination of information and propaganda emanating from Comintern field headquarters in Berlin. After September, 1931, the Comintern's efforts through the *Negro Worker* to keep Africans informed concerning the colonial revolutionary movement found an auxiliary mouthpiece in the *Anti-Imperialist Review*, a publication of the LAI's International Secretariat.[94] Similarly, the Comintern's desire to inform European activists of the details of popular unrest in Africa found an additional channel of expression in the pages of the *Information Bulletin*, another publication of the LAI Secretariat.[95]

Perhaps more significant than these journalistic activities, however, was the LAI's effort to persuade the editors of African nationalist newspapers to subscribe to the Comintern news service *Inprecorr*. The following statement which appeared in the July 22, 1930, edition of the *Nigerian Daily Telegraph* suggests that the organization was at least partially successful in this endeavor. "In order to give our readers the fullest possible information on all matters," declared the editors of the *Telegraph*, "we have opened a fresh source of supply of news by requisitioning the services of the Press Service of the LAI International Secretariat, Berlin [*Inprecorr*] to serve us with news of international interest for the publication of our paper."[96]

It was perhaps inevitable that the British government, which regarded the LAI as a "purely communist and anti-British organization,"[97] would react to such developments with distinct apprehension. Thus Governor Thompson of Nigeria warned the Secretary of State for Colonies, Lord Passfield, of the danger involved in admitting this "definitely harmful" information into Nigeria and asked for instructions concerning the preventive measures to be taken against it.[98] Although colonial office officials contemplated prohibiting altogether the entry of *Inprecorr* telegrams, they were apparently reluctant to resort to such a potentially unpopular expedient, preferring instead "to wait until they [the *Nigerian Daily Telegraph*] published something seditious in terms of the local law and then pounce on the paper".[99]

The LAI's successes in distributing communist propaganda in Africa, however, were less an annoyance to British officials than were the organization's pressure tactics in Britain itself. Following the decision of the LAI leadership in 1930 to accord special status to the

British branch of the organization,[100] the LAI-Britain became an increasingly active defender of the rights of England's African subjects. Caring little that the Colonial Office considered them "crazy fanatics,"[101] Reginald Bridgeman and his colleagues in the British LAI continually bombarded the Secretary of State for Colonies with protests concerning treatment of Africans and repeatedly prodded the British government to reveal the inner workings of its colonial administration.[102] Bent on exposing the evils of imperialist rule, the LAI became, in effect, a staunch supporter of the strivings of Africans toward full independence.

Through the instrumentality of the LAI Africans indeed possessed a unique channel for bringing pressure to bear upon the British government. Since Bridgeman and his cohorts had developed numerous contacts with the British press and, more important, had induced certain sympathetic Members of Parliament (such as the communist S. Saklatvala and the Reverend R. Sorensen) to confront the government with frequent and often embarrassing questions concerning colonial policy,[103] British officials could ill afford to ignore the repeated petitions of the LAI. African nationalists, for their part, were well aware of this fact. Organizations such as the Aborigines' Rights Protection Society (ARPS) came increasingly to rely upon the LAI to present their case in Britain,[104] and when, between 1934 and 1936, Wallace-Johnson embarked upon his campaign to form a radical nationalist party in the Gold Coast (the West African Youth League), he availed himself of the same opportunity. As one disgruntled official in the Colonial Office complained: "If anything happens in the Gold Coast, Mr. Wallace-Johnson always wishes to send a telegram off to the LAI."[105]

On occasion Bridgeman took advantage of his direct contacts with West African nationalists to spur them into greater opposition to British rule. In 1935, for example, he attempted to guide the comparatively moderate ARPS into collaboration with more radical nationalist organizations in the Gold Coast.[106] Bridgeman also took a direct and active interest in the West African Youth League, providing Wallace-Johnson with much needed support from London throughout his stormy political career in the Gold Coast and Sierra Leone.[107] But perhaps Bridgeman's single most important contribution to the cause of African nationalism was made in 1937. When in that year Wallace-Johnson, George Padmore, and other leaders of

African nationalism established a central anti-colonial directorate in London (the well-known International African Service Bureau, forerunner of the Pan-African Federation), Bridgeman was there with LAI funds to assist in the scheme.[108]

In sum, the LAI from its London offices provided an important source of support for the most radical elements within the African nationalist movement. At a time when the imperial authority of Britain and France seemed unassailable and when African nationalists could claim few friends outside the colonial world, this support was of unquestionable value not only in practical terms but in a moral and psychological sense as well.

THE COMINTERN AND FRENCH AFRICA

In order to pursue its revolutionary objectives in those areas of Negro Africa under French rule, the Comintern was able to rely not only upon the efforts of central communist organizations such as the ITUC-NW and the ILD, but also upon the services of more geographically specialized agencies whose interests in the colonial world were confined primarily to the French Empire. In this context the activities of the French Communist Party, as well as those of the League for the Defense of the Negro Race (LDRN), are worthy of special attention.

In the wake of the Sixth Comintern Congress, the French Communist Party both intensified its general campaign to promote colonial emancipation and increased its efforts to establish contacts with Negro Africans. In November, 1928, for example, the PCF Colonial Commission, under the leadership of Jacques Doriot, began publishing a monthly periodical, *Bulletin Colonial*, designed to provide party activists with information necessary to conduct a determined campaign against the "oppression and exploitation" of French colonial rule.[109] The following year Doriot himself produced a book, *The Colonies and Communism*, which sought to mobilize French communists behind the Comintern's new colonial policies and to transform the PCF into a staunch defender of the principle of colonial independence.[110] Although both the *Bulletin* and Doriot's volume dealt with the colonial world as a whole, the amount of attention which these publications devoted specifically to Negro Africa was indication of the important status this region had assumed in the operational strategy of the French party.

Indeed, the years immediately following the Sixth Congress witnessed a genuine rise in PCF concern for Negro Africans. Not only did the organization continue its drive to recruit Africans into the ranks of party membership in France, but, according to one authoritative source, in 1929 it became even "more active among Negroes, extending its work to the French colonies" themselves.[111]

Notably in Madagascar, the PCF, working in conjunction with the ILD, appears to have engaged in direct revolutionary agitation. In May, 1929, French communists led an anti-colonial demonstration of approximately 600 Madagascans in Tananarive.[112] Shortly thereafter they began publishing a local paper, Le Réveil Malgache ("Madagascan Awakening"), which succeeded in further stimulating Madagascan nationalist sentiment and in exposing "a minority" of the island's inhabitants to the influence of communist thinking.[113] In addition to Le Réveil, Comintern-inspired revolutionary tracts, some published in native dialects, were found circulating in the colony. One of these tracts reportedly referred to a separate Communist Party of Madagascar, "affiliated with Moscow"; another appealed to Madagascans to resist military conscription; yet a third gave Madagascans instructions on how to form communist cells and how to reproduce revolutionary literature.[114]

Whether such communist propaganda found its way to Africa through the efforts of the PCF alone, or whether some other Comintern agency such as the ITUC-NW was also involved, it is clear that at least in part as a result of the efforts of the PCF the inhabitants of French colonial Africa were receiving the Comintern message.

Similarly, through the work of another Paris-based organization, the LDRN, progress was being made in exposing French Africans to Moscow's revolutionary teachings. The LDRN, known officially as the Ligue Nationale de Défense des Intérêts de la Race Noire, was a direct descendent of Houénou's Ligue de Défense de la Race Nègre and of Senghor's Comité de Défense de la Race Nègre.[115] During the late twenties the new Ligue sought actively to enlarge the scope of revolutionary activity in Africa initiated by these parent organizations.* Under the

---

* By 1927 Senghor's organization had not only succeeded in distributing its journal, La Voix des Nègres, in French West Africa, but had attracted a following in Dakar and was passing out revolutionary tracts to the dock workers of the

leadership of Garan Kouyaté, who succeeded the ailing Senghor as Secretary General of the organization in the fall of 1927, the *Ligue* made a concerted effort to distribute its journal, *La Race Nègre*, and to attract a sizable following in the French colonies of Black Africa.

In order to enhance the organization's operational effectiveness in Africa, the LDRN "Action Commission" in Paris resolved in 1929 to establish branches in administrative centers and provincial capitals throughout the French colonies and to form in these territories other types of affiliated bodies such as trade union committees and *cercles d'études* ("study circles").[116] Moreover, so as to ensure regular circulation of *La Race Nègre* in West and Central Africa, Kouyaté attempted to recruit reliable distributors among African sailors in Marseilles.[117] This distribution effort, as French government surveillance discovered, was to be oriented primarily toward French Equatorial Africa where, according to LDRN calculations, popular discontent was creating a receptive atmosphere for the journal's revolutionary message.[118]

The LDRN's propaganda activity in French Africa during the late twenties was not, however, limited to the distribution of *La Race Nègre*. Combining forces with the *Association des Originaires du Congo* ("Association of Congolese Emigrés"), the *Ligue* dispatched agitators to the French Congo to preach the need for "absolute and immediate independence" for French Equatorial Africa.[119] Not only did it become involved in the serious uprisings which took place in that colony in 1929, but it appears to have had a hand in the bloody anti-colonial outbreaks which occurred in the Upper Sangha Province of Central Africa the same year. Indeed, according to the Governor General of French Equatorial Africa, the revolts which took place in that region could be linked directly to the LDRN's nationalist and "clearly communist" propaganda, thus underlining the need to impose restrictive measures on the organization's "subversive" activities.[120]

The LDRN was no less active with regard to French West Africa. From his Paris headquarters, Kouyaté was kept busy communicating with West African nationalists, urging them to support his organization and learning of their plans to oppose French rule.[121] Within

---

city. (Letter of Chef de la Sûreté [Security Chief], Dakar, to the "Administrateur en Chef de la Circonscription de Dakar [Chief government administrator of the Dakar region], August 16, 1927, in SLOTFOM, V, Box 2, File 2, subfile 54.)

West Africa itself, concerted efforts were made to ensure that *La Race Nègre* reached a significant readership. Beginning with its earliest issues, comparatively large consignments of the LDRN publication were shipped to Dakar, where distribution arrangements had been made with local inhabitants.[122] From Dakar, copies found their way to the interior of West Africa reaching African readers in Bamako and Koulouba (now the administrative capital of Mali) as well as soldiers in France's black army stationed in the region.[123] As part of its effort to recruit a loyal following in French West Africa, the LDRN also began distributing membership cards—800 in the Dakar region alone, according to one report.[124] By mid-1929, moreover, the *Ligue* had succeeded in forming sections along the Dakar-Bamako Railroad,[125] and was in the process of establishing LDRN branches in Dahomey and the French Cameroon as well.[126]

Thus, it was becoming increasingly apparent to Moscow that Kouyaté's organization possessed outstanding potential as an instrument for executing Comintern policy in French colonial Africa. There is evidence, in fact, that beginning in 1929, Moscow, both directly and through the PCF, sought to tighten its hold over the LDRN and to convert this organization into a dependent Comintern agency. The task of transforming the *Ligue* into a branch office of the Comintern, however, was not accomplished without considerable opposition from within the LDRN itself.*

The first move toward a closer Comintern relationship with the LDRN occurred in January, 1929. At this time the PCF offered to grant a substantial monthly subsidy to the *Ligue*, on the condition that the organization "place itself under the communist flag."[127] Apparently satisfied with the offer, the LDRN Executive (which for some time had been shaping *Race Nègre* editorial policy to conform to PCF wishes—reportedly in hopes that the latter organization might prove "useful to the *Ligue*") accepted the subsidy without hesitation.[128] Although the final sum agreed upon was somewhat less than the LDRN had expected, PCF assistance did make possible the publication of *La Race Nègre* on a regular monthly basis, beginning in March, 1929.[129] The new arrangement, moreover, enabled the

---

* It is interesting to note that the difficulties encountered by the Comintern in attempting to transform the *Ligue* were to prove characteristic of the problems confronted by communists in dealing with African nationalist bodies in the post-World War II period.

LDRN to utilize the distribution outlets of the PCF's own periodical *L'Humanité*.[130] In effect, the relationship between the two publications became so close that by mid-1929 *La Race Nègre* had come to be widely regarded as a subsidiary of the French party organ.[131]

Once beholden to the PCF, however, Kouyaté and his colleagues began to show symptoms of recalcitrance. When the Colonial Commission of the French party made known its desire to exercise control over the content of articles destined for publication in *La Race Nègre*, matters came to a head. Kouyaté served notice to communist leaders that regardless of their subsidy to his organization, the LDRN would not tolerate direct interference in matters which were essentially its own concern.[132]

Kouyaté's independent stand against the PCF should not be construed as a product of any nationalist-inspired disillusionment with communist domination. Rather, it appears to have been an outgrowth of his belief that material and moral support for the LDRN could be obtained from the Comintern through more direct and more ideologically respectable sources. In September, 1929, Kouyaté paid a visit to Moscow and was reportedly "well received."[133] As a result of this visit the LDRN learned not only that it could anticipate the receipt of Comintern funds before the end of the year, but that it had been designated by Moscow as the agency responsible for recruiting French-speaking Negroes to study in the Soviet Union.[134]

In the latter part of 1930 the Comintern, apparently persisting in its effort to court the favor of the LDRN, invited Kouyaté to return to the U.S.S.R., where, among other flattering experiences, he was photographed with the President of the Soviet state and was asked to address the Fifth Congress of the RILU.[135] After traveling across the entire expanse of the Soviet Union, he returned to France via Germany, where he met with officials of the Comintern's operational headquarters in Berlin. In the course of these meetings Kouyaté was reportedly commissioned to write articles on his Russian travels for Comintern publications and to undertake, upon his arrival in Paris, a reorganization of the French branch of the LAI, giving it "an organizational basis in French colonies."[136] Promised material support for this endeavor, Kouyaté returned in triumph to Paris, having, according to French surveillance reports, considerable funds at his disposal.[137]

It is particularly important to note that these visits to the U.S.S.R.

produced a marked effect not only upon the attitude of Kouyaté personally, but upon the ideological and structural development of his organization. His exposure to Russian society, for example, inspired in Kouyaté a profound admiration for the Soviet system which was communicated to his followers both in *Ligue* meetings and through the pages of *La Race Nègre*. Upon his return from the U.S.S.R. in the fall of 1930, Kouyaté enthusiastically described to assembled members of the LDRN how Russia had become "a workers' paradise."[138] Concurrently, *La Race Nègre* heralded "the magnificent and unique example" of Soviet progress, pointing out its special relevance to the economic and political development of French Negro Africa.[139]

Similarly, Kouyaté's firsthand observation of the Soviet governmental structure, as well as his more intimate understanding of the objectives of Comintern policy, had an influence upon organizational steps taken by the LDRN in late 1929. Immediately following Kouyaté's first visit to the U.S.S.R., the Soviet principle of "democratic centralism" was introduced into the LDRN organizational structure by the creation of a "central committee" as the supreme authority for *Ligue* decision-making.[140] At approximately the same time, the decision was made to extend the *Ligue*'s operational network into Africa—a move which coincided with the Comintern's emphasis on establishing branch organizations in the colonies.[141] Likewise, the LDRN's uncompromising stand on behalf of African independence, its advocacy of "mass strikes organized illegally" as the principal weapon in the political struggle, and its pointed interest in "the military question"—all these bore striking resemblance to the policies outlined by the Comintern in the years between 1928 and 1930.[142] The rationale behind the LDRN's willingness to follow faithfully the line laid down in Moscow was perhaps best summed up by Kouyaté himself, when, in the veiled but unambiguous jargon of the movement, he explained to the LDRN Executive that the organization was obliged to "follow an internationalist course, or find itself isolated and left to its own resources."[143]

The need to obtain outside assistance probably also explains the LDRN's continuing relationship with the French Communist Party. Despite Kouyaté's differences with the PCF, it should be noted that the French party managed to retain a guiding hand in the direction of *Ligue* affairs throughout the early thirties. This was accomplished primarily through the person of Stéphane Rosso, a paid functionary of the PCF who was simultaneously treasurer of the *Ligue* and Kou-yaté's principal lieutenant.[144] Himself a strong advocate of the "internationalist" approach, Rosso consistently defended Kouyaté against *Ligue* members critical of his policy of reliance upon external support.[145] When at one point Kouyaté evinced a desire to leave his post with the *Ligue* in order to concentrate his energies upon work for the LAI, it was the PCF, working through Rosso, which reported-ly cast the deciding vote inducing him to remain.[146] At various general meetings of the LDRN—some of them convened at PCF initiative—Rosso played a prominent role, praising the French party as the only true friend of the black race, soliciting subscriptions to *L'Humanité*, and delivering speeches urging Negro membership in the PCF.[147]

By 1931 the LDRN's subservience both to Moscow and to the PCF had become so pronounced that non-communist members no longer felt at home in the organization. A split in the ranks of the LDRN may have been what Kouyaté in fact intended. In November, 1930, shortly after his return from Russia, he was overheard revealing to a friend his desire to eliminate *Ligue* President Felix Faure and all other moderate elements from the organization. If denied editorial control over *La Race Nègre*, he reasoned, these individuals would un-doubtedly withdraw from the *Ligue* of their own accord, leaving the organization free to pursue its "clearly communist" course.[148]

At the LDRN executive session held November 19, 1930, Kou-yaté's plans were realized. When non-communist members began to complain that material submitted for publication in *La Race Nègre* was being altered and cut by Rosso without the consent of the authors, Kouyaté came immediately to Rosso's defense, insisting that "articles which did not conform to the *Ligue*'s established line should always be modified or suppressed."[149] Realizing that the policy of the *Ligue* had taken a sharp turn to the left, Faure served notice to the gathered delegates of his resignation as manager of *La Race Nègre*.[150] Convinced that Kouyaté and his faction had "given up . . . their independence in exchange for [communist] financial resources," Faure and his supporters formed a rival branch of the LDRN, going so far as to publish their own edition of *La Race Nègre*.[151]

Once disburdened of the more moderate LDRN elements, Kou-yaté and his colleagues were in a position to pursue unhindered their policy of close cooperation with the Comintern. In order to improve the operational efficiency of this relationship, they secretly appointed several of their number to serve as special liaison officers between the *Ligue* and the various Comintern-affiliated organizations active in France.[152] Moreover, in conformity with the Comintern's syndicalist strategy, they intensified efforts initiated in 1930 to establish a trade union organization among Negro dockers in major French ports (subsequently known as the *Union des Travailleurs Nègres*).[153] Perhaps most ambitious of all, Kouyaté and his supporters appear to have been actively planning in 1931 a nationalist insurrection in the Cameroon. Reportedly with the aim of aborting this scheme the French government not only expelled the LDRN representative from the colony, but conducted a raid on Kouyaté's headquarters in Paris, seizing plans for the insurrection.[154]

In the final analysis, however, perhaps the most revealing indication of the *Ligue*'s more radical orientation was the transformation of *La Race Nègre* into a more militant organ for espousing the Comintern line. Renamed *Le Cri des Nègres*, this revised LDRN journal first appeared in the summer of 1931 under the editorship of Rosso. Even more than its predecessor, this periodical became a virulent and doctrinaire partisan of the revolutionary struggle of Negro Africans against French colonial rule.

Publishing appeals from such organizations as the newly formed "League for the Freedom of the Peoples of Senegal and the Soudan," *Le Cri* made a substantial case for outright sedition in French African territories.[155] Moreover, recognizing the importance of stirring revolutionary sentiment on the grass roots level, the editors of the periodical made a special point of printing their message in native African dialects—urging inhabitants of the French Cameroon, for example, to "take charge" of the political destiny of their country, and instructing residents of Senegal to go from "hut to hut" in order to spread the revolutionary gospel.[156] Most interesting of all, however, was the extent to which *Le Cri des Nègres* reflected the LDRN's enchantment with the Soviet Union. Not only were readers told to "learn the lesson offered them by the ten thousand emancipated Negroes in the USSR,"* [157] but they were reminded of the values of the "free

---

* Reference was being made to the small number of people of African descent (probably no more than several hundred) living in the Republic of Abkhasia, located on the northern coast of the Black Sea near Batum. Although these people retain only traces of Negroid characteristics as a result of many years of

union of free peoples" in the Soviet federal system and of the advantages of educational and economic emancipation as achieved in Russia.[158] In sum, as demonstrated by its preoccupation with the virtues of Russian civilization as well as by its insistence on the need to protect the U.S.S.R. against the imperialist threat,[159] *Le Cri des Nègres* was by 1934 as much an apologist for the Soviet cause as it was for the cause of African independence.

Thus it appears that ultimately Moscow was successful in its efforts to transform the LDRN into an instrument of Comintern policy. By the same token, it seems that communists were in some measure successful in their attempt to use this organization to stimulate revolutionary sentiment among French-speaking Africans. Although the activities of the LDRN were limited in scope and the work of the organization did not result in any large-scale conversions to the communist faith,[160] the efforts of the *Ligue* did enable Moscow to "establish contacts" with French Africa[161] and to win a restricted number of African nationalists to its revolutionary cause.

Possibly the best indication of the success of Comintern efforts was the degree to which political observers in France took the communist threat seriously. Some, of course, were quick to point out that African Negroes—because of their "docile" character, their exposure to the Roman Catholic faith, and their limited cultural evolution—were simply incapable of absorbing the communist message.[162] Even if Moscow was able to bribe a few French Negroes into supporting communism, they argued, "the money distributed to them by the Soviets will find use nowhere else than in the [night club] establishments of Montmartre."[163]

Other French political observers, however, were considerably less inclined to optimism. The pro-government deputy from Senegal, Blaise Diagne, for example, felt compelled to warn his compatriots

---

intermarriage, they have been referred to on numerous occasions as proof that a Negro minority does live in the Soviet Union. (See L. O. G. Hanga, "Africans in Russia," in *Russia and Africa*, [Moscow, 1966]: 25–27.) Svetlana Alliluyeva [Stalin] in her book *Only One Year* (New York, 1969): 234–35, mentions the extensive though unpublished research which her friend "Bertha" (probably Hanga) conducted among the residents of Abkhasia, pointing out that the social and economic condition of these "Soviet Negroes" was considerably less enviable than officially advertized. Although described in *Le Cri des Nègres* ("Au Caméroun Une Colonie Torpilley" IV, no. 2 [September, 1930]: 3) as refugees from slave ships bound for the U.S., their origins probably date back much farther—possibly to Greek times.

to beware of the selfish designs of the PCF and to lend no credence to communist propaganda.[164] To the same end, another defender of French African rule felt it necessary to advocate major precautionary measures. Arguing that the imprisoning of communist agitators, as was done in Madagascar, was clearly insufficient, he recommended extensive surveillance operations by naval squadrons along French African coastlines in order to prevent the further dissemination of revolutionary literature.[165] Perhaps most pessimistic of all observers was French editor, François Coty, who, in warning of the "red peril in black countries," questioned whether it was not in fact already "too late to keep the Bolshevik venom from doing its work among the Negro populations" of French Africa.[166] Whatever their individual convictions, however, French political observers generally agreed that "it would be the height of foolishness and complaisance to ignore the efforts which have been undertaken by the Soviets . . . to provoke uprisings in our colonies."[167]

The French government, for its part, certainly showed no inclination to make light of the problem. Considerable official effort was expended, for example, in keeping close watch over the activities of LDRN and PCF agitators in French Africa and in preventing these individuals (either by imprisonment or expulsion from Africa) from pursuing their insurrectionary work. In West Africa, LDRN activities were considered sufficiently dangerous to warrant the surveillance of mail arriving from *Ligue* headquarters in France. On one occasion, the Governor General of French West Africa even felt it necessary to intercept a letter from Kouyaté to a follower in the Soudan and to pass this communication on directly to the Minister of Colonies in Paris.[168]

Stringent precautionary measures were undertaken as well with respect to the circulation of communist publications. Although in the case of *La Race Nègre* no general ban on distribution was enforced, close surveillance was maintained over recipients of the journal, both in France and in West Africa.[169] All governors of French African colonies were informed in advance of the appearance of new issues of the periodical and on numerous occasions shipments of *La Race Nègre* were seized by French authorities upon their arrival in Africa.[170] Following the appearance of *Le Cri des Nègres* similar restrictive measures were undertaken,[171] and beginning in 1931 LDRN members in Paris were frequently shadowed by police agents.[172]

Thus, if only on the basis of the response of the French government, it can be concluded that communist efforts were beginning to bear some fruit in French colonial Africa. In addition to stimulating restrictive policies on the part of the government, these efforts succeeded in raising the issue of communism among Negro Africans to the level of general and active debate in France. However difficult it may be to measure accurately the results of communist activity, it is possible to say with considerable certainty that the Comintern, working through the PCF and the LDRN, made its influence felt—and feared—within the French-speaking territories of Negro Africa.

THE COMINTERN AND BRITISH AFRICA

The implementational strategy employed by the Comintern with regard to the African colonies of France found certain parallels in the approach used with respect to the colonies of Britain. Comintern agitational work in the metropole, for example, was conducted in Britain, as in France, with the assistance both of central communist bodies such as the LAI and the ILD and of more localized organizations such as the British Negro Welfare Association and, to a lesser extent, the British Communist Party. In contrast to the French experience, however, it appears that the Comintern in dealing with British Africa concentrated its efforts more extensively on insurrectionary activity within African colonies themselves, and for the task relied primarily upon the services of individual African activists whose line of responsibility reached directly to ITUC-NW headquarters.

The nearest British counterpart to Kouyaté's LDRN was the London-based Negro Welfare Association (NWA). Regarded as a kind of branch office of the ITUC-NW, this organization, together with the LAI, served as a center for Comintern contacts with Africans resident in Britain. Although little information on the work of the NWA has come to light, it is known that Padmore during the early thirties referred African nationalists to this "section of our organization [ITUC-NW] in London"[173] and that the NWA responded by offering these individuals its assistance in their struggle against British imperialism. Like the LAI, the NWA felt it could make the most effective contribution to the African cause by "exposing the hypocrisy of British democracy" in the colonies through the dissemination of propaganda in England and abroad.[174] To this end, the Secretary of the organization, Arnold Ward, kept in "regular touch" both with NWA representatives in Africa and with ITUC-NW headquarters in Hamburg.[175] Becoming a contributing editor of the *Negro Worker* in early 1933, he helped this journal publicize the plight of Britain's African subjects by forwarding information concerning their deplorable living conditions.[176]

The British Communist Party, appears to have been considerably less active with regard to African work than was the Negro Welfare Association. Although the CPGB did express a certain theoretical interest in the concept of colonial liberation and its members did serve as agents for the Comintern in bringing the recalcitrant Communist Party of South Africa into line in 1929,[177] in general the British party proved a disappointment to the Comintern as far as practical work in Africa was concerned. Prodded by Moscow on numerous occasions to expand its operations in the colonial sphere, the CPGB continued throughout the mid-thirties to exhibit a dilatory approach to African revolution.[178]

No doubt as a result of CPGB inactivity, Moscow came to the realization that if progress were to be made in British Africa it would be necessary to work through individuals rather than the British party apparatus. One such individual was E. F. Small of Gambia. A founding member of the National Congress of British West Africa and the editor of Gambia's first local paper, the *Gambia Outlook*, Small had by the early 1920's already demonstrated his potential as a nationalist and anti-British activist. Although his activities had attracted the attention of the Colonial Office and of Scotland Yard prior to 1929,[179] it was in that year that Small rose to real prominence as a leader of the colonial labor movement. In May he organized one of the first important trade unions in West Africa, the Bathurst Trade Union (BTU).[180] The following November he led a general strike in Bathurst which not only resulted in armed clashes between native workers and British authorities, but succeeded in severely tying up the economy of Gambia for an eighteen-day period.[181]

From the African point of view this strike was of major importance. In an era when colonial trade unions were generally outlawed, Small's union won effective recognition from the colonial government of Gambia as well as from the commercial concerns operating in the colony.[182] Moreover, it appears that this strike served as one of the most important catalysts in causing the British government to reconsider the entire issue of the legality of colonial labor organizations. There is evidence, in fact, that the Secretary of State for Colonies, Lord Passfield (Sidney Webb), had the Gambian situation specifically in mind when he issued his well-known circular urging British colonial governments to grant legal status to trade unions in the colonies.[183] By the same token, he was most certainly thinking of such "notorious bad egg[s]" as E. F. Small when he stipulated that colonial unions be required to register with the British government in order that they might be assisted with "sympathetic guidance" and thus prevented from straying too far into the realm of revolutionary and obstructionist activity.[184]

As might have been expected, British hostility toward Small and his organization found its antipode in the sympathetic attitude of the Comintern. Indeed, a "notorious bad egg" in the British imperial basket was precisely what Moscow was hoping to find, and it was not long before the Comintern was actively cooperating with the Gambian agitator.

Even in the case of the Bathurst strike of 1929, it appears that Moscow was more than a friendly bystander. In discussing the labor disturbances in the colony, the Governor of Gambia noted that "the strikers have apparently received outside encouragement to remain on strike."[185] Although he did not specify the nature of this external assistance, other accounts of the incident identified the source of encouragement as Russia itself,[186] or, more ambiguously, as "the experience of the October Revolution."[187] However unclear may be the exact nature of Moscow's direct intervention in Gambia, what is certain is that the Comintern, acting through Bridgeman and the LAI, provided Small with valuable support in Britain. By threatening use of the Parliamentary Question, Bridgeman was able to force the Secretary of State for Colonies to conduct a full inquiry into the Gambian situation. Thus, through Comintern-sponsored efforts labor conditions in Gambia were brought to the attention of the highest circles in the British government.[188]

Whatever its initial involvement in Small's enterprise, after 1929 the Comintern became highly interested in the Gambian labor movement and sought to expand its contacts with the movement's organizer. Shortly following the strike, for example, the Fifth RILU

Congress in Moscow made a point of commenting upon the "fierce and stubborn strike in Gambia," describing it as "a fine demonstration of the . . . determination of the Negro workers to struggle against capitalism."[189] Similarly, the *Negro Worker*, which had followed closely the events of 1929, began in the spring of 1930 to contribute material to the pages of Small's *Gambia Outlook*—including such inflammatory articles as Padmore's "Africans Massacred by British Imperialism."[190] At approximately the same time, Padmore himself appeared in Gambia, making this colony one of the first stops in his clandestine tour of Africa. Although it is not known to what extent Padmore's visit brought Comintern advice and financial resources, it did result in Small's attendance at the Hamburg Negro Workers Conference the following July.[191] This Conference, Small confided to communist colleagues, opened his eyes to the possibilities of using extra-constitutional methods for challenging British authority.[192] Responding to his obvious enthusiasm, the Comintern chose to make Small a member of the ITUC-NW Executive Committee and to name him Associate Editor of the *Negro Worker*.[193] In a word, the Comintern succeeded in winning to its side a man who was both the champion of the Gambian labor struggle and one of West Africa's foremost nationalist leaders.

While Comintern circles rejoiced that the labor movement in Gambia was under "good leadership" and was bringing new elements of the population into the workers' struggle,[194] the British government reacted with expected hostility to Small's activities. In 1930 it denied a request of the Liberian government that he be appointed Liberian consul in Bathurst; in 1933 it granted various favors to a faction within the Gambian union opposed to his leadership; and in 1935 it scorned his appeals on behalf of Gambian peasants discontented with their government-supported tribal leaders.[195]

Although British officials recognized that Small enjoyed wide popular support in Gambia and they were not altogether unsympathetic to many of the issues of public welfare which he raised, it was almost certainly Small's Comintern associations which constituted the principal stumbling block to any government policy of meaningful cooperation with the Gambian leader. The government's refusal to approve Small as Liberian consul was perhaps most indicative in this regard. In making the decisive recommendation to reject Small, Acting Governor of Gambia Workman made clear to Lord

Passfield the case against the Gambian agitator. "I am not aware whether Mr. Small has definitely joined the Communist Party," Workman observed, "but his attendance at meetings of the European Congress of Working Peasants in Berlin [possibly an erroneous reference to the Hamburg Negro Workers Conference], and his correspondence with the LAI sufficiently indicate his attitude."[196]

Clearly Small's affiliation with the *Negro Worker* and his cooperation with the LAI were held against him by British authorities. Colonial officials, who might otherwise have considered seriously a conciliatory approach to the new phenomenon of labor unrest in Gambia, were deterred from cooperating with Small primarily on the basis of his communist associations. Thus, the Comintern, by inserting itself into the tenuous relationship between the British government and the Gambian nationalist, affected in an indirect though meaningful way the course of British policy in West Africa.

If E. F. Small was thus of value to the Comintern in pursuing its struggle against Britain, the organization had an even more useful African assistant in the person of I. T. A. Wallace-Johnson. Veteran of service in the British army during World War I, seafarer, strike organizer, journalist, ardent and uncompromising nationalist, Wallace-Johnson was in many respects an ideal choice for the job of Comintern activist in West Africa.

Born in Sierra Leone in 1895, Wallace-Johnson had by the mid-1920's come to the attention of Moscow as a particularly energetic labor agitator.[197] Although the exact point at which he began to work for the Comintern is not certain, it does appear that his relationship with the organization, like that of Small, became a close one following his attendance at the Hamburg Conference in 1930. Shortly after this meeting he enrolled in courses at Moscow's KUTV University.[198] The following year he departed for Nigeria on a revolutionary mission—in all probability at the express behest of the ITUC-NW.*

---

* An opportunity for revolutionary leadership in Nigeria had been created in 1931 by the death of Herbert Macauley. Like Small, Macauley had been an active participant in the Hamburg Conference and had been elected to the Executive Committee of the ITUC-NW. On his return to Africa, he had "immediately put himself the task of helping the workers of Nigeria free themselves from the reformist and petty bourgeois tendencies of the leaders of the Democratic Party and other nonworking-class organizations." ("Death of Comrade Macauley," *Negro Worker*, I, nos. 10/11 [October/November, 1931]:

Although light has still to be shed on the exact nature of Wallace-Johnson's mission to Nigeria, it is apparent from his activities in Lagos between 1931 and 1933 that he was acting in conformity with Comintern directives. The choice of Nigeria itself, for example, was unquestionably a product of the emphasis accorded British West Africa in Comintern policy after 1930. In a statement made upon his arrival in Lagos, Wallace-Johnson clearly echoed sentiments expressed earlier by Padmore. "Nigeria is the largest British possession in West Africa," he explained; "it will therefore be seen that if ever the Africans are going to be brought to a standard worthy of humanity, the work should be started in Nigeria."[199] Similarly compatible with Comintern predilections were Wallace-Johnson's efforts on behalf of various nationalist-oriented journalistic enterprises, including his service as acting editor of the *Nigerian Daily Telegraph*.[200]

But most important in terms of the Comintern's operational objectives in Africa was Wallace-Johnson's activity in the sphere of labor organization. In order to build "a broad working-class movement on the principles of the revolutionary class struggle," Wallace-Johnson, upon his arrival in Lagos, began to organize a trade union known as the African Workers' Union of Nigeria (AWUN).[201] Plans were formulated for the publication of a monthly journal "dedicated entirely to the improvement of the working class" and a special school designed for the education of agitational workers was projected.[202] By the end of 1932, when Wallace-Johnson returned to Moscow to attend the ILD Congress (and presumably also to report on his progress in Nigeria), the Comintern was able to point with satisfaction to his success in "conducting the national liberation struggle and protecting the interests of the working masses" in Nigeria.[203] In spite of stringent repressive measures on the part of British authorities, his union had succeeded in attracting several hundred active

---

42.) Not long before his death Macauley had addressed a letter to the ITUC-NW in which he requested specific Comintern assistance. "As a result of our participation in the International Negro Conference in Hamburg last year," he stated, "some of us have realized that the political methods which we have employed in the past are insufficient for the struggle for emancipation. We are sending you this first letter so that you may have information about our conditions and so that we may get in touch with you and receive your advice in the drawing up of a program for our struggle." (Letter to the editor, "The Situation in Nigeria," *Negro Worker*, I, nos. 10/11 : 39.) It may well have been in response to this appeal or as a result of Macauley's death that Wallace-Johnson was dispatched to Lagos.

members in the Lagos region and in forming two AWUN subsidiaries in provincial areas of the colony.[204]

After his departure from Russia following the ILD Conference, Wallace-Johnson proceeded to Great Britain. Establishing contact with the Negro Welfare Association in London, he returned to West Africa in February, 1933, this time as an acknowledged "representative" of both the NWA and the ITUC-NW.[205] Maintaining close communication with the latter organization, he traveled first to Sierra Leone and for a short time conducted agitational work among local inhabitants—particularly among the unemployed.[206] From there he returned to Lagos where, resuming his previous activities, he endeavored to marshall indigenous opinion behind various Comintern-sponsored causes such as that of the Scottsboro boys. Notably in the case of Nigerian women, he was apparently successful in expanding the political awareness of the local population, earning "warmest congratulations" from Padmore for his efforts.[207]

It is difficult to say how long Wallace-Johnson might have otherwise continued his agitational work in Nigeria, for in the fall of 1933 the British government resolved to clamp down on his operations. Fearing for some time that the *Negro Worker* was penetrating Nigeria and influencing indigenous political attitudes in the colony, British authorities came increasingly to suspect Wallace-Johnson of playing an instrumental role in the dissemination of this and other revolutionary literature.[208] Accordingly, in October, 1933, the local Police Magistrate authorized a raid on Wallace-Johnson's headquarters in Lagos which, according to British officials, uncovered not only copies of the *Negro Worker*, but documents revealing Wallace-Johnson's "seditious intentions" in the colony.[209]

Forced to leave Nigeria, Wallace-Johnson promptly transferred the locus of his activity to the Gold Coast, a colony with which he was personally familiar and one which he regarded as promising terrain for his revolutionary energies.* In fact, as early as 1931, when he was

---

* Wallace-Johnson himself refers to a year he spent in the Gold Coast (c. 1930) "studying the position of the working class." ("British Oppression in West Africa," *Negro Worker*, I, no. 12 [December, 1931]: 20.) On May 8, 1932, Nigerian Police headquarters in Lagos received a report from the Gold Coast (Suspect Persons Memo, no. 31931) warning that "a communist agent of a very active type, trained in Russia, is about"—an agent who was undoubtedly Wallace-Johnson.

organizing the AWUN in Lagos, he had expressed the desire to establish a branch of the union in the Gold Coast—a desire influenced by his belief that the inhabitants of that colony were eagerly awaiting "the dawn of a new era" in their struggle for freedom from British rule.[210]

Wallace-Johnson was not altogether incorrect in his assessment of the political climate in the Gold Coast. By the beginning of 1934 popular discontent with the British colonial regime had indeed begun to take new directions. Not only were depression-related economic sources of dissatisfaction still prevalent, but new unsettling factors of a sociological nature had come into play in the political equation— namely, over-production by the colony's educational system (resulting in an imbalance in the ratio of graduates to available employment) and rapid growth of the local, generally pro-nationalist press.[211] The crisis in the relationship between the British colonial government and the Gold Coast intelligentsia came to a head in the spring of 1934, when the conservative governor, Sir Thomas Shenton, introduced a series of unpopular measures including a "Sedition Ordinance" giving the government greater control over the press.[212] Although ostensibly this ordinance was designed as a means to curb only seditious literature, by granting the Governor power to determine what constituted unacceptable material, it provided him, according to his opponents, with a *de facto* "dictatorship" over censorship in the colony.[213]

It was into this political cauldron that Wallace-Johnson thrust himself. The extent to which his presence in the Gold Coast at the end of 1933 can itself be linked to the introduction of the Sedition Ordinance is not certain, but it does seem probable that his work in the colony on behalf of the ITUC-NW did have an important bearing on the government's eagerness to secure passage of the legislation. It is known, for example, that prior to the introduction of the Sedition Ordinance (March 21, 1934) the Gold Coast government was seriously concerned over the influx of issues of the *Negro Worker* coming into the colony. Copies of the ITUC-NW journal appeared more frequently than any other item on the list of government confiscations. In 1933 alone, approximately 1100 issues were seized by colonial officials, suggesting an increase in circulation possibly attributable to Wallace-Johnson's distributional efforts.[214] That the British desire to curb ITUC-NW activity in the Gold Coast was a principal reason for enactment of the Sedition Ordinance was acknowledged by the Colonial Secretary himself in a meeting with representatives of the ARPS and the NCBWA in July, 1934. Citing examples of Comintern propaganda which had penetrated the colony, he told the visiting delegation in unambiguous terms that the purpose of the legislation was "to prevent the importation of subversive (Communist) literature from Russia" into the Gold Coast.[215]

Whatever his role in bringing about the enactment of the Sedition Ordinance, there is little question that Wallace-Johnson exploited to the full indigenous political unrest sparked by the legislation. Indeed, mounting opposition to British authority provided him with an ideal opportunity to test his theory that the Gold Coast was ready for mass political action. To the consternation of the colonial government, he organized large meetings in Accra—ostensibly to garner support for the Scottsboro boys—in all probability to mobilize opposition to British rule in the colony.[216] "Down with Howardian legislation" (Howard was the Gold Coast Attorney General responsible for drafting the Sedition Ordinance) became his battle cry as he carried his campaign from the streets of Accra to the remote areas of the Gold Coast interior.[217]

If women had been the particular object of his attention in Nigeria, in the Gold Coast it was the youth of the colony which constituted his principal target. With the avowed purpose of developing "a feeling of self-determination among the inhabitants of the country especially Youth," he founded in early 1934 an organization known as the West African Youth League (WAYL). Intended as a kind of prototype for a pan-West African political party, this organization became in the course of the 1930's an inveterate proponent of the most radical, uncompromising variety of African nationalism.[218]

Although during its first year of existence in the Gold Coast the WAYL demonstrated itself to be an energetic supporter of such popular causes as the safety of native workers in the mining industry, it was not until the following year that the organization first achieved recognition as a political force in the colony. In the spring of 1935, elections were held for a native member of the Gold Coast Legislative Council. In the course of these elections Wallace-Johnson was able to increase significantly the influence of the Youth League and to expand its organizational network into the provincial areas of the colony. One observer notes:

Wallace-Johnson toured the colony, made speeches, held mass meetings, and extended the influence of the League to every major town. The League attracted trade unions, young people's clubs, literary societies, ex-servicemen's groups; an organizer for women was appointed and an effort was made to engage the Muslim communities.[219]

The immediate effect of these efforts was apparent in the outcome of the 1935 elections. Despite significant support from British authorities, the pro-government candidate, Dr. Nanka Bruce, was defeated by a substantial margin.[220] By contributing to the election of Bruce's opponent, Kojo Thompson, the WAYL was thus able to register its first major political victory in the struggle against British power in the Gold Coast.

Wallace-Johnson's initial accomplishments in the colony, however, were attributable to more than simply his ability to pick a winning candidate in local elections. One key factor in his success was the assistance he received from a fellow graduate of Moscow's KUTV University, Bankole Awoonor-Renner. A native of the Gold Coast, Awoonor-Renner combined communist convictions and unbridled enthusiasm for the U.S.S.R. with talents as a lawyer and journalist.* Serving as President of the WAYL, he assisted Wallace-Johnson in attracting a popular following throughout the colony. As founder of the Ashanti Freedom Society, he was particularly useful in winning support for the League in Ashanti—a region long recognized as the stronghold of indigenous opposition to British rule in the Gold Coast. In this way, he made a significant contribution to Wallace-Johnson's effort to make the League a viable anti-British coalition between educated radicals on the coast and the residents of Ashanti.[221]

---

* One of the five Negroes sent to Moscow in 1925 following the ANLC Congress in Chicago, Awoonor-Renner's experience as a student in the U.S.S.R. between 1925 and 1928 enamored him of everything Soviet. (See his poem, "The Red Army" and his ode to Stalin in *This Africa* [London, 1943]: 66–67.) In a biographical note to *This Africa*, the renowned Gold Coast nationalist, J. B. Danquah, described him thus: "In the sabbatical and satiric years of delusion— in the years before the Second World War—when Soviet Russian politics could only be mentioned *sub rosa* and to be found with Russian literature was accounted seditious—Bankole Awoonor-Renner openly and courageously declared himself a Communist, nay, even a Bolshevik!" (*Ibid.*: 7.) If Awoonor-Renner was a "pioneer" and a "man of vision" to Danquah, to the British government he was clearly "open to suspicion" and his movements were followed both by Scotland Yard and the M.I.5. (See C.O. 96/679/6106.) After his return to the Gold Coast from Russia he succeeded Casely Hayford (founder of the NCBWA) as editor of the *Gold Coast Leader*, and during the 1940's he became a member of the Accra Municipal Council. (*This Africa, op. cit.*: 3ff.)

In addition to utilizing effectively the services of such militants as Awoonor-Renner, Wallace-Johnson demonstrated himself to be an astute politician by the way in which he dealt with the Aborigines' Rights Protection Society, probably the largest of the pro-nationalist groups active in the Gold Coast in the early 1930's. Although the political orientation of the ARPS was comparatively moderate, Wallace-Johnson earned the Society's friendship (as in the case of the 1935 elections) by supporting it on a variety of fundamental issues. Moreover, by exploiting the Society's growing hostility toward the rival nationalist movement led by Dr. J. B. Danquah, he was able to consolidate further his working alliance with the ARPS.[222] In short, according to one student of Gold Coast politics of the mid-1930's, "the politician who showed himself best able to take advantage of the changing atmosphere was not Danquah, but Wallace-Johnson."[223]

Apart from his forensic abilities, Wallace-Johnson's principal weapon in the Gold Coast was the local press. Although his efforts found consistent and sympathetic support in the pages of the *Gold Coast Independent* and the *Gold Coast Spectator*, he decided at the beginning of 1935 to collaborate with Nnamdi Azikiwe in bringing out a new nationalist organ, the *African Morning Post*. Operating under the slogan "Independent in All Things and Neutral in Nothing Affecting the Destiny of Africa," this daily newspaper provided Wallace-Johnson with a convenient new channel through which to express his views and give publicity to the activities of his Youth League.[224]

Thus, by the time of the First Annual Conference of the WAYL in March, 1936, Wallace-Johnson could justifiably boast that his organization had become "a power to reckon with" in Gold Coast politics.[225] The truth of this statement was amply revealed in the changing attitude of Sir Arnold Hodson, Governor of the Gold Coast. Whereas in 1934 Hodson had felt confident that he could "nullify the efforts of Wallace-Johnson and other subversives by broadcast propaganda and other devices," after touring the colony in 1935 he had become considerably less certain of his ability to curb such activities.[226] By January, 1936, the situation had progressed to such a point that Hodson felt compelled to request advice from London. "I do wish you could suggest some plan whereby I could get rid of Wallace-Johnson," he wrote candidly to the Assistant Undersecretary of State for Colonies; "he is in the employ of the Bolsheviks and is doing a

certain amount of harm by getting hold of the young men for his
'Youth League.' "[227]

In hopes of finding grounds upon which to convict Wallace-
Johnson of sedition, the British government thereupon began sending
native plain clothes policemen to take notes at WAYL meetings.[228]
Moreover, on the basis of Hodson's accusation that the Gold Coast
press was "controlled by the Red element" and was "in direct touch
with the Bolsheviks whose one aim and object is to stir up trouble and
break up the Empire," the government began to keep closer watch
over the activities conducted by Wallace-Johnson and his colleagues
through the local press.[229] In brief, by early 1936 British authorities
both in London and Accra were no longer debating whether to
prosecute Wallace-Johnson, but simply how to proceed with a case
against him. Largely on the basis of his communist connections they
had determined that, whatever the repercussions, he had to be eliminated from the Gold Coast political scene.

But Wallace-Johnson was an elusive quarry. "He sails pretty near
the wind," complained one Colonial Office official, "but never so
close that a conviction could be predicted with confidence."[230] It
was not in fact until June, 1936, that the government felt it had
collected sufficient evidence to enable it to bring charges of sedition.
On May 31, the Accra Post Office seized packets, reportedly containing seditious writing, which Wallace-Johnson had addressed to the
NWA and the LAI in London.[231] Two days later a police raid on his
office yielded evidence to the effect that Wallace-Johnson was the
author of a "seditious" article ("Has the African a God?") which had
appeared in the *African Morning Post* several weeks before.[232] Forth-
with he was arrested and—in face of protests from the LAI, hostile
questions in Parliament, and even the non-concurrence of the two
African members of the jury—was convicted on two counts of sedition.[233]

This conviction, the first of its kind in the history of the colony, at
once made Wallace-Johnson the hero of Gold Coast nationalists.
Outside the courthouse, crowds gathered to cheer the WAYL leader;
his article, "Has the African a God?," became famous as far away as
Central America and the West Indies; and membership of the Youth
League doubled.[234]

Wallace-Johnson himself exploited the situation to the full, appealing his case first in the Gold Coast and finally carrying the appeal all

the way to the Privy Council in Britain. There he won even greater publicity, raising *in forma pauperis* the issue of the right of colonial subjects to equal justice under British law.[235] Although he lost this appeal, Wallace-Johnson had the satisfaction of observing high-ranking members of the legally scrupulous British administration devote an astonishing amount of time and energy to his case as well as the pleasure of witnessing Governor Hodson subjected to the humiliation of having to pay the costs of his litigation.[236]

Wallace-Johnson's revolutionary career, however, was not to end with his adventures in the Gold Coast. Indeed, in his native Sierra Leone he continued his insurrectionary activity until the very outset of World War II. Organizing a section of the WAYL in 1938, he had by the eve of the war attracted a mass following (42,000 by the League's own estimate) and had provoked widespread popular opposition to British rule.[237] Even more certainly than he had in Nigeria or the Gold Coast, Wallace-Johnson attained a position of power in Sierra Leone sufficient to cause the gravest apprehension on the part of the British government. Particularly after its decision to convert Freetown into a defended port immediately prior to World War II, the government realized that Wallace-Johnson's "continued presence" in Sierra Leone was "a menace not only to local interests but to the Empire" itself.[238] Whether or not he was receiving funds from outside sources, government officials concluded, "he is certainly rendering signal service to any power hostile to the Empire or to its system of government."[239]

Although it is difficult to determine the extent to which Wallace-Johnson was still operating under Comintern direction in the late 1930's,[240] it is clear that his activities in Sierra Leone, like those in Nigeria and the Gold Coast, followed the pattern of revolutionary activism dictated by Moscow in the earlier years of the decade. In terms of the British response to Wallace-Johnson's revolutionary exploits, the scenarios of his three successive experiences were surprisingly similar. Each ended with a police raid upon his headquarters. Each resulted in the imposition of restrictive counter-measures which served to provoke widespread opposition to colonial authority. In the Gold Coast the British colonial administration, primarily on the basis of its experience with Wallace-Johnson, was led to enact new measures to control the local press and to restrict the immigration of "undesirable" colonial subjects.[241] In Sierra Leone the colonial government, realizing that no African jury would hand down a verdict against Wallace-Johnson, felt obliged to introduce an even greater variety of legislation in order to put a stop to his activities— legislation which ultimately brought about the detention of Wallace-Johnson for the duration of World War II.[242]

In a word, the British Empire with its slow-working system of constitutional democracy had met a formidable adversary in Wallace-Johnson—an individual who was able to apply with considerable efficacy modern techniques of labor organization and political agitation. Conversely, the Comintern had found in Wallace-Johnson a highly effective anti-imperialist weapon—a man who by following closely the revolutionary guidelines delineated by Moscow had helped to undermine the stability of British rule in West Africa.

In the final analysis, however, Wallace-Johnson's activities in Africa in the late thirties must be viewed as an exception to the pattern of Comintern activism during the period. It appears, in fact, that after 1935 the most intensive phase of Comintern involvement in Black Africa had drawn to a close. Although other parts of the continent such as the Belgian Congo had attracted the attention of Moscow during the years following the Sixth Comintern Congress,*

---

* At its Fourth Congress in 1929, the Belgian Communist Party (PCB) endorsed the principle of Congolese independence and called for "aggressive intervention" in behalf of the rights of Congolese Negroes. Shortly thereafter, reports began to circulate of a 'Bolshevik organization" operating at Thysville, center of the religio-political Kibangist movement. (See W. Maesschalck, "La Situation au Congo Belge," *Correspondance Internationale*, X, no. 35 [April 23, 1930]: 423. See also Henri, "Le IVe Congres du P.C. de Belgique," *Correspondance Internationale*, IX, no. 25 [March 20, 1929]: 342.) By 1930 Padmore was able to point with pride to "growing class consciousness" in the Congo and to cite a Belgian press dispatch referring to a settlement near Brazzaville as "the operative base of native Communist elements." (Padmore, *Life and Struggles of Negro Toilers* [London, 1931]: 100.) Cunard (*Negro Anthology* [London, 1934]: 794-95) cited "Extracts from a Pamphlet [of Comintern inspiration] circulating in the Congo" which appealed to Congolese natives in "the villages," "work centers," and "army camps," instructing them to follow the example of Russia and join "the strikes and risings that are breaking out everywhere in the Congo." Perhaps the most interesting feature of this pamphlet was the light it shed upon the anti-tribal, modernizing thrust of Comintern propaganda in Africa. In simple language the various Congolese tribes were addressed individually by name and told to "unite all together" as the only effective means of attaining freedom. (*Loc. cit.*) In the course of the Congolese revolt in 1931 the PCB engaged in a number of activities in Belgium designed to lend support to the insurgents and to bring the plight of Congolese natives to the attention of the Belgian public. Progress of the revolt and accounts of government atrocities in the colony were reported in the party paper, *Le Drapeau Rouge*, and in special PCB leaflets. Various protest meetings and demonstrations were organized, and, through the

it was unquestionably the colonies of Britain and France which had constituted the principal object of Moscow's revolutionary ambitions. The preponderance of communist effort directed toward these colonies, in turn, was testimony to the fact that Comintern policy toward Africa was largely determined by Russian hostility toward Britain and France. It was the realignment of Soviet policy toward these two powers in the mid-thirties which perhaps best explains the relative decline in Africa's importance as an object of Comintern revolutionary priority.

---

efforts of Communist Deputy Jacquemotte, representations were made to the Belgian Minister of Colonies and the issue of Congolese independence was raised before the Belgian Parliament. (See A. Z. Zusmanovich, ed., *Prinuditnel 'nyi Trud i Profdvizhenie v Negritianskoi Afrike* [Moscow, 1933]: 107, 110f; and *Negro Worker*, I, no. 8 [August, 1931]: 7.) In 1934 the LAI also took up the cause of Belgium's Congolese subjects. Insisting that "while slavery exists in the Congo there will be no possibility for Belgian workers to free themselves from exploitation," the League urged that organizational unity be promoted between Congolese and Belgian workers. Toward this end, a national section of the LAI was to be established in Belgium. (See "The Situation in the Belgian Congo: Statement by the League Against Imperialism," *Inprecorr*, XIV, no. 4: 87–88.)

10

The Emergence of the Fascist Threat and the Reappraisal of Comintern Policy Toward Africa

In September, 1931, the Japanese army invaded Manchuria. In January, 1933, Hitler came to power in Germany. Each of these events had a marked impact upon Comintern policy toward the imperialist world, and each, in turn, produced a decisive effect upon the course of Comintern relations with Negro Africa. Whereas prior to these events Germany and Japan had been regarded as only minor participants in the worldwide game of imperialist politics, after 1933 they, together with fascist Italy, came increasingly to be identified as principal ringleaders in the imperialist plot against the security of the Soviet state.

In the case of Japan, the reappraisal of Comintern policy was comparatively prompt. Immediately after the outbreak of hostilities in Manchuria the ECCI issued a general warning to the Comintern concerning the situation in the Far East. The Japanese invasion, it was explained, could be regarded both as an initial step in the imperialist plan to invade the U.S.S.R. and as a prelude to a new imperialist war.[1] Throughout the Comintern organizational network the alarm was sounded. The ITUC-NW, for its part, responded with particular zeal, giving the war issue detailed coverage in the pages of the *Negro Worker*. Under the slogan, "China Today—Africa Tomorrow," the journal made a determined attempt to convince Africans that their own security would ultimately be threatened by Japanese imperialism and that they should redouble their efforts to "fight against the intervention" aimed at the U.S.S.R.[2] "The War is Here," declared Padmore, insisting that Manchuria was nothing less than the "jumping off ground for the attack against the Soviet Union."[3] In other words, the anti-Soviet war so long prophesied by the Comintern was actually at hand, and now, more than ever before, the assistance of Africans was needed for the defense of the Soviet state.

It is interesting that the Japanese invasion of Manchuria was exploited by the *Negro Worker* as prime evidence that imperialism, in keeping with its universal and immutable character, "knows no colour-line." Just as the Chinese in Manchuria had been forced to suffer under the oppression of their racial kinsmen, so African Negroes could expect to suffer exploitation at the hands of their black imperialist brothers.[4] By the same token, Japanese attempts to appeal to Negroes on the basis of a "united front of darker races" were heartily condemned by Comintern writers, who portrayed Japanese imperialists as every bit as ruthless as their white European counterparts.[5] In effect, whatever had been its previous utility, by the mid-1930's the Comintern's racially oriented appeal to Africans was no longer considered a workable approach. Calls to racial identity had become the voice of the enemy and "racial chauvinism" was counted among the worst of heresies.

Compared with the new hostility toward Japan, the change in the Comintern policy toward Germany was both slower to materialize and more profound in its ultimate effects. Although the Soviet Union had by no means been blind to Germany's revanchist tendencies during the period of the Weimar Republic, the two powers had been able to cooperate with considerable ease in a variety of important spheres. In matters concerning the colonial world this cooperative approach was particularly apparent. With regard to British and French colonies in Africa and especially with regard to former German territories such as the Cameroon, the relationship amounted to virtual collusion.[6] Whether it was out of secret revanchist ambitions or as a result of longstanding hostility toward Britain and France, both Berlin and Moscow were clearly anxious to drive a wedge between the imperial powers and their African subjects. There is perhaps no better indication of this compatibility of subversive intentions than the fact that Weimar Germany tolerated for so long the anti-colonial activities of the Comintern. In the face of the obvious displeasure of Britain and France, the entire panoply of Comintern-sponsored organizations—the RILU, the LAI, the ISH—was allowed to publish propaganda, hold congresses, and maintain worldwide revolutionary communications from German soil.[7]

Suddenly, with the Nazi takeover in Germany, the fabric of Soviet-German rapprochement was destroyed. Although Comintern leaders, and especially Stalin himself, had been slow to recognize the threat of German fascism in the early thirties, after the spring of 1933 it had become apparent to all that Germany's policy toward the Comintern had undergone a drastic change. Almost overnight the political environment which had accommodated Comintern operations in Germany disappeared. Throughout the country KPD offices were sacked and in Berlin the headquarters of the Comintern was raided.[8] In Hamburg the lightning struck the ITUC-NW with no less severity. Padmore's offices, though they had been fortified to resist the attack, were seriously damaged and the presses of the *Negro Worker* ground to a halt.[9] In accordance with the new racial policy of rounding up and evicting all Negroes in Germany, Padmore himself was dragged out of bed by Nazi police and thrown into prison for several weeks.[10] Thus graphically forewarned of the terror to come, the ITUC-NW, together with other German-based Comintern organizations, quickly transferred operations from Germany to Copenhagen. There the *Negro Worker* resumed publication, now directing its wrath toward a new enemy—the Nazi Reich.[11]

Despite Moscow's original reluctance to alter its comparatively friendly relationship with Germany, ultimately it was obliged to follow the path of anti-Nazism which had been forced upon Comintern affiliates operating in Hamburg and Berlin. As Germany and Japan moved toward entente in the course of 1934, so Germany and Russia inevitably drifted farther apart.[12] Before the end of the year, in fact, the Kremlin appears to have come to the realization that Nazi Germany constituted a more immediate threat to Soviet security than either of the two imperialist powers against which the forces of the Comintern had hitherto been unleashed.

It was in this context that Moscow redefined its policy toward Britain and France. While there is no evidence that Russia abandoned altogether its enmity toward these two powers, there are unmistakable indications that after 1933 Soviet leaders increasingly began to realize that they shared common interests with Britain and France vis-à-vis the fascist states. Although there were to be significant reversals in Soviet policy before the final anti-fascist coalition was forged during World War II, this first recognition of shared interest in the mid-thirties unquestionably served to take the sharp edge off Russia's hostility toward its former adversaries.

Russia's desire to embark upon a more conciliatory approach was most readily apparent with respect to France. As early as the summer of 1933, an atmosphere of greater cordiality could be detected in the relations between the two powers. By the spring of 1934, talks concerning a mutual Franco-Soviet security arrangement had begun in earnest and by June a draft agreement had been prepared.[13] In keeping with the new spirit of anti-fascist entente, the Communist Party of France, presumably acting on orders from Moscow, made a radical policy shift in favor of cooperation with French socialists.[14] Similarly, in line with the new cooperative approach, Russia chose to comply with French wishes and join the League of Nations in September, 1934.[15] Finally, on May 2, 1935, French and Russian representatives signed the Franco-Soviet Pact, thus formalizing the new policy of mutual defense which had emerged between their respective countries.[16]

With respect to Great Britain, Soviet policy appears to have undergone a similar, though less easily traceable, transformation. Although Anglo-Soviet relations were both complicated and tenuous, by the beginning of 1934 it was nonetheless possible to discern the outlines of an emerging rapprochement between London and Moscow. In January of that year the Anglo-Soviet Trade Agreement was signed and the following summer Britain actively supported Soviet entry into the League of Nations.[17] By March, 1935, when Anthony Eden visited Moscow to assure the Soviets of Britain's friendly intentions, relations between the two countries had reached a high point.[18]

In effect, Soviet foreign policy had made a marked shift in the direction of supporting the international status quo. Primarily out of fear that this status quo—and with it Soviet security—might be seriously jeopardized by Nazi Germany, Moscow was actively pursuing protective alliances, even with such former enemies as Britain and France. Such a conscious reappraisal of strategy on the part of the Kremlin was bound to have its effect not only upon Comintern policy in Europe, but upon Comintern revolutionary activism in the colonial world.

At the Seventh Comintern Congress held in Moscow in July and August, 1935, the imperatives of the new Soviet foreign policy were translated into the program of the Communist International. Never before, in fact, had Comintern policy been so obviously molded to correspond to calculations of Soviet national interest. Primed for almost a decade to pursue the solitary course of proletarian orthodoxy, world communism at the time of the Seventh Congress was, in effect, rerouted onto the cooperative path of anti-fascist coalition.

Recognizing the threat posed by Nazi Germany, the Seventh Congress formally abandoned the "United Front from Below" approach, replacing it with a policy of relatively indiscriminate cooperation with elements sympathetic to the anti-fascist cause. Comintern sections were instructed to follow the example of the PCF and take the unprecedented step of making peace with their former arch-rivals, the socialists. Catholics, reformists, heretics of all stripes were to be accepted as allies, provided they were willing to contribute to the battle against the new enemy. The errors of the past were condemned and the possibility of achieving revolutionary success by independent proletarian action was rejected.[19] In short, an entire era of left-wing tactics in international communism had come to an end. Under the slogan "People's Anti-Fascist Front" a conservative, even nationally-oriented approach reigned supreme.[20]

The new approach was by no means designed to call a halt to the communist campaign for colonial independence, but it did require a fundamental shift in Comintern strategy. In an abrupt reversal of previous policy, communists were called upon to "draw the widest masses" of the colonial population into the anti-imperialist struggle and to "take an active part in the mass anti-imperialist movements headed by the national-revolutionary and national-reformist organizations."[21] Although the traditional appeals were issued to Comintern followers urging them to support the national liberation struggle in colonial countries, the emphasis was clearly on the establishment of an "anti-imperialist people's front."* [22]

That the new anti-fascist strategy did not involve an abandonment of communist interest in Negro Africa was amply demonstrated both during and after the Seventh Congress by the Comintern's vigorous support of Ethiopia's struggle against Italian aggression. Even prior to the Congress, the Ethiopian situation had attracted considerable attention both in the Soviet and the Comintern press. Aware that

---

* Insofar as Negro liberation was concerned, the new pragmatism even involved a rekindling of Moscow's earlier desire to cooperate with Garveyism. In a remarkable display of political opportunism, Ford explained to communists: "Of course there are many points in the programs of the two movements [i.e. communism and Garveyism] which differ. But both are agreed that black men should be freed from the domination of imperialists in Africa and throughout the world . . . Mr. Garvey has shown the way by cooperating with the Anti-Imperialist League in England." (Ford, "Can Garveyism and Communism Mix?," in Ford, The Communists and the Struggle for Negro Liberation [Harlem section of CPUSA, n.d.]: 6, 8.)

Ethiopia's struggle to maintain its independence was full of import for nationalist strivings elsewhere in Negro Africa,[23] Moscow had resolved to undertake a bipartisan international campaign involving the establishment of Ethiopian defense committees within a variety of noncommunist organizations.[24] In his remarks at the Seventh Congress, James Ford discussed the progress of these efforts, making particular reference to the establishment of a "Provisional Committee for the Defense of Ethiopia" in the U.S. Citing the American committee as an example, he called upon British and French communists to form similar organizations and thereby mobilize support in their countries for the international campaign on behalf of the Ethiopian people.[25]

Shortly after the Congress, the ECCI, fearing that the situation in Ethiopia might soon develop into a "world war," took the hitherto unthinkable step of appealing to the Comintern's old enemy, the Second (socialist) International, to join in action to forestall hostilities.[26] Although this appeal was rejected, Moscow persevered in its effort to mobilize worldwide support for the Ethiopian cause. Following the Italian invasion in October, 1935, committees of the sort projected by the Comintern were established in Africa, London, and Paris.[27] However extensive was the Comintern's role in the actual formation of these committees, it can be said that the organization provided a continual source of support and inspiration to the "defense of Ethiopia" campaign. Not only did the Italian invasion enable the Comintern to endorse a cause highly popular among the world's Negroes, it provided Moscow with an opportunity to pursue its traditional support of African independence in a manner less antithetical to the interests of Britain and France.

Thus, on the basis of the general statements made at the Seventh Congress and the support extended Ethiopia in its struggle for independence, it can be argued that the Comintern retained, throughout the mid-thirties, both its theoretical desire for colonial revolution and its active interest in Negro Africa. On the other hand, however, there are clear indications that the realignment in Soviet foreign policy which occurred during this period was accompanied by a corresponding decline in Comintern operational concern for the colonial world. Even in the resolutions of the Seventh Congress there was a conspicuous absence of discussion of colonial matters. Similarly, in the Comintern press, articles dealing with colonial revolution—

of which there had been an abundance in the late twenties and early thirties—became infrequent as attention increasingly focused on the fascist threat in Europe and the Far East.

As far as colonial Africa was concerned, the most dramatic indication of the shift in revolutionary priorities was the Comintern's behavior toward the *Negro Worker* and its editor, George Padmore. Although the *Negro Worker* had been able to resume publication in Copenhagen following the Nazi raid on ITUC-NW headquarters in Hamburg, it was obliged for financial reasons to publish on a restricted, bimonthly basis. Despite insistent pleas for contributions from readers, the economic plight of the *Negro Worker* became progressively more desperate until, in the fall of 1933, Padmore was forced to admit that the journal was bankrupt.[28] Apparently Moscow, in order to reorient or to terminate ITUC-NW activity, had resorted to the well-established practice of undermining a Comintern affiliate by witholding subsidies necessary for operating costs. In retrospect, it can be concluded, the sudden assault which the ITUC-NW had experienced at the hands of the Nazi police was of only minor significance compared with the gradual suffocation which the organization suffered at the hands of its former patron, the Comintern.*

Certainly Padmore was not prepared to accept such treatment passively. Reportedly informed in August, 1933, of the official decision to disband the ITUC-NW,[29] he reacted violently to what he considered the Comintern's repudiation of the Negro liberation struggle. Moscow, in turn, responded with a thoroughgoing attack on the ITUC-NW Secretary. Charging that he had failed to surrender files and "other properties of the Committee,"[30] that he had associated with the "exposed provocateur" Kouyaté,[31] that he had provided Nazi police with names and addresses of Negro seamen cooperating with the movement,[32] and, most egregious of all, that he had "slipped down into the mire of counter-revolutionary petty-bourgeois nationalism" and "black chauvinism,"[33] the Comintern in February,

---

* Although the *Negro Worker* reappeared under different management in May, 1934, and continued publication until October, 1937, it never regained the revolutionary stature it had under Padmore. During this period, moreover, it led a fleeting existence, moving editorial offices from Copenhagen to Brussels, then to Harlem, and finally to Paris. The ITUC-NW also resumed limited operations in 1934—first under the secretaryship of Charles Woodson and later under that of Otto Huiswood. (See J. R. Hooker, *Black Revolutionary* [New York, 1967]: 32–33.)

1934, formally expelled Padmore from the communist movement.[34]

Whatever truth there may have been in these allegations, Padmore, for his part, made clear what he believed to be the real motivation for the radical shift in the Comintern attitude toward him and his Committee. The decision to disband the ITUC-NW, he charged publicly, had been taken "in order not to offend the British Foreign Office which has been bringing pressure to bear on Soviet diplomacy because of the tremendous indignation which our work has aroused among the Negro masses in Africa."[35] The about-face he had witnessed in Comintern policy, together with the harsh treatment he had experienced in Nazi Germany, had served to convince Padmore that the interests of his race were not necessarily served by intimate cooperation with Moscow. "The Comintern's treatment of me after eight years of loyally serving the cause of the liberation of my race is indicative of what we can expect when it has the power to decide the fate of the Negroes of the world," he declared defiantly.[36] "Let us never forget," he admonished, "that a people are respected in proportion as they help themselves. It is high time for the Negroes to stop depending on other people to fight their battles."[37]

Profound indeed had been George Padmore's disillusionment with the Comintern. During the period following the Sixth Congress he, and numerous Africans with him, had faithfully pursued the arduous path of Comintern activism in the colonies. But when the Comintern was "called upon not only to endorse the new policy of the Soviet government, but to put a brake upon the anti-imperialist work of its affiliate sections and thereby sacrifice the young national liberation movements in Asia and Africa,"[38] these once loyal devotees of Moscow were obliged to question the advantages of a continuing relationship with their revolutionary Mecca. Although many Negro activists such as James Ford and Wallace-Johnson appear to have retained their affiliation with the Comintern after 1934, the purge of Padmore unquestionably provoked a significant defection in the ranks of world communism's African sympathizers.[39]

In short, whether it was purely a product of the changing Soviet attitude toward Britain and France as Padmore suggests, or whether it was also the result of the new wave of Stalinian repression in the U.S.S.R., the Comintern's execution of the ITUC-NW forced a number of African communists to choose between devotion to Moscow and allegiance to their own race. In selecting the latter, they did not necessarily become anti-communist or even anti-Soviet. In fact some, like Padmore, were to conduct revolutionary activity along Marxist-Leninist lines for many years to come. What they did receive as a result of their disillusioning experience of the mid-thirties, however, was a sudden exposure to the underlying features of Comintern policy and a graphic demonstration of the extent to which this policy was shaped by considerations of Soviet national interest.

*   *   *

The decade following the Sixth Comintern Congress in 1928 saw the high point of Comintern involvement in Black Africa. After 1933, it also witnessed a significant reordering of revolutionary priorities away from the region in light of the new requirements of Soviet foreign policy. Because the decade after 1928 thus incorporated both extremes in Russia's African policy, it can perhaps be regarded as the most interesting period in the entire history of Russian relations with Black Africa before World War II.

Despite the dramatic changes in revolutionary strategy which were announced at the time of the Sixth Comintern Congress, the period following this Congress was marked by a conspicuous intensification of Comintern activity in the colonial world. With regard to Black Africa in particular, a genuine effort was made to carry out the revolutionary directives issued by the Congress and to expand upon many of the activities begun in the mid-twenties. Although the underlying rationale for Comintern interest in Africa remained essentially the same as it had been prior to the Sixth Congress, Comintern operational strategy in the years after 1928 became more concerted and purposeful in nature. The experimentation and adventurism which had characterized the earlier period had given way to a more deliberate and methodical approach.

Perhaps the best example of the new orientation was the Comintern's reliance upon the services of a small number of trusted revolutionaries, all of whom undertook missions in Africa itself and all of whom were associated with a single revolutionary directorate—the ITUC-NW. Although Moscow relied on a variety of other instrumentalities to implement Comintern policies in Black Africa (e.g. European communist parties and Comintern-affiliated international bodies such as the ISH, the ILD, and the LAI), it was the ITUC-NW which served as the central coordinating agency for world communism's activity among Negroes. Accordingly, to this organization can be assigned the primary responsibility for the success or failure of Comintern efforts in Africa during the half-decade following 1928.

To say that Moscow was largely successful in achieving its revolutionary objectives in Negro Africa would be misleading. The general anti-colonial uprising, so eagerly anticipated in Comintern writings, did not take place before World War II. By the same token, the Comintern message never reached the majority of Negro Africans during this period. Even the ITUC-NW, spawned by the RILU as an international center for agitation among Negroes, never developed into the African revolutionary headquarters which its sponsors had hoped it would become. In brief, the Comintern, throughout the interwar period, had been profoundly mistaken in the assumption that the colonial system in Africa could be demolished by frontal assault.

Notwithstanding its obvious failings, however, the Comintern could claim certain tangible revolutionary achievements in Black Africa in the years following the Sixth Congress. Although the flames of revolt did not spread throughout Africa, seeds of radical thought were planted—especially in the coastal areas of West Africa. Under Comintern guidance, the roots of revolutionary trade unionism began to develop in such port cities as Bathurst and Lagos, and the foundations for a radical political movement were established in at least two colonies, the Gold Coast and Sierra Leone. Although Comintern propaganda did not reach the masses, it did penetrate colonial Africa in sufficient quantity to create considerable anxiety on the part of both the British and the French governments. In certain cases this propaganda gave Africans their first outside source of information on world affairs. Inevitably it encouraged them to question the motivations of their European overlords and helped them to believe in their own ability to shape the economic and political destiny of their colonies.

The revolutionary progress which Moscow could legitimately claim in Negro Africa was largely attributable to the insight into African affairs which Comintern policy-makers had succeeded in acquiring. Although Padmore and his colleagues in the ITUC-NW have been criticized for devoting too little attention to African problems and for basing their programs too much on the Soviet and Asian experiences,[40] there is little evidence to indicate that they either ignored or seriously misjudged the importance of Africa's unique political and social conditions. On the contrary, as Wallace-Johnson's experiences in West Africa suggest, Comintern directives were based upon a fairly realistic assessment of the existing political situation in various African colonies and upon a comparatively sophisticated calculation of the most effective methods to be used for exploiting indigenous anti-colonial sentiment.

Undoubtedly the Comintern's awareness of African political realities and its consequent ability to translate Marxist-Leninist policy into programs of action relevant to African conditions was facilitated in large measure by Moscow's success in enlisting the services of West Africans, who, like Small and Wallace-Johnson, were highly familiar with the political ways of their compatriots. Similarly, information gathered by Padmore on his travels in Africa, together with data obtained from African seamen and students visiting Hamburg and Moscow, was useful in sharpening Comintern perceptions. In effect, the Comintern was able to enjoy a comparatively steady flow of information from the field—a resource, it may be assumed, which was of value not only to the Russian leaders of the Comintern, but also to the new school of Soviet Africanists which had evolved in Moscow in the period following the Sixth Congress. By relying upon this channel of information, Moscow was able to gain perspectives on the political development of Black Africa often unavailable in Western European capitals. Predisposed by their ideological convictions to look behind the facade of official data relating to the region, communists often discovered what colonial authorities were able to perceive only after a long and painful series of confrontations with their colonial subjects. In short, the Comintern may have exaggerated the extent of nationalist discontent and over-estimated the intensity of popular disillusionment with the existing political and economic order in Africa, but it did manage to keep surprisingly well informed concerning the basic direction of African political sentiment and to apply this knowledge to the promotion of its revolutionary objectives.

Whatever the ultimate success or failure of the Comintern's revolutionary efforts in Black Africa in the years after 1928, it is remarkable that communists did actively devote their attention and energy to agitational work in what was considered so remote and backward a corner of the world. Basing their activity on the presumption that revolution in Africa would undermine the political, economic, and military foundations of British and French power and thereby contribute to the security of the Soviet state, they pursued their involvement in the region up to the point at which confrontation with fascism in Europe forced them to reevaluate their traditional hostility toward Britain and France. Although it must be acknowledged that the Comintern's experiment in Black Africa in the decade following the Sixth Congress was of limited significance in terms of any immediate revolutionary impact, the pattern of relationships established, the organizations inspired, and the personal associations formed during these years were to prove of unquestionable value to the development of Soviet relations with the region in the post-independence era.

PART IV

EVALUATION OF THE RUSSIAN EXPERIENCE

11
The Basic Character of the Russian Relationship with Black Africa before World War II

It is widely held by observers of Soviet affairs that Russia pursued no serious interest in Black Africa until after World War II. Believing, with Harrison Salisbury, that "historically Russians never had contact with the peoples of Africa,"[1] these observers have overlooked the important Czarist and Bolshevik antecedents to postwar Soviet involvement in the region. Even contemporary scholars who have devoted detailed attention to the subject of Russian policy in Africa have remained largely unaware of the historical origins of Soviet activity. Arguing that before World War II "Africa remained for Moscow the orphan continent,"[2] they have concluded that not until the post-Stalinian shifts in Soviet foreign policy and the concurrent appearance of independent African states did Russia demonstrate any interest or exert any influence in regions south of the Sahara.[3] One student of the subject goes so far as to maintain that Moscow's postwar aspirations in Africa were "conditioned by the long period during which Soviet leaders knew or cared little about developments in this area" and that more recent Russian difficulties in the region have been "in large part an outcome of the [prewar] years of neglect."[4]

The present study demonstrates that Russia did display an active interest in Black Africa for at least a half century prior to World War II. Although the region played only a peripheral role in the Kremlin's foreign policy calculations, it nonetheless was the object of relatively uninterrupted and specific Russian attention beginning in the latter decades of the nineteenth century. Moreover this concern for Africa had visible manifestations and a discernible rationale. In sum, it is appropriate to speak of a conscious and distinct African policy on the part of the Russian government during both the Czarist and prewar Soviet eras.

The early Czarist concern for northeastern Africa was expanded in the first decade of Soviet power to include the colonial territories of central and West Africa. Emerging first as a combined product of Moscow's interest in the world's Negroes and the world's colonial peoples, concern for the region became after 1928 a separate focus of world communism's revolutionary program. Nowhere was this concern more apparent than in the African orientation of the Comintern's Negro revolutionary directorate, the ITUC-NW. The amount of energy devoted to agitation in Africa by this and other Comintern affiliates, together with the attention directed toward the region in communist pronouncements, literature and scholarship during the twenties and thirties, all provide clear evidence that Africa, in its own right, had found a conspicuous place in Russian thinking long before the era of independence.

PURSUIT OF NATIONAL SECURITY

The primary motivation for Russian involvement in Africa was concern for the security of the Russian state. Although Africa's distance from Russia might at first glance have made its relevance to Russian security seem somewhat obscure, Kremlin leaders in both the Czarist and early Soviet periods nonetheless found ample reason to conceive of activity in Africa in terms of Russia's national interests.

During the Czarist period, for example, Africa played a dual role in Russian strategic calculations. In the first place, Czarist leaders were anxious to safeguard Russian maritime communications with the Far East. Particularly after the construction of the Suez Canal, it was recognized that a Russian presence near the mouth of the Red Sea would protect Russian shipping and prevent rival imperial powers—principally Great Britain—from obtaining a permanent foothold in north-eastern Africa and thereby threatening Russia's freedom of movement along the Suez route. At the same time, Czarist activity in Africa promised to contribute to a second strategic objective—weakening the imperial strength of Russia's adversaries. Notably in the context of heightened Anglo-Russian antagonism in the late nineteenth century, Czarist involvement in northeastern Africa presented the Kremlin with the opportunity both to gain allies against the British and to threaten Britain's all-important maritime route to India. The mere possibility of Russian moves at a point so vulnerable and so critical to the prosperity of the British Empire, it was felt, was sufficient to exact concessions at Britain's expense in areas more immediately vital to Russian interests—namely, Central Asia and the Far East.

Similar calculations figured significantly in the thinking of Soviet strategists.* However, the Soviets found additional, even stronger security-related justifications for active Russian involvement in the continent. After the Allied intervention in Russia, the task of preventing an imperialist attack against the Soviet Union by weakening the military position of Britain and France became a matter of highest priority. One method of dealing with the problem was to attempt to convince Negro colonial troops, who formed large contingents in the armies of both Britain and France, to refuse to serve in the armed forces of imperialism. Another far more ambitious approach was to promote widespread revolution in Negro African territories in the hope of weakening the hold of the imperialist powers over their colonies. In general, it was believed that by separating the colonial powers from their African sources of economic and military strength, Moscow could enhance the security of the Soviet Union and at the same time alter the world strategic balance in favor of the forces of socialism.

Thus, Russian security interests, whether they were manifested in the form of Czarist preventive imperialism or Soviet anti-imperialism, were the primary stimulus for Russian involvement in Africa. In certain fundamental respects, moreover, these interests produced a pattern of behavior toward Africa which was surprisingly uniform

---

* It is interesting, for example, that the strategic arguments presented in connection with the establishment of a Russian sphere of influence in Ethiopia during the Czarist period found renewed prominence in the writings of Soviet observers during the Italian-Ethiopian conflict in the 1930's. Probably in part as a result of their exposure to earlier Russian thinking, Soviet observers displayed not only a keen awareness of Ethiopia's importance as a "powerful lever for pressure against England," but also a precise knowledge of the ways in which this lever might be used to threaten the British position in Egypt and to interrupt Britain's communications with colonial Africa and India. (See P. Lisovskii, *Abissinskaia Avantiura Italianskogo Fashizma* [Moscow, 1936]: 129; G. Kreitner, *Abissiniia* [Moscow, 1932]: 32–35; and D. A. Ol'derogge, ed., *Abissiniia: Sbornik Statei* [Moscow, 1936]: 473ff. See also numerous articles on the Italian-Ethiopian war appearing in *Revoliutsionnyi Vostok* in 1935, especially Zusmanovich, "Italo-Abissinskaia Voinai; Pod'em Natsional'nogo Osvoboditel'nogo Odvizheniia," [nos. 2, 1935] and B. Aleksandrov, "Abissiniia" [no. 2: 138–51].)

over time. Both in the Czarist and in the prewar Soviet eras, for example, Russian involvement in Africa was largely a response to moves on the part of other powers. Just as the fear of European competition led Peter I and Uspensky to plan for the establishment of a Russian presence in Madagascar and Ethiopia, so European colonial entrenchment in Negro Africa provoked the Soviet regime to pursue revolutionary activity within the territories of its imperialist enemies. In neither the Czarist nor the Soviet period were unilateral Russian initiatives in Africa essential to even the most ambitious conception of Russia's strategic requirements.

In addition to its derivative character, Czarist and Soviet involvement in Africa was also remarkably constant in its anti-British orientation. Although the Soviets departed from Czarist practice by including France among Russia's enemies on the continent, they consistently upheld the tradition of Russian opposition to British power. During both the Czarist and the Soviet periods the most active phases of Russian involvement in Africa largely coincided with the years of most intense hostility toward Britain. In both periods it was only when relations with the British improved that Russians seemed willing to reconsider the fundamental premises of their African approach. In short, whether it was under the leadership of Czars or commissars, Russian energies in Africa were above all directed toward the destruction of the British Empire.

Finally, Czarist and Soviet policies in Africa were strikingly similar in the way in which ideology was used as the handmaiden for the pursuit of political objectives. Certainly it would be incorrect to insist that ideology as such played no part whatsoever in stimulating Russian involvement in Africa. On the contrary, both Slavophilism and communism were of real importance in predisposing Russians to take an active interest in this and other distant territories. The universalist pretensions of these faiths, moreover, served to convince Russians that they should concern themselves with the moral and political life of indigenous peoples and that they had a unique contribution to make to the social and cultural development of the Third World. What the Russian experience in Africa demonstrated, however, was that ideology served more often as an instrument than as a primary determinant of Kremlin policy. Not only was it adapted to conform to Russia's more concrete national objectives, but, as in the case of the Orthodox "church reunification" concept, it was consciously used as a cloak for concealing the less altruistic ambitions of the Russian state. As Uspensky, the apostle of Orthodox involvement in Africa, and Pavlovich, the prophet of communist penetration, so clearly recognized, Russia's military and political interests provided the major rationale for Russian activity beyond its territorial borders. The principal function of ideology, in effect, was to legitimize policies of realpolitik undertaken by Russian leaders and to reassure these leaders that in pursuing their nation's interests they were in step with the inexorable march of history.

PROMOTION OF INDIGENOUS NATIONALISM

In addition to betraying the security motives for Russian involvement in Black Africa, the prewar history of Czarist and Soviet activity in the region exposes the importance of indigenous nationalism as an instrument used by Russians to promote the objectives of their African policy. Indeed, from the time of Catherine the Great Russians demonstrated both an awareness of the disruptive potential of African nationalist sentiment and a practical ability to exploit this sentiment to the detriment of their imperial adversaries.

In terms of their intellectual background, Russians seemed particularly well qualified to become protagonists of African nationalism. Their readiness to accord it sympathetic recognition as a valid political phenomenon stemmed from essentially three sources. The first was the early Russian liberal belief, typified by the writings of Kovalevsky, that Negroes were human beings capable of political expression and cultural development. The second was the Russian inclination, in part an outgrowth of the Asiatic element in the Russian psychology, to question the intrinsic superiority of Western culture and to challenge the basic value of Europe's civilizing mission in the colonial world. Finally, there was the Russian conviction, as expounded by Lenin, that all peoples had an inherent right to national self-determination. All these things, coupled with a characteristic Russian empathy for the world's downtrodden, predisposed Russians to side emotionally with Negro Africans—a people, they discovered, who were the victims of an unusual coincidence of racial, political, and economic discrimination. Similarly, these attitudes enabled Russians to identify at an early stage the specific causes of

African discontent. More readily than other European observers, Russians were able to calculate the immense political and psychological effect upon Africans of such cataclysmic events as the First World War and the depression.

Also in terms of their practical experience, Russians historically were prepared to become active supporters of African nationalism. Although Czarist activities in Africa produced few lasting political rewards, Imperial Russia's involvement with the Mameluks, Mahdists, and Boers was useful in first exposing the Kremlin to the dynamics of African nationalism. Of still greater utility was Russia's experience in cooperating with Ethiopia. The relatively close relationship which developed between the Czarist and Ethiopian governments during the latter decades of the nineteenth century provided Russians with a first hand knowledge of African topography, customs, and political behavior. Perhaps most important of all, it made Russians graphically aware of the intensity of the African desire to be independent of European authority.

Possibly in part as a result of the Czarist experience, Russians after the revolution demonstrated an uncanny ability to detect early signs of anti-colonial discontent in Africa. During the first decade of Soviet power, they became vocal advocates of the cause of Negro nationalism and after 1928 became responsible, through the agency of the Comintern, for a series of enterprises designed to give operational support to the struggle for African self-determination. By the eve of World War II, in sum, Russia had become remarkably well-practiced in the technique of using African nationalism as a weapon in the political and ideological battle against European imperialism.

In order to establish contact with Negro Africans and give concrete expression to its pro-nationalist stand, Russia found it expedient to work through a variety of instrumentalities. Although support for the African nationalist cause was publicly expressed through journalistic and diplomatic channels, the real substance of Russia's African policy was communicated and executed in more indirect and covert ways.

In this context the importance of "front" organizations and clandestine agents is noteworthy. Used in connection with the earliest Czarist contacts with Negro Africa, these instruments were employed with varying success both before and after 1917. Just as the Kremlin used the Russian Geographical Society and the Palestine Society to camouflage its activities in northeastern Africa during the Czarist era, so the Comintern, itself an arm of the Kremlin, used the LAI, the ISH, and similar front organizations to shield its ambitions in colonial Africa during the period of Soviet rule. Russia's clandestine agents served a similar function. Whether they were secret envoys of the Czar, like Mashkov and Artamonov, or special agents of the Comintern, like Padmore and Wallace-Johnson, these individuals made important direct and indirect contributions to the Russian effort in Black Africa. Not only did they gather information on the region useful to Russian policy-makers, but they carried the message of Russian friendship into the interior of the continent.

With the expansion of Russian interest in Africa following the Bolshevik Revolution, additional strategies were devised for promoting the cause of African nationalism. In particular, given the lack of sufficient Russian cadres to conduct agitational work in Black Africa, the Soviets found it necessary to rely upon various groups of non-Russian activists who could be expected to advance Moscow's revolutionary and anti-colonial objectives.

The first persons to achieve prominence in this connection were American Negroes. Regarded as politically and socially more advanced than their African kinsmen, black Americans were accorded an important place in Comintern plans at the time of the Fourth Congress in 1922. Reliance upon American Negroes for revolutionary activity in Africa (which was in part an outgrowth of the policy of cooperation with the "nationalist bourgeoisie") was epitomized in the Comintern's attempt to forge ties with the Garveyite movement. Partially as a result of the problems encountered in this effort, Moscow came to realize the extent of ideological and practical difficulty involved in cooperating with black Americans. The Comintern soon began to recognize that American Negroes were far too concerned with their own racial problems and too much inclined to view African activity in terms of the American experience to be effective instruments for its purposes.

Largely unsuccessful in their attempt to use American Negroes, the Soviets turned to European communists as agents of revolution in Black Africa. Although the Comintern relied upon the efforts of European communists in varying degrees throughout the prewar period, it was during the years immediately following the Fifth Congress in 1924 that the revolutionary role of this group was accorded highest priority. In certain respects European communists seemed well qualified for their African assignment. As citizens of the metropolitan countries, these individuals enjoyed the advantage of comparatively easy access into African colonies. Moreover, as residents of the metropoles, they were in a position to conduct agitational work among the relatively large number of Negro Africans living in the capitals and port cities of Europe. Despite these advantages, however, European communists seem never to have fulfilled the Comintern's expectations in the years before World War II. Whereas the PCF could boast certain revolutionary successes in Negro Africa (particularly in Madagascar), the CPGB, at least until the late thirties, appears to have been almost totally negligent in pursuing its colonial duties. Throughout the prewar period both parties were the object of persistent Comintern criticism for their dilatory approach to colonial projects. Not only were their efforts in Africa hindered by the anti-European sentiments of the local population, but their devotion to the cause of colonial independence was clouded by their own national loyalties and by their desire to concentrate on the seemingly more important task of communist agitation at home.

Finally, discouragement with the performance of European communists led to Comintern reliance upon Africans themselves for implementation. Attempts had been made in the mid-twenties to recruit revolutionary workers from among the ranks of Negro Africans (cooperation with Tovalou Houénou was a case in point), but it was primarily after the Sixth Comintern Congress and the establishment of the ITUC-NW that emphasis was placed upon the direct training and use of African agitators. As part of the Comintern's more centralized and ideologically orthodox approach to the colonial world, the employment of trusted African revolutionaries became a distinguishing characteristic of Moscow's operational involvement in Africa during the early 1930's.

Combined with the propaganda and advisory activities of the RILU, Moscow's use of trained African agents proved to be the most successful of its revolutionary tactics. Through the efforts of the ITUC-NW and other Comintern front organizations, Moscow was able to recruit such influential African nationalists as Garan Kouyaté, E. F. Small, and I. T. A. Wallace-Johnson. After study in Russia and exposure to Comintern policy, these men became staunch supporters of the communist cause and avid admirers of the Soviet system. In the course of their subsequent organizational work among Africans in London, Paris, and West Africa, they communicated these attitudes together with many of the Comintern's more specific teachings. As colonial subjects, they were neither hindered by a pro-European orientation nor confronted by latent hostility and racial antagonism on the part of the black Africans among whom they worked. With this entrée into the African milieu, they were helpful as distributors of the *Negro Worker* and other Comintern propaganda. By the same token, as frequent voyagers between Moscow and Black Africa, they were a prime source of information on African conditions. It is not surprising, therefore, that the years of greatest Comintern reliance upon African agitators were also the years of greatest Comintern awareness of the political situation in colonial Africa.

Without denying the value of their contributions, however, it must be noted that the work of Moscow's African converts would have been virtually impossible without the combined efforts of a variety of auxiliary organizations and individuals. Reginald Bridgeman and the British LAI, for example, provided important moral and material support to E. F. Small and Wallace-Johnson in the course of their revolutionary activity in British West Africa. Similarly, the French Communist Party and the ILD gave continuing assistance to Garan Kouyaté and his followers in the LDRN, supporting them both financially and legally in their agitational efforts among French-speaking Africans. Ultimately, however, the most important organization in terms of its effect upon the course of Comintern activism in Black Africa was Moscow's Negro revolutionary directorate, the ITUC-NW. Through this instrumentality, George Padmore and his superiors in the RILU were able to plan and coordinate world communism's African initiatives. Moreover, during the period of most intensive Comintern involvement, Moscow was able to use this agency both as a command station to direct the work of its African representatives, and as a central headquarters for its ambitious propaganda effort in the Negro world.

Moscow's use of this broad spectrum of covert and indirect instrumentalities to conduct activities in Africa was testimony to the pragmatism of the Russian approach. It was also an acknowledgement of the formidable obstacles that prevented a more straightforward pursuit of Russian national objectives. To comprehend the nature of the Russian effort, it is necessary to recognize the magnitude of these obstacles and to understand the limitations which they imposed upon the conduct of Russian policy.

Certainly Africa's topography as well as its distance from Russia were factors which limited the scope of Russian involvement during both the Czarist and the Soviet periods. In addition, Russia was confronted by a series of political impediments of an equal, if not greater magnitude. Of these, perhaps the most aggravating were the anti-Russian policies of European powers.

Except for the brief period during which Nicholas II maintained a mission in Addis Ababa, Russia at no time before World War II possessed a diplomatic establishment in sub-Saharan Africa. Moreover, despite the attempts of the Czarist government to establish a foothold in Eritrea, Russia never occupied a territorial base which could be used as a source of supply for penetration of the interior. Thus, Russians always found themselves at the mercy of the colonial powers, who, more often than not, sought to exclude them altogether from their African possessions. Only by cooperating with the French were Russians able to establish a presence in Ethiopia at the end of the nineteenth century. By the same token, after 1917, British and French restrictions made it necessary for Russia to go to considerable lengths to ensure entry of Russian propaganda and agents into African colonies.

These external factors, however, proved less of a deterrent than Russia's own domestic problems. Throughout the entire prewar period, Russian projects in Africa were continually thwarted by competing demands upon Russia's human and material resources. Although the lack of resources does not appear to have curbed the nation's enthusiasm for African adventure, eventually the practical requirements of other foreign and domestic commitments were allowed to take precedence over allocations for African schemes. In short, whether it was war in the Far East during the Czarist period, or civil war, Stalinian purges, and anti-fascist preparations during the years of Soviet rule, Russia's foreign and domestic problems made it impossible for Russia to sustain a continuing involvement in regions as distant as Black Africa.

Finally, and ultimately perhaps most important, were the obstacles presented by Africans themselves. In this context observers of Soviet and African affairs have often singled out both the dearth of an African proletariat and the educational backwardness of the

African population as primary impediments to Russian penetration.[5] The Kremlin was, after all, addressing a people the vast majority of whom could neither read nor understand its political message. By the same token, Africa's class structure (the Comintern's optimistic assertions to the contrary notwithstanding) remained sufficiently primitive to present a continual stumbling block to communist efforts throughout the prewar period. But neither of these conditions can be considered as potentially preclusive to the spread of Russian influence as a third obstacle, perhaps less obvious than the rest. Ironically, this was the very force which Russians considered to be their greatest weapon—the desire of Africans for independence from external authority.

If Africans were opposed to European colonial domination of their continent, they were not likely to accept with equanimity the substitution of Russian for European control. Indeed, African nationalist thought contained, from its very inception, an element of independent-mindedness which created among Africans a healthy suspicion regarding the practical implications of Russian friendship. Whether reflected in the efforts of Ethiopia's Menelik II to preserve his freedom of maneuver when surrounded by Russian advisors,[6] or in the fears of members of the LDRN, the ARPS, and the NCBWA concerning Comintern influence over the policy of their organizations,[7] this suspicion of Russia's ultimate intentions was an important factor in circumscribing the success of Russian efforts and in predisposing Africans to question Russia's motives in the post-colonial era.

In sum, Russians were faced with a series of obstacles which made it extremely difficult to exploit African nationalism for their own political ends. The existence of these obstacles explains in large part the covert nature of Russia's African projects, as well as their apparently uncoordinated and sporadic character. Indeed, given the magnitude of these obstacles, it is remarkable that Russians were able to pursue any active involvement whatsoever on the African continent. That they attempted over a considerable period of time to influence the course of African politics was testimony not only to their spirit of adventurism and ideological fervor, but to their conviction that events in this distant land were relevant to their own national security. However valid this conviction, it explains, more than anything else, the significant record of Russian activism in Negro Africa before World War II.

12

Legacies of the Russian Experience

Although Russia's pre-1939 experience in Black Africa is of independent historical interest, the ultimate significance of this experience
rests in large measure upon its relevance to the development of
Soviet-African relations in the period after 1945. It is possible to
identify a number of ways in which Russia's prewar contacts, despite
their relatively limited scope, did have a concrete bearing upon the
ensuing course of Black Africa's political development and upon subsequent Soviet behavior toward the region. Thus, both from the
African and from the Russian point of view, the years before 1940
supplied a valuable historical prologue to the unfolding political
drama of the independence era.

THE IMPACT ON AFRICANS

In terms of its ultimate impact upon African political thought, Russia's prewar experience was not altogether unproductive. Although
many Africans were never exposed to Russian teachings, and others
were inclined to reject the revolutionary implications of Moscow's
political message, on balance the result of Russia's African venture
was to promote among a number of nationalist leaders both radical
political attitudes and a willingness to emulate the Soviet example.
In large measure, Moscow's success in this regard was attributable to
the efforts of the former ITUC-NW Secretary, George Padmore.

Much has been written concerning Padmore's break with the
Comintern and his consequent ability to give an anti-communist
direction to the thinking of virtually the entire first generation of
African independence leaders.[1] Padmore himself contributed heavily
to this impression in his cold war study *Pan-Africanism or Communism?*
(London, 1956). Primarily an attempt to wring Western economic
support for Africa by invoking the threat of communist penetration,

this book obscured both the real nature of Padmore's political convictions and the character of the advice which he gave to Africans during the period following his Moscow sojourn.[2]

In the years after 1934 Padmore retained his distrust of the Comintern and his distaste for the tyrannical aspects of Stalinian rule. Yet never did he allow himself to become an anti-communist. Although in later years he reportedly received attractive offers to divulge the details of his work for the Comintern, he always refused to do so, fearing that this information would be misused by Moscow's enemies.[3] Not only did he persist in using the Marxist-Leninist rhetoric characteristic of his Comintern years, but he remained until his death in 1959 both a devoted admirer of the Soviet system and a convinced disciple of Marx and Lenin.[4]

Through his writings and his close associations with influential African nationalists Padmore was able to bring these pro-communist sentiments to bear upon the central current of African political thought. Not long after his break with Moscow, he published a book entitled *Africa and World Peace* which, though banned in such British colonies as the Gold Coast, was widely read by the educated strata of English-speaking Africans.[5] Rather than an attack upon the Comintern, this book actually amounted to a renewal of the Comintern appeal to Africans to defend the Soviet Union by waging an "anti-imperialist fight" against the colonial powers.[6] In its pages Padmore sought both to apply Lenin's theory of imperialism to Africa and to present a bipolar view of international politics which depicted the socialist system as the source of peace and progress and the capitalist system as the source of strife and exploitation.[7]

Similarly, in his volume *How Russia Transformed Her Colonial Empire* (London, 1946), Padmore extolled the virtues of the socialist system, underscoring in particular the merits of the Soviet model of development. Impressed by Russia's military achievements during the war, Padmore explained Russia's wartime strength in terms of the country's ability to enlist active support from its national minorities, the former subject peoples of the Czarist Empire. As a result of the enlightened policies pursued by the Soviets, he maintained, these once primitive peoples of Central Asia had come to recognize the advantages to be derived from supporting the Soviet system and defending the U.S.S.R. against foreign aggression. In distinct contrast to the subject peoples of the British Empire, they had thrown themselves wholeheartedly into the war effort. In short, in Padmore's estimation World War II served to highlight the progress achieved by the Soviet system in underdeveloped regions and to confirm his belief that in education, economic organization, and race relations, the Soviet record was worthy of emulation.[8]

The continued allegiance to the communist cause which Padmore evinced in his writings after 1934 was also revealed in his activity among African nationalists. While living in London during the thirties and forties, Padmore clearly demonstrated that he had neither disassociated himself from his former Comintern colleagues nor abandoned his struggle for African revolution.*

It appears that Padmore's efforts during the years immediately following his rupture with Moscow were directed largely toward the formation of an organization which could replace the ITUC-NW as a command center for revolutionary operations in Africa. As early as 1934 he was at work with Garan Kouyaté in Paris, promoting the establishment of a body known as the Pan-African Brotherhood.[9] The same year he was also in contact with two of his other former associates, Wallace-Johnson and Azikiwe, who were then engaged in agitational work as "pioneers of Pan-Africanism" in the Gold Coast.[10] In conjunction with his efforts in their behalf, Padmore formed in London an ad hoc committee to support the demands of Gold Coast nationalists. Following the Italian invasion of Ethiopia in 1935, this ad hoc committee was reconstituted as the International African Friends of Abyssinia (IAFA). In 1937 the IAFA served, in turn, as the organizational framework through which Padmore coordinated the efforts of Wallace-Johnson, Kenyatta, C. L. R. James, and other

---

* Although the evidence is somewhat unclear, it is possible that Padmore even retained his connections with the CPGB after 1934. Hooker (*Black Revolutionary* [New York, 1967]: 56), for example, notes that Padmore refrained from criticizing the CPGB, while Coleman (*Nigeria: Background*: 208) makes an interesting reference to a break between Padmore and the British Communist Party in 1938. It is likely, moreover, that the British and American governments would have altered their attitude toward Padmore had he renounced his earlier communist associations. Instead, both remained highly suspicious of the former Comintern agitator. While the American government refused him entry into the U.S., the British government kept his activities under close surveillance. (See Roi Ottley, *No Green Pastures* [New York, 1951]: 68, and C.O. 323/1517/7046/3, no. 20, which notes that the M.I.5 maintained a watch on Padmore's London flat.) St. Clair Drake remembers that some persons in the British Foreign Office even went so far as to believe that Padmore's much heralded break with the Comintern was actually a calculated deception on his part. (Drake, interview.)

prominent Negro nationalists and formed a functional equivalent for the ITUC-NW—the International African Service Bureau (IASB).[11]

Although Padmore later insisted that the IASB was inherently neutral in its political orientation,[12] given the communist connections of its General Secretary, Wallace-Johnson, as well as the financial support it received from the communist-dominated LAI, it seems safe to conclude that the organization possessed a definite communist complexion. Not only was this noted by British police officials,[13] but it was revealed clearly in the IASB's own policy statements. The following manifesto issued by the IASB Executive in September, 1938, was typical of the organization's subversive propaganda among Africans:

> You are about to take part in an evil war. We denounce the whole gang of European robbers and enslavers of colonial peoples. . . . The Blacks everywhere under whatever flag, in war as in peace know but one goal— Independence. We call upon you to organize yourselves and be ready to seize the opportunity when it comes.[14]

Certainly such statements differed in no significant way from the revolutionary propaganda directed at Negroes from Comintern headquarters in Moscow.

Although little scholarly attention has been devoted to the IASB, it appears that the work of this organization was of fundamental importance in preparing the ground for African independence. Through the efforts of its General Secretary, Wallace-Johnson, for example, the IASB was able to carry its radical nationalist message to large numbers of West Africans, particularly in the Gold Coast and Sierra Leone.[15] Through branches in Brussels, Paris, and New York, moreover, it was able to establish contact with other Negro organizations and mobilize support for the African nationalist cause.[16] In London, it should be noted, the IASB did much to condition British public opinion to be sympathetic to the aims of African leaders. In this connection it published an information bulletin entitled *Africa and the World* (subsequently superseded by the *African Sentinel* and *International African Opinion*); it formed a bureau to provide speakers for public meetings—particularly labor gatherings, and, with the assistance of friendly Members of Parliament, it used the device of the parliamentary question to draw the attention of British officials to the plight of their African subjects.[17] Most important of all, however, was the role of the IASB in fostering the Pan-African movement.

Combining forces with W. E. DuBois' Pan-African Congress movement in 1944, it played an instrumental part in convening the famous Fifth Pan-African Conference in Manchester the following year. It was at this conference, in turn, that the concept of Pan-Africanism took on practical meaning and the independence movement in Negro Africa became a recognized political force on the international scene.[18]

In sum, through his activities in London, Padmore had succeeded in forming an organization which effectively carried on the tradition of revolutionary leadership established in the early 1930's by the ITUC-NW. Indeed, in all the IASB's varied undertakings the guiding hand of Padmore was ever-present. Whether it was in editing the organization's publications or in preparing the Manchester Conference, he applied his Comintern experience and injected his Marxist-Leninist faith into what increasingly became the program of African nationalism. If it would be too much to assert with C. L. R. James that "up to 1945 there was hardly a single African leader still active who had not passed through the school of thought and organization which George directed from Moscow,"[19] then it can at least be affirmed that from his London-based extension of that school Padmore brought his radical political influence to bear upon many of the individuals responsible for Black Africa's emancipation in the 1950's.*

Among these, none was more important than Kwame Nkrumah. The intimate personal and political relationship between Padmore and the Gold Coast nationalist first developed in London in early 1945. Introduced by their mutual friend James, the two men soon discovered that they shared much in terms of their ultimate ambitions for Africa. Nkrumah, fresh from his studies in the U.S., had become an ardent convert to the cause of African independence. In Padmore he found a reservoir of political knowledge and practical experience. As James observed, "nowhere else could Nkrumah have found such

---

* It should be noted that Padmore's position as Chairman of the IASB was by no means the only capacity in which he influenced African nationalists in London after 1934. In addition to his role as an author, Padmore was active as a political instructor both formally at the Independent Labor Party Summer School and informally at his London flat. He was also active in supporting the West African Students Union based in London, and undoubtedly exerted considerable influence over the radically nationalist and pro-Soviet positions taken by that body. (See Hooker, *op. cit.*: 46, 64.)

a combination of information and theory all centered on African emancipation."[20] For his part, Padmore saw in Nkrumah a source of energetic leadership for the realization of his long-cherished revolutionary objectives in West Africa.

In short, Padmore took Nkrumah under his wing—in both an ideological and a practical political sense. The effects of Padmore's tutoring were first apparent at the Manchester Conference of 1945 where Nkrumah, Co-Secretary of the meeting, delivered the major speech on the political situation in West Africa. Not only did this discourse reveal the influence of Padmore's Marxist-Leninist teachings, but it reflected Padmore's long-standing emphasis on West Africa as the principal starting point for the revolutionary movement in the rest of the continent.[21]

Almost certainly it was Padmore who put Nkrumah in touch with important left-wing elements in London. Through his efforts, Nkrumah met members of the radical West African Student Union and may well have made contact with representatives of the British Communist Party.[22] Probably as a result of Padmore's initiatives, Nkrumah was introduced to some of the more experienced African revolutionaries like Wallace-Johnson and Awoonor-Renner, who were temporarily in Britain following the Manchester Conference. It was largely as an outgrowth of these associations, in turn, that Nkrumah was able to establish, with Padmore's active support, a successor organization to the IASB, the West African National Secretariat (WANS).

Although the headquarters of the new organization was in London and its founders were principally English-speaking Africans, the scope of WANS activity was intended to encompass the entirety of West Africa, including the French territories.[23] Like the IASB, WANS could trace its ideological and organizational lineage directly to the ITUC-NW. In the tradition of the *Negro Worker*, for example, it published a pro-Soviet journal, *The New African*, under the editorship of Nkrumah. Similarly, in accordance with Leninist strategy, it formed within its leadership an elite corps of dedicated revolutionaries, known as "The Circle."[24] Clearly, if the West African Secretariat was not organized at the explicit instruction of Moscow, it conformed in structure and policy to the Comintern model of a European-based Negro revolutionary directorate.

Undoubtedly Padmore's influence was important in shaping the organizational structure and revolutionary strategy of Nkrumah's Secretariat. In addition, his pro-Soviet sentiments appear to have been influential in determining the organization's ultimate political objectives. Although Nkrumah, in his *Autobiography*, insists that the ambition of WANS at the time of its formation was to create a "Union of West African Socialist Republics," it seems more likely that the real objective of the organization was to establish what Padmore described as "a *Soviet* form of multi-national state."[25] Even Nkrumah himself, at his sedition trial in 1950, reportedly admitted that while in London he had made plans to form a "West African Soviet Republic."[26] In addition, his organization had, in 1946, published a short volume entitled *West African Soviet Union*, written by one of WANS co-founders, Awoonor-Renner. Not only did this book contain frequent citations from the Soviet Constitution and numerous laudatory references to the Soviet federal system, but it included a detailed program for an independent "federated peoples' " state of West Africa. Emphasizing the applicability of the Soviet multi-national structure, this program set forth, point by point, a precise political platform on behalf of "the exiled government" of West Africa—presumably WANS.[27]

In sum, Nkrumah's early contacts with Padmore and other former Comintern agents in London unquestionably influenced his political thinking on a number of critical issues. As British government sources observed, his "communist affiliations" in Britain imbued him with "a communist ideology which only political expedience" could blur.[28] Whether he later altered his position on the specific subject of a West African Soviet Republic is not of real significance. What is important, however, is that as a result of his London associations he acquired a marked sympathy for the communist system which remained with him throughout the years of his political prominence.

Although Padmore probably exerted his greatest influence over Nkrumah's political thinking during their years of association in London, his role as ideological and political mentor to the Gold Coast leader by no means ended after Nkrumah's return to Africa. It appears, in fact, that in 1947 Padmore was instrumental in persuading Nkrumah to take the fateful step of accepting the invitation of Danquah's United Gold Coast Convention Party to return to his native colony as secretary of the UGCC.[29] In 1950 Padmore himself was invited to Africa to witness the elections which propelled

Nkrumah's own Convention People's Party into power.[30] Although the exact extent of his advisory role at this time is not clear, he did keep in close and frequent touch with the Gold Coast leader during this crucial stage in the colony's political history. Whether it was in London, at Padmore's flat, or in the Gold Coast, where Padmore returned to tour the colony with the soon-to-be-installed Prime Minister, the two men were often together.[31] Shortly after the political successes of 1951, moreover, Padmore's counsel extended to the point of advising Nkrumah to opt for immediate independence, "even if such a course demanded armed insurrection."[32] Although Nkrumah did not heed this particular suggestion at the time, he later confided his feeling that perhaps Padmore had been right all along and that he had been wrong in allowing the British to procrastinate for another half decade before granting the Gold Coast full independence.[33]

With the emergence of the independent state of Ghana in 1957, Padmore assumed a position in the office of the Prime Minister. In this capacity he exerted a powerful influence over the early course of Ghanaian foreign policy.[34] Not only did he assist Nkrumah in his efforts to give leadership to the independence movement in the remaining colonial areas of Black Africa, but he aided the Ghanaian Prime Minister in his endeavors to create unity among the newly independent African states.[35] Toward these ends, he helped to convene the First Congress of Independent African States and was the principal organizer of the All-African Peoples' Conference, both of which were held in Accra in 1958.

Padmore's days of power were numbered, however, for in July, 1959, following a trip with Nkrumah to neighboring West African states, he became seriously ill and died shortly thereafter. By the time of his death, Padmore had become, in a very real sense, the "elder statesman" of the national revolutionary movement in Negro Africa. To his initiatives could be traced some of the most significant foreign policy undertakings of Nkrumah's new government. The Ghana-Guinea Union (later joined by Mali), for example, could be viewed in part as a product of Padmore's efforts.[36] Similarly, Ghana's clandestine attempts to promote revolution in other parts of Negro Africa were conducted in the conspiratorial tradition which Padmore had established and by the very office which he had created.[37] Nkrumah himself, who was not known for giving credit to others, recognized publicly on the occasion of Padmore's death the personal debt which he owed the Trinidadian revolutionary. "There existed between us," he declared, "that rare affinity for which one searches so long but seldom finds in another human being."[38] "One day," he prophesied, "the whole of Africa will surely be free and united and when the final tale is told the significance of George Padmore's work will be revealed."[39]

In a sense Nkrumah was not speaking for himself alone when he acknowledged his attachment to the fallen Pan-Africanist leader. Indeed, many of the Africans prominent in the national independence movement during the postwar period, like Nkrumah, owed a very profound ideological debt to the efforts of Padmore. Even those who had not known him personally were exposed, through his writings, to Marxist-Leninist ideology and in particular to the Leninist interpretation of imperialism. On this basis they in turn were able to construct a comprehensive theory of international politics which reflected Padmore's two-camp view of world affairs as well as his fundamental sympathy for the communist system.

In a broader context, Africa's debt to Padmore was also a debt to the world communist movement and to its efforts among Africans in the prewar period. Although Padmore's devotion to the cause of Negro liberation and his enthusiasm for the Pan-Africanist movement were not inspired solely by his work in Moscow, certainly his profound adherence to Marxism-Leninism and his commitment to African revolution were a direct outgrowth of his Comintern experience. It was in Moscow, for example, that Padmore became convinced of the notion that "imperialism divides; socialism unites."[40] It was there, moreover, that he came to recognize both the importance of concerted, pre-planned revolutionary action and the futility of isolated and spontaneous resort to force. In the final analysis, perhaps the most important lesson which Padmore learned from his period of Comintern activism was that Black Africa, more than any other region, was the logical starting point for the revolutionary movement which would ultimately lead to the liberation of his race. It was this belief, in turn, which enabled Padmore, long after his break with the Comintern, to dedicate his life to the cause of African independence.

Thus, largely through the efforts of Padmore and other former Comintern activists, Moscow was able to impart radical attitudes, if not a pro-Soviet political orientation, to a number of leaders of

African independence. In addition to influencing their political thought, however, Moscow was also able to transmit to Africans a knowledge of operational techniques and organizational strategy which was useful in the conduct of the struggle for independence. Although Africans no doubt learned many of the same techniques and received much the same tactical instruction from other, non-communist sources as well, by and large the Comintern legacy of practical operational advice was an important factor in shaping the subsequent pattern of African political behavior.

In the first place, as a result of their exposure to the Comintern, Africans learned important lessons in the use of political propaganda. Emphasis on establishing an independent press organ, for example, was a Leninist stricture which they obviously took to heart. Possibly as an outcome of association with Comintern representatives, many African nationalists such as Nkrumah and Azikiwe came to recognize the importance of forming local newspapers and of becoming themselves journalists in behalf of the cause of African independence. Even more significant, they came to understand certain fundamental axioms of an effective propaganda effort. If their ideas were to reach the widest possible audience, it was necessary that their message be reduced to direct and simple themes. By the same token, if they were to mobilize widespread popular support, it was important that they rely upon a series of brief but rousing political slogans. Finally, if they were to overcome colonial restrictions on their propaganda, it was imperative that they operate in the best tradition of clandestine activism. When the distribution of nationalist journals was curtailed by colonial authorities in the early postwar period, it was undoubtedly a source of inspiration as well as practical utility for Africans to recall the covert but effective manner in which Moscow had been able to circulate the *Negro Worker* during the difficult years of the 1930's.

Besides introducing Africans to the art of revolutionary propaganda, the Comintern experience was also instrumental in familiarizing them with another stratagem of modern politics—the use of international conferences. Although a number of African nationalists participated in Comintern-sponsored gatherings in the years before World War II, it was primarily through the efforts of George Padmore that Africa's leaders in the independence period came to know the more subtle techniques of conference management. Playing an active role in the preparation of the Hamburg Negro Workers' Conference in 1930 and the Moscow ILD Conference in 1932, Padmore had, by the time of his break with Moscow, acquired considerable skill as a conference organizer. He had learned, for example, that advance planning was essential if the conference was to follow a desired political line. In order to ensure that specific issues were discussed or that a given policy was adopted, resolutions had to be prepared in advance and the proceedings of the conference had to be carefully manipulated. In addition to proper planning, Padmore had come to recognize the indispensable role of a well-managed conference secretariat. Such a secretariat could both determine the political direction of the conference and ensure its own perpetuation as an ongoing institution. In short, Padmore had acquired a fund of knowledge and experience which he was able to apply at the pivotal Manchester Pan-African Conference of 1945 as well as at the widely-attended Conference of Independent African States and the All-African Peoples' Conference of 1958. Indeed, it is difficult to estimate the number of African leaders who were made aware of the art of conference organization as a result of this application of Padmore's Comintern experience.

Apart from their exposure to propaganda and conference techniques, Africans in the postwar period also appear to have been in some measure indebted to Moscow for another, more general lesson in operational strategy—emphasis on trade unionism as a primary political weapon. Partially as a result of the efforts of Wallace-Johnson and the activities of the French communist trade union, the Confédération Générale du Travail (CGT), nationalist leaders in both British and French West Africa came to recognize that labor agitation could indeed provide the principal ladder for the attainment of political power.

In British West Africa it was Wallace-Johnson, more than any other single individual, who put into practice the Comintern's syndicalist teachings. Beginning his activity in Nigeria in 1932, he had, by the time of World War II, amassed an impressive record of labor organization. In his native colony of Sierra Leone, for example, he had succeeded in establishing an entire network of labor unions, some of which were able to increase their membership and expand their base of political power during the war.[41] Although detained by the British during the course of the hostilities, Wallace-Johnson resumed his earlier organizational work in 1945, helping to establish the World Federation of Trade Unions (WFTU) in London and advising the British Trades Union Congress on questions of colonial policy.[42] Soon he became once again the object of widespread attention among West African nationalists.* In Nigeria, where left-wing trade unionism gained considerable momentum in the decade following the war, he was remembered for his pioneering role in the indigenous labor movement. Similarly, in Sierra Leone, in part as a result of his prewar organizational efforts, he found himself in a position of political prominence.[43] Although he never lived to see his native colony achieve independence (he died in Ghana in 1957, presumably while advising Nkrumah), he was able to communicate much of his activist political philosophy to the subsequent leadership of Sierra Leone under the Presidency of Siaka Stevens—men who consciously acknowledge their spiritual and practical debt to the former Comintern agitator.[44]

In French West Africa the Comintern's syndicalist approach was, if anything, applied on a broader basis than in the British colonies. This was largely a result of the efforts of the CGT, which embarked upon an energetic program of trade union organization in West Africa immediately following the war. So vigorous was this campaign, in fact, that by 1952 nearly half the 68,550 unionized French West Africans were affiliated with the French communist body.[45] In many territories CGT-inspired unions were the first indigenous organizations to attract a mass popular following.[46] From these unions, in turn, the nationalist movement in French Africa drew a large portion of its leadership. This close relationship between communist-led trade unionism and the nationalist movement was not accidental, however,

---

* For example, Wallace-Johnson appears to have won the particular esteem of Nkrumah, who described him as "the first labor organizer in West Africa." (*The Autobiography of Kwame Nkrumah* [Edinburgh, 1957]: 22.) Like his contemporaries in the Gold Coast, Nkrumah was very much impressed by Wallace-Johnson's article, "Has the African a God?," which he characterized as "the first warning puff of smoke that a fire had been lit, a fire that would prove impossible to extinguish." (*Ibid.*: 23.) Not only did Nkrumah work with Wallace-Johnson at Manchester and in WANS in London, but he found it useful to stop off in Sierra Leone to confer with his African colleague in the course of his return voyage to the Gold Coast in 1947—a visit which produced, in Nkrumah's words, "some important political contacts." (*Ibid.*: 64.) In sum, it seems safe to say that for Nkrumah, Wallace-Johnson, like Padmore, was a source both of moral inspiration and practical advice for the independence struggle.

for the CGT, in the early postwar period, had undertaken a series of measures designed to train African cadres not only for labor agitation, but also for political roles in the anti-colonial struggle. Acting in conjunction with WFTU, the CGT had organized conferences of African trade unionists (often in West Africa itself), opened a special "Ecole des Cadres" outside Paris, and offered scholarships for study in Eastern Europe to promising African students.[47] Although these efforts were comparatively limited in scope, they often produced striking political results. Sékou Touré, for example, who received CGT-sponsored training in Czechoslovakia, went on to become not only a coordinator of communist trade union activities in West Africa,[48] but the leader of Guinean independence and a friend of the communist world. Like many of his colleagues taught in communist schools, he owed much of his political success to the careful cultivation in his colony of a solid base of radical trade union support.

In addition to encouraging African nationalists to devote energy to the organization of trade unions in their respective colonies, Comintern teachings also helped to predispose them to concentrate attention on the mobilization of women and youth. Hardly a single nationalist party came to power in the postwar period which did not establish special branches to cultivate support from these two segments of the indigenous population. Although it is impossible to determine the extent to which this policy was influenced by Comintern teachings, it is probable that as a result of ITUC-NW propaganda and the prewar agitational efforts of Wallace-Johnson, many African leaders came to recognize the potential political power of the two groups. There is little question, for example, that the activities of the Youth League, with its special women's auxiliary, set important precedents for subsequent political development in both the Gold Coast and Sierra Leone. Its success in mobilizing a mass political following, moreover, may well have been responsible for encouraging Moscow to stress even more vigorously the politicization of women and youth in the postwar period.

Among those forms of organization recommended by the Comintern for the mobilization of youth, the "study circle" was particularly noteworthy in terms of its subsequent role in the African nationalist movement. Although there is little evidence that Africans followed the Comintern's recommendations concerning the establishment of such circles during the prewar period, immediately after the war several study groups of the type projected were formed among African nationalists and soon became important building blocks in the organizational structure of the independence movement.

For example, Nkrumah's well-known "Circle" (formed within WANS in London in 1946) began as just such a group of students. Formed ostensibly for the purposes of study and discussion, Nkrumah's circle became in reality the training ground for a corps of revolutionary activists.[49] Upon his return to the Gold Coast in 1947, one of Nkrumah's first moves was to establish a similar "Youth Study Group" in Accra. It was this organization, in turn, which served as the nucleus for Nkrumah's pioneering nationalist movement—the Convention People's Party.[50]

Similarly in French Africa, study groups along the lines recommended by the Comintern began to appear in the early postwar period. Largely as a result of the efforts of French communists, organizations known as *Groupes d'Etudes Communistes* (GEC) were formed in the urban centers of West and Equatorial Africa. In a political context in which the formation of communist parties was impossible, these groups served both as training centers for an important segment of the nationalist leadership[51] and as the spawning ground for a number of French Africa's mass political parties. In the French Congo (now the Congo People's Republic), for example, they formed the core of the *Parti Progressiste Congolais*, which dominated the politics of that colony between 1946 and 1955.[52] In Guinea and the French Soudan (now Mali) they figured significantly in the early development of the *Parti Progressiste de Guinée* and the *Parti Démocratique Soudanais*.[53] Most important of all, however, these communist study groups were instrumental in the formation and early policy direction of the *Rassemblement Démocratique Africain* (RDA), French Africa's first interterritorial political organization and the parent body to an impressive number of French West Africa's parties of national independence.[54]

It was largely through the RDA, in turn, that world communism made its most important organizational contribution to the postwar political development of Negro Africa. In structure as well as internal policy, the RDA resembled closely the model of the CPSU. Its principal founder, Gabriel d'Arboussier, like the organizers of the LDRN and the WAYL before him, was a confirmed Marxist-Leninist and an admirer of the Soviet political structure.[55] Accordingly, he induced the RDA to adopt concepts of elitist leadership and centralized authoritarian control borrowed largely from the PCF and the CPSU. In an effort to mobilize support from all segments of the French African population, moreover, he persuaded the organization to establish, in line with communist practice, RDA subcommittees in villages and districts, coordinating bodies on the territorial level, and a powerful politburo to direct the work of the entire party apparatus.[56] In a word, the RDA appears to have taken to heart Stalin's insistence on the need for a tightly controlled party structure. Thus the RDA Charter of Organization began by quoting the maxim made famous by the Soviet leader: "When the correct political line is laid down, organizational work determines everything, including the fate of the political line itself—its realization or its failure."[57] Indeed, the faith which it placed in the power of efficient organization to achieve political ends was evidence that the RDA had inherited not only the structure, but also the operational philosophy of the CPSU.

If the RDA represented a replica of the communist party apparatus, then the nationalist political parties which grew out of its regional sections mirrored correspondingly the Soviet-inspired organizational structure of their parent body. The *Parti Démocratique de la Côte d'Ivoire*, for example, began as the Ivory Coast section of the RDA and became, under the leadership of Félix Houphouet-Boigny, an effective nation-building party organized along communist lines.[58] Similarly, the *Union Soudanaise*, the *Parti Démocratique de Guinée*, the *Union Démocratique Nigérienne* (renamed *Sawaba*), and the *Union des Populations du Cameroun* all developed out of RDA sections and consequently owed their centralized party structure to the tightly-controlled organization from which they evolved.[59]

Thus, in form, if not in operational policy, African parties in the independence era were influenced significantly by the Soviet political model. To what extent this was a result of Moscow's prewar efforts to popularize Russia's achievements among Africans is of course difficult to say. Undoubtedly the willingness of certain nationalist leaders to form political structures according to the Soviet pattern was in part an outgrowth of postwar communist efforts in Africa as well as of the desire of Africans themselves to borrow organizational concepts from more developed political movements. Yet, whatever the ultimate explanation, it seems safe to assume that Moscow's relatively extensive propaganda effort in Black Africa before 1945 at least gave African leaders an initial acquaintance with the nature of the communist system and inclined them to look with favor upon the Soviet model of political development.

In sum, through the activities of the Comintern and its representatives, Moscow helped to transmit to Negro Africans radical political attitudes, a supporting ideology and a knowledge of specific techniques and strategies which were useful in the structural organization and practical conduct of the independence movement. In terms of such contributions alone, it can be argued, Russia's prewar experience had the effect of accelerating the pace of African political development. In addition, there were other, more general ways in which Russia, acting through the Comintern, served as a catalyst for the modernization process in Negro Africa. In evaluating the effect of Russia's prewar experience upon African politics, the importance of world communism's role as an agent of rapid political change should indeed be underscored.

There seems little question, for example, that the Comintern, with its emphasis upon reaching the majority of Africans, played an important part in politicizing new elements of the indigenous population. Its concentration upon labor organization and agitational work among women and youth was clearly a significant factor in bringing new strata of African society into the political system. As in the case of Wallace-Johnson's activities in Nigeria, the Gold Coast, and Sierra Leone, the Comintern helped to start the process of party organization in Negro Africa and contributed to the gathering momentum of anti-colonial feeling across a broad segment of African opinion.

The Comintern was also responsible for suggesting to Africans extra-constitutional shortcuts for achieving independence. As African participants at the Hamburg Conference of 1930 acknowledged, the Comintern opened their eyes to a whole new approach to the emancipation problem, the starting point of which lay well beyond the European systems of constitutional democracy. Whether or not Nkrumah followed Padmore's advice to opt for complete independence in the Gold Coast six years before it was constitutionally granted, or nationalist leaders in Sierra Leone accepted Wallace-Johnson's scheme for uncompromising struggle against colonial rule in that colony, as a result of communist teachings these and other African leaders came to realize that radical options were indeed open to them. They did not always heed the Comintern's advice, but the awareness of new and radical formulas for political action undoubtedly affected their conventional thinking and probably their subsequent political activity as well.

Perhaps even more significant as a catalyst for African emancipation was the role of the Comintern in facilitating intercommunication among African nationalists and in providing them with a nonimperial source of information on the outside world. At Comintern-sponsored gatherings in Western Europe and Russia, Africans from different colonies were able to meet and exchange views on political issues. Similarly, by their joint membership in the ITUC-NW and other Comintern-affiliated bodies, they were able to pool their knowledge of African conditions and give coordinated direction to the independence movement. Still more important as a channel of political communication was the relatively extensive Comintern propaganda network which Africans found at their disposal. In particular, the *Negro Worker*, with its clandestine system of distribution, served as an invaluable organ through which nationalists could transmit information and keep abreast of the progress of the independence struggle in other parts of the continent. By means of this and other Comintern publications, moreover, educated Africans were able to obtain a source of information on world affairs which was highly critical of the colonial system. By presenting them with the communist interpretation of the nature of imperialism, Comintern propaganda encouraged Africans to conceive of their problems in global terms. At the same time, by familiarizing them with the ideological and political issues of East-West conflict, this propaganda helped to prepare them for the bipolar international environment in which they were forced to operate during the early years of independence.

Finally, the Comintern added to the momentum of the independence movement by helping to break down tribal and religious barriers to political integration in African societies. Encouraging Africans to reject traditional institutions, Moscow repeatedly pointed out the importance of abandoning tribal animosities and of overcoming the conservative influence of Western religion. In place of the familiar loyalties to tribe and church, Africans were counseled to develop new faith in themselves as citizens of the twentieth century, capable of wielding both economic and political power. By helping to convince them that, as Wallace-Johnson put it, "we Africans are our own trustees,"[60] Moscow in a sense made its most important single contribution to the ideological progress of the liberation movement.

Thus, on balance, the effect of the Comintern effort was, from the African point of view, a modernizing one. Although Moscow's prewar revolutionary message did not provide the primary inspiration for Africa's rapid political evolution in the postwar period, it did serve as an influential factor in convincing Africans that national independence was not beyond their reach. The political thinking which Africans absorbed, the organizational and operational techniques which they inherited, and the modernizing political influences to which they were exposed as a result of Comintern efforts all left their mark upon the African elite and upon African attitudes toward colonial authority. Moscow may not have provided the original stimulus for the independence movement in Negro Africa, but it did unquestionably help to accelerate this movement and to incline it toward radical political solutions.

THE HERITAGE FOR RUSSIANS

The legacies which Africans inherited as a result of their relations with Russia in the prewar period belonged, in a real sense, to Russians as well. Clearly the Comintern's success in radicalizing elite African thought and in accelerating the African independence movement redounded to Russia's advantage in the post-World War II era. In addition to sharing the fruits of Africa's political development, however, there were other ways in which Russia benefited independently as a result of its long cultivation of African nationalism. Although on the surface Russia's rewards do not seem commensurate with the energy expended, in a broader sense its prewar experience can be viewed as essential preparation for subsequent Soviet involvement in the politics of independent Africa.

If only in terms of the knowledge and experience they acquired, Russians reaped significant benefits from their prewar interest in Negro Africa. As early as the mid-nineteenth century, Russians, like other Europeans, began to collect substantial amounts of data on the region, most of which was later published. Through the efforts of such explorers as Kovalevsky, Junker, and Eliseev, Russians gained detailed, firsthand information on the ethnology and economic life of northeastern Africa. Through the observations of yet other Russian travelers, notably officers like Artamonov and Bulatovich, they learned important strategic facts concerning the geography of the region and the military capabilities of its inhabitants. Most significant, from these early contacts, Russians acquired an understanding of political realities in Negro Africa and, in particular, an unusual appreciation of the extent to which Africans valued independence from European rule. Although after the revolution the Kremlin was no longer able to obtain information directly from Russian representatives in the field, through the covert channels of the Comintern it nonetheless managed to maintain an effective flow of data from Black Africa and to form a reasonably accurate estimate of the intensity of African nationalist sentiment. In effect, by World War II Russians had amassed a significant body of recorded information on Black Africa—one which was of subsequent academic and practical political use.

Of equal utility after 1945 was the practical experience in promoting African nationalism accumulated by Russians in the prewar period. Long before the era of Soviet military aid programs in Africa, Russians were assisting Ethiopians to draw up military plans, inviting them to tour Russia's own defense establishment, and exporting to them sizable consignments of the latest weapons. Similarly, a full quarter century before the massive Soviet propaganda campaign in Africa, Russians were training nationalist leaders in Moscow, appealing to Africans to follow the Soviet model of development, and sending communist agitators into African territories to distribute literature and otherwise incite anti-colonial unrest. However meager the immediate fruits of these efforts, they undoubtedly contributed to the evolution of Russian expertise in courting the favor of African leaders in the independence era.

The prewar interest which gave rise to a body of information and experience relating to Black Africa also generated the formation in Moscow after 1929 of a group of Soviet African specialists. Pursuing the path of Soviet academic interest in Negro Africa pioneered by Pavlovich, these men had, by the time of World War II, developed considerable skill in analyzing the region. They had made a particular effort to learn its languages; they had inquired in depth into its sociological peculiarities; they had carefully prognosticated its political future. Hence it was hardly surprising that these same African specialists were able to supply the leadership for the sudden expansion of Soviet academic interest in Black Africa in the mid-1950's and to provide practical counseling on African affairs to the post-Stalinian Kremlin leadership. By relying for advice upon such experts as Potekhin and Zusmanovich, the Khrushchev regime was able to benefit not only from the extensive background of knowledge on African politics which these individuals had absorbed, but presumably also from the personal contacts with nationalist leaders which they had established during the Comintern period. Surely it was not altogether by coincidence that within months of Ghana's independence Potekhin, the new dean of Soviet Africanists and a former Comintern colleague of Padmore, became the first Soviet scholar allowed to pursue research in Black Africa itself.[61]

The welcome accorded Potekhin in Ghana suggests a final advantage which the Soviets derived from their prewar support of African nationalism—the development of a political climate in Negro Africa which was conducive to further Russian involvement in the region. Although prewar Russian support for African nationalism by no means supplies a comprehensive explanation for the friendliness exhibited by Africans toward Russia immediately following independence, it does account for some of the emotional and even institutional foundations for the rapid proliferation of Soviet-African ties during the postwar era.

As noted previously, Africans developed in the early postwar period a number of political and trade union organizations similar to those existing in the U.S.S.R. What this meant for Russians in the independence era was the existence of an institutional framework through which they could easily establish fraternal ties with African organizations. Clearly, reciprocal exchanges were facilitated when African youth leagues could trade visits with parallel youth bodies in the U.S.S.R., when African trade unionists could compare notes with representatives from identical workers' organizations in the Soviet Union, and when delegations from African women's organizations could attend international conferences sponsored by similarly-constituted women's groups in Russia. In a way, Moscow appeared to be reaping the benefits of its earlier agitation in Africa. The trade union, youth, and women's organizations advocated by the Comintern in the prewar period had in fact come into being as national institutions in the independent African states. These, in turn, provided Russians with a series of political channels through which to extend their influence among the newly organized elements of the African population.

In addition to establishing fraternal ties with African organizations, Moscow also found it useful in the postwar period to do business with African leaders who had either received training in the U.S.S.R. or come into contact with former Comintern activists in Europe and Africa. Possibly as a result of the communist propaganda to which they had been exposed, many of these leaders seemed automatically inclined to suspect the motives of Western governments and to attribute friendly intentions to the Soviets. Indeed, the emergence of a cadre of nationalist leaders sympathetic to the communist message was one of the most significant rewards which Russia could claim as a result of its prewar activities among Africans.

Finally, even those African leaders least sympathetic to the communist system nonetheless evinced a certain spirit of appreciation toward Russia for the prewar support which it had accorded the nationalist cause. When Haile Selassie of Ethiopia visited Moscow in 1959 he specifically recalled the valuable aid which Czarist Russia had extended his country at a critical point in its struggle to maintain independence from European domination.[62] By the same token, West African nationalists in the postwar period by no means forgot the moral and material assistance which Soviet Russia had given them during a period when success seemed beyond their grasp. In short, by actively supporting African nationalism at a time when its friends were few, Russians created for themselves a reservoir of trust and goodwill upon which they could draw in the years after Africa had taken its independent place in the international arena. As much as anything else, the mood of friendliness engendered by Russians during the prewar period explains the receptivity of black Africans to a Soviet presence in their region in the years following the collapse of colonial rule.

Thus, the path of Russia's first steps in independent Africa was paved by many years of diligent courtship of African nationalism. After the death of Stalin, when Russia emerged as an open competitor for the ideological and political allegiance of the Third World, it came to Black Africa not as a stranger to the politics of the region but as a tested defender of the struggle of Africans for liberation from imperial rule. This advantage may not have been enough to ensure the success of communist revolution in Africa, but it was sufficient to provide Russia with a valuable entrée in the post-independence African political scene. It was perhaps in this respect that the Soviets ultimately derived their most significant practical reward from the Russian relationship with Black Africa before World War II.

A Note on Sources

Despite the inaccessibility of Russian government archives, a considerable amount of authoritative material is available which sheds light on the political contours of both Czarist and prewar Soviet involvement in Africa. With respect to the period before 1917, much useful information can be found by consulting the works of various Soviet scholars, who, although writing on essentially non-political subjects, based their research upon Czarist archival sources. Among primary materials, of particular value are the detailed diaries of Count V. N. Lamsdorff (principal adviser to Foreign Minister de Giers and himself Russian Foreign Minister from 1900 to 1906), and the diplomatic records of the French government (compiled in *Documents Diplomatiques Français*). Perhaps most illuminating of all are the travel diaries kept by the Russians who visited Africa in the course of the nineteenth century. An impressive number of these diaries, both in published and manuscript form, is to be found in the Library of Congress in Washington, D.C.

Material for the post-1917 period, was obtained from three sources: specialized Soviet literature on Black Africa; publications of the Comintern and its affiliates (including official accounts of Comintern gatherings); and documents contained in the colonial archives of the British and French governments.

Of special importance in tracing the evolution of Soviet attitudes toward Black Africa were articles contained in Russian journals devoted to the problems of the Third World. Among these, *Zhizn Natsional'nostei* ("Life of the Nationalities"), *Novyi Vostok* ("New East"), and *Revoliutsionnyi Vostok* ("The Revolutionary East") proved particularly useful. Similarly, books written by men like M. P. Pavlovich and A. Z. Zusmanovich, who were closely associated with the formation of Soviet policy, were extremely valuable in exploring the nature of early Soviet attitudes.

For understanding the contours of early Soviet policy, the wide variety of Comintern publications dealing either directly or indirectly with Black Africa provided the prime source. For example, the stenographic accounts of relevant Comintern Congresses (notably the Fifth and Sixth) proved most useful in revealing the content of

Comintern policy. Similarly, specialized periodicals subsidized by the Comintern such as the *Negro Worker* and *Le Cri des Nègres* were of value in shedding light upon Moscow's attitudes toward Black Africa and in revealing the outlines of Comintern activism in the region. Also of importance were Comintern-sponsored books and pamphlets such as James Ford's *Economic Struggle of Negro Workers* and George Padmore's *Negro Workers and the Imperialist War.* Perhaps the single most valuable source for determining the substance of Moscow's relationship with Black Africa was the *International Press Correspondence of the Comintern (Inprecorr)*, published bi-weekly in English, French, and German from 1921 through 1937. Essentially a compilation of articles and news releases emanating from Comintern headquarters, *Inprecorr* supplied journals around the world with information concerning the progress of the revolutionary movement. Particularly from 1928 through 1935 it contained a considerable quantity of material relating to Black Africa.

Probably the most reliable source of information on the actual implementation of Comintern policy is the material contained in the archives of the British Colonial Office in London and the French Ministry of Colonies in Paris. With regard to this material, however, a problem of concealment exists. If the British and French were diligent in their efforts to keep informed concerning unrest in their colonies (by sending native informers to African political gatherings, by keeping close watch over the African press, etc.), they were no less energetic in their attempts to shield this information from outside observers. The British authorities in particular seem to have been eager to "destroy under statute" politically sensitive material relating to subversive activities in their colonies. Despite these efforts, however, much material has survived in the form of newspaper clippings, surveillance reports on African political agitation, confidential departmental notes, and secret communications between officials of the Colonial Ministries and administrators in the field. Since this material provides a unique view both of the nature of communist activity and the extent of British and French fears concerning the effects of Comintern agitation, it was essential for this study.

Newspapers published by African nationalists during the prewar period provided useful information concerning Comintern policy implementation. Incomplete sets of these papers are to be found in the newspaper collections of the Bibliothèque Nationale in Paris and

Versailles and of the British Museum in Colindale. Some of the more important articles from these papers are contained in the British and French colonial archives.

NOTES

PART I

CHAPTER ONE

1 It is interesting to note that in the year 1001 the famous Kievan Prince Vladimir is believed to have sent an ambassador as far south as Egypt. (See Makarii, Bishop of Kharkov, *Istoriia Russkoi Tserkvi*, I [2nd ed.; St. Petersburg, 1868]: 230.)

2 Letter of instruction from Peter I to Admiral Wilster, British Museum, addition no. 21259/71. Peter asked the Admiral to persuade the Madagascan king to pay a visit to Russia and "by all means to learn from him whether he wishes to have commerce with us." (*Ibid.*: paragraphs 5, 6.)

3 A. I. Zaozerskii, "Ekspeditsiia na Madagaskar pri Petre Velikom," *Rossiia i Zapad*, I (1923): 95.

4 *Ibid.*: 96, quoting Peter's instructions to Wilster.

5 *Loc. cit.* This conclusion is that of Zaozerskii.

6 It is probable that the indefatigable Czar, had he lived longer, would have pursued this enterprise. It is known that he received the news of the failure of the mission very badly, insisting that the vessels either be repaired or replaced. (*Ibid.*: 101.)

7 *Ibid.*: 92–94.

8 See M. de Taube, "Paul Ier et l'Ordre de Malte," *Revue d'Histoire Moderne*, 1930, no. 27: 161–77.

9 See Sergius Yakobson, "Russia and Africa," in I. J. Lederer, ed., *Russian Foreign Policy* (New Haven, 1962): 456. The Russian government was closely associated with the formation of the "Septinsular Republic" in the Ionian Islands (1800–07). The British government, which subsequently seized the islands, recognized their strategic importance as part of "a chain of Mediterranean garrisons which secured our Indian Empire." (D. A. Farnie, *East and West of Suez* [Oxford, 1969]: 4, quoting Disraeli.)

10 M. G. Kokovtsov, *Opisanie Arkhipelaga i Varvariiskago Berega* ("Description of the Aegean and the Barbary Coast") (St. Petersburg, 1786): i. Theoretically at least, this was an important precedent for later Russian support of the Negro liberation movement in Africa. Such a parallel was in fact drawn by Alexander Pushkin, himself descended from an African Negro. In June, 1824, when the issue of Greek independence was again current, he wrote to Prince Viasemski, "It is permissible to judge the Greek question like that of my Negro brethren, desiring for both deliverance from an intolerable slavery." (Quoted by Harold Acton, "Pushkin and Peter the Great's Negro," in Nancy Cunard, ed., *Negro Anthology* [London, 1934]: 570.)

11 Kokovtsov, *op. cit.*: 82, 127. It is possible that Russia was anxious to acquire its own port facilities on the southern shore of the Mediterranean even at this early date.

12 See D. Urquart, *The Progress of Russia in the West, North, and South* (London, 1853): 412, who reports that Catherine regarded Greece and Egypt as the two "horns of the crescent, of both of which that luminary had to be shorn before . . . it could lapse into her amorous embrace."

13 Yakobson, "Russia and Africa," *Slavonic Review, op. cit.*: 10.

14 F. J. Cox, "Khedive Ismail and Panslavism," *Slavonic and East European Review*, December, 1953: 153.

15 Gabriel Hanotaux, ed., *Histoire de la Nation Egyptienne* (7 vols.; Paris, 1931), V: 194.

16 Halford Hoskins, *British Routes to India* (New York, 1966): 37, citing India Office, London, Factory Records VI, September 24, 1787.

17 Yakobson, "Russia and Africa," in Lederer, *op. cit.*: 456. See also Hanotaux, *op. cit.*: 194–95, and Cheikh Abd-el-Rahman El Djabarti, *Merveilles Biographiques et Historiques* (9 vols.; Cairo, 1890), IV: 173.

18 See El Djabarti, V, *ibid.*: 37–38. The text of Catherine's letter was approximately as follows: "Be careful of yourselves and throw out the Ottomans who are going to implant themselves in your country; place yourselves under our protection, select leaders from among yourselves, fortify your ports, keep whoever tries from entering them, unless it is for commercial purposes; do not fear anyone, for we are capable of protecting you against everyone. Name governors to act in your behalf in Syria, as you did before, and leave us the ports. We are sending you enough ships and enough sailors and soldiers; we have all the money and all the men that you will ask of us, and even more than you can imagine." (*Ibid.*: 39. Catherine's letter appears in this source paraphrased in French. Hanotaux, *op. cit.*: 195, also refers to this letter.) Although a Russian frigate and two troop transports arrived at Damietta in mid 1788, they were too late to give effective assistance to the Egyptians. (See El Djabarti, V, *op. cit.*: 32, 38.) Moreover de Thonus, who made the mistake of persisting in the effort to create an anti-Turkish alliance with the Egyptians, was murdered for his role in the intrigues. (See Hanotaux, *op. cit.*: 195.)

19 On October 27, 1788, for example, the French Consul in Egypt, a M. Magallon, reported to his government that "the Russians have had designs on this rich kingdom for some time. If the Mameluk government is not overthrown altogether by its [Ottoman] overlord, they will one day find the means for accomplishing their project." (Cited in Hanotaux, *loc. cit.*)

20 See Urquart, *op. cit.*: 413, 416.

21 Yakobson, "Russia and Africa," *Slavonic Review, op. cit.*: 15.

22 *Loc. cit.*

23 *Loc. cit.*

24 See D. Tsvetaev, "Snosheniiia s Abissiniei," *Russkii Arkhiv*, 1888, no. 2: 206–09.

25 *Loc. cit.*

26 See Y. M. Kobishchanov, "From the History of Relations between the Peoples of Russia and Ethiopia," in *Russia and Africa* (Moscow,

26 1966): 160–61. See also S. L. Miliavskaia, "Information about Africa in 18th Century Russia," *Russia and Africa, ibid.*: 41–42.

27 Miliavskaia, *op. cit.*: 42–43.

28 See Kobishchanov, *op. cit.*: 162 and Carlo Conti Rossini, *Italia ed Etiopia dal Trattato d'Ucciali alla Battaglia di Adua* (Rome, 1935): 107.

29 V. Federov (V. F. Mashkov), *Abissiniia* (St. Petersburg, 1889): 36. F. Volgin, *V Strane Chernykh Khristian* (St. Petersburg, 1895): 54 refers to another letter which passed between the two emperors—one from Nicholas to Theodore.

30 Vicomte de Constantin, "Une Expédition Réligieuse en Abyssinie," *Nouvelle Revue*, February 1, 1891: 463.

31 The bulk of Uspensky's writing on Ethiopia is contained in a four-part article entitled "Tserkovnoe i Politicheskoe Sostoianie Abissinii s Drevneishikh Vremen do Nashikh Dnei" ("The Ecclesiastical and Political Status of Abyssinia from Earliest Times until the Present"), in *Trudy Kievskoi Dukhovnoi Akademii*, 1866, nos. 3–6.

32 *Ibid.*, no. 5: 5.

33 *Ibid.*: 6–7.

34 See, for example, *ibid.*, no. 4: 556–604 and no. 5: 3–32.

35 Uspensky, "Uchastie Rossii v Sud'be Abissinii," in *Trudy Kievskoi Dukhovnoi Akademii*, 1866, no. 8: 415–40.

36 Jesman, *op. cit.*: 39.

37 Uspensky, "Sostoianie Abissinii," *op. cit.*, no. 4: 556f.

38 See Uspensky, "Uchastie Rossii," *op. cit.*: 420–38.

39 Uspensky, "Sostoianie Abissinii," *op. cit.*, no. 3: 344.

40 Uspensky, "Uchastie Rossii," *op. cit.*: 424–25.

41 *Loc. cit.*

42 *Loc. cit.* In arguing against the proposed visit to Ethiopia of Bishop Cyril, his successor in Jerusalem, Uspensky indicated that the Ethiopian Emperor was far more interested in building a gunpowder mill and a canon foundry than in engaging in theological dialogues with the Russians. (*Ibid.*: 434.)

43 In addition to the mutual exchange of official ecclesiastical emissaries, Uspensky probably had in mind the ordination in Russia of several Ethiopian bishops. He emphasized, however, that the theological foundations for such a solemn step toward union be well prepared in advance. (*Ibid.*: 431f.)

44 *Ibid.*: 432.

45 *Ibid.*: 422.

46 Uspensky, "Sostoianie Abissinii," *op. cit.*, no. 5: 6f.

47 *Ibid.*: 6.

48 See Uspensky, "Uspekhi i Neudachi Nemetskikh Missionerov vo Vnutrennei Afrike," in *Trudy Kievskoi Dukhovnoi Akademii*, 1866, no. 10: 289ff.

49 See E. P. Kovalevsky, *Puteshestvie vo Vnutrenniuiu Afriku* ("Travels in the Interior of Africa"), (2 vols.; St. Petersburg, 1849), I: 144–45, who observed of Father Rylo's plans, "if religious ideas do play a part in them, then only incidentally, as a means but not an aim." In a conversation with Rylo in Khartoum, Kovalevsky learned that the priest was contemplating the establishment of a colony in a spot which is now on the border of Ethiopia and the Sudan.

50 Uspensky, "Sostoianie Abissinii," *op. cit.*, no. 6: 167.
51 Uspensky, "Uchastie Rossii," *op. cit.*: 416.
52 Uspensky, "Sostoianie Abissinii," *op. cit.*, no. 6: 164.
53 Uspensky, "Uchastie Rossii," *op. cit.*: 416.
54 Uspensky, "Sostoianie Abissinii," *op. cit.*, no. 6: 164.
55 Uspensky, "Uchastie Rossii," *op. cit.*: 416–17.
56 Uspensky, "Sostoianie Abissinii," *op. cit.*, no. 5: 17–18.
57 Uspensky, "Uchastie Rosii," *op. cit.*, 418. In 1865 Theodore imprisoned the new bishop sent from Alexandria to head the Ethopian church. (Jesman, *op. cit.*: 38.)
58 Uspensky, "Uchastie Rossii," *op. cit.*: 418.
59 *Loc. cit.*
60 *Loc. cit.* See also: 428.
61 See Jesman, *op. cit.*: 44.
62 Foreign Minister Nesselrode had, for example, received reports from Russia's Consul General in Alexandria, Colonel Duhamel, concerning the incursions of Ethiopian military forces into Upper Egypt and the inability of the Egyptians to expel them. (Dispatch dated October 2, 1837, in René Cattaui, ed., *Le Règne de Mohammed Aly d'après les Archives Russes en Egypte* [3 vols.; Rome, 1931–36], II: 476.)
63 Letter in the Central Government Historical Archives, Leningrad, quoted in Maria Rait, "Russkie Ekspeditsii v Efiopii v Seredine XIX—Nachale XX vv." in I. I. Potekhin, ed., *Afrikanskii Etnograficheskii Sbornik*, I (*Trudy Instituta Etnografii*, XXXIV) (Moscow, 1956): 230. This article makes extensive use of Russian government archives, including the archives of the Czarist Foreign Ministry.
64 These included, for example, the Military-Topographical Department of the Army and the Hydrographic Department of the Navy. (See L. S. Berg, *Vsesoiuznoe Geograficheskoe Obshchestvo za Sto Let, 1845–1945* [Moscow, 1946]: 35, 37, 39.)
65 On January 12, 1849, he read a report on his African travels to one of its general meetings. (See Russkoe Geograficheskoe Obshchestvo, *Izvestiia* [Imperial Russian Geographical Society, "News"], 1849, no. 1: 9–15.)
66 See Nesselrode to Vronchenko, in Rait, *op. cit.*: 230. This passage is quoted in L. Y. Kubbel, "The Expedition of Y. P. Kovalevsky to Egypt and the Sudan in 1847–48," in *Russia and Africa, op. cit.*: 119.
67 See Kubbel, *ibid.*: 120.
68 Rait, *op. cit.*: 227.
69 A. A. Shiik, "Iz Istorii Russkoi Afrikanistiki," *Sovetskaia Etnografiia*, 1946, no. 2: 174.
70 Uspensky, *Kniga Bytiia Moego* (St. Petersburg, 1896): 306. See also B. A. Val'skaia, *Puteshestviia Egora Petrovicha Kovalevskogo* (Moscow, 1956): 119.
71 Alan Moorehead, *The Blue Nile* (New York, 1962): 201.
72 Kovalevsky, II, *op. cit.*: 39.
73 M. P. Zabrodskaia, *Russkie Puteshestvenniki po Afrike* (Moscow, 1955): 18–19.
74 *Loc. cit.*
75 Kovalevsky, II, *op. cit.*: 36.
76 *Ibid.*: 54ff.

77 *Ibid.*: 35–36.
78 F. I. Tiutchev, "Russkaia Geografiia," in *Polnoe Sobranie Stikhot-vorenia*, II (Moscow, 1934): 13.
79 See Sir Peter Wyche, ed., *A Short Relation of the River Nile, or its Source and Current* (London, 1669). The Blue Nile originates in Lake Tana, situated in the mountains of northwestern Ethiopia.
80 Moorehead, *op. cit.*: 201.
81 See *Bibliografiia Afriki* (Moscow, Institut Afriki, 1964): 151 for numerous titles relating to Baker's explorations, including, for example, *Puteshestvie S. U. Bakera k Istokam Nila* (3rd ed.; Moscow, 1887).
82 "Pokhod Anglichan v Abissinii v 1867–68 Godakh," *Voennyi Sbornik*, Vol. 74 (1870): 35–58, 253–81, and Vol. 75 (1871): 59–88.
83 Farnie, *ibid.*: 149–50. The S. S. *Nakhimoff* of the Odessa-based Russian Steam Navigation Company arrived in Bombay in March, 1876, Farnie observed, "ending the British monopoly of the eastern seas and causing more concern to the Government of India than any other vessel using the canal." (*Loc. cit.*)
84 Russia occupied the Amur region in 1858 and established Vladivostok in 1860. It is to be remembered in this context that through service on the Trans-Siberian Railroad was not inaugurated until 1903.
85 Farnie, *op. cit.*: 237–38.
86 See Cox. *op. cit.*: 151–67.
87 Farnie, *op. cit.*: 242.
88 Yakobson, "Russia and Africa," in Lederer, *op. cit.*: 457.
89 Farnie, *op. cit.*: 278–79.
90 On July 5, 1877, Ismail closed the canal to all Russian vessels. (*Ibid.*: 264.)
91 Letter of Foreign Minister de Giers to the Russian Consul General in Egypt, I. M. Lex, December 10, 1881, as cited in G. A. Nersesov, "The Egyptian Crisis of 1881–82 and Russian Diplomacy (from Archival Material)," *Russia and Africa, op. cit.*: 312.
92 Foreign Minister Lobanov-Rostovsky, quoted in Hanotaux, *op. cit.*, VII: 182.
93 Curzon, *op. cit.*: 112.
94 Quoted in Tsvetaev, *op. cit.*: 205.

CHAPTER TWO

1 Sergius Yakobson, "Russia and Africa" (part 2), *Slavonic and East European Review*, XIX, 1939–40: 164.
2 See Czeslaw Jesman, *The Russians in Ethiopia* (London, 1958): 26f.
3 Cited in Vicomte de Constantin, "Une Expédition Réligieuse en Abyssinie," (part 2), *Nouvelle Revue*, February 15, 1891: 681.
4 See F. Volgin, *V Strane Chernykh Khristian* (St. Petersburg, 1895): 545, and Jesman, *op. cit.*: 21.
5 Constantin (part 2), *op. cit.*: 690, quoting a speech delivered by the French consul in Jidda, January 12, 1889, welcoming the stopover of Ashinov's colonial expedition.
6 Letter from French Foreign Minister Goblet, May 22, 1888, to M. Laboulaye, French Ambassador in St. Petersburg, citing information

furnished him by the Russian Minister of the Navy, Admiral Krantz.
Documents Diplomatiques Français (hereafter DDF), Série 1ᵉ (1871–1900), VII: 132.

7 Letter of Pobedonostsev to Alexander III, July 16, 1888, in K. P. Pobedonostsev, *Pisma Pobedonostseva k Aleksandru III* ("Letters of Pobedonostsev to Alexander III"), II (Moscow, 1925): 187.

8 *Loc. cit.*

9 Letter from Baranov, September 20, 1888, to Alexander, quoted verbatim in V. N. Lamsdorff, *Dnevnik* ["*Diary*"], *1886–1890* (Moscow, 1926): 132–33.

10 *Ibid.*: 133.

11 *Loc. cit.*

12 K. P. Pobedonostsev, *Pisma i Zapiski* ("Letters and Notes"), II (Moscow, 1923): 828.

13 Lamsdorff, *op. cit.*: 132.

14 *Ibid.*: 134.

15 Jesman, *op. cit.*: 15, 28. Whether the *Manjur* under Captain Shchukin, which arrived in Aden at the time Ashinov's followers were setting up New Moscow, was sent in order to furnish protection to the Russian colonists, or whether it was sent on an independent investigative mission, is unclear. In any case, Shestakov's sudden death and his replacement by a non-Slavophile Naval Minister put an end to such measures in behalf of Russian expansionism. (*Loc. cit.*)

16 Viscomte de Constantin, "Une Expédition Réligieuse en Abyssinie," *Nouvelle Revue* (Part I), February 1, 1891: 474. See also Pobedonostsev, *Zapiski, op. cit.*: 846–47.

17 See T. G. Stavrou, *Russian Interests in Palestine, 1882–1914* (Thessaloniki, 1963).

18 *Ibid.*: 126.

19 See Jesman, *op. cit.*: 9ff.

20 See, for example, the excellent biography by Robert Byrnes, *Pobedonostsev, His Life and Thought* (Bloomington, Indiana, 1968): 237, which notes that "Pobedonostsev had been an eager supporter of the expedition."

21 Volgin, *op. cit.*: 56–57.

22 Pobedonostsev, *Pisma k Aleksandru, op. cit.*: 187.

23 Pobedonostsev, *Zapiski, op. cit.*: 903.

24 Letter from Baranov to Alexander, cited in Lamsdorff, *op. cit.*: 132–33.

25 L. Nikolaev (a member of Ashinov's expedition), *Ashinovskaia Ekspeditsiia* (Odessa, 1889): 10. On the way to Tajura, members of the expedition reconnoitered British and Italian naval vessels and on several occasions were asked to be prepared to meet any hostile action with gunfire. (*Loc. cit.*)

26 Lamsdorff notes that the Russian Ambassador in Paris heard reports to this effect. (Lamsdorff, *op. cit.*: 148.) French diplomatic documents reveal, moreover, that the Italian government did not hesitate to keep France fully informed concerning Ashinov's movements— probably in hopes that the latter would prevent disembarkation of the Cossacks. (DDF, VII: 314.)

27 See William Langer, *The Franco-Russian Alliance, 1890–1894* (New York, reprinted 1967) for a discussion of this subject.

28 *Ibid.*: 346.
29 Constantin (part 2), *op. cit.*: 684.
30 *Loc. cit.* Constantin maintains that French Prime Minister Floquet approved of the scheme—at least to the extent that he did not act to prevent the departure of the Ashinov expedition.
31 Nikolaev, *op. cit.*: 43.
32 Jesman, *op. cit.*: 15.
33 Lamsdorff, *op. cit.*: 108. A similar text appears in DDF, VII: 335, dated February 6, 1889.
34 Telegram from Foreign Minister Goblet to Ambassador Laboulaye, February 20, 1889, DDF, VII: 347.
35 Lamsdorff, *op. cit.*: 124.
36 Lamsdorff, *op. cit.*: 124. According to de Giers, the Czar's annoyance with Ashinov reached the point of wishing that the French might do away with the adventurer altogether. (*Loc. cit.*)
37 *Ibid.*: 125.
38 See DDF, VII: 345ff.
39 Telegram of Goblet to Laboulaye, February 20, 1889, DDF, VII: 347. French soldiers supervising the evacuation of Sagallo told the Russians: "Your government left it to us to deal with you as with pirates." (Nikolaev, *op. cit.*: 57.)
40 Goblet to Laboulaye, *op. cit.*, DDF, VII: 346.
41 Jesman, *op. cit.*: 13. See DDF, VII: 345, for the text of the telegram sent by de Giers to the Russian Chargé d'Affairs in Paris, February 4, 1889, asking that the French government be informed of the Russian decision and reminded that it would take a certain amount of time to put it into effect.
42 See Jesman, *op. cit.*: 15–16.
43 Lamsdorff, *op. cit.*: 128.
44 An article to this effect, personally approved by the Czar, appeared in the *Pravitel'stvennyi Vestnik* ("The Government Herald"), c. February 24, 1889. It is referred to by Lamsdorff, *op. cit.*: 128–29, and a partial text appears in DDF, VII: 350–51.
45 For example, unflattering diplomatic dispatches about Ashinov were released by the government for publication in the *Kronshadtskii Vestnik.* (Lamsdorff, *op. cit.*: 124.)
46 Laboulaye to Spuller, French Foreign Minister, March 20, 1889, DDF, VII: 352.
47 Nikolaev, *op. cit.*: 60.
48 Lamsdorff, *op. cit.*: 135, quoting his colleague, Nikonov.
49 *Ibid.*: 122, 146.
50 See Pobedonostsev, *Zapiski, op. cit.*: 903, for the text of Pobedonostsev's letter to the Czar, January 12, 1889, in which he protested that he never gave approval to Ashinov's schemes and even failed to respond to Ashinov's letters.
51 Volgin, *op. cit.*: 3, 56.
52 Some observers went so far as to see in Father Paissi's mission "a pledge for future permanent relations with Abyssinia." (*Ibid.*: 3.)
53 Letter dated February 24, 1889, from I. Soloviev to Pobedonostsev, in Pobedonostsev, *Zapiski, op. cit.*: 922.
54 Lamsdorff, *op. cit.*: 168.

55 Dispatch from Consul General Koyander, c. the beginning of March, 1889, cited in *loc. cit.*

56 *Loc. cit.*

57 *Loc. cit.* The same diplomatic dispatch mentioned above also brought the Czar's attention to the first African mission of Lieutenant V. F. Mashkov. Lamsdorff makes note of de Giers' recollection that the Ministry of War had intended to send an officer to Africa. (*Loc. cit.*)

58 "Russia in Africa—the Abyssinian Expedition," the *Times* (London), July 25, 1891: 5.

59 *Loc. cit.*

60 *Loc. cit.*

61 This book, which was probably written in 1888, was published in St. Petersburg in 1889. Maria Rait, "Russkie Ekspeditsii v Efiopii v Seredine XIX—Nachale XX vv." in I. I. Potekhin, ed., *Afrikanskii Etnograficheskii Sbornik*, I (Trudy Instituta Etnografii, XXXIV) (Moscow, 1956): 237, is responsible for having traced the identity of the author.

62 Mashkov (writing as V. Fedorov), *Abissiniia*, (St. Petersburg, 1886): 63.

63 *Ibid.*, 61–62.

64 *Ibid.*: 61.

65 *Loc. cit.*

66 *Loc. cit.*

67 *Loc. cit.*

68 *Loc. cit.*

69 *Loc. cit.*

70 "Russia in Africa," *op. cit.*: 5. The author of this *Times* article seems to have been privy to a substantial amount of inside information.

71 *Loc. cit.* The article describes the proposal as one "for the gradual reduction of Abyssinia to the position of a vassal state under the protection of Russia," and states that the original copy of the proposal was to be found in the archives of the Russian Ministry of War.

72 *Loc. cit.*

73 The *Times* account indicates that Menelik intimated to Mashkov that he would be grateful for any assistance from Moscow in this regard. (*Loc. cit.*)

74 *Loc. cit.*

75 *Loc. cit.*

76 Lamsdorff, *op. cit.*: 256 (Entry for December 30, 1889).

77 "Russia in Africa," *op. cit.*: 5.

78 *Loc. cit.*

79 This quotation from the letter is supplied by Father Efrem, to whom the letter was shown by Menelik at the time of Efrem's visit to Ethiopia in 1895). Archimandrite Efrem, *Poezdka v Abissiniiu* [St. Petersburg, 1901]: 106.)

80 man, Jes*op. cit.*: 82, citing Edoardo Scarfoglio, *Abissinia, 1889–1896*: 320.

81 Rait, *op. cit.*: 221. This source refers to extensive correspondence between these departments concerning the mission.

82 "Russia in Africa," *op. cit.*: 5.

83 Telegram, February 18, 1891, from Ambassador Laboulaye to Foreign Minister Ribot, DDF, VIII: 371–72.

84 V. N. Lamsdorff, *Dnevnik, 1891–1892* (Moscow, 1934): 48. (Entry for February 19, 1891.)
85 Lamsdorff, *Dnevnik, 1886–1890, op. cit.*: 233.
86 William Langer, *The Diplomacy of Imperialism, 1890–1902* (New York, 1951): 272.
87 Volgin, *op. cit.*: 86–87.
88 V. F. Mashkov, "Puteshestvie v Stranu Chernykh Khristian v 1891–1892 gg." (part 2) in *Novoe Vremia* (St. Petersburg) February 16, 1893: 3.
89 Volgin, *op. cit.*: 103, citing Mashkov's account. Mashkov's articles are contained in *Novoe Vremia*, nos. 6069, 6095 and 6102. Since, however, Volgin includes a more concise and easily accessible extract of these accounts, subsequent references will be to his volume.
90 Volgin, *loc. cit.*
91 Rait, *op. cit.*: 237. It is interesting to note that in 1887, newspapers had reported that Italians in Massawa had seized an entire Ethiopian embassy on its way to Russia to seek Russian aid." (Mashkov, *Abissiniia, op. cit.*: 62.)
92 "Soobshchenie V. F. Mashkova ob Abissinii," *Russkiia Viedomosti,* April 5, 1893: 2.
93 Mashkov had anticipated that this transfer would be accomplished by "sending [Russian] instructors and training a regular army in Ethiopia under the leadership of Russian officers." (Mashkov, *Abissiniia, op. cit.*: 63.)
94 "Russia in Africa—the Abyssinian Expedition" (part 2), the *Times* (London), July 28, 1891: 13. Evidently recalling Kovalevsky's gold mining projects, the *Times* went on to observe: "This is not the first occasion on which Russia has cast longing eyes on the gold of Africa." (*Loc. cit.*)
95 See Mashkov, *Abissiniia, op. cit.*: 63. In this connection it is interesting to note that Mashkov was aware of Uspensky's writings on Ethiopia and that he correctly regarded him as the initiator of the proposal for Russian relations with Ethiopia. (*Loc. cit.*)
96 "Russia in Africa" (part 2), *op. cit.*: 13. From Mashkov's own accounts it is possible to see that the example of Russian Orthodox activity in the Balkans appeared to him to be relevant to Russia's future in Abyssinia. (See Mashkov, "Puteshestvie," in Volgin, *op. cit.*: 110.)
97 Volgin, *loc. cit.*
98 Rait, *op. cit.*: 237. This source refers to reports which Mashkov sent to the Ministry of War, which were then forwarded to the Foreign Ministry. (*Ibid.*: 225.)
99 Volgin, *op. cit.*: 115.
100 "Russia in Africa" (part 2), *op. cit.*: 13.
101 Mashkov, "Puteshestvie" in Volgin, *op. cit.*: 144.
102 *Loc. cit.*
103 "Russia in Africa" (part 1), *op. cit.*: 5.
104 The *Times* article notes that Mashkov's expedition was "the immediate work of the Russian government which was only partially true of of the Atchinoff [*sic*.] expedition." (*Loc. cit.*)
105 *Loc. cit.*

106 *Loc. cit.*
107 "Russia in Africa" (part 2), *op. cit.*: 13.
108 *Loc. cit.*
109 *Loc. cit.*
110 Volgin, *op. cit.*: 84–85.
111 Lamsdorff, *Dnevnik, 1891–1892, op. cit.*: 368.
112 While Jesman consecrates two chapters to Ashinov, he devotes only two pages to Mashkov's second expedition. (See Jesman, *op. cit.*: 82–83.)
113 K. S. Zviagin (a member of the Eliseev expedition to Ethiopia), *Ocherk Sovremennoi Abissinii* ("A Sketch of Contemporary Abyssinia") (St. Petersburg, 1895): 62.
114 See his account of this venture: A. V. Eliseev, "Makhdizm i Sovremennoe Polozhenie Del v Sudane" ("Mahdism and the Contemporary State of Affairs in the Sudan"). Russkoe Geograficheskoe Obshchestvo, *Izvestiia*, XXX (1894), no. 4: 604–66.
115 See Eliseev's own account of this expedition in A. V. Eliseev, *Po Belu-Svetu* ("Around the World"), IV (published posthumously in St. Petersburg, 1898): 268ff.
116 Eliseev, *Ibid.*, 270.
117 See *Ibid.*: 268, Jesman, *op. cit.*: 84, and Rait, *op. cit.*: 221.
118 Rait, *op. cit.*: 268.
119 Efrem, *op. cit.*: 31.
120 Eliseev, *Po Belu-Svetu, op. cit.*: 302.
121 Rait, *op. cit.*: 240, refers to this factor as a reason for Menelik's readiness to greet Eliseev's arrival in Ethiopia, and Eliseev himself credits the Ethiopians with possessing an astonishing degree of political acumen in cultivating Russian friendship. (Eliseev, *Po Belu-Svetu, op. cit.*: 309.)
122 Eliseev, *Po Belu-Svetu, op. cit.*: 301. Also Efrem, *op. cit.*: 41ff.
123 Efrem, *ibid.*: 45, notes that the matter was broached by the Ethiopians in their first conversations with the Russians at Harrar.
124 Eliseev himself is rather guarded in explaining his abrupt return to Russia, but does concede that his departure became imperative after contact had been made with officials of the Ethiopian government. (Eliseev, *Po Belu-Svetu, op. cit.*: 309.) See also P. P. Semenov-Tian'-shanskii, *Istoriia Poluvekovoi Deiatelnosti Imperatorskago Russkago Geograficheskago Obshchestva, 1854–1895* (St. Petersburg, 1896), III: 1197, which indicates that Eliseev returned to St. Petersburg with a commission from Ras Makonnen.
125 The preface to Eliseev's *Po Belu-Svetu*, written by a friend, mentions these events (*op. cit.*: xiv) and describes the circumstances of his death. Thus Eliseev's influence on the development of Russo-Ethiopian relations was not, as Jesman would have us believe, nullified by his premature death from sunstroke while in Africa. (See Jesman, *op. cit.*: 86, 113.)
126 Efrem, *op. cit.*: 168.
127 Volgin, *op. cit.*: 120. According to Efrem, LaGarde had "sincere sympathy for the goals of our expedition," having been forewarned of its arrival by the President of France himself. (Efrem, *op. cit.*: 28–29.)

128 Eliseev, *Po Belu-Svetu, op. cit.*: 310. Father Efrem felt that his efforts in Ethiopia had been successful in preparing the final ground for union between the Russian and Ethiopian Churches. "Now all that is lacking is the occasion on which God will find it appropriate to perform this great historic event," he declared. (Efrem, *op. cit.*: 168.)

129 See IU. Elets (possibly a pseudonym for N. S. Leontiev), *Imperator Menelik i Voina Ego s Italiei* ("Emperor Menelik and His War with Italy") (St. Petersburg, 1898), an account from Leontiev's travel diary.

130 Cited from Eliseev's notes by Efrem, *op. cit.*: 72. A similar text of Makonnen's remarks is in Eliseev's *Po Belu-Svetu, op. cit.*: 309–10.

131 See Elets, *op. cit.*: 34.

132 Father Efrem refers to visits between the Ethiopians and various high officers of the Russian General Staff, including Lt. General Protsenko and Adjutant General Obruchev. He also notes that on one occasion Prince Damto communicated with the Minister of War, General Vannovski, by telegram. (Efrem, *op. cit.*: 158ff, 162.)

133 See *ibid.*: 164.

134 Jesman, *op. cit.*: 88, reports that this consisted of 400,000 rubles and a large consignment of rifles, machine guns, and cavalry sabres.

135 See Efrem's description. (Efrem, *op. cit.*: 136–63.)

136 See Jesman, *op. cit.*: 87.

137 Efrem, *op. cit.*: 156–59.

138 *Ibid.*: 136.

139 *Ibid.*: 144f.

140 I. I. Vasin, "From the History of Russo-Ethiopian Relations at the End of the 19th Century," *Russia and Africa*, (Moscow, 1966): 188, quoting the report of Lobanov-Rostovski to Nicholas II, June 22, 1895, concerning his conversation with the Italian Minister Selvestri. The year before, the Russian government had also taken exception to the Anglo-Italian accord of May 5, 1894 which recognized Ethiopia as falling within the Italian sphere of influence. (See Montebello, French Ambassador to St. Petersburg, to Hanotaux, French Foreign Minister, June 26, 1894, DDF, XI: 255–56, for a résumé of the statement of Foreign Minister de Giers to the Italian Ambassador in St. Petersburg.

141 Italian military moves toward Adowa appeared to be, at least in part, influenced by news of the Russo-Ethiopian rapprochement. (See Efrem, *op. cit.*: 131, and Elets, *op. cit.*: 27.)

142 Elets, *ibid.*: 38, indicates that promptly upon receipt of the account of his emissaries, Menelik "energetically undertook the arrangements for the attack against the Italians." The Battle of Adowa took place only a few months after the return of the mission, and several of the members of the embassy played prominent roles in the fighting. (*Loc. cit.*)

143 See Langer, *Diplomacy of Imperialism, op. cit.*: 280.

144 Sir Evelyn Baring (Lord Cromer), *Modern Egypt*, II (London, 1908): 83.

145 See Chancellor von Hohenlohe to Count von Hatzfeldt, German Ambassador in London, March 4, 1896, *Die Grosse Politik der Europaischen Kabinette* (1871–1914), XI: 236. The German Kaiser reminded

the English of their precarious position and therefore urged them to come to the rescue of the Italians in north-eastern Africa.

146 Winston S. Churchill, "The Fashoda Incident," *North American Review,* CLXVII (1898): 742.

147 Winston S. Churchill, *The River War* (London, 1902): 363.

148 Ernest Work, *Ethiopia, A Pawn in European Diplomacy* (New York, 1935): 269.

149 *Ibid.*: 166, citing Ward and Gooch, *The Cambridge History of British Foreign Policy,* III: 250.

150 Gabrial Hanotaux, *Le Partage de l'Afrique—Fachoda* (Paris, 1909): 104, describes the expedition as a direct reply to Britain's Dongola Expedition. See also Work, *op. cit.*: 185.

151 See DDF, XIII: 63.

152 See Work, *op. cit.*: 250f, for a good account of French plans.

153 *Loc. cit.*

154 See Churchill, River War, *op. cit.*: 312, and Jesman, *op. cit.*: 71.

155 See Elets, *op. cit.*: 80f.

156 Mashkov, in *Abissiniia, op. cit.*: 58ff., had predicted that the Ethiopians were likely to win a defensive war with the Italians largely because of the favorable nature of their native topography.

157 Elets, *op. cit.*: 261f.

158 *Ibid.*: 284.

159 Rait, *op. cit.*: 242.

160 *Ibid.*: 242–43.

161 Augustus Wylde, *Modern Abyssinia* (London, 1901): 417.

162 Rait, *op. cit.*: 243.

163 *Ibid.*: 243–44.

164 *Ibid.*: 245.

165 See Vasin, *op. cit.*: 191.

166 See M. V. Right (probably Maria Rait), "Russian Red Cross Expedition to Ethiopia," in *Russia and Africa, op. cit.*: 169–70, and Elets, *op. cit.*: 261.

167 Hanotaux to M. Vauvineux, French Chargé d'Affairs in St. Petersburg, November 5, 1896, DDF, XIII: 30–31, relaying information supplied to him by M. Shishkin, acting Russian Foreign Minister.

168 Hanotaux to Montebello, July 29, 1894, and August 18, 1894, DDF, XI: 301.

169 Hanotaux to Vauvineaux, November 5, 1896, DDF, XIII: 30.

170 Hanotaux to Montebello, French Ambassador in St. Petersburg, "very confidential," January 31, 1897, DDF, XIII: 158.

171 Text of note, dated September 10, 1897, DDF, XIII: 533–54. Evidently the coordination of instructions had been agreed to in the course of a visit between Hanotaux and Muraviev. (Hanotaux to Vauvineux, September 9, 1897, DDF, XIII: 532.)

172 *Ibid.*: 534.

173 N. Notovitch to Hanotaux, May 12, 1898, DDF, XIV: 283, reporting a conversation with Vlassov, who was in route to Addis Ababa. Notovitch asserted that he was transmitting the very words used by the Czar.

174 A. K. Bulatovich, *S Voiskami Menelika II* ("With the Armies of Menelik II") (St. Petersburg, 1900): 1.

175 See M. Prompt's proposals to this effect. (Langer, *Diplomacy of Imperialism, op. cit.*: 135, 575.)

176 In coming to this conclusion the British government was no doubt influenced by pressure from the British in India who were concerned about the security of Egypt. In particular, they were apprehensive lest Russia in its desire for a position on the Red Sea, might allow its enthusiasm for Ethiopia to go "far beyond the bounds of political decency." (Klobukowski, French Consul General in Calcutta, to Hanotaux, April 1, 1897, DDF, XIII: 307–09.)

177 Prince Henri d'Orléans, *Une Visite à l'Empereur Ménélick* (Paris, 1898): 159.

178 Rodd to Salisbury, confidential letter, May 10, 1897, F.O. 1/32 (Foreign Office Archives in Public Records Office, London): 221–22.

179 *Ibid.*: 222.

180 Churchill, *River War, op. cit.*: 312.

181 Rodd to Salisbury, May 10, 1897, F.O. 1/32: 235–36.

182 On the basis of information gained by members of the mission, the British Prime Minister was advised that "the early seizure of Khartoum and an attempt to establish communication by water with the British protectorate in Uganda and Unyoro, or at least, to effectively occupy the Nile valley as far south as Fashoda . . . would appear to be the immediately essential steps to be taken." (Memorandum by Lt. Colonel F. R. Wingate, Chief of Egyptian Intelligence Services, May 9, 1897, F.O. 1/32: 237.)

183 See Rennell Rodd, *Social and Diplomatic Memories, 1894–1901*, Second Series (London, 1923): 186–87.

184 Hanotaux to French Colonial Minister Lebon, February 28, 1897, DDF, XIII: 239–40. Also Lebon to Lagarde, March 14, 1897, DDF, XIII: 262–63.

185 The full text appears in DDF, XIII: 278–79.

186 *Ibid.*: 278, Article 2.

187 Lagarde to Hanotaux, December 24, 1897, DDF, XIII: 645.

188 Chargé Vauvineux to Hanotaux, December 15, 1896, DDF, XIII: 81. In a conversation with the French Chargé in St. Petersburg, Leontiev indicated that he planned to take part in the Ethiopian expedition himself. (*Loc. cit.*)

189 See d'Orléans, *Une Visite, op. cit.*: 260, also Work, *op. cit.*: 257.

190 D'Orléans, *Une Visite, op. cit.*: 195–96.

191 See Elets, *op. cit.*: ii.

192 Rait, *op. cit.*: 241.

193 Serge Julievich, Count Witte, *Vospominaniia* ("Memoires") (Berlin, 1922): 116.

194 Lebon to Hanotaux, March 2, 1898, DDF, XIV: 119. At one point the French Foreign Minister appeared to have been tempted to assist Leontiev with funds as well. (Lebon to Hanotaux, March 24, 1898, DDF, XIV: 336.)

195 Russian Foreign Minister Muraviev had warned Hanotaux about Leontiev when they met in Paris in 1897. (Hanotaux to Montebello, January 31, 1897, DDF, XIII: 158. See also Lebon to Lagarde, April 12, 1898, DDF, XIII: 348.)

196 Lagarde to Hanotaux, December 24, 1897, DDF, XIII: 647n.

197 Notovitch to Hanotaux, *op. cit.*: in DDF, XIII: 283–84.
198 Hanotaux to Geoffray, French Chargé in London, June 18, 1898, DDF, XIV: 337.
199 *Loc. cit.*
200 *Ibid.*: 338.
201 Rodd had cast doubts on French intentions in this connection when he reminded Menelik that "it might be disadvantageous for his kingdom to constitute the only break in a trans-African road from east to west which another country might eventually be ambitious to establish." (Rodd, *Memories, op. cit.*: 199.) Lagarde had indeed been suspiciously zealous in promoting the project for a French railroad which was to proceed westward from Djibouti.
202 See A. K. Bulatovich, *Ot Entoto do Reki Baro* (St. Petersburg, 1897.) Also Rait, *op. cit.*: 254.
203 See Bulatovich, *S Voiskami, op. cit.*: 7. Vlassov gave his permission for Bulatovich's trip, but the original idea was probably Menelik's.
204 See *Russkii Invalid*, no. 195, 1899.
205 A. I. Kokhanovskii, "Imperator Menelik II i Sovremennaia Abissiniia," *Novyi Vostok*, no. 1, 1922: 321, attributes the English about-face entirely to Bulatovich. Although Bulatovich himself (*S Voiskami, op. cit.*) mentions no actual hostilities with the British, the presence of an Ethiopian force of nearly 30,000 men may nonetheless have acted as an effective deterrent to MacDonald's forces.
206 Bulatovich, *S Voiskami, ibid.*: 270. See also his report to the Imperial Russian Geographical Society, January 13, 1899, which appears in its journal *Izvestiia*, XXXV, no. 3, 1899: 259–83: A. K. Bulatovich, "Iz Abissinii Cherez Strany Kaffa na Ozeru Rudolfa."
207 I. S. Katznelson, "Alexander Bulatovich: Man of Unusual Destiny," in *Russia and Africa, op. cit.*: 181. Katznelson observes that Bulatovich was really the unofficial commander of the vanguard units of the Giorgis army and was largely responsible for reconnaissance.
208 P. N. Krasnov, *Kazaki v Abissinii* ("Cossacks in Abyssinia") (St. Petersburg, 1900).
209 Rait, *op. cit.*: 225. In this connection it is interesting that Bulatovich's book, *S Voiskami Menelika II*, was published by order of the Commission on Military Science of the Russian General Staff.
210 See Rait, *op. cit.*: 273.
211 Jesman, *op. cit.*: 123, citing a conversation with Babitchev, a Russian officer who accompanied Leontiev on the expedition.
212 Bulatovich, *S Voiskami, op. cit.*: ii.
213 L. K. Artamonov, "Kratkii Otchet o Puteshestvie" ("A Short Account of My Travels"): 1f., an article prepared for publication by the Imperial Russian Geographical Society, 1899. (Papers of L. K. Artamonov, Library of Congress, Acquisition no. 14, 897.)
214 See Rait, *op. cit.*: 264.
215 Artamonov, "Kratkii Otchet," *op. cit.*: 1f.
216 Vasily Arkhipov's notes on the expedition as dictated and translated into English: 35. (Artamonov Papers, *op. cit.*) Arkhipov was one of the Cossacks accompanying Artamonov.
217 See Artamonov, "Kratkii Otchet," *op. cit.*: 30ff.
218 Arkhipov, *op. cit.*: 52.

219 Montebello to Delcassé, December 22, 1898, DDF, XIV: 883.
220 Toutain, French Chargé in St. Petersburg, to Delcassé, 10-12-98, DDF, XIV: 542.
221 Vauvineux to Delcassé, November 12, 1898, DDF, XIV: 796-98.
222 Quoted in Vauvineux to Delcassé, October 27, 1898, DDF, XIV: 717.
223 Montebello to Delcassé, January 18, 1899, DDF, XIV: 40, and Montebello to Delcassé, January 19, 1900, DDF, XIV: 80.
224 Gabriel Hanotaux, ed., *Histoire de la Nation Egyptienne* (7 vol.; Paris, 1931), VII: 189. See also Langer, *Diplomacy of Imperialism, op. cit.*: 563 for information on the Muraviev-Delcassé discussions of October, 1898. Subsequently Muraviev expressed his thorough approval of the the conciliatory fashion in which France handled the affair. (French Ambassador to Berlin, Noailles, to Delcassé, November 13, 1898, DDF, XIV: 798-99.)
225 "France, Russia and the Nile," *The Contemporary Review*; London), Vol. 74, December, 1898: 766.
226 Montebello to Delcassé, June 9, 1899, DDF, XV: 362.
227 Lagarde to Delcassé, November 18, 1898, DDF, XV: 362.
228 Rait, *op. cit.*: 266. Ethiopia had not been as easily deterred from its territorial ambitions as had France. Leontiev's expedition in 1899 serves as evidence that Ethiopia was still attempting to expand its frontiers in the direction of the Nile.
229 Russian observers were inclined to believe that as a result of Kitchener's victory at Omdurman, "the projects of the English to seize and control the entire expanse of land between Capetown and Alexandria came close to realization." (I. T. Bok, "Uspekhi Evropeitsev v Vostochnoi Polovine Afriki za Poslednie Gody" ["The Success of Europeans in the Eastern Half of Africa in Recent Years"], Russkoe Geograficheskoe Obshchestvo, *Izvestiia*, XXXV, no. 4, 1899: 476.)
230 Kokhanovskii, *op. cit.*: 326.
231 See Vasin, *op. cit.*: 189-90. In the latter activity Leontiev was apparently active as well.
232 See D. S. Vlassov, "Zametka ob Abissinii (Donesenie iz Addis-Abeby)" ("A Note on Abyssinia [Dispatch from Addis Ababa]") in *Sbornik Konsul'skikh Donesenii* (published by the Imperial Russian Ministry of Foreign Affairs, St. Petersburg), no. 2, 1899: 99-106. Presumably Vlassov obtained much of his military information from Russian officers like Artamonov, who spent considerable time in the field and who drew up detailed studies of Ethiopia's military organization. (See Artamonov's Papers, *op. cit.*, for a 56-page report by Artamonov entitled "Abissinskaia Armiia.")
233 Early in 1899 a number of officers attached to the Russian mission were in the field and one or more of them appear to have visited Urail, Menelik's headquarters for the campaign against Mangasha. Worthy of note in this connection are Captains Bulatovich and Dragomirov and Lieutenants Arnoldi and Davydov. (See Rait, *op. cit.*: 270-73.)
234 Vasin, *op. cit.*: 191.
235 Langer, *Diplomacy of Imperialism, op. cit.*: 571.
236 As late as June, 1914, St. Petersburg was still receiving dispatches

from Russian representatives in Addis Ababa. The last Imperial Russian Chargé left Ethiopia in 1919. (Jesmen, *op. cit.*: 143.)

237 Kokhanovskii, *op. cit.*: 333. This article in *Novyi Vostok* purports to be the text of the report of Kokhanovskii submitted to Sazonov on June 1, 1913, concerning his mission to Ethiopia.

238 The last meaningful exchange on this subject actually took place in 1902, when the Abuna was received in Russia by the Czar and members of the Imperial family. (Grand Duke Alexander of Russia, *Always a Grand Duke* [New York, 1935]: 157ff.)

239 "Russia in Africa" (part 2), *op. cit.*: 13. Wylde, *op. cit.*: 50–51, suggests that Russia would have been willing to accept either a small island on the coast near Perim or a foothold at Obok in return for further assistance to France.

240 "France, Russia and the Nile," *op. cit.*: 773. (Anonymous)

241 Uspensky, "Tserkovnoe i Politicheskoe Sostoianie Abissinii s Drevneishikh Vremen do Nashikh Dnei" ("The Ecclesiastical and Political Status of Abyssinia from Earliest Times until The Present"), in *Trudy Kievskoi Dukhovnoi Akademii*, 1866, no. 5: 10–19. Uspensky takes note of Ethiopia's intention to seize islands in the Red Sea as well as recent British and French territorial acquisitions in the area. (*Ibid.*: 15, 17.)

242 Mashkov, *Abissiniia*, *op. cit.*: 47ff.

243 Rait, *op. cit.*: 228, refers to a manuscript of 306 pages which Nesterov wrote describing this area. Eliseev, *Po Belu-Svetu*, *op. cit.*, also devotes considerable attention to its geography and inhabitants.

244 See "Map of Localities Adjacent to the Tajura Inlet," Mashkov, *Abissiniia*, *op. cit.*: 63.

245 A. S. Troianskii, *Eritreiskaia Koloniia Italii* (St. Petersburg, 1893): 18ff.

246 Eliseev, *Po Belu-Svetu*, *op. cit.*: 270. Zviagin (*op. cit.*: 9), who was also on this visit remarked upon the excellence of the harbor at Tajura.

247 Letter of John Jopp, British Resident in Aden, to the India Office, February 19, 1898 (F.O. 78/4676) reporting information gathered in Obok by Commander Story of HMS *Lapwing*.

248 Eliseev, *Po Belu-Svetu*, *op. cit.*: 316.

249 Jesman, *op. cit.*: 105–07. These efforts were without success.

250 *Ibid.*: 104–05.

251 Baron von Marschall, March 4, 1896, *Die Grosse Politik*, *op. cit.*, XI: 237.

252 Hanotaux to Montebello, February 25, 1897, DDF, XIII: 228.

253 The Czar had evidently complied with the French appeal by recalling Ensign Babitchev from the Danakil coast. (*Loc. cit.*)

254 *Loc. cit.*

255 Lagarde to Hanotaux, December 24, 1897, DDF, XIII: 647.

256 M. P. Zabrodskaia, *Russkie Puteshestvenniki po Afrike* (Moscow, 1955): 66–67.

257 See Krasnov, *op. cit.*, ch. 9. (Krasnov was in charge of the military convoy of the Vlassov mission.)

258 L. K. Artamonov, "Ruskie v Abissinii," text of an address delivered November 29, 1899, to the Society of Promoters of Military Knowledge, St. Petersburg. (Artamonov Papers, *op. cit.*)

259 Lagarde to Delcassé, December 23, 1898, DDF, XIV: 887.
260 Delcassé to Montebello, December 30, 1898, DDF, XIV: 889.
261 *Loc. cit.*
262 *Loc. cit.*, footnote 2. This had been in the context of a conversation concerning the possible Russian intention to seize Raheita.
263 As they had in Djibouti, the Russians turned to the French for coaling facilities in the Persian Gulf. Vlassov, who had earlier been the Russian Consul in Meshed, was asked in 1902 to return as Minister to Persia. In this capacity he presided over efforts to extend Russian railroads through Persia to the Indian Ocean. (Bompard, French Ambassador in St. Petersburg, to Delcassé, August 28, 1903, DDF, Serie 2e [1901–11], III: 549.)
264 See D. A. Farnie, *East and West of Suez* (Oxford, 1969): 491.
265 Not only was Rozhdestvensky unable to use Djibouti to regroup his forces, but while he was in Dakar he had so much difficulty obtaining authorization to coal his vessels that the Russian government at one point thought it might be necessary for him to turn back to Russia. (Bompard to Delcassé, December 3, 1904, DDF, 2e, V: 561.)
266 See David Woodward, *The Russians at Sea* (New York, 1965): 140ff.
267 "And from where will the English get their reinforcements," he asked, "if not from India?" ("Nikolai Romanov ob Anglo-Burskoi Voine," *Krasnyi Arkhiv*, no. 63 [1934]: 125.) Indian troops were, in fact, required for the Boer War—as they had been for the Sudan campaign.
268 *Loc. cit.*
269 Montebello to Delcassé, January 19, 1900, DDF, 1e, XVI: 80.
270 Langer, *Diplomacy of Imperialism, op. cit.*: 666–67.
271 *Ibid.*: 652, quoting Sir Edmund Monson, the British Ambassador in Paris, to this effect. See also "Nikolai Romanov," *op. cit.*: 125.
272 The Boer War stimulated the publication of a considerable amount of literature in Russia. See *Bibliografiia Afriki* (Moscow, Institut Afriki, 1964): 176–79.
273 V. I. Gere, "Pochemu Sleduet Zhelat Uspekha Buram?" *Russkiia Viedomosti*, no. 29, January 29, 1900: 3.
274 V. I. Romeiko-Gurko, *Voina Anglii s IUzhno-Afrikanskimi Respublikami, 1899–1901* ("England's War with the South African Republics") (St. Petersburg, 1901): 302.
275 A list of 25 of these officers appears in *ibid.*: 303f.
276 *Ibid.*: 34.
277 The Russian medical mission, which participated in the task of collecting information on dead and wounded in the field, provided data which enabled Russians to follow closely the progress of the fighting. (See *ibid.*: 122–23.)
278 "Nikolai Romanov," *op. cit.*: 125. In the same context he expressed satisfaction over the capture of two English battalions by the Boers.
279 "Anglo-Burskaia Voina v Doneseniiakh Ruskogo Voennogo Agenta," ("The Boer War in the Dispatches of a Russian Military Agent"), *Krasnyi Arkhiv*, no. 103, 1940: 148. The Czar must have been pleased with Romeiko-Gurko's performance, for he was subsequently asked to command Russian armies in World War I. As Chief of the Russian General Staff in 1917, he was for several months the closest assistant

of the Czar in the high command. (See General Basil Gourko [*sic.*], *Memories and Impressions of War and Revolution in Russia* [London, 1918].)
280 See Romeiko-Gurko, *Voina, op. cit.*: 262–88.
281 Marked "not to be made public," the report was drawn up by "Imperial command" and was seen both by General Sakharov of the General Staff and by Grand Duke Vladimir Alexandrovich. (Notes on copy of the report at New York Public Library, *ibid.*: title page.)
282 *Ibid.*: 257f.
283 Langer, *Diplomacy of Imperialism, op. cit.*: 669.
284 "Anglo-Burskaia Voina v Doneseniiakh," *op. cit.*: 148. Maksimov sought to convince the Boer President that peace initiatives to England were not the only hope. Should these fail, he advised that the Boers should send a delegation to Europe—including on its itinerary not only Paris and Berlin, but St. Petersburg as well. This the Boers did in the fall of 1900. However, in September the British were able to put an end to the Transvaal's independent existence by annexing the republic. (Langer, *Diplomacy of Imperialism, op. cit.*: 651.)
285 D. Zaslavskii, "Nikolai II—Imperator Kafrov," *Krasnyi Arkhiv*, no. 67/70 (1935): 255.
286 *Ibid.*: 253–54.
287 See, for example, P. IA. Zhuber [*sic.*], *Transvaal. Istoriia ego Stradanii pod Angliiskim Vladychestvom* (St. Petersburg, 1900).
288 Letter from Joubert to the Russian government (no. 8), transmitted by Lamsdorff to the Czar, March 5, 1905, and quoted by Zaslavskii, *op. cit.*: 248. In talks with African leaders in the Gold Coast, Joubert reportedly received specific promises of assistance.
289 *Loc. cit.*
290 *Ibid.*: 243.
291 Lamsdorff to Koyander, March 8, 1905, secret dispatch, quoted in *ibid.*: 249.
292 *Ibid.*: 252.
293 *Ibid.*: 242.
294 *Ibid.*: 251.
295 *Loc. cit.*
296 Kokhanovskii, *op. cit.*: 332.
297 See Zviagin, *op. cit.*: 63ff., for a discussion of these factors.
298 Churchill, *The River War, op. cit.*: 313–14.
299 "France, Russia and the Nile," *op. cit.*: 778.

PART II

CHAPTER THREE

1 Thus, according to Marx, eighteenth century Liverpool was constructed upon the bodies of African Negroes. (*Das Kapital*, I: 642 [Russian edition] cited in *K. Marx and F. Engels on Colonialism* [Moscow n.d.]: 300.)
2 F. Engels, Supplement to *Kapital*, III, cited in *ibid.*: 306.
3 V. I. Lenin, *Imperialism: the Highest Stage of Capitalism* (New York, 1939): 76, 124.
4 *Ibid.*: 79. Engels, in a letter to Kautsky, September 12, 1882, had

already marvelled at how "the workers daily share in the feast of England's . . . colonies." (*Marx and Engels on Colonialism, op. cit.*: 340.)

5 See Lenin, *Imperialism, op. cit.*: 120–25.

6 N. Gavrilov, *Le Mouvement de Libération Nationale en Afrique Occidentale* (Moscow, n.d.): 27, refers, for example, to French African troops stationed in Romania.

7 On more than one occasion he asserted: "Marxists cannot ignore the powerful factors that give rise to the aspiration to create national states." (See V. I. Lenin, "The Right of Nations to Self-Determination," *Selected Works* [Moscow, 1946], I: 564–95.)

8 N. Bukharin, speech at the Eighth Communist Party Congress, March, 1919, *Vos'moi S'ezd Kommunisticheskoi Partii: Protokoly* (Moscow, 1959): 47–48. It is interesting that in this context Bukharin mentioned Negroes specifically.

9 M. Pavlovich, "Lenin i Narody Vostoka," ("Lenin and the Peoples of the East") in *Lenin i Vostok* (Moscow, 1925): 16–21.

10 V. I. Lenin, *The National Liberation Movement in the East* (Moscow, 1969): 333, reproducing "Better Fewer but Better," *Pravda*, no. 49, March 4, 1923.

11 Lenin's speech at the opening session of the Second Comintern Congress, July 28, 1920, quoted in Jane Degras, ed., *The Communist International, 1919–1943: Documents* (3 vols.; London, 1956–65), I: 139.

CHAPTER FOUR

1 Turaev's *Istoriia Drevnogo Vostoka* (1913) was published again in Leningrad in 1935, and during the 1930's the Soviet Institute of Eastern Studies published a number of his prerevolutionary collections of Ethiopian and Egyptian manuscripts. See also Turaev's posthumous publication *Russkaia Nauka o Drevnom Vostoke do 1917 goda* (Leningrad, 1927).

2 See, for example, *Chto Dokazala Anglo-Burskaia Voina* ("What did the Anglo-Boer War Prove?") (Odessa, 1901) and *Velikie Zhelezno-Dorozhnye i Morskie Puti Budushchago* ("The Great Railroad and Maritime Routes of the Future") (St. Petersburg, 1913). This latter study was expanded upon by Pavlovich in *Mirovaia Voina i Bor'ba za Razdel Chernogo Kontinenta* ("The World War and the Struggle for the Division of the Black Continent"), published by the All-Russian Central Executive Committee of the Soviet of Workers' and Soldiers' Deputies in Moscow in 1918.

3 Pavlovich was a Menshevik well before 1917 and it is likely that he became acquainted with Lenin as early as 1904–05, in Geneva, where the Russian Social Democratic Working Party's press "Iskra" published his book on the Russo-Japanese War (*Russko-Iaponskaia Voina*). Pavlovich also contributed a series of articles to *Iskra* under the pseudonym Volunter. It is known that Pavlovich's writings were read by Lenin himself and there is good reason to believe that they contributed to Lenin's thinking on the subject of imperialism. (Louis Fisher, *Life of Lenin* [New York, 1964]: 661.)

4 *Zhizn Natsional'nostei*, no. 1, 1923: 268.

5   See Russkoe Geograficheskoe Obshchestvo, *Izvestiia*, issues 1914–20.
6   See *Revue du Monde Musulman*, Vol. 51 (October, 1922): 53.
7   Pavlovich, *Velikie Puti, op. cit.*: 171.
8   *Ibid.*: 180–83.
9   *Ibid.*: 186.
10 *Ibid.*: 185–86.
11 *Ibid.*: 185.
12 *Ibid.*: 184f.
13 *Ibid.*: 184.
14 *Ibid.*: 186.
15 This volume (*Mirovaia Voina i Bor'ba za Razdel Chernogo Kontinenta, op. cit.*) formed a part of a series of works entitled *Osnovy Imperialisticheskoi Politiki i Mirovaia Voina* ("The Principles of Imperialist Politics and the World War").
16 Pavlovich, *Razdel Chernogo Kontinenta, ibid.*: 12.
17 M. Pavlovich, *Bor'ba za Aziiu i Afriku* ("The Struggle for Asia and Africa") (Moscow, 1923): 122.
18 *Ibid.*: 118.
19 K. M. Troianskii, "Novyi Peredel Afriki posle Versal'skogo Mire," ("The New Redivision of Africa following the Peace of Versailles"), *Novyi Vostok*, no. 1, 1922: 86.
20 A. Krikkel, "Novaia Afrika" ("The New Africa"), *Vestnik Narkomindela*, January/March, 1922: 85.
21 Pavlovich, *Bor'ba za Aziiu i Afriku, op. cit.*: 214, and K. M. Troianskii, *op. cit.*: 86ff. By 1924 Pavlovich was warning of an "approaching European war which threatens to become a world war" and was pointing the finger of blame at Anglo-French antagonism. (Pavlovich, "The Coming of War," *Inprecorr*, IV, no. 35 [June 19, 1924]: 356.)
22 G. Chicherin, "The International Situation," *Inprecorr*, III, no. 22 (March 1, 1923): 168.
23 The British government, at least, appeared apprehensive concerning Soviet intentions. A stipulation was, in fact, included in the Anglo-Soviet Trade Agreement of March 16, 1921, to the effect that Russia would refrain from encouraging the peoples of Asia—and especially those of Afghanistan and India—from engaging in activities hostile to British interests. (Louis Fischer, *The Soviets in World Affairs* (Vintage edition, New York, 1960): 213.
24 Pavlovich, *Sovetskaia Rossiia i Kapitalisticheskaia Angliia* (Moscow, 1925): 3.
25 See, for example, V. Khudadov, "Zheleznye Dorogi Afriki" ("The Railroads of Africa"), *Novyi Vostok*, no. 5, 1925: 168–70, and V. D. Kaisarov, "Zheleznye Dorogi v Afrike" ("Railroads in Africa"), *Novyi Vostok*, no. 6, 1924; 184–86.
26 Pavlovich, *Bor'ba za Aziiu i Afriku, op. cit.*: 220.
27 Khudadov, *op. cit.*: 184.
28 Pavlovich, *Bor'ba za Aziiu i Afriku, op. cit.*: 221.
29 The writings of V. Markov are a good case in point. See his *Iskusstvo Negrov* (Petrograd, 1919), written before the revolution, in which he praises the achievements of West African artists. (*Ibid.*: 16–17.) See also P. G. Mizhuev's textbook, *Istoriia Kolonial'noi Imperii i Kolonial'noi Politiki Anglii* (St. Petersburg, 1902), which is as sympathetic in its

discussion of Negro Africans as it is unsympathetic in its treatment of the British—the carriers of "many of the vile aspects of civilization" into central Africa. (*Ibid.*: 169.)

30 Pavlovich, *Velikie Puti, op. cit.*: 180ff.

31 *Ibid.*: 189. See also: 190–91.

32 Pavlovich, *Razdel Chernogo Kontinenta, op. cit.*: 15.

33 Pavlovich, *Velikie Puti, op. cit.*: 192.

34 *Loc. cit.*

35 *Ibid.*: 191.

36 Pavlovich, *Bor'ba za Aziiu i Afriku, op. cit.*: 138, citing *Journal Officiel de l'Afrique Occidentale Française*, January, 1917.

37 Sir J. E. Bruce, *A Tribute for the Negro Soldier* (New York, 1918): 6–9. (Also published in French.) The *tirailleurs Sénégalais* were particularly valuable to France after Russia's withdrawal from the war. Bruce estimates that including Africans, altogether half a million Negroes served in the war.

38 R. L. Buell, *The Native Problem in Africa*, II (New York, 1928): 14.

39 Bruce, *op. cit.*: 48.

40 The *Gold Coast Independent*, I, no. 1 (June 8, 1918): 3, noted "there is a distinct public opinion taking shape in West African affairs today; it may be crude, rough-hewn, but it is growing and developing vigorously." See also N. S. Russell, "The Negro in the British Empire," *Les Continents*, I, no. 3 (June 15, 1924): 3, which discusses the role of Britain's Negro Africans in the war and refers to "dangerous revolutionary tendencies" among them.

41 *Gold Coast Independent*, I, no. 1, *op. cit.*: 4.

42 *Gold Coast Independent*, I, no. 2 (June 13, 1918): 23.

43 L. R. E. Denzer, "The National Congress of British West Africa, Gold Coast Section," (unpublished M.A. thesis, written for the Institute of African Studies, University of Ghana, Legon, 1965): 3.

44 The *Gold Coast Independent* (October 1, 1921) greeted the establishment of the NCBWA in the following terms: "Nationhood has dawned on the West African horizon."

45 Separatist outbreaks had, for example, occurred in Madagascar as early as 1913. (See François Coty, *Sauvons Nos Colonies: Le Péril Rouge au Pays Noir* [Paris, 1931]: 67–68.)

46 *Le Libéré* (November 15, 1923): 4.

47 K. Tovalou Houénou, "Simple Histoire," *Action Coloniale*, I, no. 3 (June 15, 1924): 1.

48 See Houénou, "Le Problème de la Race Noire," *Action Coloniale*, VII, no. 107 (March 25, 1924): 1. In this article, as in other writings, Houénou betrayed a certain revolutionary bent, referring to the Ministry of Colonies as a "Bastille to be taken," and warning that "wherever there are men who suffer, there are men who will revolt." (The latter quote comes from, Houénou, "La Grande Pitié des Colonies," *Les Continents*, I, no. 2 [June 1, 1924]: 1.)

49 Houénou, "La Grande Pitié," *ibid.*: 1.

50 Houénou, "Le Problème de la Race Noire," *op. cit.*: 1.

51 See "Bulletin d'Adhésion: Buts de la Ligue," in the LDRN's paper *Les Continents*, I, no. 2 (June 1, 1924): 4, for a description of some of the LDRN's objectives.

52 See, for example, "Amérique: Le Plan Garvey," *Les Continents*, I, no. 1 (May 15, 1924): 3.

53 T. Houénou, "Paris, Coeur de la Race Noir," *Les Continents*, I, no. 10 (October 1, 1924): 1.

54 The French government maintained surveillance over the activities of the LDRN by means of secret agents. A collection of their reports appears in the archives of the Ministry of Colonies, SLOTFOM, Series V, Box 2, File 1, subfile 106 under the title "Une Entreprise Garveyiste en France."

55 Not only did the LDRN consider itself responsible for representing the interests of African Negroes at the League of Nations, it called for admission of French colonies such as Senegal into the international body. (*Les Continents*, I, no. 10 [October 1, 1924]: 24, and *Les Continents*, I, no. 5 [July 15, 1924]: 1.) The LDRN also objected to the international transfer of colonial possessions and, by implication, to their original acquisition. (See "Bulletin d'Adhésion," *op. cit.*)

56 *Les Continents* began publication in May, 1924, and in January, 1925, after producing over a dozen issues, it absorbed *Le Libéré*. Copies of *Les Continents* were sent to such destinations as Madagascar, Dahomey, and the Ivory Coast, and at the end of 1924 were known to be circulating freely in Dakar. (*Les Continents*, I, no. 12 [November 1, 1924]: 3.)

57 Leon Trotsky, *The First Five Years of the Communist International*, I (New York, 1945): 24.

58 Krikkel, *op. cit.*: 90, 86. The above remarks of Krikkel are also cited in Pavlovich, *Bor'ba za Aziiu i Afriku, op. cit.*: 206, 213.

59 Krikkel, *op. cit.*: 93. Typical among these notions, Krikkel observes, was the belief that the French and Belgians would be relatively easy to deal with since African troops had already beaten the much stronger Germans.

60 Krikkel, *ibid.*: 91, for example, felt that the French assimilationist approach was politically and racially less biased against African Negroes than was current British colonial policy.

61 *Ibid.*: 90–91.

62 *Loc. cit.*

63 A. T., "K Volneniiam sredi Negrov Kenii," *Zhizn Natsional'nostei*, no. 11 (June 1, 1922): 13.

64 See "V Angliiskikh Koloniakh Tropicheskoi Afriki" ("In the English Colonies of Tropical Africa"), *Zhizn Natsional'nostei*, no. 6/7 (April 14, 1922): 21.

65 Krikkel, *op. cit.*: 90.

66 Pavlovich, *Bor'ba za Aziiu i Afriku, op. cit.*: 207.

67 I. Trainin, "Na Chernom Kontinente," *Zhizn Natsional'nostei*, no. 20 (October 3, 1921): 1.

68 *Ibid.*: 1. In this context Trainin quoted Garvey as having given Africans the following exhortation in a speech: "Negroes fought on all fronts [in World War I] for the interests of others. We learned how to kill and how to die . . . Now we can at least die for our own interests." (*Loc. cit.*)

69 Krikkel, *op. cit.*: 92ff.

70 *Ibid.*: 93.

71 Trainin, *op. cit.*: 1.
72 Krikkel, *op. cit.*: 93. This authorization was evidently granted at a Garveyite congress held in the United States in August, 1921.
73 At the Paris session, Krikkel notes, as many as 400 delegates were convened, representing not only the independent Negro states of Africa (Liberia and Ethiopia) but also the British and French colonies, the Belgian Congo, etc. (*Loc. cit.*)
74 In particular, they looked with disdain upon the activities of Blaise Diagne, a Senegalese deputy to the French Parliament who chaired sessions of the World Negro Congress in Brussels. Diagne had been responsible for the recruitment of France's West African troops during World War I and was now, they seemed to believe, assisting Britain and France in attempts to induce the Congress to adopt moderate and loyalist positions. (Krikkel, *ibid.*: 94, and Trainin, *op. cit.*: 1.)
75 Krikkel, *op. cit.*: 93–94. Although Krikkel refers to him as a West Indian, the leftist mentioned was almost certainly W. E. B. DuBois, founder of the NAACP and well-known American leader of Pan-Africanism.
76 *Ibid.*: 94.
77 *Ibid.*: 95.
78 Trainin, *op. cit.*: 1.
79 Pavlovich, *Bor'ba za Aziiu i Afriku, op. cit.*: 205, 211. Pavlovich was referring specifically to a statement made by French Professor Charles Gide warning of the imminent victory of Bolshevism in Africa. Gide's statements appeared in Russian translation in the *Vestnik Narkomindel*, no. 8, 1920, and were reproduced by Pavlovich in *ibid.*: 203–06.
80 Trainin, *op. cit.*: 1, and Krikkel, *op. cit.*: 86.
81 Pavlovich, *Bor'ba za Aziiu i Afriku, op. cit.*: 205–06.
82 Krikkel, *op. cit.*: 86.

CHAPTER FIVE

1 E. H. Carr, *The Bolshevik Revolution: 1917–23* (London, 1953): 448.
2 As Dmitri Boersner points out in *The Bolsheviks and the National and Colonial Question* (Geneva, 1957): 97, Russian dominance in the Comintern could be detected in the organization's positions on colonial matters as early as 1921, and by the following year it was "completely obvious."
3 See David Ivon Jones, "Communism in South Africa," *The Communist Review* (a monthly journal of the Communist Party of Great Britain) I, no. 3, July, 1921: 15.
4 See Lenin, "Première Esquisse des Thèses sur les Questions Nationales et Coloniales," article 1, *L'Internationale Communiste* (the theoretical journal of the Comintern; English edition known as *The Communist International*), I (1920): 1769; see also articles 4, 12, and Boersner, *op. cit.*: 79, quoting Lenin's report on "The Present World Situation and the Tasks of the Comintern" at the Second Congress.
5 It appears that the term "Achilles heel" was first used by Karl Radek and subsequently by Pavlovich and other Bolshevik writers to describe the position of the colonies vis-à-vis British imperialism. (See

Jane Degras, ed. *The Communist International, 1919–1943: Documents* [3 Vols.; London, 1956–65], I: 139.)

6 V. I. Lenin, *Selected Works* (London, 1936) V: 305, cited in Roger E. Kanet, "The Soviet Union and Sub-Saharan Africa: Communist Policy toward Africa, 1917–1965" (unpublished Ph.D. dissertation, Princeton University, 1966): 48.

7 See Lenin, "Première Esquisse des Thèses," *op. cit.*, articles 6, 9: 1769–70.

8 *Ibid.*, article 11.

9 *Ibid.*: 1767–68.

10 *Ibid.*, article 6: 1769.

11 *Protokoll des II Weltkongresses der Kommunistichen Internationale* (Hamburg, 1921): 154–57, cited in Boersner, *op. cit.*: 87.

12 Mikhail Pavlovich, *Voprosy Kolonial'noi i National'noi Politiki i IIIi Internatsional* ("Questions of National and Colonial Politics and The Third International") (Moscow, Ind. Kommunisticheskogo Internatsionala, 1920): 46.

13 *Ibid.*: 46–49.

14 *Ibid.*: 46–47. Chicherin, in "Vospominaniia o M. P. Vel'tmane-Pavloviche," *Novyi Vostok*, no. 18, 1927: 6, refers to Pavlovich as a champion of the concept of linkage between the revolutionary fortunes of the European proletariat and the peoples of the Third World.

15 See *Zhizn Natsional'nostei*, no. 6, 1922: 2, and no. 1, 1923: 261–67, for information on the establishment of this institute.

16 See T. Ryskulov, "Pavlovich i Ugnetennye Narody Vostoka," *Novyi Vostok*, no. 18, 1927: 12. This source also indicates that Pavlovich lectured to those present at Baku on the evils of imperialism in the colonies.

17 M. Pavlovich, *Bor'ba za Aziiu i Afriku* ("The Struggle for Asia and Africa") (Moscow, 1923): 209.

18 I. Steklov, "The Awakening of a Race," *Inprecorr*, II, no. 102 (November 24, 1922): 825–26, and I. Trainin, "Na Chernom Kontinente," *Zhizn Natsional'nostei*, no. 20 (October 3, 1921): 1.

19 "David Ivon Jones" (obituary), *Inprecorr*, IV, no. 35 (June 19, 1924): 360. Jones was one of the founders of the International Socialist League in South Africa (which was established in 1916 and which subsequently became the CPSA) and was editor of its weekly journal, *The Internationalist*.

20 Jones, "Communism in South Africa," (part 2), *The Communist Review*, I, no. 4 (August, 1921): 66f.

21 See Sydney Bunting, "The Labour Movement in South Africa," *Inprecorr*, II, no. 98 (November 13, 1922): 787–88.

22 Jones, "Communism in South Africa" (part 1), *op. cit.*: 15.

23 Jones, "Communism in South Africa" (part 2), *op. cit.*: 70–71.

24 Boersner, *op. cit.*: 110. This was done at the specific request of the South African delegation (i.e. probably Jones).

25 See, for example, the following articles by Jones: "The Crisis in the South African Labour Movement" which appears under the title "Les Problèmes du Travail en Afrique du Sud" in the French edition of *Inprecorr*, *La Correspondance Internationale*, II, no. 17 (March 4, 1922): 128–29; "American Imperialism and the Negro," *The Communist*

Review, III, no. 5 (September, 1922): 225–28 (appears also in *Inprecorr*, II, no. 56 [June 30, 1922]: 412–13); and "Africa's Awakening," *Inprecorr*, III, no. 25 (June 14, 1923): 421–22.

26 "Death of David Ivon Jones," *The Communist Review*, V, no. 3 (July, 1924): 136.

27 See Jones, "Les Problèmes," *op. cit.*: 128.

28 Jones, "Africa's Awakening," *op. cit.*: 422.

29 Steklov, *op. cit.*: 825.

30 Address of Comrade McKay at the Fourth Comintern Congress, reproduced in *Inprecorr*, III, no. 2 (January 5, 1923): 16.

31 *Ibid.*: 17.

32 Steklov, *op. cit.*: 825.

33 Jones, "Africa's Awakening," *op. cit.*: 422.

34 "Trotzky on the Negro Question (A Letter from Comrade Trotzky to Comrade McKay)," *Inprecorr*, III, no. 25 (March 13, 1923): 197.

35 *Loc. cit.*

36 See N. Bukharin, "The Occupation of the Ruhr and Soviet Russia," *Inprecorr*, III, no. 21 (February 27, 1923): 159–60.

37 Trotsky, "Letter to McKay," *op. cit.*: 197.

38 "Report and Resolution on the Negro Question," read by Rose P. Stokes (pseudonym "Sasha"), *Inprecorr*, III, no. 2 (January 5, 1923): 21–22.

39 *Ibid.*: 21.

40 *Ibid.*: 22. In this context the Comintern resolution dealt specifically with Africa, referring to the continent as capitalism's "reservoir of human labor" and warning that: "Just as in the Pacific the danger of another war has become acute owing to the competition of imperialist powers . . . so Africa looms ominously as the object of their rival ambitions." (*Ibid.*: 21, 22.)

41 Zinoviev, in a postmortem description of the Congress (*Inprecorr*, III, no. 1 [January, 1923]: 2), made a point of mentioning the presence of the Negroes, adding that "they brought reports full of interest to us." See also Jones, "Africa's Awakening," *op. cit.*: 422, and Steklov, *op. cit.*: 825.

42 Stekov, *loc. cit.*

43 *Loc. cit.*

44 *Loc. cit.*

45 Jones, "Africa's Awakening," *op. cit.*: 422.

46 *Loc. cit.*

47 *Ibid.*: 421.

48 *Loc. cit.*

49 Jones, "Africa's Awakening," *op. cit.*: 422.

50 "Resolution on the Negro Question," *op. cit.*: 21–22.

51 *Ibid.*: 21.

52 *Loc. cit.*

53 Jones, "Africa's Awakening," *op. cit.*: 422.

54 Trotsky, "Letter to McKay," *op. cit.*: 197.

55 Otto Huiswood (pseudonym Billings), "Report on the Negro Question," *Inprecorr*, III, no. 2 (January 5, 1923): 15.

56 "Resolution on the Negro Question," *op. cit.*: 22, article 6, section 3.

57 *Loc. cit.*, article 6, section 4.
58 *Ibid.*, article 6, section 1.
59 *Ibid.*: 21, article 2.
60 See Claude McKay, "The Racial Issue in the USA," *Inprecorr*, II, no. 101 (November 21, 1922): 817.
61 In the opinion of French journalist François Coty, the cultural attachment which American Negroes had to Africa rendered them for communists "an indispensable human lever for action in that Africa which has never ceased to preoccupy them as the cradle of their race." (François Coty, *Sauvons Nos Colonies: Le Péril Rouge au Pays Noir* [Paris, 1931]: 40.)
62 Steklov, *op. cit.*: 826.
63 Huiswood, *op. cit.*: 15.
64 *Loc. cit.*
65 Specifically this program declared that "no opportunity should be lost for propagandizing the native soldiers in the 'colonial armies' and for organizing secretly a great Pan-African army in the same way that Sinn Fein built up the Irish army under the very nose of England . . . Using the more able and developed Negroes" in the coastal districts for leadership, the program went on to insist that "modern arms must be smuggled into Africa; men sent into Africa in the guise of missionaries, etc., to establish relations with the Senussi, the various tribes of the interior, and to study the topography of the country." Ultimately, it was believed, "all the Negro organizations in each of the African countries" would be brought into a worldwide "Negro Federation." ("Programme of the African Blood Brotherhood," *The Communist Review*, II, no. 6 [April, 1922]: 450–51.)
66 *Ibid.*: 449, 454.
67 Jones, "American Imperialism and the Negro," *op. cit.*, (September, 1922): 228.
68 Trotsky, "Letter to McKay," *op. cit.*: 197. In the same letter Trotsky went on to express his conviction that "every ten Negroes who gather round the flag of revolution and unite to form a group for practical work among the Negroes are worth a hundred times more than dozens of resolutions."
69 Steklov, *op. cit.*: 826. As suggested by the program of the ABB, communists at this time may have felt that American missionaries might furnish them useful opportunities for the penetration of Africa. Coty (*op. cit.*: 40ff.) takes note of this possibility, pointing out the advantages such as color, religious dignity, and a detailed knowledge of African territory which black American missionaries might possess for communists.
70 I. Amter, "Les Victimes Noires de l'Impérialisme," *L'Internationale Communiste*, IV, nos. 26–27 (July 9, 1923): 62.
71 To M. N. Roy's protests at the Third Comintern Congress were added the interventions of the Tunisian delegate at the Fourth Congress and Ho Chi Minh at the Fifth. The latter (pseudonym Nguyen ai Quac) warned that communists who de-emphasize the importance of agitation in the colonies would be contradicting Leninism and would earn for themselves the brand of counter-revolutionaries from Stalin. (*Piatyi Vsemirnyi Kongress Kommunisticheskogo Internatsionala:*

Stenograficheskii Otchet [stenographic record of the Fifth Comintern Congress] [2 vols; Moscow, 1925], I: 653f.)

72 Degras, I, *op. cit.*: 326–27.
73 *Ibid.*: 327.
74 Comintern, *Armiia Kommunisticheskogo Internatsionala* (Petrograd, 1921): 85. See also remarks of Louis Sellier at the 22nd Session of the Fifth Comintern Congress (July 1, 1924) in *Piatyi Kongress*, I, *op. cit.*: 643.
75 See, for example, the following articles appearing in 1922 in *L'Afrique Française (Bulletin Mensuel du Comité de l'Afrique Française et du Comité du Maroc)*: "La Crise Tunisienne et le Communisme dans l'Afrique du Nord," July, 1922: 326–33; and Maurice Delafosse, "Les Points Sombres de l'Horizon en Afrique Occidentale," June, 1922: 271–85.
76 "Manifesto of the Comintern on the Liberation of Algiers and Tunis," *Inprecorr*, II, no. 53 (June 23, 1922): 394. According to "La Crise Tunisienne," *op. cit.*: 330, the French edition of this *Inprecorr* issue was distributed in Tunis.
77 "Manifesto of the Comintern on the Liberation of Algiers and Tunis," *op. cit.*: 394.
78 *Loc. cit.*
79 Article 9, "Programme d'Action du PCF," *Correspondance Internationale*, II, no. 96 (December 13, 1922): 728.
80 T. A. Jackson, "The British Empire," *The Communist* (London: a continuation of *The Call*) no. 48 (July 2, 1921): 4–11.
81 H. S. Ryde, "Review of E. D. Morel, "The Black Man's Burden," *The Call*, April 22, 1920: 12.
82 Article 16, "The Draft Programme of the CPGB to the Comintern," *The Communist Review*, V, no. 1 (May, 1924): 99–100.
83 "The Draft Program Criticized," *The Communist Review*, V, no. 4 (August, 1924): 187.
84 P. Vaillant-Couturier in "Northern Africa and Communism," *Inprecorr*, II, no. 38 (May 19, 1922): 303, points to "bad blood among races" as an impediment to PCF work even in North Africa.
85 A. Lozovsky, "The National Question and the Trade Union Movement," *Inprecorr*, III, no. 53 (July 26, 1923): 564.
86 "Le Cinquième Congrès de l'Internationale Communiste," *Correspondance Internationale*, IV, no. 60 (August 27, 1924): 635.
87 *Loc. cit.* One suspects that the intensity of Manuilsky's criticism of the PCF for its failure to turn colonial troops against the metropolitan bourgeoisie was conditioned by the anxiety that these same contingents could be used against Russia.
88 *Piatyi Kongress*, I, *op. cit.*: 676.
89 *Ibid.*: 642.
90 *Ibid.*: 644.
91 *Loc. cit.* Sellier was probably referring to the "Council on Propaganda and Agitation for Eastern Peoples" established at Baku.
92 *Loc. cit.* Another entirely different source, "La Propagande Communiste dans les Colonies Françaises," *Les Continents*, I, no. 9 (September 15, 1924): 3, describes an identical communist plan of action in sub-Saharan Africa.
93 *Piatyi Kongress*, I, *op. cit.*: 676.

94 *Ibid.*: 675.
95 *Rasshirennyi Plenum Ispolkoma: Kratkii Protokol* (July 12, 1924), *Piatyi Kongress, ibid.*, II: 9.
96 "La Propagande Communiste," *op. cit.*: 3.

CHAPTER SIX

1 RILU, *The Tasks of the International Trade Union Movement (Resolutions and Decisions of the Third World Congress of the RILU, Moscow, July, 1924)* (London, 1924), article 6: 48.
2 *Loc. cit.*
3 L. Gelber, "The Labor Movement in the Colonial and Semi-Colonial Countries," *Inprecorr*, V, no. 18 (March 5, 1925): 261–62.
4 G. Gautherot, *Le Bolshévisme aux Colonies et l'Impérialisme Rouge* (Paris, 1930): 66.
5 RILU, *Resolutions of Third World Congress, op. cit.*: 48.
6 Gautherot, *op. cit.*: 106.
7 RILU, *Resolutions of Third World Congress, op. cit.*, article 9: 48.
8 *Loc. cit.*
9 Rabinovitch, "Le Congrès des Ouvriers Noirs Américains," *Correspondance Internationale*, V, no. 125 (December 23, 1925): 1076.
10 *Loc. cit.*
11 Cites in S. W. Johns, "Marxism-Leninism in a Multi-Racial Environment" (Ph.D. dissertation, Harvard University, 1965.): 429. Jane Degras, ed. *The Communist International, 1919–1943: Documents* (3 vols.; London, 1956–65), II: 187, notes that the congress established a national committee to convene a world congress of Negroes.
12 L. F., "The Influence of the Comintern among Negroes," *The Negro Worker*, II, no. 2 (March/April, 1929): 1. The ANLC continued its formal existence until 1930, but with little grass roots support.
13 Wilson Record, *The Negro and The Communist Party* (Chapel Hill, 1951): 34f. See also H. Stassova, "Dix Années de Secours Rouge International," *Correspondance Internationale*, XII, no. 91 (November 1, 1932): 1037–38.
14 Record, *op. cit.*: 35.
15 George Padmore, *Pan-Africanism or Communism?* (London, 1956): 303.
16 *Ibid.*: 318.
17 Johns, *op. cit.*: 431. See also Theodore Draper, *American Communism and Soviet Russia* (New York, 1960): 332–33. The Gold Coast student mentioned was almost certainly Awoonor-Renner, who later became an avowed communist and an associate of Nkrumah. (See subsequent discussion of this individual.) One of the Americans was probably William L. Patterson, who was later Executive Secretary of the ILD and an influential member of the CPUSA. (See Record, *op. cit.*: 34–35, 107–08.)
18 François Coty, *Sauvons Nos Colonies: Le Péril Rouge au Pays Noir* (Paris, 1931): 46, claims that the Soviet government asked its representative in New York City "Rietchensky" to assist DuBois in forming an organization called the American Colored Men's Federation which would be directed "less toward action in the US" than toward the promotion internationally of the "issue of black labor in the colonies."

19 DuBois, editorial in *Crisis* (organ of the NAACP), XXXIII (November, 1926): 8, cited in Dorothy Nelkin, "Socialist Sources of Pan-African Ideology," in W. F. Friedland and C. G. Rosberg, *African Socialism* (Stanford, 1964): 65. In the same vein DuBois' Fourth Pan-African Congress in 1927 closed by thanking "the Soviet Government of Russia for its liberal attitude toward the colored races and for the help which it [had] extended to them." (*Loc. cit.*)

20 "Le Procès Fantôme," *Les Continents*, I, nos. 13–14 (November 15/December 1, 1924): 1.

21 Coty, *op. cit.*: 140.

22 French government surveillance revealed, for example, that the former colonial editor of the PCF's *Humanité*, Charles Lussy, had been helpful in the establishment of *Les Continents*. (Note of Agent "Désiré," July 28, 1924, in SLOTFOM, V, Box 2, File 1, subfile 106.)

23 Coty, *op. cit.*: 140ff.

24 See *Les Continents*, I, no. 9 (September 15, 1924): 1, and *Les Continents*, I, no. 13–14 (November 15/December 1, 1924): 1, 5.

25 Coty, *op. cit.*: 144–45, and Gautherot, *op. cit.*: 273.

26 Coty, *op. cit.*: 144–45.

27 Wounded three times in the war, Senghor had been given the *Croix de Guerre* for his services as a *tirailleur Sénégalais*. ("Le Procès Fantôme," *op. cit.*: 1.)

28 Senghor had been asked by the editors of *Les Continents* to testify against Diagne in the latter's suit for defamation of character. (*Loc. cit.*) Senghor was not only a member of the PCF, but he had, in 1924, run for election as a PCF candidate in Paris. (See "La Ligue est en Deuil: Lamine Senghor est Mort," *La Race Nègre*, I, no. 5 [May, 1928]: 1. See also SLOTFOM, V, Box 3, File 73, subfile 51, "Notes des Agents Relatives au Journal *La Race Nègre*," note dated September 24, 1927.)

29 Coty, *op. cit.*: 159, 257–58.

30 Fernand Huré, "Le Mouvement Pan-Noir et le Bolchévisme," *Le Temps Coloniale*, October 7, 1930.

31 *La Voix des Nègres*, I, no. 1 (January, 1927): 4, notes, for example, that in October, 1926, the *Comité* was in the process of establishing a section in Le Havre. See also Senghor, "Debout les Nègres," *La Race Nègre* (the continuation of *La Voix des Nègres*), I, no. 1 (July, 1927) 1.

32 See note of Agent Désiré dated April 27, 1927, SLOTFOM, V, Box 3, File 73, subfile 51, which refers to a refusal on the part of the PCF to furnish further funds to *La Voix des Nègres*.

33 Senghor, "Ce Qu'est Notre Comité," *La Voix des Nègres*, I, no. 1 (January, 1927): 1.

34 Lt. Governor of Dahomey to Governor General of French West Africa, Confidential Report dated September 1, 1927: 2 (forwarded by the latter to the Minister of Colonies on October 6, 1927), in SLOTFOM, V, Box 3, File 73, subfile 51, "La Voix des Nègres."

35 Willy Munzenberg, "Pour une Conférence Coloniale," *Correspondance Internationale*, VI, no. 9 (August 14, 1926): 1011.

36 J. R. Hooker, *Black Revolutionary: George Padmore's Path from Communism to Pan-Africanism* (New York, 1967): 11, suggests that

the Comintern's ILD provided some of the funds for the Brussels Conference.

37 See Munzenberg, "La Première Conférence Mondiale contre la Politique Coloniale Impérialiste," *Correspondance Internationale*, VII, no. 17 (February 5, 1927): 232.

38 Munzenberg, "Pour une Conférence Coloniale," *op. cit.*: 1011.

39 *Loc. cit.* See also "Liste des Organizations et Délégués ayant Apporté leur Concours au Congrès International de Bruxelles," *La Voix des Nègres*, I, no. 3 (March, 1927): 4.

40 See X. Eudin and R. C. North, *Soviet Russia and the East* (Stanford, California, 1957): 265.

41 "Liste des Organisations et Délégués," *op. cit.*: 4. The *Comité* was also represented by Narcisse Danae.

42 The text of Senghor's speech to the conference appears in *La Voix des Nègres*, I, no. 3 (March, 1927): 2. It was accurately summarized in "The Revolutionary Movement in the Colonies: The International Congress against Colonial Oppression in Brussels," *Inprecorr*, VII, no. 16 (February 25, 1927): 328–29. Padmore (*op. cit.*: 324) refers to the address by Senghor as "memorable and prophetic."

43 Degras, *op. cit.*, II: 354. See also Eudin and North, *op. cit.*: 265.

44 Coty, *op. cit.*: 196, for example, refers to Melnichansky as "the right hand of the Muscovite management."

45 "Contre l'Impérialisme: Pour la Libération Nationale: (Manifeste du Congrès de Bruxelles)," *Correspondance Internationale*, VII, no. 27 (February 26, 1927): 368.

46 *Loc. cit.*

47 See "Les Décisions du Congrès: Résolution Commune sur la Question Nègre," *La Voix des Nègres*, I, no. 3 (March, 1927): 3.

48 *Loc. cit.*

49 *Loc. cit.*

50 Circular of invitation to the Brussels Conference cited by Munzenberg, "Pour une Conférence Coloniale," *op. cit.*: 1011.

51 "The International Congress against Colonial Oppression in Brussels," *op. cit.*: 331. See also LAI, *Statutes* (LAI International Secretariat, Berlin, 1929): 4–8.

52 See "La Deuxième Conférence de Bruxelles de la Ligue Anti-Impérialiste," *Correspondance Internationale*, VII, no. 127 (December 21, 1927): 1952.

53 During the summer of 1927 Senghor was active in connection with the establishment of an LAI office in Paris. In August, for example, French governmental surveillance discovered that he had come to the city at LAI expense to participate in a meeting of the branch. (Note of Agent Désiré, August 11, 1927, SLOTFOM, V, Box 3, File 73, subfile 51.) Bridgeman's activity will be discussed subsequently.

54 The Soviet government appeared anxious to place the Africans on public display. Richards, for example, was asked to join Clara Zetkin and Lenin's wife Krupskaya in presiding over a congress of "The Friends of Soviet Russia." (Munzenberg, "A la Veille de la Deuxième Conférence de la Ligue Anti-Impérialiste," *Correspondance Internationale*, VII, no. 122 [December 7, 1927]: 1822.) The South Africans, for their part, returned home enthusiastic about their experience in

the U.S.S.R. and were reportedly anxious to apply the model of Soviet development in South Africa. (See CPGB, *The Comintern between the Fifth and Sixth Congresses* [London, 1928]: 490, and Johns, *op. cit.*: 387.)

55 Munzenberg, "A la Veille," *op. cit.*: 1822.

PART III

CHAPTER SEVEN

1 See Isaac Deutscher, *Stalin* (New York, 1960): 309–10.
2 See Dmitri Boersner, *The Bolsheviks and the National and Colonial Question* (Geneva, 1957): 259.
3 "Le VIe Congrès de l'Internationale Communiste," *Internationale Communiste*, VIII, no. 14 (July 1, 1928): 1006. See also "Bilan et Perspectives sur le Premier Point d'Ordre du Jour du VIe Congrès de l'Internationale Communiste," *Internationale Communiste*, VIII, no. 18 (September 1, 1928): 1379.
4 Particularly with regard to trade union work in Negro Africa, the conviction had been gaining ground in Comintern circles that "there must be no putting off or delaying; or else this work of organization will take place without us and consequently against us." (RILU, *Report of the Fourth Congress* [London, 1928]: 24.) At the Sixth Congress both Edward Roux of South Africa and Alexander Lozovsky, head of the Profintern, stressed the point that the Second International and other "social imperialists" were already making efforts to penetrate Black Africa. (See *Correspondance Internationale*, VIII, no. 83 [August 16, 1928]: 872, and no. 135 [November 11, 1928]: 1492, for their respective remarks.)
5 See P. V. Kitaigorodskii, *Ugroza Voiny na Sredizemnoe More* ("The Threat of War in the Mediterranean") (Moscow, 1928): 6; also E. E. Shvede, "Suetskii Kanal" ("The Suez Canal"), in Pavlovich, ed. *Sredizemnoe More; Politiko-Strategicheskii Ocherk* ("The Mediterranean Sea: A Politiko-Strategic Essay") (Moscow, 1927): 101–75; and J. Humbert-Droz, "La Réorganization Militaire de l'Impérialisme Français," *Internationale Communiste*, no. 13 (July 1, 1927): 845.
6 "Program of the Communist International," Jane Degras, ed., *The Communist International, 1919–1943: Documents* (3 Vols.; London, 1956–65), II: 521.
7 *Stenograficheskii Otchet VI Kongressa Kominterna* ("Stenographic Account of the Sixth Comintern Congress") (6 vols.; Moscow, 1929), III: 186.
8 *Ibid.*, IV: 111.
9 See *Inprecorr*, VIII, no. 49 (August 13, 1928): 867.
10 *Stenograficheskii Otchet VI Kongressa*, IV, *op. cit.*: 212.
11 *Loc. cit.* See also Ford, "Les Nègres dans la Prochaine Guerre," *Correspondance Internationale*, VII, no. 103 (September 15, 1928): 1097.
12 *Inprecorr*, VIII, no. 41 (July 30, 1928): 735.
13 *The Revolutionary Movement in the Colonies: Theses on the Revolutionary Movement in the Colonies and Semi-Colonies, Adopted by the Sixth World Congress of the Comintern, 1928* (London, 1929): 61.
14 Kuusinen revealed in an article entitled "A Leninist View of the

Colonial Problem" (*The Communist*, VIII [1929]: 3, cited in Kanet, *op. cit.*: 86), that in preparing the "Theses on the Revolutionary Movement in Colonial and Semi-Colonial Countries," he had been concerned most of all with clarifying "the independent role of the proletariat in the revolutionary movement of the colonial countries, the attaining of the hegemony of the proletariat, including as well, the leading role of the Communist Party."

15 See "Extracts from the Resolution of the Ninth ECCI Plenum on the Chinese Question" (February, 1928), Degras, II, *op. cit.*: 438.

16 "Program," Degras, II, *ibid.*: 520.

17 "Theses on the Revolutionary Movement in Colonial and Semi-Colonial Countries," cited in Degras, II, *ibid.*: 542.

18 "Theses," Degras, II, *ibid.*: 542.

19 "Program," Degras, II, *ibid.*: 480.

20 *Loc. cit.*

21 "Theses," Degras, II, *ibid.*: 543.

22 *Ibid.*: 539.

23 *The Revolutionary Movement in the Colonies*, *op. cit.*: 56–58.

24 Jones, "Les Nègres dans le Mouvement Prolétarien," *Correspondance Internationale*, I, no. 22 (1921): 178. See also Jones, "American Imperialism and the Negro," *op. cit.*: 228.

25 See, for example, Harry Haywood, "La Question Nègre aux Etats-Unis et la Tâche du Parti Communiste," *Internationale Communiste*, no. 19 (September 15, 1928): 1588; and Chiik [Shiik], "Le Programme de l'Internationale Communiste et la Question des Races," *Internationale Communiste*, no. 16 (August 1, 1928): 1165.

26 "Program," Degras, II, *op. cit.*: 519.

27 Theodore Draper, *American Communism and Soviet Russia* (New York, 1960): 343.

28 According to one of the group, Otto Hall (a former Garveyite and brother of the better known American Negro communist Harry Haywood), Stalin had on that occasion asked the students why the CPUSA did not include more Negro members. Moreover, he had expressed his belief that American Negroes constituted "a national minority with some characteristics of a nation." (*Ibid.* [Draper, interview with Hall]: 334.)

29 *Stenograficheskii Otchet VI Kongressa*, *op. cit.*, VI: 157. See also "Résolution sur l'Afrique du Sud," *Internationale Communiste*, 1928: 1935–42; and "Resolution on the Negro Question in the United States," *Communist International*, VIII, no. 2 (January 15, 1931); 65–74, for fuller description of the scheme.

30 "Program," Degras, II, *op. cit.*: 506.

31 *The Revolutionary Movement in the Colonies*, *op. cit.*: 60.

32 "Theses," Degras, II, *op. cit.*: 547.

33 Text of Theses in Béla Kun, ed., *Kommunisticheskii Internatsional v Dokumentakh* (Moscow, 1933): 857.

34 Hence Kuusinen criticized the PCF for having established sections in Algeria and Tunisia rather than permitting communists in these colonies to form autonomous party organizations. (See Kuusinen, "Rapport de la Commission Coloniale," [August 29, 1928] *Correspondance Internationale*, VIII, no. 145 [November 30, 1928]: 1663.)

35 "Theses," Degras, II, *op. cit.*: 542.
36 *Loc. cit.*
37 *Ibid.*: 543.
38 "Theses," *Stenografcheskii Otchet VI Kongressa*, VI, *op. cit.*: 150–51. The latter emphasis was apparently prompted by the need to combat the work of heavily subsidized "reactionaries", (i.e. missionaries, etc.) among these segments of the colonial population. (*Loc. cit.*)
39 "Program," Degras, II, *op. cit.*: 506.
40 *Correspondance Internationale*, VIII, no. 130 (October 30, 1928): 1418.
41 *Loc. cit.* Hall somewhat misleadingly referred to the organization as a "colonial bureau concerned with the Negro question."
42 *Loc. cit.*
43 *Stenografcheskii Otchet VI Kongressa*, IV, *op. cit.*: 128.
44 *Loc. cit.*
45 *Correspondance Internationale*, VIII, no. 83 (August 16, 1928): 872.
46 *Loc. cit.* It is interesting that Roux made particular note of the emergence of a stratum of skilled Negro workers in British West Africa. Both he and J. Jacquemotte, representative of the Communist Party of Belgium, drew attention to the development of a large indigenous proletariat in the Belgian Congo. (See *Correspondance Internationale*. VIII, no. 124 [October 18, 1928]: 1345.)
47 *Correspondance Internationale*, VIII, no. 135 (November 12, 1928): 1492.
48 *Correspondance Internationale*, VIII, no. 145 (November 30, 1928): 1663, reproducing Kuusinen's statements on behalf of the Colonial Commission at the 4th Session, August 29, 1928.
49 *Stenografcheskii Otchet VI Kongressa*, VI, *op. cit.*: 158.
50 RILU, *Report of the Fourth Congress*, *op. cit.*: 30.
51 *Ibid.*: 187. See also RILU, "Rabota Profinterna sredi Negritianskogo Proletariata" ("The Work of the Profintern among the Negro Proletariat"), in *Mirovoe Revoliutsionnoe Profdvizhenie ot IV do V Kongressa Profinterna, 1928–1930* (Moscow, 1930): 241.
52 RILU, "Rabota Profinterna," *ibid.*: 241. See also "Comité Syndical International des Ouvriers Nègres," *Correspondance Internationale*, VIII, no. 85 (August 18, 1928): 900. It is interesting that the French CGTU was also represented at the meeting.
53 See "Comité Syndical," *loc. cit.* A full text of the resolution appears in this source and an abbreviated form appears also in *La Race Nègre*, I, no. 6 (November, 1928): 2.
54 RILU, "Rabota Profinterna," *op. cit.*: 241; see also 220–25.
55 "Comité Syndical," *op. cit.*: 900.
56 *Loc. cit.*
57 *Loc. cit.*
58 See the *Negro Worker*, I, no. 1 (July 15, 1928). Appearing both in English and French (*l'Ouvrier Nègre*), this bulletin carried in its first issue a statement by Alexander Lozovsky pledging "every [possible] aid" of the RILU to Negro organizational efforts of this nature. (*Ibid.*: 5.)
59 *Stenografcheskii Otchet VI Kongressa*, IV, *op. cit.*: 212. (Italics mine.)
60 "The Aims and Purposes of the 'Negro Worker,' " *Negro Worker*, I, no. 1 (July, 1928): 3.

61 See, for example, articles such as that by William Wilson, "Imperialism, War, and the Negro Toilers," *Negro Worker*, I, no. 4 (December, 1928): 10–12. According to the editors, one of the basic purposes of the journal was "to expose preparations for a new imperialist war especially designed against the Soviet Union." (*Ouvrier Nègre*, I, no. 4 [December, 1928]: 16.)

62 This program appeared both in the *Negro Worker* ("A Trade Union Program of Action for Negro Workers"), II, no. 2 (March/April, 1929): 2–6, and in *Correspondance Internationale* ("Un Programme d'Action Syndicale pour les Ouvriers Nègres"), IX, no. 37 (May 4, 1929): 525–26.

63 "Programme d'Action," *ibid.*: 526.

64 See "Pod Kontrol," *op. cit.*: 1.

65 *Correspondance Internationale*, VIII, no. 124 (October 18, 1928): 1342.

66 "Theses on the International Situation," *Stenograficheskii Otchet VI Kongressa*, VI, *op. cit.*: 72. This decision undoubtedly came as a gratification to Munzenberg, who had been working hard during the preceding year to "support within the League a number of proletarian-revolutionary minded classes and groups and to promote their influence in the League." (W. Munzenberg, "Growing Revolutionary Militancy among Colonial Peoples," *Inprecorr*, VII, no. 72 [December 22, 1927]: 1633.)

67 See "The Brussels Conference of the LAI," *Inprecorr*, VII, no. 71 (December 15, 1927): 1622.

68 In order not to embarrass nationalist organizations still affiliated with the LAI, the organization adopted a resolution, denying these accusations at a second meeting in Brussels, December 10, 1927. (*Loc. cit.*)

69 Speaking before the LAI Executive, Melnichansky emphasized the importance of a proletarian-led revolution and stressed the need to struggle against conscious traitors in the workers' movement." ("Speech of Comrade Melnichansky at Cologne Meeting of the LAI," *Inprecorr*, IX, no. 5 [January 25, 1929]: 78–80.) Munzenberg himself noted that the Cologne meeting marked the first active participation of Russians in an executive session of the LAI. ("La Conférence de Cologne de la Ligue Anti-Impérialiste," *Correspondance Internationale*, IX, no. 7 [January 23, 1929]: 75.) G. Gautherot, *Le Bolshévisme aux Colonies et l'Impérialisme Rouge* (Paris, 1930): 77, refers to the Soviet trade union personnel as the "new majority" in the LAI following the Cologne meeting.

70 V. Vil'son [William Wilson], "Vtoroi Kongress Ligi Borby s Imperializmom" ("Second Congress of the League Against Imperialism"), *Revoliutsionnyi Vostok*, no. 8 (1930): 252. See also "Résolutions de la Session de Cologne de la Ligue Contre L'Impérialisme," *Correspondance Internationale*, IX, no. 8 (January 26, 1929): 85.

71 As Munzenberg put it: "In comparison with the Brussels Congress, the Frankfurt Congress represents a considerable move to the left. The main weight of the League Against Imperialism no longer rests on the liberal and intellectual men and women as individuals as it did at the time of its formation, but upon the broad masses of workers and peasants affiliated with the League in the oppressed countries."

(Munzenberg, "The Frankfurt Congress of the LAI," *Inprecorr*, IX, no. 38 [August 9, 1929]: 813.)

72 See "The League against Imperialism: Its Congress and Its New Tasks," *Communist International*, VI, no. 24 (November 1, 1929): 975.

73 "Speech of Comrade Kouyaté (of French West Africa) at the Congress of the League against Imperialism," *Negro Worker*, II, no. 4 (August, 1929): 23, 26.

74 Comrade Ford, "Report to the Second World Congress of the LAI," *Negro Worker*, II, no. 4 (August, 1929): 20.

75 "Manifeste du Deuxième Congrès Mondiale de la Ligue Anti-Impérialiste," *Correspondance Internationale*, IX, no. 68: 936.

76 Vil'son, "Vtoroi Kongress," *op. cit.*: 257.

77 In the course of several special gatherings held in the corridors of the LAI meeting place, Ford was able, for example, to induce the Negro delegates to discuss "the problems and the question of trade union organization amongst the Negro workers." (ITUC-NW, *A Report of Proceedings and Decisions of the First Conference of Negro Workers* [Hamburg, 1930]: 9. See also Ford, "Report to the Second World Congress," *op. cit.*: 1.)

78 François Coty, *Sauvons Nos Colonies: Le Péril Rouge en Pays Noir* (Paris, 1931): 60, citing documents captured in Durban and Johannesburg.

79 *Negro Worker*, II, no. 4 (August, 1929): 1. This Committee has been widely referred to as the Provisional ITUC-NW.

80 See V. Vil'son, "Pervaia Mezhdunarodnaia Negritianskaia Rabochaia Konferentsiia" ("First International Negro Workers' Conference"), *Revoliutsionnyi Vostok*, no. 9/10, 1930: 294. Wilson appears to have been a close colleague of Ford when the latter worked for the CPUSA in New York City.

81 François Coty, "Le Péril Rouge en Pays Noir," *L'Ami du Peuple* (December 15, 1930): 3.

82 CH. [V. Chattopadhyaya], "La Première Conférence Internationale des Ouvriers Nègres," *Correspondance Internationale*, X, no. 62 (July 23, 1930): 742.

83 See Ford, "La Conférence Syndicale Internationale des Ouvriers Nègres à Londres," *Correspondance Internationale*, X, no. 46 (May 31, 1930): 543, for pre-conference statements attacking the behavior of the MacDonald Government toward Africans in the colonies.

84 Coty, for example, described the German attitude as follows: "Apart from the obligations imposed by its policy of cooperation with the Soviets [i.e. that inaugurated at Rapallo] . . . Germany, as a country which no longer has colonies, cannot look with disfavor upon the agitation among Negroes which the agents of Moscow are fomenting in the colonies of its former enemies." (Coty, "Le Péril Rouge," *op. cit.*: 3.)

85 ITUC-NW, *A Report of Proceedings*, *op. cit.*: 1, 3, 5.

86 ITUC-NW, *Report of Proceedings*, *op. cit.*: 1. Wallace-Johnson, reported by J. R. Hooker (*Black Revolutionary: George Padmore's Path from Communism to Pan-Africanism* [New York, 1967]: 51) as having attended the Conference, was officially listed as E. Richards, representative of the Railway Workers' Union of Sierra Leone. Kenyatta's presence at the Conference is noted in the [F.D.] Corfield Report: *Historical Survey of the Origins and Growth of Mau Mau* (London, 1960): 42.

87 Cited both in Vil'son, "Pervaia," *op. cit.*: 297–98, and A. Z. Zusmanovich, ed., *Prinuditel'nyi Trud i Profdvizhenie v Negritianskoi Afrike* (Moscow, 1933): 149. It is not clear whether this program was a separate document, or simply an uncirculated version of "A Trade Union Program of Action for Negro Workers," *op. cit.*

88 Chattopadhyaya, *op. cit.*: 743.

89 James A. Ford, *The Economic Struggle of Negro Workers: A Trade Union Program of Action* (Provisional ITUC-NW, New York, 1930): 4–5.

90 *Loc. cit.*

91 ITUC-NW, *Report of Proceedings, op. cit.*: 29–35.

92 *Ibid.*: 35–37. Frank Macauley represented the NNDP on behalf of his father, the well-known Nigerian nationalist Herbert Macauley. (See *Negro Worker*, I, no. 10/11 [October/November, 1931]: 42.)

93 Zusmanovich, ed., *op. cit.*: 149.

94 RILU, "Rabota Profinterna," *op. cit.*: 242.

95 Zusmanovich, ed., *op. cit.*: 149.

96 Zusmanovich, ed., *op. cit.*: 149.

97 Coty, "Le Péril Rouge," *op. cit.*; 1, 3.

98 ITUC-NW, *Report of Proceedings, op. cit.*: 40.

99 *Loc. cit.*

100 Chattopadhyaya, *op. cit.*: 743.

101 Coty, "Le Péril Rouge," *op. cit.*: 3. Kouyaté arrived in Moscow on August 25, 1930, somewhat later than the others. (Report of Agent Joe, November 20, 1930, SLOTFOM, V, Box 3, File 73, subfile 51.)

102 Coty, "Le Péril Rouge," *op. cit.*: 3. Specifically Padmore was charged with the task of publishing and distributing revolutionary literature among Negroes and fomenting revolt among the black troops of colonial powers. (*Loc. cit.*)

103 Vil'son, "Pervaia," *op. cit.*: 301. See also Zusmanovich, ed., *op. cit.*: 148.

104 This was presumably the same M. E. Burns (probably a member of the left-wing Independent Labor Party) listed as a member of Ford's Provisional Executive Committee. (ITUC-NW, *Report of Proceedings, op. cit.*: 1.)

105 See IU. IUg, "Imperializm na Chornom Kontinente," in E. Pashukanis and B. Vinogradov, *Mirovaia Politika* cited in *Bibliografiia Afriki* (Moscow, Institut Afriki, 1964): 47. See also in the same series, Hué Duval, "Frantsyzskii Imperializm v Koloniakh."

106 A. Shiik, "K Postanovke Marksistkogo Izucheniia Sotsial 'no-Ekonomicheskikh Problem Chernoi Afriki" ("Toward the Organization of Marxist Study of the Socio-Economic Problems of Black Africa"), *Revoliutsionnyi Vostok*, no. 8, 1930: 85–100. See especially footnote: 85. Since the time of the Sixth Comintern Congress Shiik had been regarded as something of an authority on the general question of Negroes. (See his article "The Comintern Program and the Racial Problem" in the *Communist International*, V, no. 16 [August 15, 1928]: 407ff, and his study *Rasovaia Problema i Marksizm* [*Trudy* NIANKP, no. 6, 1930]). By his use of the term "Black Africa" in his speech to the NIANKP meeting, Shiik revealed his belief that this region indeed constituted a separate entity, worthy of being investigated apart from the continent as a whole.

107 Shiik, "Marksistkogo Izucheniia," *op. cit.*: 85.

108 *Ibid.*: 88.
109 *Loc. cit.*
110 *Ibid.*: 88–89.
111 *Ibid.*: 92. The political history of the region—whether it involved the activities of ancient Black African states or the post-World War I development of the anti-imperialist liberation movement—was to be the principal object of attention.
112 *Ibid.*: 95. Also of possible interest, Shiik noted, would be an investigation of the different forms of capitalist exploitation and an assessment of their impact upon Africa's economic production and upon its sociological development. (*Ibid.*: 94.)
113 *Ibid.*: 97. In so doing, he advised, it would be convenient to consider sub-regions, or groups of nations with similar characteristics (nations here to be interpreted not in the European sense of colonial divisions, but rather as ethnic, tribally constituted entities). (*Loc. cit.*)
114 *Ibid.*: 89.
115 *Ibid.*: 88–89, 98.
116 A remarkable number of the research topics first suggested by Shiik formed the subjects of subsequent studies by Soviet Africanists. For example, I. I. Potekhin, widely regarded as the father of Soviet African studies, wrote his doctoral dissertation on "The Formation of National Communities by the Southern African Bantu" (see *Bibliografiia Afriki, op. cit.*: 170)—a subject which followed faithfully the format laid down by Shiik.
117 See NIANKP, *Materialy po Natsional'no-Kolonial'nym Problemam*, nos. 3–6, 9, for 1934, and nos. 1–3 for 1935.
118 Luba A. Holowaty, "Selected Bibliography of the Works of I. I. Potekhin, Soviet Africanist, 1947–1964," *African Studies Bulletin*, XII, no. 3 (December, 1969): 315. In 1934, Potekhin led an ideological house-cleaning operation in the Soviet African Studies program, revealing himself to be an ardent Stalinist as well as a proponent of increased Soviet attention to Black Africa. (See Potekhin, "Afrika v Osveshchenii Maloi Sovetskoi Entsiklopedii," *Revoliutsionnyi Vostok*, no. 3 [1934]: 252–56.)
119 See George Skorov, "Ivan Potekhin—Man, Scientist and Friend of Africa," *Journal of Modern African Studies*, II, no. 3 (1964): 444.
120 Zusmanovich, ed., *op. cit.* This was the first Soviet volume devoted entirely to Black Africa.
121 In particular, Potekhin and Zusmanovich analyzed the socio-economic status of Africa by regions and attempted to apply the new data drawn from Africa to the Marxist model of the "most backward" society, as proposed by Shiik. (See *ibid.*: 163ff.)
122 *Ibid.*: 79.
123 "Soveshchanie po Afrikanskim IAzykam," *Revoliutsionnyi Vostok*, no. 2, 1934: 207–08. Affiliated with the NIANKP and under the supervision of Shiik and two other original directors, the center reportedly attracted a number of new scholars into the field. (*Loc. cit.*) Their subsequent efforts included such publications as that on Swahili by P. S. Kuznetsov: "Ob Immenoi Klassifikatsii i Sisteme Soglasovanii v Suakhili" in *IAzyki Zarubezhnogo Vostoka* (Moscow, Izd., NIANKP, 1935).
124 *Loc. cit.*

CHAPTER EIGHT

1 See, for example, statements made at the Fourth Congress of the RILU (RILU, *Report of the Fourth Congress* [London, 1928]: 30) and discussions at the Sixth Comintern Congress (*Stenograficheskii Otchet VI Kongressa Kominterna* ["Stenographic Account of The Sixth Comintern Congress"] [6 vols.; Moscow, 1929], IV: 128.)

2 See "O Rabota sredi Negrov-Rabochikh" ("Work Among Negro Workers"), RILU, *Rezoliutsii i Postanovleniia V Kongressa* (Moscow, 1930): 153, which describes Negro workers as "the last remaining proletarian reserve" of capitalism. See also Otto Huiswood, "The Economic Crisis and the Negro Workers" (Report to RILU Executive Plenum), *Negro Worker*, II, no. 3 (March, 1932): 19.

3 A. Z. Zusmanovich, ed., *Prinuditel'nyi Trud i Profdvizhenie v Negritianskoi Afrike* (Moscow, 1933): 21.

4 G. Safarov, "The World Economic Crisis and the Development of Revolutionary Ferment in the Colonies," *Communist International*, VI, no. 31 (February 15, 1930): 1235. See also Motilev, "A Year of World Crisis," *Communist International*, VII, no. 14 (December 1, 1930): 326, for an analysis of the initial effects of the depression on Africa, notably the drop in prices for such products as tin and rubber.

5 See George Padmore, "The Agrarian Crisis in British West Africa," *Communist International*, VIII, no. 13 (July 1, 1931): 373.

6 Safarov, *op. cit.*: 1234.

7 This phrase was used by Padmore in "L'Impérialisme Britannique au Nigéria," *Correspondance Internationale*, X, no. 67 (August 9, 1930): 847. See James Ford, *Economic Struggle of Negro Workers* (New York, 1930): 13, and Huiswood, "The Economic Crisis," *op. cit.*: 19, for descriptions of the effects of the depression on Negro Africa.

8 Zusmanovich, for one, went so far as to equate the condition of Africa's Negroes during the depression with their deplorable state during the days of legalized slavery. (*Op. cit.*: 58–59.)

9 See, for example, statements in the *Gold Coast Spectator* (March 12, 1932) which referred to "misrule in the world" and "something wrong with our society," cited in A. J. Egyir-Benyarku, "Socialism is Only a Matter of Time," *Negro Worker*, II, no. 5 (May, 1932): 26.

10 See, for example, Zusmanovich, ed., *op. cit.*: 104, and Padmore, "L'Impérialisme Britannique," *op. cit.*: 847.

11 A. Shiik, "Chernaia Afrika na Revoliutsionnom Puti" ("Black Africa on the Revolutionary Path"), *Revoliutsionnyi Vostok*, no. 8, 1930: 250.

12 Padmore, *The Life and Struggles of Negro Toilers* (London, 1931): 87; see also: 85–86.

13 See, for example, Padmore, "The Agrarian Crisis," *op. cit.*: 375, and RILU, "Rabota Profinterna sredi Negritianskogo Proletariata" ("The Work of the Profintern among the Negro Proletariat"), in *Mirovoe Revoliutsionnoe Profdvizhenie ot IV do V Kongressa Profinterna, 1928–1930* (Moscow, 1930): 243.

14 See, for example, Nguyen ai Quac (pseudonym for Ho Chi Minh), "Colonialisme Condamné: L'Expérience de l'Afrique Equatoriale Française," *Correspondance Internationale*, IV, no. 73 (October 28, 1924): 811–12.

15 See M. Joubert, "L'Insurrection des Nègres de l'Afrique Equatoriale Française," *Correspondance Internationale*, IX, no. 11 (February 6,

1929): 113. See also R. Bishop, "La Situation des Ouvriers Nègres dans les Colonies Britanniques d'Afrique," *Correspondance Internationale*, XII, no. 83 (October 5, 1932): 932, which developed the argument that all imperialism—whether French, British, or Belgian —was bringing about the progressive disappearance of Black Africa's indigenous population.

16 Ford, *The Economic Struggle of Negro Workers, op. cit.*: 10; Padmore, *Life and Struggles, op. cit.*: 98; RILU, "Rabota Profinterna," *op. cit.*: 242–43.

17 See especially Zusmanovich, ed., *op. cit.*: 164f.

18 See "La Souffrance des Noirs aux Etats-Unis et en Afrique," by Jim Crow, *Correspondance Internationale*, VIII, no. 34 (April 4, 1928): 452.

19 I. Rikhter, "Kavirondskoe Zoloto," *Materialy po Natsional'no· Kolonial'nym Problemam*, NIANKP, no. 3, 1933: 110.

20 J. Kenyatta, "An African Looks at British Imperialism," *Negro Worker*, III, no. 1 (January, 1933): 21.

21 Shiik, "Chernaia Afrika," *op. cit.*: 251, citing Kenyatta's remarks printed in the *Sunday Worker* of the CPGB (October 27, 1929): 1.

22 See, for example, "Résolution sur l'Afrique du Sud" (of the ECCI), *Internationale Communiste*, no. 25 (December 15, 1928): 1935–36, which refers to an industrial labor force in South Africa composed of 420,000 Negroes—a figure which was seen to be "mounting rapidly." (See also Zusmanovich, *op. cit.*: 152ff.)

23 Afrikanskii Kabinet NIANKP, "Zoloto v Afrike," *Materialy*, no. 4, 1934: 152, and Afrikanskii Kabinet NIANKP, "Bel'giiskoe Kongo," *Materialy*, no. 1, 1935: 111.

24 Afrikanskii Kabinet NIANKP, "Zoloto v Afrike," *op. cit.*: 155–56.

25 Padmore, "Agrarian Crisis," *op. cit.*: 374.

26 See Zusmanovich, ed., *op. cit.*: 146–47.

27 Thomas Ring, "The Revolutionary Forces of Africa," *Negro Worker*, I, no. 1 (January, 1931): 14.

28 Afrikanskii Kabinet NIANKP, "Emigratsiia i Immigratsiia v Afrike," *Materialy*, no. 9, 1934: 115ff, and Afrikanskii Kabinet NIANKP, "Bel'giiskoe Kongo," *op. cit.*: 111.

29 "Bel'giiskoe Kongo," *loc. cit.* Kuusinen had pointed out as early as the Sixth Comintern Congress that this recently proletarianized stratum of colonial populations was worthy of particular revolutionary interest. (*Stenograficheskii Otchet VI Kongressa*, IV, *op. cit.*: 23.)

30 See *Correspondance Internationale*, VIII, no. 124 (October 18, 1928): 1345, and Afrikanskii Kabinet NIANKP, "Emigratsiia," *op. cit.*: 115f.

31 Afrikanskii Kabinet NIANKP, "Bel'giiskoe Kongo," *op. cit.*: 109.

32 *Ibid.*: 106.

33 Padmore, "Agrarian Crisis," *op. cit.*: 373. See also Zusmanovich, ed., *op. cit.*: 145, citing report of Governor General of Gold Coast for 1932. As Zusmanovich observed, the psychological and political effects of unemployment in West Africa were most significant among recent graduates and formerly employed civil service workers.

34 Zusmanovich, ed., *ibid.*: 119.

35 *Stenograficheskii Otchet XI Plenum IKKI* ("Stenographic Account of the Eleventh Plenum of the ECCI"), no. 2 (Moscow, 1931): 129.

36 "Report of Lozovsky to the Fifth Congress of the RILU," *Negro Worker*, I, nos. 4/5 (April/May, 1931): 17.

37 See *Correspondance Internationale*, X, no. 69 (August 15, 1930): 887.

38 "Report of Lozovsky," *op. cit.*: 17.

39 RILU, "O Rabote sredi Negrov-Rabochikh," *op. cit.*: 149, 152.

40 Report of Joe (November 20, 1930), SLOTFOM, V, Box 3, File 73, subfile 51: 3–4, citing confidential report of Kouyaté on the Congress to the executive meeting of the LDRN, Paris.

41 *Ibid.*: 3.

42 RILU, "Negritianskaia Afrika," in RILU, *Rezoliutsii i Postanovleniia V Kongressa, op. cit.*: 65.

43 *Loc. cit.*

44 *Loc. cit.*

45 See Ford, "Negro Seamen and the Revolutionary Movement in Africa," *Negro Worker*, I, nos. 4/5 (April/May, 1931): 10.

46 *Loc. cit.* See also Padmore, "The Revolutionary Movement in Africa," *Negro Worker*, I, no. 6 (June, 1931): 5.

47 See Padmore, "Agrarian Crisis," *op. cit.*: 374. See also Padmore, "The Fight for Bread," *Negro Worker*, III, nos. 6/7 (June/July, 1933): 2f.

48 See RILU, "Negritianskaia Afrika," *op. cit.*: 65.

49 Padmore, "Agrarian Crisis," *op. cit.*: 375.

50 RILU, "Negritianskaia Afrika," *op. cit.*: 65–66.

51 "An Appeal to the Negro Workers and Toilers," *Negro Worker*, VI, no. 2 (April, 1936): 20.

52 Padmore, "Agrarian Crisis," *op. cit.*: 375.

53 RILU, "Negritianskaia Afrika," *op. cit.*: 66.

54 Padmore, "Agrarian Crisis," *op. cit.*: 375.

55 Padmore, *American Imperialism Enslaves Liberia* (Moscow, 1931): 34.

56 Padmore, *Life and Struggles, op. cit.*: 27, and "L'Impérialisme Britannique au Nigéria," *op. cit.*: 847.

57 Resolution of the ECCI to the CPSA, 1930, cited in S. W. Johns, "Marxism-Leninism in a Multi-Racial Environment." (Ph.D. dissertation, Harvard University, 1965): 535.

58 "Plan of Work of the International Trade Union Committee of Negro Workers of the RILU," *Negro Worker*, I, no. 4 (December, 1928): 2.

59 See Zusmanovich, ed., *op. cit.*: 180.

60 See, for example, Padmore, *Life and Struggles, op. cit.*: 125, and Padmore, *The Negro Workers and the Imperialist War—Intervention in the Soviet Union* (ITUC-NW, Hamburg, 1931): 15.

61 Padmore, *Negro Workers and Imperialist War, ibid.*: 14–15.

62 Padmore, *American Imperialism Enslaves Liberia, op. cit.*: 34. It may be supposed with some justification that the Comintern's final abandonment of the American-based "Back to Africa" scheme as a path toward African revolution coincided with the general decrease in Comintern reliance upon American Negroes as leaders of Negro African revolution.

63 Padmore, *Life and Struggles, op. cit.*: 125. See also Cyril Briggs, "How Garvey Betrayed the Negroes," *Negro Worker*, II, no. 6 (June, 1932): 14–17.

64 See Hermann Remmele, "On the Defence of the Soviet Union," *Communist International*, VIII, no. 14 (August 1, 1931): 389, and "War against War," *Inprecorr*, XIV, no. 43: 1111.

65 Remmele, *op. cit.*: 389.

66 As Padmore explained it ("The World Today," *Negro Worker*, I, no. 8 [August, 1931]: 2), the imperialists "want to turn the Soviet Union into a colony which they would loot and rape as they are doing in Africa." Cyril Briggs ("War in the East: Negro Workers Fight Against Intervention," *Negro Worker*, II, no. 5 [May, 1932]: 6) further suggested that the riches of the Soviet Union might provide imperialists with cause to forget their differences—in favor of a combined exploitative effort.

67 Remmele, *op. cit.*: 389.

68 See R. Page Arnot, "British Imperialism Preparing for War and Its Colonial Contradictions," *Communist International*, XI, no. 14 (July 20, 1934): 470; Padmore, *Negro Workers and the Imperialist War, op. cit.*: 2; and "Our Aims," *Negro Worker*, I, no. 1 (January, 1931): 5.

69 *Stenograficheskii Otchet XI Plenum, op. cit.*: 14ff. These remarks were also published in English under the title *War Preparations against the Soviet Union* (New York, 1931).

70 *Stenograficheskii Otchet XI Plenum, ibid.*: 17. The theory of imperialist collusion was also explained to Africans in the *Negro Worker*. In "The Study Corner" (*Negro Worker*, II, no. 5 [May, 1932]: 32), it was asserted that "the more they are driven to quarrel among themselves, the more the policy of dropping their quarrels in favor of an attack on the USSR leading to the opening up of Russia as a market for capitalism finds favor."

71 See Yobe, "Le Pacte Franco-Britannique et l'Oppression Coloniale," *Correspondance Internationale*, XII, no. 64 (August 3, 1932): 711.

72 Isaac Deutscher, *Stalin* (New York, 1960): 408. See also A. Vassiliev, "The Communist Parties on the Anti-Militarist Front," *Communist International*, VIII, no. 14 (August 1, 1931): 385, concerning France's role as "chief organizer" of the intervention.

73 Padmore, *The Life and Struggles, op. cit.*: 112.

74 *Stenograficheskii Otchet XI Plenum, op. cit.*: 14.

75 Padmore, *Life and Struggles, op. cit.*: 32. See also Padmore, "How the Imperialists are Civilizing Africa," *Negro Worker*, II, no. 3 (March, 1932): 11–14.

76 Padmore, *Life and Struggles, op. cit.*: 32.

77 Padmore, *Negro Workers and the Imperialist War, op. cit.*: 10. Zusmano-vich, ed., *op. cit.*: 50, directly accused the Belgians of instructing their Negro African subjects in the techniques of warfare in order to prepare them for service in Europe—"for example, in a war against Russia."

78 See Karine, "L'Armée Coloniale de l'Impérialisme Français," *Correspondance Internationale*, XI, no. 57 (July 1, 1931): 735, and Ford "Les Ouvriers Nègres et le Premier Mai," *Correspondance Internationale*, IX, no. 36 (May 1, 1929): 520.

79 *Afrikanskii Kabinet NIANKP*, "Kolonialnye Voiska v Afrike," *Materialy*, no. 5, 1934: 143. This study also undertook a detailed analysis of the geographical deployment of French and British units composed of African troops.

80 *Ibid.*: 150ff. In the Comintern view, by employing Anglo-Saxons from the British dominions in such places as Negro Africa, Britain was in effect endeavoring "to make out of the 'White Empire' a garrison to hold down the 'Coored Empire.' " (Page Arnot, *op. cit.*: 470.)

81 H. A., "La Croisade contre L'URSS et les Peuples Coloniaux," *Correspondance Internationale*, X, no. 24 (March 15, 1930): 267.

82 Afrikanskii Kabinet NIANKP, "Kolonialnye Voiska," *op. cit.*: 149–50.

83 Shiik, "Chernaia Afrika," *op. cit.*: 236, noted that opposition to conscription was a motive factor behind the 1929 native uprisings in Kenya. Other incidents were noted in Afrikanskii Kabinet NIANKP, "Kolonialnye Voiska," *op. cit.*: 154–56.

84 Page Arnot, *op. cit.*: 468. See also H. A., "La Croisade," *op. cit.*: 267.

85 Report of Joe (citing report of Kouyaté), November 20, 1930, SLOT-FOM, V, Box 3, File 73, subfile 51: 3. Among its public resolutions the Congress included a call for "systematic agitational-propaganda work" among those Negroes who were "being used by the imperialists for the creation of Negro armies." (RILU, *Rezoliutsii i Postanovleniia V Kongressa, op. cit.*: 152.)

86 Huiswood remarks at ECCI meeting April 9, 1931, *Stenograficheskii Otchet XI Plenum, op. cit.*: 129. "Why have not the French comrades as far as I know not published heretofore a single proclamation for distribution among the African soldiers in the French army?" he complained.

87 *Loc. cit.* Huiswood felt certain that Negroes would respond to Comintern appeals, including those for the defense of the U.S.S.R. He characterized "the contemporary situation in the colonies of imperialist countries" as one which "opens before us brilliant perspectives in the task of bringing the Negro workers into our movement."

88 Vassiliev, *op. cit.*: 385–87. The latter move was prompted by the belief that imperialist governments, prior to the attack on the U.S.S.R., would conduct a general crack down on known communist organizations. (See *Strenograficheskii Otchet XI Plenum, op. cit.*: 39.)

89 Vassiliev, *op. cit.*: 388. See also "Appeal to the Black Soldiers of France," *Negro Worker*, I, no. 1 (January, 1931): 20–22, which warned that "a new war is very near" and advised France's African troops that "the example of the Red Army of the Soviet Union is yours to follow. War against imperialist war." This appeal was addressed specifically to soldiers of French Equatorial Africa, asking them "where have five million of your population gone?" and reminding them of the revolt of their compatriots in 1928–29. ("Appeal to Black Soldiers," *ibid.*: 21.)

90 See, for example, such articles as "Colonial Toilers Used as Cannon Fodder," *Negro Worker*, I, no. 7 (July, 1931): 6, and Cyril Briggs, "Negro Workers Fight against Intervention," *op. cit.*: 6–8.

91 Copies of this pamphlet were sent by the French government on October 6, 1931, to all governors of French colonies in Negro Africa. (SLOTFOM, V, Box 70, document nos. 1156–62.)

92 Padmore, "The World Today," *Negro Worker*, II, no. 3 (August, 1932): 4. This appeal was designed to promote attitudes such as that

held by Kouyaté, who, when asked what he would do in case France went to war, responded unhesitatingly that he would "openly preach insubordination and military disobedience." (Report of Joe, November 20, 1930, SLOTFOM, V, Box 3, File 73, subfile 51: 3.)

93 Padmore, "The War is Here," *Negro Worker*, II, nos. 1/2 (January/February, 1932): 10. Similar statements appear in Padmore, *Negro Workers and the Imperialist War, op. cit.*: 9. In urging Africans not to allow the history of the First World War to repeat itself, it is interesting that Padmore used essentially the same arguments employed by Houénou at the beginning of the 1920's, i.e. that Africans had given their lives only to be cruelly deceived in postwar political arrangements. (Padmore, "The World Today," *op. cit.*: 4.)

94 Bernier, "La Crise de l'Empire Français," *Correspondance Internationale*, XIII, nos. 39/40 (May 20, 1933): 495.

CHAPTER NINE

1 See, for example, such articles as "Zabastovka Zheleznodorozhnikov v IUzhnoi Rodezii," in *Mezhdunarodnoe Rabochee Dvizhenie* (RILU weekly, Moscow), no. 14 (April 5, 1929): 14–16, and articles in *Krasnyi Internatsional Profsoiuzov* (monthly organ of the RILU Executive Committee, Moscow; also published in London as the *R.I.L.U.* magazine).

2 Both *Kolonialnyi Mir: Spravochnik Dlia Propagandista* ("The Colonial World: Handbook for the Propagandist") (Leningrad, 1929), and *Mirovoe Professional'noe Dvizhenie: Spravochnik Profinterna* (Moscow, 1927), VII: 127–302, deal with Africa.

3 RILU, "Rabota Profinterna Sredi Negritianskogo Proletariata" ("The Work of the Profintern among the Negro Proletariat"), in *Mirovoe Revoliutsionnoe Profdvizhenie ot do v Kongressa Profinterna, 1928–1930* (Moscow, 1930): 242.

4 These included such titles (in French editions) as "Les Syndicats et la Situation de la Classe Ouvrière dans l'URSS" and "Les Syndicats Russes et la Nouvelle Politique." (See Nancy Cunard, ed., *Negro Anthology* [London, 1934]: 567.)

5 The preface to this pamphlet, written by Lozovsky, appears in *Negro Worker*, I, no. 7 (July, 1931): 11–13.

6 C. L. R. James, "Notes on George Padmore" (MSS): 12, 19f.

7 J. R. Hooker, *Black Revolutionary: George Padmore's Path from Communism to Pan-Africanism* (New York, 1967): 27.

8 Austin Worth, "Some Negro Workers in the Soviet Union," *Negro Worker*, VII, no. 6 (June, 1937): 10, and James, *op. cit.*: 15.

9 James, *ibid.*: 19.

10 Padmore, *How Russia Transformed Her Colonial Empire* (London, 1946): x, and James, *op. cit.*: 2ff. In this context it is interesting to note that KUTV sources themselves refer to the introduction of "a course on the Negro movement" at the University in 1929. (See "O Rabote i Ocherednykh Zadachakh," *Revoliutsionnyi Vostok*, no. 7, 1929: 360.)

11 See T. Jackson, "Under the Banner of the ILD in Africa," *Negro Worker*, III, nos. 2/3 (February/March, 1933): 27.

12 See Samuel Rohdie, "The Gold Coast Aborigines Abroad," *Journal*

of African History, VI, no. 3 (1965): 396, citing correspondence between Padmore and Sekyi contained in the Ghanaian National Archives.

13 See Hooker, *op. cit.*: 154–56, for an enumeration of the "most important articles by Padmore." This list omits, however, such significant articles as "The Agrarian Crisis in West Africa", in *Communist International*, VIII, no. 13 (July 1, 1931), as well as all of Padmore's contributions to the *Negro Worker*.

14 Titles listed in Hooker, *op. cit.*: 22. Padmore's contribution to Nancy Cunard's communist-oriented *Negro Anthology* (*op. cit.*) is also worthy of mention in this context. Not only did he send his own writings for inclusion in the text, but he was instrumental in putting Miss Cunard in touch with other contributors. (Hooker, *op. cit.*: 28.) Contributors to the volume included many leading figures in the Negro movement for political and cultural emancipation—Nnamdi Azikiwe, Johnstone Kenyatta, Countee Cullen, Langston Hughes, James Ford, and William E. DuBois—making the final work a landmark in the recorded history of the movement.

15 See George Skorov, "Ivan Potekhin—Man, Scientist and Friend of Africa," *Journal of Modern African Studies*, II, no. 3 (1964): 444.

16 As a contributor to the *Negro Worker* Potekhin himself became part of the system of Soviet control over the periodical. When, for example, he submitted such apparently authoritative articles as "How to Build the Unemployed Movement" (*Negro Worker*, II, nos. 11/12 [November/December, 1932]: 17–24), they found almost immediate echoes in editorial statements written by Padmore. (See Padmore's editorial, "What Must Be Done," *Negro Worker*, III, nos. 6/7 [June/July, 1933]: 2.)

17 I. I. Potekhin, interview with Rolf Italiaander in the latter's *Schwarze Haut im Roten Griff* (Dusseldorf, 1962): 74.

18 Padmore, "Fifteen Years of Soviet Russia," *Negro Worker*, II, nos. 11/12 (November/December, 1932): 28. Similar statements were made at approximately the same time by Zusmanovich and Potekhin in their study of Black Africa. The region, they felt, had reached a decisive crossroads in its development. Either it could take the option of increased pauperization or it could follow the revolutionary example of Russia and China: "The October Revolution in Russia, the fifteen year existence of the USSR, and the Soviet movement in China —all these conditions are an obvious indication of where the path to freedom is to be found." (A. Z. Zusmanovich, ed., *Prinuditel'nyi Trud i Profdvizhenie v Negritianskoi Afrike* [Moscow, 1933]: 163.) See also James Ford, "Communism and the Negro," in Cunard, *op. cit.*: 287, who, offering the same reasons, admonishes "our brothers in Africa" to "embrace communism."

19 Title of regular section in the *Negro Worker*. See, for example, "In the Land of Socialism: Education in the Soviet Union," *Negro Worker*, II, nos. 9/10 (September/October, 1932): 19–21.

20 See, for example, Cyril Briggs, "The World Situation and the Negro," *Worker*, II, no. 6 (June, 1932): 27ff.

21 "How to Organize for Mass Action (The Example of Russian Workers)," *Negro Worker*, I, no. 2 (February, 1931): 21–22.

22 See J. B., "The Union of Free Soviet Republics," *Negro Worker*, I, no. 12 (December, 1931): 15, and M. J. Olgin, "A Brotherhood of Nationalities," *Negro Worker*, I, no. 6 (June, 1931): 20ff.

23 The *Negro Worker* helped to popularize this argument by devoting attention to such incidents as that involving the nephew of the Nigerian Prince of Abeokutu who was unable to find rooms in London because of racial discrimination. ("Believe It or Not," *Negro Worker*, II, no. 5 [May, 1932]: 21.)

24 Although this theme was a recurrent one in the pages of the *Negro Worker*, it was perhaps most fully developed in Nancy Cunard's *Negro Anthology*. After a visit to the U.S.S.R. she declared: "Today in Russia alone is the Negro a free man, one hundred per cent equal," with the same certitude she asserted that "the world communist order is the solution of the race problem for the Negro." (Cunard, *op. cit.*: iv, iii.)

25 See Worth, *op. cit.*: 10; George Padmore, *Negro Workers and the Imperialist War—Intervention in the Soviet Union* (Hamburg, 1931): 4–5; and *La Race Nègre*, IV, no. 2 (September, 1930): 4, for accounts of the incident.

26 Padmore, *Negro Workers and the Imperialist War, op. cit.*: 5. Padmore was reportedly asked by Manuilsky to serve on the commission of inquiry which investigated the incident. (See Hooker, *op. cit.*: 35.)

27 See, for example, Padmore, "Soviets for Peace—Capitalists for War," *Negro Worker*, II, no. 5 (May, 1932): 1–6.

28 See Padmore, "How the Empire is Governed," *Negro Worker*, II, no. 7 (July, 1932): 1–6.

29 See Padmore's writings: "Soviets for Peace," *op. cit.*: 3–4; "How the Empire is Governed," *op. cit.*: 1–6; and *The Life and Struggles of Negro Toilers* (London, 1931): 99. See also J. Bile (Secretary, LDRN-Cameroon), "How the Workers Live in Cameroon," *Negro Worker*, II, no. 7 (July, 1932): 28–30. This article describes how life in the Cameroon under British and French tutelage was really no different than it had been previously under German rule.

30 See Padmore, *Negro Workers and the Imperialist War, op. cit.*: 8.

31 Caption appearing beneath a picture of a Negro missionary in Africa (*Negro Worker*, II, nos. 9/10 [September/October, 1932]: 11). In an article on the adjacent page, for example, the conclusion was reached that "beyond doubt the Christian church and missionary societies in Nigeria are the biggest exploiting agencies in the country." (Yuraba, "Religion in the Service of Imperialism," *Negro Worker*, II, nos. 9/10 [September/October, 1932]: 10.)

32 "To Our Brothers in Kenya," *Negro Worker*, III, nos. 8/9 (August/September, 1933): 22. This criticism was directed specifically to the KCA in Kenya which had been devoting energy to drawing up legal petitions, etc. It should be noted, however, that Kenyatta and his colleagues in the KCA were regarded by Padmore and other Comintern leaders as belonging to the category of revolutionists rather than reformists. (See A. Shiik, *"Chernaia Afrika na Revoliutsionnom Puti"* ["Black Africa on the Revolutionary Path"], *Revoliutsionnyi Vostok*, no. 8, 1930: 251.) For example, after publishing Kenyatta's virulently anti-British article, "An African Looks at British Imperialism"

(*Negro Worker*, III, no. 1 [January, 1933]: 18–22), Padmore observed: "We hope to be able in the future, with the assistance of Comrade Kenyatta, to go more fully into the situation in Kenya in order to render the maximum assistance at our disposal in this fight of the Kenya toiling masses against imperialism." ("Editor's Note," *Negro Worker*, III, no. 1 [January, 1933]: 23.)

33 Padmore, "Notes and Comments," *Negro Worker*, III, nos. 8/9 (August/September, 1933): 15.

34 Padmore letter to Sekyi, September 7, 1932, cited in Rohdie, *op. cit.*: 394. (Italics mine.)

35 See "Our Study Corner," *Negro Worker*, I, no. 2 (February, 1931): 21–22, and *Negro Worker*, I, no. 1 (January, 1931): 26–27.

36 "Study Corner," (February, 1931), *op. cit.*: 25. See also W. Sworakowsky, ed., *The Comintern and Its Front Organizations* (Stanford, 1965): 363, for a listing of these correspondence courses.

37 See "Our Study Corner: The Organization of Workers' Defence Corps," *Negro Worker*, I, no. 3 (March, 1931): 19.

38 "How to Organize the Unemployed," *Negro Worker*, V, no. 4 (April, 1935): 17.

39 See "To Our Brothers in Kenya," *op. cit.*: 24, and Padmore, "Editor's Note," *op. cit.*: 23–24.

40 James, *op. cit.*: 18. See also Padmore's article, "Hands Off Liberia" (*Negro Worker*, I, nos. 10/11 [October/November, 1931]: 5–11) in which he recommended a series of organizational measures for Liberian workers and made a general appeal for trade union formation in large coastal cities of West Africa. See also request from Nigeria for revolutionary instructions. (Letter to the Editor, *Negro Worker*, I, nos. 10/11 [October/November, 1931]: 39.)

41 "What the Workers of Sierra Leone Should Do: Open Letter from the ITUC-NW to the Workers of Sierra Leone," *Negro Worker*, I, no. 9 (September 15, 1931): 17–19. This was also issued by the ITUC-NW as a special pamphlet.

42 *Ibid.*: 18.

43 *Ibid.*: 18–19.

44 *Ibid.*: 18.

45 See "Our First Anniversary," *Negro Worker*, II, nos. 1/2 (January/February, 1932): 3.

46 *Loc. cit.* Particularly among sailors the motto was to be "every reader —a writer and distributor." (*Loc. cit.*)

47 *Loc. cit.* See also "Liberians Inspired by 'Negro Worker,' " *Negro Worker*, II, no. 3 (March, 1932): 32; and K. Tamba, "Liberia and the Labor Problem," *Negro Worker*, II, no. 6 (June, 1932): 3, which refer to the establishment of a section of the ITUC-NW in Liberia.

48 Unsigned letters (presumably from government agents engaged in surveillance over LDRN activities in France) dated March 16, 1929, and June 15, 1932, in SLOTFOM, V, Box 2, File 1, subfile 50, document 676.

49 See "Letter to the Editor" from Liberia, *Negro Worker*, VI, no. 1 (March, 1936): 24, which refers to "our journal" having reached "the two extremes of this country" and having "penetrated the Firestone plantations."

50 Hooker, *op. cit.*: 26, cites 4000 as the maximum figure for the *Negro Worker*'s circulation in the colonies.

51 *Negro Worker*, VII, nos. 7/8 (September/October, 1937): 2.

52 See "Our First Anniversary," *op. cit.*: 2–3. For example, it was noted that "every ship carrying a black crew which arrives in the harbour of Freetown is immediately raided by the native police, under ex-CID officers, and searched for the *Negro Worker*." (*Ibid.*: 3.)

53 "Bosses Afraid of the *Negro Worker*," *Negro Worker*, I, nos. 10/11 (October/November, 1931): 40–41. A resident of Nigeria reported (*loc. cit.*) that despite government efforts, "we are still receiving it [the *Negro Worker*]" and whatever the penalties "we will never turn back and stop reading the *Negro Worker*."

54 Padmore, "The Agrarian Crisis," *op. cit.*: 374. Padmore uses approximately the same citation in *Life and Struggles, op. cit.*: 90.

55 For example, according to a letter to the editor printed in the *Negro Worker*, a Liberian was able to find encouragement in the example of the national liberation struggle of workers in South Africa. (*Negro Worker*, VI, no. 1 [March, 1936]: 5.) See also statements of Macauley concerning the effects of the journal on nationalist sentiment in Nigeria. ("The Situation in Nigeria," *Negro Worker*, nos. 10/11 [October/November, 1931]: 38.)

56 James, *op. cit.*: 11.

57 Letters to Sekyi, June 9 and July 9, 1932, cited in Rohdie, *op. cit.*: 393. Although Padmore did not say so directly, the educational institution he had in mind was KUTV University. Padmore's correspondence with Sekyi is also interesting in that it indicates the key role of African sailors in the conduct of the ITUC-NW's covert activities. As Padmore wrote Sekyi from Hamburg, it was from "the African seamen calling at this port" that we "first received your address." (Letter to Sekyi, March 23, 1932, Rohdie, *ibid.*: 392.)

58 James, *op. cit.*: 22. For further reference to the recruitment activities of the LDRN see subsequent discussion of policy implementation in French Africa.

59 Russell Howe, "George Padmore," *Encounter*, XIII, no. 6 (December, 1959): 53. An abbreviated version of this article appeared in the *Washington Post* (October 11, 1959): E3, under the title "Africa Owes a Lot to the Major." Similar information regarding Padmore's clandestine activities is presented in Roi Ottley's *No Green Pastures* (New York, 1951): 62ff. Both accounts appear to be based upon conversations with Padmore himself (Howe in Ghana c. 1958; Ottley in London c. 1950)—hence any exaggerations may be Padmore's own.

60 Secret Minute Paper prepared by Colonial Secretary (Bathurst) for Governor of Gambia (Gambia Archives, file no. 438 for 1930).

61 James, *op. cit.*: 2.

62 Padmore, *New Leader*, October 3, 1942, cited in Hooker, *op. cit.*: 16.

63 Ottley, *op. cit.*: 66.

64 *Ibid.*: 62.

65 See James, *op. cit.*: 11, for reference to Padmore's use of aliases and disguises.

66 *Northern Provinces Nigeria, Police Intelligence Report for Quarter Ending*

March, 1930, "Political and Religious influences," paragraph 3, in Colonial Office Archives (C.O.), Series 583, Box 174, File 864.

67 *Northern Provinces Nigeria, Police Intelligence Report for Quarter Ending June, 1930,* "External Bolshevik Propaganda," paragraph 21, in C.O. 583/174/864. Enlisting the assistance of both the British Consul in Tunis and the S.I.S., British investigators uncovered the account of the agreement with Moscow from several independent Tunisian sources.

68 Reportedly £10,000 in cash was reserved for the Sultan of Sokoto alone. (*Northern Nigeria Intelligence Report March, 1930, op. cit.*: paragraph 7.)

69 *Ibid.*: paragraph 4.

70 Secret letter from Lieutenant Governor of Northern Nigeria, H. R. Palmer, to Government Chief Secretary, Lagos, March 5, 1930, in C.O. 583/174/864. See also C.O. 583/160/237. The latter file contains a letter dated May 7, 1928, from the French Minister of Foreign Affairs to the British Ambassador in Paris regarding the assassinations.

71 *Northern Nigeria Intelligence Report March, 1930, op. cit.*: paragraph 1.

72 It is interesting that both Mahdist and communist connections were apparent in the backgrounds of the conspirators themselves. One of the terrorists, for example, had fought with the forces of the Mahdi against Britain in the Sudan, while another reportedly worked for Moscow in establishing the communist trade union movement in Tunisia. (*Northern Nigeria Intelligence Report June, 1930, op. cit.*: paragraph 3.) According to Palmer, all confessed they were "out to destroy all European power" in Africa. (Palmer, appendix to letter, March 5, 1930, *op. cit.*)

73 See Palmer, *ibid.* See also notation to this letter by A. Cooke (Colonial Office), May 23, 1930 (C.O. 583/174/864). In this context, it is interesting to recall the Comintern's expectation during the early 1920's that Bolshevism might be transmitted from North Africa across the Sahara into West Africa.

74 Palmer letter, *op. cit.*

75 A personal exposure to African conditions seems, for example, to be discernible in Padmore's writings after the spring of 1930. Both "The Agrarian Crisis in West Africa," *op. cit.* and *American Imperialism Enslaves Liberia* (Moscow, 1931), appear to reflect a detailed knowledge of West Africa—a knowledge which would have been extremely difficult to acquire simply by study in Moscow and Hamburg.

76 Jan Valtin (pseudonym for Richard Krebs), *Out of the Night* (an autobiography of his career as a professional Comintern agent) (New York, 1940): 241. It is interesting that Krebs, who attended the ISH organizational conference in Moscow in 1930, also refers to "a special department for agitation among Negroes" as being part of the initial plans for the ISH. (*Loc. cit.*)

77 Georgi Dimitrov, the operational boss of the Comintern, revealed the thinking behind the Comintern's emphasis on maritime work when he told Krebs "nothing is better for taming the capitalist shark than to cut off his exports and imports." (*Ibid.*: 238.) In this connection see also the *Negro Worker*'s exhortation: "Negro slaves in Africa: refuse to

load and unload ammunition and armies destined to massacre your class brothers in the East." (*Negro Worker*, II, no. 4 [August, 1929]: 23.)

78 See, for example, Kouyaté's articles "Black and White Seamen Organize for Struggle," *Negro Worker*, I, no. 12 (December, 1931): 19–20, and "Solidarity between White and Colored Sailors," *Negro Worker*, II, no. 3 (March, 1932): 27–28. Working through the International Seamen's Club in Marseilles, Kouyaté was particularly active in organizing African sailors in that French port. (See Director of Sûreté Générale [the French internal security agency] to Minister of Colonies, Confidential Report, March 6, 1930, in SLOTFOM, V, Box 2, File 2, subfile 54, and *Negro Worker*, I, nos. 10/11 [October/November, 1931]: 36.)

79 See ISH Executive, "New Organizations for Negro Seamen," *Negro Worker*, I, nos. 10/11 (October/November, 1931): 27–28.

80 *Loc. cit.* See also Zusmanovich, ed., *op. cit.*: 148.

81 See Zusmanovich, ed., *loc. cit.*, and ISH, "Appeal to Negro Seamen and Dockers," *Negro Worker*, II, no. 4 (April, 1932): 20–24. See also "Colonial Toilers Used as Cannon Fodder," *op. cit.* (*Negro Worker*, I, no. 7 [July, 1931]: 6.)

82 See "World Congress of Seamen," *Negro Worker*, II, no. 6 (June, 1932): 23–25.

83 *Loc. cit.* The Congress passed a resolution calling for an immediate campaign to organize colored seamen in the metropoles and in the colonies. (*Ibid.*: 25.)

84 See Padmore, "Speech at the World Congress of the ILD," *Negro Worker*, III, nos. 2/3 (February/March, 1933): 4.

85 François Coty, *Sauvons Nos Colonies: Le Péril Rouge au Pays Noir* (Paris, 1931): 87, and Jackson, "Under the Banner of the ILD in Africa," *op. cit.*: 27–28. A letter from Cayla in Tananarive, September 2, 1930, to the French Minister of Colonies refers to the visit to Madagascar in May, 1930, of the French lawyer Foissin, who performed organizational work for the ILD in the course of his stay. (SLOTFOM, V, Box 2, File 1, subfile 133, document 1015.)

86 H. Stassova, "Dix Années de Secours Rouge International," *Correspondance Internationale*, XII, no. 91 (November 1, 1932): 1038, and Jackson, "Under the Banner," *op. cit.*: 27.

87 Padmore, "Speech," *op. cit.*: 4, and Jackson, "The ILD and the Negro Peoples," *Negro Worker*, III, nos. 2/3 (February/March, 1933): 12.

88 Stassova, "Le Congrès Mondial du Secours Rouge," *Correspondance Internationale*, XIII, no. 1 (January 4, 1933): 4, and Jackson, "ILD," *op. cit.*: 9.

89 This mimeographed periodical is not to be confused with the *Bulletin Colonial* of the PCF which it resembles.

90 See "Renforçons Immédiatement Notre Action Contre la Terreur dans les Colonies!" *Bulletin Colonial*, no. 4 (February/March, 1933): 1–2. See also "Introduction," *Bulletin Colonial*, no. 1 (April, 1934): 1, for an enumeration of the objectives of the periodical.

91 See *Le Cri des Nègres*, II, no. 1 (July/August, 1933): 1, and Cunard, *op. cit.*: 567.

92 See *Bulletin Colonial*, no. 4 (February/March, 1933): 5.

93 For example, the ILD's journal *Défense* (French edition) devoted attention to the separatist movement in Madagascar and was subjected to government confiscation upon its arrival on the island. (*Bulletin Colonial* [PCF], II, no. 11 [February, 1933]: 29.)

94 See "La Revue Anti-Impérialiste," *Correspondance Internationale*, XI, no. 102: 1148.

95 See, for example, (LAI) *Information Bulletin*, no. 3, 1933: 7, which describes the details of popular unrest in the Gold Coast.

96 The *Nigerian Daily Telegraph*, July 22, 1930: 4. See issue dated July 21, 1930: 5, for an example of one of the dispatches emanating from Berlin.

97 Notes of G. L. M. Clauson, Colonial Office, dated October 5, 1930, C.O. 583/174/864.

98 Thompson to Passfield, confidential letter, August 15, 1930, C.O. 583/174/864, no. 7.

99 Clauson, notes, *op. cit.*

100 The decision to make the British section of the LAI a "particularly influential" one was taken at a meeting of the LAI Secretariat in Berlin, May 10, 1930. ("La Ligue Anti-Impérialiste pour le Soutien de la Lutte Libératrice aux Indes," *Correspondance Internationale*, X, no. 43 [May 21, 1930]: 504.) George Padmore, *Pan-Africanism or Communism?* (London, 1956): 328, notes that the LAI-Britain was subsequently "run from behind the scene" by members of the CPGB.

101 A. Fiddian (Senior Assistant to Secretary of State for Colonies, in charge of West African Department), note dated October 2, 1935, C.O. 96/724/31198. See also C.O. 583/173/852.

102 See LAI correspondence with the Colonial Office in C.O. 96/724/ 31163, 31198 and C.O. 583/173/852. Padmore (*Pan-Africanism, op. cit.*: 328) notes that other activities of the LAI-Britain included the organization of public meetings, conferences, and demonstrations, and the publication of popular pamphlets on such topics as British rule in Africa.

103 See Rohdie, *op. cit.*: 394, for reference to the LAI's contacts with the *Manchester Guardian*, etc. Bridgeman also published his protests to the British government in the *Negro Worker* (*Negro Worker*, II, no. 3 [March, 1932]: 30–31). See C.O. 323/1517/7046/3, no. 13 and C.O. 96/731/31230, for parliamentary questions posed by Sorensen on the basis of information received from West Africa by Bridgeman.

104 In August, 1935, for example, the ARPS submitted to Bridgeman "for your perusal and immediate action" a report concerning popular discontent in the Gold Coast (Bridgeman letter, August 12, 1935, to Secretary of State for Colonies MacDonald, C.O. 96/724/31163, no. 3). The same year Wuta Ofei, Editor of the *Gold Coast Spectator*, forwarded to Bridgeman an article concerning riots at Appam (allegedly provoked by the local British District Commissioner) with the request: "Please see whether the matter cannot be taken up with the Colonial Office through Parliament." (Ofei, letter to Bridgeman, cited by Colonel Sir Vernon Kell [British Intelligence officer evidently responsible for screening Bridgeman's mail] in a letter to F. J. Howard, Colonial Office, dated September 2, 1935, C.O. 96/724/ 31198.)

105 Mr. Creasy, Colonial Office, Notes dated June 9, 1936, C.O. 96/731/
31230. See also C.O. 96/740/31230/1.

106 See Rohdie, *op. cit.*: 405. Bridgeman had in mind Awoonor-Renner's
Ashanti Freedom Society, to be discussed later. See also Bridgeman
letter to Editor, *Gold Coast Spectator*, January 6, 1935, cited in Rohdie,
ibid.: 404.

107 See, for example, *Negro Worker*, VI, nos. 3/4 (May/June, 1936): 11,
reproducing a letter from Bridgeman urging support for WAYL candidates in the Gold Coast elections. Upon Wallace-Johnson's arrival
in London from West Africa in March, 1937, moreover, he contacted
Bridgeman immediately and thereafter, British intelligence observed,
the two remained "closely in touch." (C.O. 323/1517/7046/3, nos. 5,
9.) Bridgeman's liaison services for the WAYL included the facilitation of communication between Wallace-Johnson and his followers in
the Gold Coast. (See messages both to and from the Gold Coast which
went via Bridgeman [C.O. 323/1517/7046/3].) Wallace-Johnson's
organizational work for the WAYL in the Gold Coast (1934–36) and
in Sierra Leone (1938–39) will be discussed subsequently.

108 Colonel Kell, secret letter to F. J. Howard, June 21, 1937, C.O.
323/1517/7046/3, no. 9. According to this intelligence source, the
money financed initial issues of the IASB's monthly paper, *Africa and
the World*. The same source notes that the offices of the IASB and
those of the LAI were next door. Members of the IASB cited previously in this study included C. L. R. James, Jomo Kenyatta, Nancy
Cunard, and the Reverend Sorensen. (*Ibid.*: no. 16.) For a description
of the IASB see Padmore, *Pan-Africanism, op. cit.*: 146ff.

109 See "A Nos Lecteurs," *Bulletin Colonial*, II, no. 15 (June, 1933). Discussions of the economic plight of black Africans occupied a prominent place in the *Bulletin*'s regular survey of French colonial injustices.
In addition, this periodical also dealt with political exploitation of
Africans, discussing such subjects as the extent of anti-colonial unrest
in Madagascar and the coming conscription of military manpower
from West Africa via the Trans-Saharan railroad. (See, for example,
section on French West Africa and French Equatorial Africa in
Bulletin Colonial, II, no. 13 [March, 1933]: 19a. See also "Préparation
à la Guerre," *Bulletin Colonial*, II, no. 12 [March, 1933]: 5, and
"Résistance des Travailleurs," in same issue: 19c–21.)

110 Jacques Doriot, *Les Colonies et le Communisme* (Paris, 1929). In urging
unconditional support for colonial emancipation, Doriot made a
point of attacking the position of the reformist-minded socialists, who
wanted to reserve for themselves the right to decide when colonial
peoples were ready for independence. Using Africa as an example, he
argued that regardless how backward were subject peoples, self-
government could be no more detrimental to them than imperialist
rule. "Could Congolese Negroes," he asked dramatically, "if they
took affairs into their own hands, really do worse than imperialism
which brought about the disappearance of two out of four million
men [in the colony] in the span of only a decade?" (*Ibid.*: 100; see
also *ibid.*: 40.)

111 Ford, "The Influence of the Comintern among Negroes," *Negro
Worker*, II, no. 2 (March/April, 1929): 2.

112 See "Une Manifestation Révolutionnaire à Tananarive," *Action Française* (July 3, 1929): 2, which remarks of the demonstration: "the effect upon the indigenous population cannot fail to be considerable."

113 *Le Réveil Malgache*, I, no. 3 (August 16, 1929), makes this claim. Subsequently *Le Réveil* was replaced by another violently nationalist organ edited by French communists, *L'Aurore Malgache*.

114 See Georges G. Joutel, "Les Menées Communistes à Madagascar" ("Communist Plots in Madagascar"), *La Presse Coloniale* (November 28, 1930): 1.

115 Although differing in name, the new *Ligue* was generally referred to in French government documents and elsewhere by the same initials as Houénou's organization—LDRN.

116 See "Vox Africae," *La Race Nègre*, II, no. 2 (April, 1929): 1, and Report of Paul, October 14, 1929, SLOTFOM, V, Box 3, File 73, subfile 51.

117 Marseilles representative of CAI (Service de Contrôle et d'Assistance en France des Indigènes des Colonies, Ministère des Colonies [special branch of Colonial Ministry responsible for surveillance over natives of French colonies resident in France]), secret letter to Director of Political Affairs, French Ministry of Colonies, January 4, 1930, SLOTFOM, V, Box 2, File 2, subfile 54.

118 *Loc. cit.*

119 Note of Agent (Désiré?), dated August 13, 1929, SLOTFOM, V, Box 3, File 73, subfile 51.

120 R. Antonetti, Governor General of French Equatorial Africa, confidential letter, June 17, 1929, to Minister of Colonies, SLOTFOM, Box 2, File 2, subfile 54. In the course of these revolts, the inhabitants of the Upper Sangha Province (now the Central African Republic) actually achieved independence from French rule for several days.

121 Reports of Désiré, September 10, 1927, June 3, 1928, and October 18, 1929, SLOTFOM, V, Box 3, File 73, subfile 51. These reports mention, for example, conversations between Kouyaté and Lamine Guèye of Senegal concerning the latter's plans to oppose France politically. (Guèye, together with Leopold Senghor, was subsequently elected to the French Parliament and became a prominent figure in post-independence Senegalese politics.) The reports also refer to letters received by Kouyaté from friends in Dahomey, announcing their plans to establish an LDRN branch in that colony, and to circulars sent by Kouyaté to African students urging them to support the work of his organization.

122 Report of Désiré, August 11, 1927, SLOTFOM, V, Box 3, File 73, subfile 51. See also Governor General of French Equatorial Africa to Political Affairs Department of Ministry of Colonies, August 30, 1927, SLOTFOM, V, Box 2, File 2, subfile 54. Large numbers of copies were also sent to the international sailors' clubs established with RILU funds in Bordeaux and Marseilles. (Report dated October 22, 1927, in SLOTFOM, V, Box 3, File 73, subfile 51.)

123 Letter from Commandant, Deuxième Brigade, Troupes du Groupe de L'AOF, Kati, to Political Affairs Department of Ministry of Colonies, Paris, October 9, 1927, SLOTFOM, V, Box 2, File 2, subfile 54. *La Race Nègre* also appears to have reached readers on the grass

roots level in the Ivory Coast and in the Cameroon. (*Loc. cit.*, and Coty, *Le Péril, op. cit.*: 238.)

124 Report of Désiré, November 28, 1928 (probably based on LDRN claims), SLOTFOM, V, Box 3, File 73, subfile 51.

125 Kouyaté, "Speech at the Congress of LAI," *Negro Worker*, II, no. 4 (August, 1929): 3.

126 See Report of Désiré, September 10, 1927, SLOTFOM, V, Box 3, File 73, subfile 51, and Coty, *Le Péril, op. cit.*: 237–38, who refers to LDRN recruitment activities in the Cameroon.

127 Report of "Rosso" to LDRN executive meeting, Paris, January 10, 1929, cited in Report of Désiré, January 12, 1929, SLOTFOM, V, Box 3, File 73, subfile 51. This source (SLOTFOM, *ibid.*) contains numerous reports of government informants who, it should be noted, attended LDRN meetings. The proceedings of these meetings provided a major part of their information on *Ligue* activities.

128 Report of Désiré, May 21, 1928, in *ibid.*

129 Report of Désiré, March 9, 1929, in *ibid.* The sum agreed upon was half of the regular expenses of *La Race Nègre*, plus 800 francs monthly.

130 Report of Coco, July 5, 1929, in *ibid.*

131 This was the opinion of the French government and PCF officials. (*Loc. cit.*)

132 Reports of Paul, October 26, and November 1, 1929, in *ibid.*

133 Report of Paul, October 11, 1929, in *ibid.*

134 *Loc. cit.*, and Report of Paul, December 21, 1929, in *ibid.* Whereas according to the first directive only ten students were to be sent, after Kouyaté's second visit to Moscow the LDRN was commissioned to recruit on an annual basis as many as 300 students for study in Soviet institutions. (Report of Désiré, November 18, 1930, in *ibid.*)

135 Report of Désiré, November 18, 1930, in *ibid.* For a text of Kouyaté's remarks at the Fifth Congress of the RILU, see "Un Discours Nègre au Congrès de L'I.S.R.," *La Race Nègre*, IV, no. 1 (July, 1930).

136 Reports of Claude, June 15, 1931, and Désiré, November 18, 1930, in SLOTFOM, V, Box 3, File 73, subfile 51.

137 *Loc. cit.*

138 Report of Désiré, November 18, 1930, in *ibid.* (The exact words may have been Désiré's.)

139 S. R. (probably Stéphane Rosso), "Les Misères et les Souffrances de Tout un Peuple Nègre," *La Race Nègre*, IV, no. 2 (September, 1930): 2.

140 Report of Paul, October 14, 1929, SLOTFOM, V, Box 3, File 73, subfile 51.

141 *Loc. cit.*

142 See numerous articles in *La Race Nègre* demanding African independence, for example: "La Jeune Afrique et Ses Luttes," III, no. 2 (February/March, 1930): 3–4; S. R., "En A.O.F.," IV, no. 3 (November/December, 1930): 3–4; and "Chose du Caméroun," IV, no. 3, *ibid.*: 1. In this latter issue see also Kouyaté, "Conquête des Larges Masses Nègres": 1, in which Kouyaté declares, "The strike —that is our weapon especially in Africa, where it takes on a clearly political character." See Report of Paul, October 14, 1929, SLOTFOM, V, Box 3, File 73, subfile 51, which refers to LDRN

interest in the military question. A text of the LDRN program appears in Fernand Huré, "Le Mouvement Pan-Noir et le Bolchevisme," *Le Temps Coloniale*, October 7, 1930.

143 Report of Paul, November 20, 1930, SLOTFOM, V, Box 3, File 73, subfile 51.

144 See Report of Paul, April 17, 1930, in *ibid.*

145 In one LDRN executive meeting, for example, Rosso declared that "all alone the *Ligue* would be helpless. What it needs is the support of a strong party." (Report of Joe, May 10, 1931, in *ibid.*)

146 Report of Désiré, November 18, 1930, in *ibid.*

147 One such meeting, held December 20, 1929, is described both in the Report of Joe, December 22, 1929 and the Report of Guillaume, December 21, 1929, in *ibid.*

148 Report of Désiré, November 18, 1930, in *ibid.* See also Report of Paul, November 25, 1930, in *ibid.*, which notes, "the objective pursued by Kouyaté is the disorganization of the *Ligue* and the creation of a new organization which he will place under the aegis of the Communist Party."

149 Report of Joe, November 20, 1930, in *ibid.*

150 *Loc. cit.*

151 See *La Race Nègre* (Faure), IV, no. 4 (April, 1931), which appeared simultaneously with *La Race Nègre*, IV, no. 4 (April, 1931), published by Kouyaté and Rosso. Although this first editorial effort was short-lived, the Faure branch of the LDRN did persist in its drive to oppose Kouyaté and to promote the cause of African independence. In addition to distributing in Africa tracts calling for the establishment of a "Negro African Republic" ("Appel Fraternel aux Nègres du Monde Entier," *La Race Nègre* [Faure], no. 1 [July, 1935]), this organization at the end of 1934 revived its version of *La Race Nègre* and included in it repeated demands for the granting of independent status to French West Africa. (See "Notre Ligne Politique," *La Race Nègre* [Faure], VII, no. 1 [November/December, 1934]: 1.)

152 Report of Joe, April 5, 1931, in SLOTFOM, V, Box 3, File 73, subfile 51. The organizations designated were the PCF, the LAI, the ILD, and the French communist trade union organization—the *Confédération Générale du Travail Unitaire* (CGTU, the forerunner of the CGT.)

153 See reports of Paul, February 14, and November 12, 1930, in *ibid.*, and *Le Cri des Nègres*, II, no. 3 (November/December, 1933): 2. Although this was not formally an LDRN project, it was conducted with LDRN funds.

154 See "A Tous nos Abonnés, Membres et Lecteurs," *La Race Nègre*, IV, no. 4 (April, 1931): 1. See also Report of Paul, May 25, 1930, in SLOTFOM, V, Box 3, File 73, subfile 51; Coty, *Le Péril, op. cit.*: 235–39; and "Au Caméroun: Une Colonie Torpille," *La Race Nègre*, IV, no. 2 (September, 1930): 1.

155 See "Manifeste de la Ligue de Lutte pour la Liberté des Peuples du Sénégal et du Soudan," *Le Cri des Nègres*, II, no. 5 (April/May, 1934): 4, continued in *Le Cri des Nègres*, II, no. 6 (June, 1934): 4.

156 "Au Caméroun: Les Nègres Doivent Prendre la Direction de Leur Pays: Un Example Qui Nous Vient de l'Union Soviétique," *Le Cri*

des Nègres, IV, no. 11 (November, 1934): 3, and "Manifeste de la Ligue" (part 1), *op. cit.*: 4.

157 "Aux Cameroun, *op. cit.*: 3.
158 "Manifeste de la Ligue" (part 2), *op. cit.*: 4; "M. Herriot a Visité l'Union Soviétique," *Le Cri des Nègres*, II, no. 2 (September, 1933): and "Au Caméroun," *op. cit.*: 3.
159 See, for example, "L'Union Soviétique est à la Tête de la Civilisation," *Le Cri des Nègres*, II, no. 8 (August, 1934): 4. See also in same issue Julians, "A la Veille d'Une Nouvelle Guerre": 1, and "Les Nègres dans l'Armée Impérialiste," *Le Cri des Nègres*, II, no. 2 (September, 1933): 1.
160 Although Fernand Huré in "Le Mouvement Pan-Noir et le Bolchevisme," *op. cit.* does refer to the LDRN having obtained "thousands of adherents in all the colonies," this was probably an exaggeration.
161 Zusmanovich, ed., *op. cit.*: 151, referring to the achievements of *Le Cri des Nègres* in Central Africa. See also "The 'Cri des Nègres' Penetrates the Belgian Congo," *Negro Worker*, IV, no. 8 (December, 1934): 24.
162 The hasty and insistent nature of these assertions, however, suggests that even their authors were concerned about the threat of communism in French Africa. See Maurice Satineau, "Le Communisme et l'Opinion Indigène," *La Dépêche Africaine*, III, nos. 29/30 (October/November, 1930): 1; "Les Colonies Françaises et le Communisme: Les Malgaches Ne Sont Pas Communistes," *La Dépêche Africaine*, III, no. 20 (January 15, 1930): 5; and Satineau, "Christianisme et Communisme," *La Dépêche Africaine*, IV, no. 34 (March 15, 1931): 6.
163 Satineau, "Le Communisme et l'Opinion Indigène," *op. cit.*: 1.
164 Charles Cros, ed., *La Parole est à M. Blaise Diagne* (Paris, 1961): 62.
165 Joutel, *op. cit.*: 1.
166 Coty, *Le Péril*, *op. cit.*: 239.
167 Yvon Delbos, *L'Expérience Rouge* (Paris, 1933): 229.
168 The Governor General of French West Africa to Minister of Colonies, secret communication dated January 19, 1931, SLOTFOM, V, Box 2, File 2, subfile 54.
169 See reports on *La Race Nègre* by Paris Prefecture of Police such as that dated March 13, 1929, in SLOTFOM, V, Box 2, File 2, subfile 54, and correspondence between Director of the French Sûreté Générale and the Minister of Colonies, 1929–30, in *ibid.*
170 See, for example, telegrams of Minister of Colonies, June 8, 1928, in SLOTFOM, V, Box 2, File 2, subfile 54, and covering letters of December, 1929, accompanying copies of *La Race Nègre*, III, no. 1 (January, 1930) in *ibid.* See also "La Ligue de Défense de la Race Nègre Proteste Contre les Saisies de Son Journal," *L'Humanité* (January 31, 1929), which refers to seizures of *La Race Nègre* in Dahomey, the Ivory Coast, Togo, and French Guinea. Désiré (Report January 12, 1929, SLOTFOM, V, Box 3, File 73, subfile 51) describes a complaint received by the LDRN from one subscriber—a postal worker on the Guinean railroad—who had been refused delivery of the paper by his superiors in the post office.
171 Governor General of French West Africa communication to Political Affairs Director, Ministry of Colonies, dated December 26, 1935

(SLOTFOM, V, Box 2, File 2, subfile 54) noting that all recipients of *Le Cri* had been placed under surveillance.

172 See Report of Joe, May 10, 1931, SLOTFOM, V, Box 3, File 73, subfile 51.

173 Padmore to Sekyi, June 9, 1932, cited in Rohdie, *op. cit.*: 393.

174 *Ibid.*: 395, citing correspondence between the Secretary of the NWA (Ward) and Sekyi, 1932. The NWA also appears to have extended assistance to Negro children and unemployed seamen in London, and to have had a share in the ILD campaign on behalf of "the Scottsboro boys" in Britain.

175 *Loc. cit.*

176 Ward was listed as a "Contributing Editor" in the *Negro Worker*, III, nos. 2/3 (February/March, 1933). See, for example, such articles in the *Negro Worker* as Ward, "The Negro Situation in England," *Negro Worker*, IV, nos. 6/7 (October/November, 1934): 7–9.

177 See S. W. Johns, "Marxism-Leninism in a Multi-Racial Environment" (Ph.D. dissertation, Harvard University, 1965): 502.

178 See Valtin, *op. cit.*: 382f., who accuses the leaders of the CPGB of extreme corruption in the early 1930's. Manuilsky, who had scolded the CPGB for laxity in colonial work at the Fifth Comintern Congress, was obliged to repeat his recriminations before the English Commission of the ECCI in 1932. (See K. McKenzie, *The Comintern and World Revolution* [New York, 1963]: 199.) It was not until 1937 that the Communist Party of Britain followed the example of its counterpart in France by publishing a *Colonial Information Bulletin* (see vol. I, no. 1, April 15, 1937) and by issuing directives to district party committees to emphasize colonial work. (See CPGB circular, April 16, 1937, "To All District Party Committees," in C.O. 323/1517/7046/1.)

179 See I. J. T. Turbett (Attorney General, Sierra Leone) report on NCBWA in C.O. 267/655/32157, and C.O. 87/225/XF8054.

180 See articles of incorporation submitted by BTU General Secretary, T. C. Fye, to British Colonial Secretary, Bathurst, in a letter dated September 28, 1929 (C.O. 87/229/12167).

181 For a detailed description of the strike see proceedings of government inquiry held at the end of November, 1929, in C.O. 87/230/12182.

182 See confidential letters to Secretary of State for Colonies, Lord Passfield, from Governor of Gambia, Sir Edward Denham, December 12, 1929 (C.O. 87/229/12167, no. 22), and from Acting Governor Workman, January 24, 1930 (C.O. 87/230/12182, no. 1).

183 See C.O. 87/238/2388, no. 3, for Passfield circular dated September 17, 1930. After reviewing the case of the Gambian trade union, Dr. T. Drummond Shiels, then Parliamentary Undersecretary of State for Colonies, proposed that the government "look into this class of legislation generally in our colonies." He further noted that "trade unions are likely to arise, even in West Africa. I hope they will be under better guidance than in Gambia, as I don't trust Mr. Small." (T. D. S. Shiels, note dated March 8, 1930, in C.O. 87/230/12182.)

184 See Walter Bowen, *Colonial Trade Unions* (London, 1954): 4f., for further description of the Passfield circular. See also note by member of Colonial Office referring to Small in C.O. 87/230/12223. In a meeting with the "Chief Traveling Inspector" of Gambia, Shiels

learned that Small's "personal character is high. He lives an ascetic life and is respected locally by the black people. His politics, however, are definitely on communist lines." (C.O. 87/230/12223.)

185 Governor Denham to Flood, Colonial Office, November 5, 1929, C.O. 87/229/12167.

186 Coty, *Le Péril, op. cit.*: 25, citing prisoner interrogations in Bathurst.

187 Smeral [Small?], "Les Expériences de la Révolution d'Octobre et la Lutte d'Emancipation des Colonies," *Correspondance Internationale*, X, no. 94 (November 12, 1930): 1212.

188 Prior to his meeting with Bridgeman, the Secretary of State for Colonies had apparently been unaware of the situation in Gambia. Confronted with the information which Bridgeman had received from Small, he promptly demanded of the local Governor "what the trouble is" in Gambia. (See Small telegram to LAI, November 4, 1929, regarding labor conditions in Gambia and unsigned reply from the organization promising support in Great Britain. See also Bridgeman's approaches to the Colonial Office and Passfield communication to Governor Denham, November 8, 1929, all contained in C.O. 87/229/12167.)

189 RILU, "O Rabote sredi Negrov-Rabochikh," ("Work Among Negro Workers"), *Rezoliutsii i Postanovleniia v Kongressa* (Moscow, 1930): 148. See also RILU, "Rabota Profinterna," *op. cit.*: 243, for reference to the events in Gambia.

190 See *Gambia Outlook*, April 5, 1930. Another article borrowed from the *Negro Worker* was John Reed's "Anti-Imperialist Struggles of Negro Workers" (*Gambia Outlook*, March 29, 1930).

191 ITUC-NW, *A Report of Proceedings and Decisions of the First Conference of Negro Workers* (Hamburg, 1930): 21. See also Secret Minute Paper (Bathurst), *op. cit.*

192 See Smeral, [*sic.*] *op. cit.*: 1212. ITUC-NW, *Report of Proceedings, op. cit.*: 21–23, contains Small's statements at the Hamburg Conference. His remarks were republished as "Situation of Workers and Peasants in Gambia," *Negro Worker*, I, no. 1 (January, 1931): 22–24.

193 ITUC-NW, *Report of Proceedings, op. cit.*: 40.

194 Zusmanovich, ed., *op. cit.*: 158.

195 See C.O. 87/230/12223; C.O. 87/238/2388; and C.O. 87/241/33075.

196 Workman to Passfield, letter dated June 2, 1930, C.O. 87/230/12223, no. 1: 2–3. Lord Passfield, proceeding "upon the advice of the Acting Governor of Gambia," asked the British Foreign Secretary, Arthur Henderson, to inform the Liberian Minister in London that the British government did "not consider desirable" Small's appointment. (Letter from Downing Street, June 11, 1930, C.O. 87/230/12223, no. 2: 3.)

197 In 1926 he led a strike of Sierra Leone railroad workers which James Ford (*Economic Struggle of Negro Workers* [New York, 1930]: 10) described as "the first serious attempt at trade union organization in West Africa." Blacklisted by the government, he went to sea (See Hooker, *op. cit.*: 51) and appeared the following year at the first congress of the LAI in Brussels. It was at this gathering that Wallace-Johnson presumably first came into contact with the Soviets and was invited to visit Russia in late 1927.

198 See Chin Sheng-Pao, "The Gold Coast Delegations to Britain in 1934: the Political Background," *National Chengchi University Studies in African Affairs*, no. 2 (Taipei, 1970): 17.

199 See "British Oppression in West Africa," by "A Sierra Leone Correspondent" [Wallace-Johnson], *Negro Worker*, I, no. 12 (December, 1931): 21.

200 James Coleman, *Nigeria: Background to Nationalism* (Berkeley, 1958): 208.

201 "Death of Macauley," *Negro Worker*, I, nos. 10/11 (October/November, 1931): 43.

202 *West African Nationhood* (organ of the Lagos branch of the NCBWA), October 13, 1931, cited by Coleman, *op. cit.*: 458, footnote 17. See also "British Oppression in West Africa," *op. cit.*: 23f., for further discussion of AWUN objectives.

203 Zusmanovich, ed., *op. cit.*: 118.

204 *Loc. cit.* Reportedly the British even resorted to sending police spies to AWUN meetings. (*Loc. cit.*)

205 Padmore, "Notes and Comments," *op. cit.* (*Negro Worker*, III, nos. 8/9): 26–28. See also Governor Jardine of Sierra Leone to Secretary of State for Colonies, Malcolm MacDonald, secret letter, June 30, 1938, giving background information on Wallace-Johnson, in C.O. 267/665/32208, no. 7.

206 Wallace-Johnson's correspondence with Hamburg was intercepted by British authorities (see Jardine letter, *ibid.*: 2). In advance of Wallace-Johnson's arrival in Sierra Leone (February 18, 1933), the *Negro Worker* published his article (written under the pseudonym Wal. Daniels), "Unemployment in Sierra Leone and the Way Out," *Negro Worker*, III, no. 1 (January, 1933): 26–28.

207 Padmore, "Notes and Comments," *op. cit.*: 14.

208 Governor of Nigeria, letter dated December 5, 1933, to Secretary of State for Colonies, Sir Philip Cunliffe-Lister, C.O. 583/195/21029.

209 Note by A. Fiddian, January 20, 1934, C.O. 583/195/21029.

210 "British Oppression in West Africa," *op. cit.*: 20.

211 See Sheng-Pao, *op. cit.*: 11, and Jones-Quartey, "Press and Nationalism in Ghana," *United Asia*, IX, no. 1 (1957): 58.

212 See IU. IUg, "Zolotoi Bereg v 1934g." *Materialy* (NIANKP), no. 3, 1935: 108–15, for a detailed discussion of this ordinance and its political effects.

213 *Ibid.*: 110.

214 Sheng-Pao, *op. cit.*: 13, citing "official sources"—presumably memos from the Gold Coast government contained in C.O. 96/716/21729.

215 "This Sedition Business," *African Sentinel* (nationalist paper published by Wallace-Johnson in London), I, no. 2 (November/December, 1937): 7–8. See also record of meeting of Secretary of State for Colonies, Sir Philip Cunliffe-Lister, with Gold Coast and Ashanti Delegation at the Colonial Office, July 7, 1934, C.O. 96/717/21750/3. The material cited by the Colonial Secretary was a passage from one of the ITUC-NW exhortations concerning the importance of "turning the [coming] imperialist war into a civil war" as a step towards attaining the freedom of Africa.

216 See Sheng-Pao, *op. cit.*: 19, citing C.O. 96/714/21639.

217 Wallace-Johnson, "Down with the Howardian Legislation," *Gold Coast Spectator*, February 17, 1934.

218 See Wallace-Johnson, "The West African Youth League: Its Origin, Aims and Objects," *Negro Worker*, VII, no. 5 (May, 1937): 9. See also William L. Patterson, "West African Youth and the People's Front," *Negro Worker*, VII, no. 3 (March, 1937): 13.

219 Rohdie, *op. cit.*: 408. By the end of 1935, Rohdie notes, the WAYL was able to boast twenty branch committees in the Gold Coast. (*Ibid.*: 406.)

220 The British government conducted a rerun of the first election in order to give Bruce an opportunity to reverse his initial defeat. After his second loss the government named him to represent the Gold Coast at the coronation and awarded him an O.B.E.—signifying, according to Wallace-Johnson's sarcastic interpretation, "obedient boy of the Empire." (Personal letter from Edna Horton, former First Secretary of Wallace-Johnson's WAYL in Sierra Leone, January 10, 1970. See C.O. 96/740/31230/1 for information on the election. See also Charles Woodson's article, "People's Candidate—Victor in Gold Coast," *Inprecorr*, XV, no. 71, [December 28, 1935]: 1750–51.)

221 See Sheng-Pao, *op. cit.*: 38–39.

222 *Loc. cit.* Danquah is generally recognized as having been the first major leader of Gold Coast nationalism.

223 *Loc. cit.*

224 See, for example, "Youths' League Meeting," *African Morning Post*, July 16, 1935: 1, 8, which describes the proceedings and resolutions of a WAYL meeting held in Accra. In addition to Wallace-Johnson and Azikiwe, another frequent contributor to the *African Morning Post* was Padmore. See, for example, his article, "Anglo-Boer Conflict in South Africa," IV, *African Morning Post*, June 4, 1935: 5–6.

225 Wallace-Johnson, "West African Youth League," *op. cit.*: 14.

226 A. Fiddian (Colonial Office) note, September 5, 1935, C.O. 96/731/31230.

227 Hodson to Bottomley, confidential personal letter, January 14, 1936, C.O. 96/731/31230.

228 Unsigned note, March 27, 1936, C.O. 96/731/31230.

229 Hodson to Bottomley, confidential personal letter, February 12, 1936, C.O. 96/729/31205.

230 Unsigned note dated March 27, 1936, C.O. 96/731/31230. In a similar context Hodson complained to Bottomley (personal letter, January 14, 1936, *op. cit.* [C.O. 96/731/31230]) that Wallace-Johnson "just keeps within the law, but only just. At many of his meetings he says outrageous and criminal things, but the law officers tell me it is almost impossible to get a conviction on spoken word. There is something wrong with our Constitution which allows these sort [*sic.*] of people to be at large. The French would not tolerate it for one second."

231 See "Wallace-Johnson Trial Ends Before Magistrate," *Gold Coast Spectator*, July 4, 1936.

232 See Report of Gold Coast Inspector General of Police, C.O. 96/731/31230. The same file contains a copy of the article. Although it did nothing more than question the morality of the European civilizing mission in Africa (albeit at times bitterly), the article was officially

regarded as "bringing the government into hatred." (Hodson to Secretary of State for Colonies, telegram, June 12, 1936, C.O. 96/731/31230, no. 7.)

233 See C.O. 96/731/31230, nos. 3, 16. Azikiwe was also charged with sedition, but he was eventually acquitted. (See *African Morning Post*, March 25, 1937: 1.)

234 Reprints of "Has the African a God?" appeared in such distant papers as the *Panama Tribune* (November 22, 1936). See C.O. 96/731/31230, and Wallace-Johnson, "West African Youth League," *op. cit.*: 9, which claims that WAYL membership, estimated at three to four thousand in June, 1936, had swollen to seven thousand by the end of the year.

235 The *London Times*, May 27, 1939, reports that Sir Stafford Cripps, who became famous in connection with the liquidation of the British Empire after World War II, appeared on Wallace-Johnson's behalf at the appeal hearing. Wallace-Johnson received public support in Britain from such organizations as the British Trades Union Council and the National Council for Civil Liberties. The latter organization was quoted as declaring (*Gold Coast Spectator*, July 30, 1938): "The Wallace-Johnson case which has naturally aroused very great interest in the Gold Coast . . . will tend to restrict the intellectual awakening which is taking place amongst the colonial peoples and is, therefore, of importance throughout the British Empire."

236 Although he had first refused to bear the costs of the case (Hodson letter to MacDonald, January 4, 1939, C.O. 96/759/31230/2), Governor Hodson was ultimately obliged to comply with the request of the Secretary of State that the funds be supplied by the Gold Coast government. (MacDonald telegram to Hodson, July 3, 1939, and Hodson telegram to MacDonald, July 4, 1939, in C.O. 96/759/31230/2.) Shortly before his request to Hodson, MacDonald had expressed his opinion on the issue: "It seems to me that we are in danger of depriving colonial citizens of equal justice." (Note in MacDonald's hand, June 29, 1939, C.O. 96/759/31230/2.) See C.O. 96/759/31230/2, no. 56, for text of final judgement against Wallace-Johnson.

237 Even the Governor of Sierra Leone, Sir Douglas Jardine, was forced to admit that Wallace-Johnson had "considerable personal magnetism for the masses" and that in attracting popular support he had succeeded "far beyond our expectations." (Jardine, secret letters to MacDonald, November 28, 1938, and June 30, 1938, C.O. 267/666/32216, and C.O. 267/665/32208.) Upon the request of Jardine, the Colonial Secretary was even obliged to issue a formal statement disavowing the claim of the WAYL to speak for the entire population of Sierra Leone. (See secret [coded] telegram, no. 103, Jardine to MacDonald [c. June, 1939] and secret telegram, no. 143, MacDonald to Jardine, both in C.O. 267/672/32254/1.) See the *African Standard* (organ of the WAYL—Sierra Leone), June 23, 1939, for League estimates of its own strength.

238 Acting Governor Blood to Secretary of State for Colonies MacDonald, secret letter, February 9, 1939, C.O. 267/670/32210/2, part I. Freetown was recognized as an important halfway point on the strategic supply route between Britain and Latin America. By October,

1939, the port had become the headquarters of the South Atlantic Command of the British Navy.

239 Acting Attorney General of Sierra Leone, Charles Abbott, memorandum, February 5, 1939, in C.O. 267/670/32210.

240 It should be noted, however, that in 1938 the British government had information confirming that Wallace-Johnson was "an adherent of the Communist Party" in Britain. (See Jardine to MacDonald, secret letter, November 28, 1938, *op. cit.* [C.O. 267/666/32216].) He was, moreover, a contributing editor of the *Negro Worker* between 1934 and 1937.

241 See C.O. 96/731/31230, and C.O. 96/729/31205. See also note by Colonial Office official, C.O. 96/731/31230/1, which observed that according to the new Amendment of the Immigration Restriction Ordinance, 1936, introduced specifically to deal with Wallace-Johnson, the Sierra Leonean agitator was to be denied re-entry to the Gold Coast as an "undesirable" British subject, not native to the Gold Coast.

242 In response to Wallace-Johnson's activity in Sierra Leone, the colonial government introduced four new ordinances in June and July, 1939: the Undesirable British Subjects Control Ordinance, the Sedition Ordinance, the Undesirable Publications Ordinance, and the Incitement to Disaffection Ordinance. (See "Draft Brief for the Secretary of State when He Receives the Deputation Regarding Certain Sierra Leone Ordinances," C.O. 267/673/32254/8, no. 15B.) Following the introduction of the first of these ordinances, sympathy for Wallace-Johnson ran so high in Freetown that the Governor felt it necessary to request that a British warship come in order to help support the government. (*Loc. cit.*) In October, 1938, the Sierra Leone government had sought to convict Wallace-Johnson of criminal libel, but, armed with the assistance of a battery of local lawyers (eighteen of the colony's twenty-one lawyers were reported to be members of the WAYL), he won the case and subjected the government to considerable embarrassment. (See C.O. 267/671/32221.) The government, however, managed to have the last word when it raided Wallace-Johnson's headquarters (September 3, 1939) and placed the WAYL Secretary under detention under the provisions of the new legislation. (Jardine to MacDonald, telegram, September 5, 1939, and secret letter, September 23, 1939, C.O. 267/670/32210/2.)

CHAPTER TEN

1 See Jane Degras, *The Communist International, 1919–1943: Documents* (3 vols., London, 1956–65): 176–80, for a partial text of this and a subsequent ECCI appeal.

2 See Cyril Briggs, "War in the East: Negro Workers Fight against Intervention," *Negro Worker*, II, no. 5 (May, 1932): 6–8, and *Negro Worker*, III, no. 1 (January, 1933): 17. The same theme was also taken up by *Le Cri des Nègres* which insisted: "Let us establish a guard around Russia." ("Contre Impérialismes: Montons la Garde autour de la République des Soviets," *Le Cri des Nègres*, I, no. 3 [October, 1931]: 2.)

3 George Padmore, "The War is Here," *Negro Worker*, II, nos. 1/2 (January/February, 1932): 4, and Padmore, "The World Today," *Negro Worker*, I, no. 8 (August, 1931): 2.

4 Padmore, *Negro Workers and the Imperialist War—Intervention in the Soviet Union* (Hamburg, 1931): 9. See also Padmore, "The War is Here," *op. cit.*: 8.

5 In particular, the Comintern was responding to the Japanese attempt in 1932 to gain concessions from the Ethiopians by convincing them that it was "in the interests of both coloured nations to establish the closest ties against white imperialism." (See Padmore, "Ethiopia Today," in Nancy Cunard, ed., *Negro Anthology* [London, 1934]: 17.) To this Padmore responded: "Although it might suit their present needs to pose as the 'defenders' and 'champions' of the darker races, Japanese imperialists are quite as ruthless as the white imperialist nations." (*Loc. cit.*) In the same vein, American Negro communists fought bitterly Japan's efforts to win support for its "Pacific Movement of the Eastern World" among American Negroes—contending that the recent interest of the Japanese in the world's Negroes was simply a function of their anti-Soviet military plans. (See Harry Haywood's report to the Eighth Convention of the CPUSA, Cleveland, April, 1934, in *The Road to Negro Liberation* [New York, 1934]: 46.)

6 Not only such observers as François Coty (*Sauvons Nos Colonies: Le Péril Rouge au Pays Noir* [Paris, 1931]: 232–34), but also the French government itself was aware of this fact. See confidential report of Director of Sûreté Générale to Minister of Colonies, December 16, 1930, SLOTFOM, V, Box 2, File 2, subfile 54, in which Germany is accused of "behind the scenes" support of Comintern agitation among the population of French West Africa. It is even possible, as suggested by Coty (*Le Péril, op. cit.*: 254ff.) that in such places as the Cameroon German-Comintern cooperation actually extended to an operational level.

7 Despite repeated British protests concerning the seditious effects of ITUC-NW propaganda in Negro Africa, the ITUC-NW was allowed to continue its activities after only the most perfunctory of restrictive measures by the German police. (See Jan Valtin, *Out of the Night* [New York, 1940]: 360, and Rolf Italiaander, *Schwarze Haut im Roten Griff* [Dusseldorf, 1962]: 70.) Clearly, had the Weimar government been so inclined, it could easily have disowned and evicted such enterprises—as the Nazis later demonstrated.

8 See Valtin, *op. cit.*: 385–416, for a good description of the early Nazi crackdown on communists.

9 See Italiaander, *op. cit.*: 57, which cites an eyewitness account to the effect that machine gun emplacements, etc., had been set up in the upper stories of the building.

10 See Editorial, "Fascist Terror against Negroes in Germany," *Negro Worker*, III, nos. 4/5 (April/May, 1933): 2.

11 See *ibid.*: 1–3.

12 See Max Beloff, *The Foreign Policy of Soviet Russia, 1929–1941*, I (London, 1949), Chapter VIII: "Russia and the Nazi Reich": 94–105.

13 *Ibid.*: 139–42.
14 See Roger Kanet, "The Soviet Union and Sub-Saharan Africa: Communist Policy toward Africa, 1917–1965." (Ph.D. dissertation, Princeton University, 1966): 157, citing D. W. Brogan, *The Development of Modern France* (New York, 1940): 651–701.
15 Beloff, *op. cit.*: 135–37.
16 *Ibid.*: 152ff.
17 *Ibid.*: 111–12.
18 *Ibid.*: 114, and Isaac Deutscher, *Stalin: A Political Biography* (New York, 1966): 418.
19 See Beloff, *op. cit.*: 190.
20 Resolution of the Seventh Comintern Congress on "Fascism, Working-Class Unity, and the Tasks of the Comintern," cited in Degras, III, *op. cit.*: 364.
21 *Ibid.*: 367.
22 *Loc. cit.*
23 In this context, British concern lest Ethiopian resistance spark nationalist outbreaks in Britain's Negro African colonies was noted with particular interest. (See Jack Cohen, "British Imperialism in Abyssinia," *Inprecorr*, XV, no. 29 [July 13, 1935]: 756–57, and William L. Patterson, "The Abyssinian Situation and the Negro World," *Inprecorr*, XV, no. 20 [May 11, 1935]: 542–43.) For examples of Russian literature on the subject, see Zusmanovich, "Italo-Abissinskaia Voina i Pod'em Natsional'nogo Osvoboditel'nogo Dvizheniia" ("The Italo-Abyssinian War and the Rise of the National Liberation Movement"), *Revoliutsionnyi Vostok*, no. 2, 1935: 43–54, and other articles in *Revoliutsionnyi Vostok*, nos. 2, 6, for 1935.
24 "Hands Off Abyssinia" committees were to be formed in such organizations as churches, cooperatives, and labor unions. In each country a national "Committee of Friends of Abyssinian Independence" was also to be established. (See "Hands Off Abyssinia!," *Inprecorr*, XV, no. 27 [June 29, 1935]: 713–14, and William L. Patterson, "Negro Reforms, World Politics, and Ethiopia," *Inprecorr*, XV, no. 28 [July 6, 1935]: 743–45.)
25 James Ford, "The Struggle for Peace and the Independence of Ethiopia" (remarks delivered at the Seventh Comintern Congress), in *The Communists and the Struggle for Negro Liberation*, (New York, 1936): 41–47. In these remarks Ford specified: "The British communists should also help to further develop the movement which is now growing among the Negro population of London and in the British colonies. Our French communists, from the tribune of the broad Peoples Front in France, should . . . develop a broad movement in defense of the Ethiopian people." (*Ibid.*: 46.)
26 See Degras, III, *op. cit.*: 378–79, for text of ECCI telegram (September 23, 1935) to Secretariat of the Second International.
27 In the Gold Coast, for example, Wallace-Johnson's Youth League (together with African veterans groups) sponsored a local Ethiopia Defense Committee through which "funds were raised and forwarded to the Ethiopian Minister in London, in aid of distressed Ethiopians." (Wallace-Johnson, "The West African Youth League: Its Origin, Aims and Objects," *Negro Worker*, VII, no. 5 [May, 1937]: 14. See

also "While Abyssinia Groans," *African Sentinel*, I, no. 2 [November/ December, 1937]: 8–9, which describes subsequent meetings of the Gold Coast Ethiopian Defense Committee.) In London large open-air meetings were held by the International African Friends of Abyssinia. (See George Padmore, *Pan-Africanism or Communism?* [London, 1956]: 144–46, and "Les Organisations Nègres d'Angleterre," *La Race Nègre* [Faure], IX, no. 1 [January/February, 1936]: 2.) Perhaps the most active center of all was Paris. There an international headquarters known as the "International Committee for the Defense of the Abyssinian People" was established which claimed by 1936 an affiliation of two hundred organizations in various countries. Moreover, on May 9/10, 1936, presumably at the behest of the Comintern, this committee called an "International Conference of Arabs and Negroes" which attracted representatives from African organizations throughout Europe and Africa. The gathering was apparently concerned with wider issues than simply Ethiopian independence and harbored ambitions of becoming a permanent political organization uniting Arabs and Negroes. (See Adami's articles, "International Conference of Negroes and Arabs," *Inprecorr*, XVI, no. 24 [May 23, 1936]: 659, and "The Front of Negroes and Arabs in the Struggle against the Fascist War in Africa," *Inprecorr*, XVI, no. 9 [February 15, 1936]: 246.) Many of the individuals and organizations referred to previously in connection with Comintern activity—Padmore, Kenyatta, Rosso, Kouyaté, the LAI, the ITUC-NW, the UTN— were active in the campaign in behalf of Ethiopia.

28 Padmore, "Au Revoir," *Negro Worker*, III (August/September, 1933): 18.

29 J. R. Hooker, *Black Revolutionary* (New York, 1967): 31.

30 "Expulsion of George Padmore from the Revolutionary Movement," *Negro Worker*, IV, no. 2 (June, 1934): 15.

31 *Ibid.*: 14. Kouyaté was also expelled from the international communist movement at approximately the same time as Padmore.

32 Greenwood, "A Betrayer of the Negro Liberation Struggle," *Inprecorr*, XIV, no. 37 (June 29, 1934): 968.

33 See *loc. cit.*, and Haywood, *op. cit.*: 59.

34 "Expulsion of George Padmore," *op. cit.*: 14. The decision to expel Padmore was made by the Comintern's International Control Commission on February 23, 1934. Although Padmore had been asked to come to Moscow to defend his activities before Comintern leaders, he reportedly knew too well "the power of the Stalinist machine and the helplessness of the individual before it" to accept such a potentially dangerous invitation. (See C. L. R. James, "Notes on George Padmore" (MSS): 22, and Hooker, *op. cit.*: 31.) Valtin (second edition, 1941), *op. cit.*: 302–03, 317–18, describes the unhappy fate of numerous Comintern activists who accepted such invitations.

35 Padmore, "An Open Letter to Earl Browder" (Secretary of the CPUSA), *Crisis*, XXXII (October, 1935): 302. It is possible that Moscow did in fact receive a direct protest from the British government concerning ITUC-NW propaganda. The British government, it is known, took particular exception to Kenyatta's article "An African Looks at British Imperialism," which appeared in the January,

1933, issue of the *Negro Worker* (III, no. 1 [January, 1933]) and early in 1933 protested to the German government. (Italiaander, *op. cit.*: 70.) Certainly the British government had legal grounds upon which to lodge complaints. According to Article 16 of the Anglo-Soviet Treaty of 1924 (reconfirmed by exchange of notes December 21, 1929) both governments had agreed "to refrain and to restrain all persons and organizations under their direct or indirect control, including organizations in receipt of financial assistance from them, from any activity overt or covert liable in any way to endanger the tranquility or prosperity of any part of the territory of the British Empire or the USSR." (F.O. 371/14844, no. 19.)

36 Padmore, "Open Letter to Earl Browder," *op. cit.*: 302.

37 Padmore, "Au Revoir," *op. cit.*: 18.

38 Hooker, *op. cit.*: 31.

39 James, *op. cit.*: 22ff., notes that many of the Africans who were associated with Padmore in the Comintern chose to leave the movement when Padmore was ousted. James also notes that Negroes who refused to sign statements denouncing Padmore were expelled from their respective communist parties.

40 Samuel Rohdie, "The Gold Coast Aborigines Abroad," *Journal of African History*, VI, no. 3 (1965): 396–97, observes that Padmore's ideas had "little relevance to Gold Coast conditions" and therefore failed to appeal either to Sekyi or to the ARPS. In the same vein Christopher Allen, in his study of Gambian trade unionism ("The Pathology of Gambian Trade Unionism, 1929–67" [unpublished paper, Nuffield College, Oxford, 1967],) indicates that "Small's plans were foolishly ambitious and the advice he received from Britain and from the RILU (via the LAI and George Padmore) was inevitably inappropriate to the specific conditions of Gambia."

PART IV

CHAPTER ELEVEN

1 Harrison Salisbury, introduction to Homer Smith's memoir, *Black Man in Red Russia* (Chicago, 1964): x.

2 Alexander Dallin, "The Soviet Union: Political Activity," in Z. Brzezinski, ed., *Africa and the Communist World* (Stanford, 1963): 9–10. Dallin adds: "During the Stalin era Africa attracted no significant attention except in the Comintern, which did little more than deplore the absence of Communist parties in tropical Africa." (*Ibid.*: 10.)

3 See Roger Kanet, "The Soviet Union and Sub-Saharan Africa: Communist Policy toward Africa, 1917–1965." (Ph.D. dissertation, Princeton University, 1966): 473, 563, for repeated assertions to this effect.

4 Robert Legvold, *Soviet Policy in West Africa* (Cambridge, 1970): 1–2. Legvold acknowledges that Africa was included in Moscow's revolutionary exhortations, but argues that this was done principally "to preserve symmetry in the appeal." (*Ibid.*: 3.) Legvold insists further that "Soviet leaders and political analysts had done almost nothing to

learn about the nature of African society until the first wave of independent African states appeared right in front of them" and that "because the Soviet Union avoided involvement in the organization of radical African movements, it came to Africa without a reliable working knowledge of the political milieu there." (*Ibid.*: 34.)

5 See, for example, Dallin, *op. cit.*: 451; Legvold, *op. cit.*: 339, and Vernon McKay, "Communist Exploitation of Anti-Colonialism and Nationalism in Africa," in C. Grove Haines, ed., *The Threat of Soviet Imperialism* (Baltimore, 1954): 272–73.

6 Menelik treated even such trusted assistants as Lt. Bulatovich with caution lest they become too influential in Ethiopia. (See Czeslaw Jesman, *The Russians in Ethiopia* [London, 1958]: 89.) A. I. Kokhanovskii's report to Foreign Minister Sazonov ("Imperator Menelik II i Sovremennaia Abissiniia," *Novyi Vostok*, no. 1, 1922: 331) includes an interesting account of how the Ethiopian Emperor decided to heed the advice of his anti-Russian counselors (following the Russo-Japanese War) and to rely upon non-Russians for topographic work in his country. Specifically, it had been warned that Ethiopia might go the way of Manchuria which had been seized by the Russians following similar topographical undertakings.

7 The concern of the Faure group regarding excessive Comintern influence, it will be recalled, was an important issue in provoking the schism in the LDRN. Similar apprehensions undoubtedly had much to do with the reluctance of Sekyi, of the ARPS, to cooperate with Padmore in 1932. (See Sekyi letters to Padmore, cited in Samuel Rohdie, "The Gold Coast Aborigines Abroad," *Journal of African History*, VI, no. 3 [1965]: 395–96.) Doubts about the wisdom of following the Russian path were also voiced by at least one member of the NCBWA as early as 1926. At the NCBWA's Third Congress held in Bathurst that year, J. W. Kuye warned: "Russia's Bolshevism . . . stands condemned by its results. Let us take, therefore, a timely heed of the proverb which says: 'By the mistakes of others wise men correct their own.' " (J. W. Kuye, "The Right of People to Self-Determination [with special reference to British West Africa]," reprinted in the *Gambia Outlook*, November 14, 1936: 8 [part 2].)

CHAPTER TWELVE

1 See, for example, Dorothy Nelkin, "Socialist Sources of Pan-African Ideology," *African Socialism* (Stanford, 1964): 70–71, and Colin Legum, "Pan-Africanism and Communism," in C. G. Widstrand and S. Hamrell, eds., *The Soviet Bloc, China and Africa* (Uppsala, Sweden, 1964): 15ff.

2 Daniel Guerin, in a personal letter dated September 18, 1956 (George Padmore Library, Accra), reminded Padmore that his real target for criticism in *Pan-Africanism or Communism?* was Stalinism, not communism or even the Soviet system. Guerin complained that Padmore failed to make this distinction clear.

3 C. L. R. James, "Notes on George Padmore" (MSS): 15. St. Clair Drake, who also knew Padmore, corroborates this point. (Interview, Washington, December 5, 1969.)

4 For example, in a conversation with Drake in Ghana in 1959, Padmore confided that the fate he had in mind for Africa was essentially the same thing for which Russian leaders were working—presumably a continental union of states governed by the principles of Marxism-Leninism. (Drake, interview, *ibid.*)

5 Governor Hodson to Secretary of State for Colonies, Ormsby-Gore, October 15, 1937, C.O. 323/1517/7046/1. Papers like the *African Sentinel*, widely circulated among English-speaking Africans, registered protests against the banning of *Africa and World Peace*, published reviews of the book, and generally promoted its circulation. (See for example, *African Sentinel*, I, no. 3 [January, 1938]: 20.)

6 Padmore, *Africa and World Peace* (London, 1937): 258. Padmore insisted, for example, that Africans, despite their disapproval of the Stalinian purges, "must still remain loyal and devoted to the October Revolution." (*Loc. cit.*) All the old slogans were used: Africans were instructed to "turn the imperialist war into civil war;" they were assured of "the impending communist revolution," and they were encouraged to forcibly "overthrow all existing social arrangements." (*Ibid.*: 264, 271–72.)

7 See *ibid.*: 157–75 (chapter VI) and 263f.

8 Padmore, *How Russia Transformed Her Colonial Empire* (London, 1946): 87–88, Padmore also made a point of emphasizing the absence of racial discrimination in the Soviet Union. (*Ibid.*: 151ff.)

9 See J. R. Hooker, *Black Revolutionary* (New York, 1967): 43.

10 See Padmore, *The Gold Coast Revolution* (London, 1953): 46. It will be recalled that Padmore was contributing to their paper, the *African Morning Post*, at this time.

11 George Padmore, *Pan-Africanism or Communism?* (London, 1956): 144ff.

12 *Ibid.*: 147f.

13 See Sierra Leone Police Report on Wallace-Johnson, June 20, 1938, in C.O. 267/665/32208.

14 IASB Manifesto, "Europe's Difficulty is Africa's Opportunity." A copy of this manifesto, found by the government raid on Wallace-Johnson's premises in Sierra Leone, appears in C.O. 267/670/32210/2.

15 In the pages of Wallace-Johnson's widely distributed weekly, the *African Standard*, articles appeared which echoed the themes and sometimes even the very language of IASB pronouncements. See, for example, "Rewarding the African's Loyalty," *African Standard*, I, no. 18 (May 5, 1939): 3, which was evidently inspired by the IASB manifesto cited above.

16 See "A Brief Review of the Activities of the IASB for the period May through December, 1937," *African Sentinel*, I, no. 4 (March 4, 1938): 14.

17 *Loc. cit.*

18 See Immanuel Wallerstein, *Africa: the Politics of Independence* (New York, 1961): 104 and Colin Legum, *Pan-Africanism* (New York, 1965): 31–32.

19 James, *op. cit.*: 9.

20 James, *op. cit.*: 40–41.

21 Drake interview. See also Padmore, ed., *History of the Pan-African Congress* (London, 1947): 32.

22 See Hooker, *op. cit.*: 92.
23 In this context Padmore's contacts among African nationalists in Paris were helpful to Nkrumah. (James, *op. cit.*: 40.) Nkrumah indicates that following his visit to Paris he was able to persuade Leopold Senghor and Sourous Apithy to attend "the first West African conference," held jointly by WANS and WASU in London in 1946 in order to lay plans for a "Union of West African Socialist Republics." (Nkrumah, *The Autobiography of Kwame Nkrumah* [Edinburgh, 1957]: 57.)
24 Nkrumah, *ibid.*: 60–61.
25 (Italics mine.) Padmore, *How Russia Transformed, op. cit.*: 177–78. This volume argues, among other things, the applicability of the Soviet form of multinational state to Africa. See Nkrumah, *op. cit.*: 57.
26 "Plans for West African Soviet Republic," *London Times*, February 17, 1950: 3. A report to the same effect appears in *Le Monde*, February 18, 1950: 2. In describing the same trial, Nkrumah's *Autobiography* is curiously silent on this point.
27 See Awoonor-Renner, *West African Soviet Union* (London, 1946): 19–23. The author, known for his pro-Soviet and even Stalinist political orientation, had recently returned to the Gold Coast from a second period of study in the U.S.S.R.
28 Nkrumah, *op. cit.*: 85–86, citing findings of the Gold Coast Commission of Enquiry, 1948.
29 *Ibid.*: 62 and Hooker, *op. cit.*: 107, citing a letter from the Socialist MP, Fenner Brockway, indicating the extent of Padmore's influence in persuading Nkrumah to return to the Gold Coast.
30 Hooker, *ibid.*: 114.
31 See *ibid.*: 114–15 and Nkrumah, *op. cit.*: 157–58. An article by Padmore in the *Accra Evening News* (May 6, 1953): 1, describes his 1951 tour of the Gold Coast bush in the company of Nkrumah.
32 James, *op. cit.*: 57.
33 *Loc. cit.* James also deals with this subject in "Nkrumah Then and Now"—an unpublished manuscript.
34 See W. Scott Thompson, *Ghana's Foreign Policy* (Princeton, 1969): 22. Thompson contends that during the first two years of Ghana's independence no person besides Nkrumah had more to do with shaping the country's foreign policy.
35 S. I. A. Kottei (Director of the George Padmore Library, Accra), "George Padmore in the African Revolution" (MSS): 22ff.
36 *Loc. cit.* The concept of a West African union of socialist states may well have been the theoretical basis for this initiative.
37 After 1959 Padmore's office was renamed the Bureau of African Affairs, an institution which many of Ghana's neighbor states came to regard as the perpetrator of subversion against them. Russell Howe ("George Padmore," *Encounter*, XIII, no. 6 [December, 1959]: 55) observed: "One relic of the Moscow past which persisted to his last days was Padmore's love of the 'plot' atmosphere . . . for George, even an exchange of economic views between, say, Ghana and Mali, would have had to be conducted as though the Tsarist police were outside the door."

38 "Funeral Oration by Dr. Kwame Nkrumah on the Occasion of the Internment of Ashes of the Late George Padmore at Christiansborg Castle," copy of original manuscript at George Padmore Library, Accra.

39 Remarks of President Nkrumah on the Ghana Radio, cited in Hooker, *op. cit.*: 140.

40 Hooker, *ibid.*: 73, citing Padmore.

41 Specifically, he had established the Public Works Workers' Union, the War Department Amalgamated Workers' Union, the Mabella Coaling Company Workers' Union, the King Tom Docks Workers' Union, the All Seamen's Union, the Bonthe Amalgamated Workers' Union, the Pepel and Marampa Miners Workers' Union, and the Motorists' Union. On the eve of the war he was even in the process of forming a combined trade union directorate for the colony, the Sierra Leone Trades Union Congress. (See confidential letter H. R. Blood, Secretary to the Governor of Sierra Leone, to Secretary of State for Colonies, Malcolm Macdonald, August 22, 1939, in C.O. 267/666/ 32218. See also letter January 23, 1942, R. S. MacTier, Port and Transit Control officer of the Ministry of War, to T. J. Padler, Colonial Office, in C.O. 267/666/32218.)

42 While in Britain he also published *Trade Unionism in Colonial Dependent Territories* (London, 1946) and served as Chairman of Nkrumah's West African National Secretariat. (See Hooker, *op. cit.*: 86.)

43 He was, for example, one of the leaders of the opposition in the Sierra Leone Legislative Council after the war.

44 Interview with Dr. Davidson Nicol, Sierra Leone Ambassador to the U.N. (New York, November, 1969).

45 Ministère de la France d'Outre-Mer, Direction des Affaires Politiques, Deuxième Bureau, "Le Syndicalisme dans les Territoires Africains" (1954): 2, citing statistics of the government of French West Africa, January 1, 1953. The CGT was a successor of the CGTU, to be remembered for its ties with the RILU and the ITUC-NW.

46 See, for example, J. A. Ballard, "The Development of Political Parties in French Equatorial Africa" (unpublished Ph.D. dissertation, Fletcher School, 1963): 191, concerning the importance of CGT-inspired trade unions in the Cameroon.

47 Deuxième Bureau, "Le Syndicalisme," *op. cit.*: 7, 13.

48 Shortly after his return from Czechoslovakia in 1950, Sékou Touré became the Secretary-General of the CGT Coordinating Committee for French West Africa. (*Ibid.*: 10.)

49 Nkrumah, *op. cit.*: 60–61.

50 *Ibid.*: 96ff.

51 Robert Legvold (*Soviet Policy in West Africa* [Cambridge, 1970]: 35–36) notes: "In such study circles a notable list of African leaders acquired an important part of their formative political training: men like Modibo Keita, the future President of Mali; Guinea's President Sékou Touré; Idrissa Diarra later Secretary-General of Mali's dominant party, the *Union Soudanaise*; his predecessor and a founder of the party, Mamadou Konaté, Diallo Siafoulaye, Secretary-General of the *Parti Démocratique Guinéen*; the list is much longer."

52 Ballard, *op. cit.*: 619.

53 R. S. Morganthau, *Political Parties in French-Speaking West Africa* (Oxford, 1964): 225 (a useful discussion of the role of the GEC in French West Africa also appears on pages: 24ff.), and Thomas Hodgkin and R. S. Morganthau, "Mali," in J. S. Coleman and C. G. Rosberg, eds., *Political Parties and National Integration in Tropical Africa* (Los Angeles, 1964): 31.

54 The RDA was formed at a conference of French African nationalists held in Bamako on October 18–21, 1946. The GEC, which were heavily represented at the conference, had, among other things, taken the lead in many parts of French Africa in raising funds to send African delegates to Bamako. (See Ballard, *op. cit.*: 193.) French communists, led by Raymond Barbé, a member of the PCF Central Committee, also attended the conference. If they were not responsible for inspiring the formation of the organization in the first place (this is suggested by Vernon McKay's account, "Communist Exploitation of Anti-Colonialism and Nationalism in Africa," in C. Grove Haines, ed., *The Threat of Soviet Imperialism* [Baltimore, 1954]: 266), French communists were at least extremely active in their efforts to direct the development of the RDA throughout the remainder of the 1940's. (Deuxième Bureau, "Le Syndicalisme," *op. cit.*: 5.)

55 Like Kouyaté, d'Arboussier visited the Soviet Union and "was thrilled with what he saw." (*L'Essor* [journal of the *Union Soudanaise*], December 23, 1949: 1.) Roger Kanet ("The Soviet Union and Sub-Saharan Africa: Communist Policy toward Africa, 1917–1965." [Ph.D. dissertation, Princeton University, 1966]: 208, citing d'Arboussier, *Le RDA dans la Lutte Anti-Impérialiste* [Paris, 1948]) notes that d'Arboussier also appeared to be shaping the objectives of the RDA in accordance with the wishes of the PCF.

56 "Charte de l'Organisation du RDA" (mimeographed pamphlet, c. 1947). See also Morganthau, *Political Parties*, *op. cit.*: 303–04.

57 "Charte de l'Organisation," *op. cit.*: 1.

58 E. J. Schumacher in "A Political History of the RDA: 1946–58" (unpublished M.S. thesis, London School of Economics, 1964): 52, observes in this connection: "The most notable example of an RDA territorial party whose structure owed a good deal to both communist inspiration and direct assistance by French communists was the *Parti Démocratique de la Côte d'Ivoire*."

59 See Morganthau, *Political Parties*, *op. cit.*: 425, for a more complete list of RDA territorial sections.

60 See the *African Sentinel*, I, no. 4 (March–April, 1938): 9.

61 The diary which Potekhin kept on this visit to Ghana was published under the title *Gana Segodnia* ("Ghana Today") (Moscow, 1958).

62 See Maria Rait, *Efiopiia* (Moscow, 1960): 5, citing Selassie's remarks (printed in *Pravda* [July 1, 1959]: 2): "Our country remembers with eternal gratitude the timely military assistance which the people of this great country gave us at the time of our decisive struggle against imperialism in the last years of the last century." In this context it is interesting to note that Emperor Selassie's father was Ras Makonnen, the Ethiopian noble who acted as the principal liaison officer for Menelik in his dealings with the representatives of Czarist Russia.

BIBLIOGRAPHY

I. BIBLIOGRAPHIES

Bibliografiia Afriki. Moscow, ANSSSR, Institut Afriki, 1964.

Hammond, T. T., ed. *Soviet Foreign Relations and World Communism.* Princeton, Princeton University Press, 1965. See especially: 876–88.

Pischel, E. C. and Robertazzi, C. *L'Internationale Communiste et les Problèmes Coloniaux: 1919–1935.* Paris, Mouton, 1968.

II. MATERIALS RELATING TO THE CZARIST PERIOD

A. PRIMARY ACCOUNTS BY RUSSIANS WHO VISITED AFRICA BEFORE 1917 (listed chronologically)

Kokovtsov, M. G. *Opisanie Arkhipelaga i Varvariiskago Berega.* St. Petersburg, F. Tumanskii, 1786.

Kovalevsky, E. P. *Puteshestvie vo Vnutrenniuiu Afriku.* 2 vols. St. Petersburg, Edward Prats, 1849.

Petri, E. IU., ed. *Puteshestviia V. V. IUnkera po Afrike* (diaries of Junker's travels in Africa c. 1876). St. Petersburg, A. F. Devrien, 1893.

Nikolaev, L. (member of Ashinov's "New Moscow" expedition). *Ashinovskaia Ekspeditsiia.* Odessa, Izd. "I. ZH.," 1889.

Mashkov, V. F. "Puteshestvie v Stranu Chernykh Khristian v 1891–1892 gg." *Novoe Vremia* (St. Petersburg), nos. 6069, 6095, and 6102 (1893).

Eliseev, A. V. "Makhdizm i Sovremennoe Polozhenie Del v Sudane." Russkoe Geograficheskoe Obshchestvo, *Izvestiia,* XXX (1894), no. 4: 604–66.

———. *Po Belu-Svetu.* Vol. IV. St. Petersburg, Izd. Soikin, 1898.

Zviagin, K. S. (member of the Eliseev expedition to Ethiopia). *Ocherk Sovremennoi Abissinii.* St. Petersburg, P. Golike, 1895.

Efrem, Archimandrite (accompanied the Eliseev expedition to Ethiopia and the Ethiopian mission to Russia, 1895). *Poezdka v Abissiniiu.* St. Petersburg, Universitetskaia Tipografiia, 1901.

Elets, IU. *Imperator Menelik i Voina Ego s Italiei* ("According to Documents and the Field Diaries of N. S. Leontiev"). St. Petersburg, E. Eudokimova, 1898.

Krasnov, P. N. *Kazaki v Abissinii* ("Diary of the Commander of the Imperial Russian Mission to Abyssinia in 1897–98"). St. Petersburg, Isidora Gol'dberg, 1900.

Bulatovich, Captain A. K. *Ot Entoto do Reki Baro*. St. Petersburg, V. Kirshbaum, 1897.

————. *S Voiskami Menelika II* ("Diary of an Expedition from Ethiopia to Lake Rudolf"). St. Petersburg, Khudozh. Pechati, 1900.

————. "Iz Abissinii cherez Strany Kaffa na Ozeru Rudolfa." Russkoe Geograficheskoe Obshchestvo, *Izvestiia*, XXXV (1899), no. 3: 259–83.

Artamonov, Colonel L. K. "Kratkii Otchet o Puteshestvie" (MSS for publication by the Russian Geographical Society), in Artamonov papers. Library of Congress (MSS Division), Acc. no. 14,897.

————. "Russkie v Abissinii," text of an address delivered November 29, 1899, to the Society of Promoters of Military Knowledge, in Artamonov papers. Library of Congress, Acc. no. 14,897.

Arkhipov, Vasily (a Cossack who accompanied Artamonov to the Nile). "Dontsy na Belom Nile" (account of the Nile expedition), with an English translation, in Artamonov papers. Library of Congress, Acc. no. 14,897.

Shchusev, Dr. P. V. "K Istokam Golubogo Nile." Russkoe Geograficheskoe Obshchestvo, *Izvestiia*, XXXVI (1900), no. 2: 198–217.

Vlassov, D. S. (Imperial Russian Minister in Addis Ababa). "Zametka ob Abissinii" ("Dispatch from Addis Ababa"). *Sbornik Konsul' skikh Donesenii* (Russian Ministry of Foreign Affairs, St. Petersburg), no. 2, 1899: 99–106.

[Romeiko]-Gurko, Colonel V. I. *Voina Anglii s IUzhno-Afrikanskimi Respublikami, 1899–1901* (report prepared for the Russian General Staff). St. Petersburg, Voennaia Tipografiia, 1901.

Kokhanovskii, A. I. "Imperator Menelik II i Sovremennaia Abissiniia" (report [dated June, 1913] to Russian Foreign Minister Sazonov on his recent mission to Ethiopia). *Novyi Vostok*, no. 1, 1922: 316–33.

B. GOVERNMENT DOCUMENTS

France. *Documents Diplomatiques Français*, Série 1e (1871–1900), vols. VII–XVI. Série 2e (1901–11), vols. I–VI.

Germany. Johannes Lepsius, *et al.*, compilers. *Die Grosse Politik der Europaischen Kabinette (1871–1914)*, vol. XI.

Great Britain. Foreign Office Archives. Public Record Office, London. Files relating to British interests in Ethiopia and the Red Sea region, 1895–97.

Russia. Peter I, instructions to his admirals concerning naval expedition to Madagascar and India, 1723. British Museum (MSS Division), addition no. 21529.

C. BOOKS AND ARTICLES

"Anglo-Burskaia Voina v Doneseniiakh Russkogo Voennogo Agenta." *Krasnyi Arkhiv* (Moscow), no. 103 (1941): 130–59.

Berg, L. S. *Vsesoiuznoe Geograficheskoe Obshchestvo za Sto Let (1845–1945)*. Moscow, ANSSSR, 1946.

Bok, I. I. "Uspekhi Evropeitsev v Vostochnoi Polovine Afriki za Poslednie Gody." Russkoe Geograficheskoe Obshchestvo, *Izvestiia*, XXXV (1899), no. 4: 455–81.

Byrnes, R. F. *Pobedonostsev, His Life and Thought*. Bloomington, Indiana University Press, 1968.

Cattaui, René, ed. *Le Règne de Mohammed Aly d'après les Archives Russes en Egypte*. 3 vols. Rome, Institut Français d'Archéologie Orientale du Caire, 1931–36.

Churchill, Winston. "The Fashoda Incident." *North American Review*, CLXVII (1898): 736–43.

———. *The River War*. London, Longmans Green, 1902.

Constantin, Vicomte de. "Une Expédition Réligieuse en Abyssinie." *Nouvelle Revue*, LXVIII: February 1, 1891: 449–80 and February 15, 1891: 673–92.

Cox, F. J. "Khedive Ismail and Panslavism." *The Slavonic and East European Review* (London), December, 1953: 151–167.

Curzon, George. *Russia in Central Asia*. London, Frank Cass, 1967 (reprint of 1889 edition).

Darcy, Jean. *France et Angleterre. Cent Années de Rivalité Coloniale: L'Afrique*. Paris, Perrin Libraires, 1904.

El Djabarti, Cheikh Abd-el-Rahman. *Merveilles Biographiques et Historiques*. 9 vols. Cairo, Imprimerie Nationale, 1890.

Farnie, D. A. *East and West of Suez*. Oxford, Clarendon Press, 1969.

Filesi, Teobaldo. "Russi in Etiopia." *Affrica* (Rome), June, 1948: 155–56.

"France, Russia, and the Nile." *The Contemporary Review* (London), LIV, December, 1898: 761–78.

Gere, V. I. "Pochemu Sleduet Zhelat Uspekha Buram?" *Russkiia Viedomosti*, January 29, 1900: 3–4.

Hanotaux, Gabriel, ed. *Histoire de la Nation Egyptienne*. 7 vols. Paris, Librairie Plon, 1931.

Hoskins, H. L. *British Routes to India*. New York, Octagon Books, 1966.

Istoriia Afriki v XIX—Nachale XXv. Moscow, ANSSSR, Institut Afriki, 1967.

Jesman, Czeslaw. *The Russians in Ethiopia*. London, Chatto and Windus, 1958.

Lamanskii, V. I. *O Slavianakh v Maloi Azii, v Afrike, i v Ispanii*. St. Petersburg, Imp. Akad. Nauk, 1859.

Lamsdorff, V. N. *Dnevnik, 1886–1890*. Moscow, Gos. Izd., 1926.

———. *Dnevnik, 1891–1892*. Moscow, "Akademiia," 1934.

Langer, William. *The Diplomacy of Imperialism, 1890–1902*. 2nd ed. New York, Knopf, 1951.

———. *The Franco-Russian Alliance, 1890–1894*. 2nd ed. New York, Octagon Books, 1967.

Mashkov, V. F. [V. Fedorov, pseud.]. *Abissiniia, Istoriko-Geograftcheskii Ocherk*. St. Petersburg, A. Sovorin, 1889.

Mizhuev, P. G. *Istoriia Kolonial'noi Imperii i Kolonial'noi Politiki Anglii*. St. Petersburg, Brokhaus-Efron, 1902.

"Nikolai Romanov ob Anglo-Burskoi Voine." *Krasnyi Arkhiv*, LXIII (1934): 124–26.

d'Orléans, Prince Henri. *Politique Extérieure et Coloniale*. Paris, Flammarion, n.d. [c. 1900].

———. *Une Visite à l'Empereur Ménélick*. Paris, Librairie Dentu, 1898.

Pobedonostsev, K. P. *Pisma Pobedonostseva k Aleksandru III*. 2 vols. Moscow, "Novaia Moskva," 1925.

———. *Pisma i Zapiski*. 2 vols. Moscow, Gos. Izd., 1923.

"Pokhod Anglichan v Abissinii v 1867–1869 Godakh." *Voennyi Sbornik* (St. Petersburg), LXXIV (1870): 35–58, 253–81; LXXV (1871): 59–88.

Rait, M. V. "Russkie Ekspeditsii v Efiopii v Seredine XIX–Nachale XXvv." *Afrikanskii Etnograficheskii Sbornik*, I (*Trudy Instituta Etnografii, XXXIV*). Edited by I. I. Potekhin. Moscow, ANSSSR, 1956.

Rodd, Sir James Rennell. *Social and Diplomatic Memories, 1894–1901*. Second Series. London, Edward Arnold, 1923.

Romanov, Grand Duke Alexander. *Always a Grand Duke*. New York. Garden City Publishing, 1935.

Rossini, Carlo Conti. *Italia ed Etiopia dal Trattato d'Ucciali alla Battaglia di Adua*. Rome, Instituto per Oriente, 1935.

Russia and Africa ("Reports made at the Conference on the Historical

Relations of the Peoples of the Soviet Union and Africa, Moscow, May 19–21, 1965"). Moscow, "Nauka," 1966.

"Russia in Africa—the Abyssinian Expedition." *The Times* (London), July 25, 1891: 5; July 28, 1891: 13.

Shiik, A. A. "Iz Istorii Russkoi Afrikanistiki." *Sovetskaia Etnografiia,* 1946, no. 2: 173–81.

Shokal'skii, IU. M. "Afrikanskiia Vladeniia Evropeiskikh Derzhav." Russkoe Geograficheskoe Obshchestvo, *Izvestiia,* XXXIV (1898), no. 5: 721–26.

Skal'kovskii, K. A. *Suezskii Kanal i Ego Znachenie dlia Russkoi Torgovli.* St. Petersburg, "Obshchestvennaia Pol'za," 1870.

Sollogub, V. A. *Novyi Egipet.* St. Petersburg, Skariatina, 1871.

Stavrou, T. G. *Russian Interests in Palestine, 1882–1914.* Thessaloniki, Institute for Balkan Studies, 1963.

de Taube, M. "Paul Ier et l'Ordre de Malte." *Revue d'Histoire Moderne,* 1930, no. 27: 161–77.

Troianskii, A. S. *Eritreiskaia Koloniia Italii.* St. Petersburg, Kirshbaum, 1893.

Tsvetaev, D. "Snosheniia s Abissiniei." *Russkii Arkhiv,* 1888, no. 2: 205–10.

Urquart, David. *Progress of Russia in the West, North, and South.* London, Trubner, 1853.

Uspensky, Porfiry. *Kniga Bytiia Moego: Dnevniki i Avtobiograficheskiia Zapiski.* 3 vols. St. Petersburg, Imp. Akad. Nauk, 1896.

––––––. "Tserkovnoe i Politicheskoe Sostoianie Abissinii s Drevneishikh Vremen do Nashikh Dnei." *Trudy Kievskoi Dukhovnoi Akademii,* 1866, no. 3: 305–44; no. 4: 556–604; no. 5: 3–32; no. 6: 142–67.

––––––. "Uchastie Rossii v Sud'be Abissinii." *Trudy Kievskoi Dukhovnoi Akademii,* 1866, no. 8: 415–40.

––––––. "Uspekhi i Neudachi Nemetskikh Missionerov vo Vnutrennei Afrike." *Trudy Kievskoi Dukhovnoi Akademii,* 1866, no. 10: 289–304.

Val'skaia, B. A. *Puteshestviia Egora Petrovicha Kovalevskogo.* Moscow, Izd. Geog. Lit., 1956.

Volgin, F. V. *V Strane Chernykh Khristian.* St. Petersburg, Soikina, 1895.

Witte, Serge Julievich, Count. *Vospominaniia.* Vol. I. Berlin, "Slovo," 1922.

Work, Ernest. *Ethiopia, A Pawn in European Diplomacy.* New York, MacMillan, 1935.

Wylde, Augustus. *Modern Abyssinia.* London, Methuen, 1901.

Yakobson, Sergius, "Russia and Africa." *The Slavonic and East European Review*, XVII, no. 51 (April, 1939), and XIX (1939–40).

Zabrodskaia, M. P. *Russkie Puteshestvenniki po Afrike*. Moscow, Geografgiz, 1955.

Zaozerskii, A. I. "Ekspeditsiia na Madagaskar pri Petre Velikom." *Rossiia i Zapad*, I (1923): 91–102.

Zaslavskii, D. "Nikolai II—'Imperator Kafrov.'" *Krasnyi Arkhiv*, LXIX-LXX (1935): 241–52.

III. MATERIALS RELATING TO THE SOVIET PERIOD

A. REFERENCE WORKS

Degras, Jane, ed. *The Communist International, 1919–1943: Documents*. 3 vols. London, Oxford University Press, 1956–65.

Eudin, X., and North, R. C. *Soviet Russia and the East, 1920–1927*. Stanford, Stanford University Press, 1957.

Kun, Béla, ed. *Kommunisticheskii Internatsional v Dokumentakh, 1919–1932*. Moscow, Partiinoe Izd., 1933.

Sworakowski, W. S. *The Comintern and Its Front Organizations—A Research Guide*. Stanford, Hoover Institution, 1965.

B. COMINTERN PUBLICATIONS

1. OFFICIAL ACCOUNTS OF COMINTERN CONGRESSES AND ECCI PLENUMS (listed chronologically)

Piatyi Vsemirnyi Kongress Kommunisticheskogo Internatsionala: Stenograficheskii Otchet. 2 vols. Moscow, Gos. Izd., 1925. (Vol. II entitled *Rasshirennyi Plenum Ispolkoma [Kratkii Protokol]*.)

Stenograficheskii Otchet VI Kongressa Kominterna. Vols. III–VI. Moscow, Gos. Izd., 1929. (For English text of the "Theses on the Revolutionary Movement in the Colonies and Semi-Colonies" adopted at the Sixth Congress see *The Revolutionary Movement in the Colonies*. London, Modern Books, 1929.)

Stenograficheskii Otchet XI Plenum IKKI. Moscow, Gos. Izd., 1931. (For English text of remarks by Cachin see Marcel Cachin, *War Preparations against the Soviet Union*. New York, Workers' Library, 1931.)

2. BOOKS AND PAMPHLETS PUBLISHED BY THE COMINTERN AND ITS AFFILIATES

Armiia Kommunisticheskogo Internatsionala. Petrograd, 1921.

The Comintern between the Fifth and the Sixth World Congresses, 1924–8. London, CPGB, 1928.

Ford, James. *The Communists and the Struggle for Negro Liberation.* New York, Harlem Division CPUSA, 1936.

——. *Economic Struggle of Negro Workers.* New York, Provisional ITUC-NW, 1930.

——. *Imperialism Destroys the People of Africa.* New York, Harlem Division CPUSA, n.d.

Haywood, Harry. *The Road to Negro Liberation.* New York, Workers' Library, 1934.

ITUC-NW. *A Report of Proceedings and Decisions of the First International Conference of Negro Workers.* Hamburg, ITUC-NW, 1930.

Lozovsky, Alexander, ed. *Kolonial'nyi Mir: Spravochnik dlia Propagandista.* Leningrad, Gos. Izd., 1929.

Padmore, George. *American Imperialism Enslaves Liberia.* Moscow, Centrizdat, 1931.

——. *The Life and Struggles of Negro Toilers.* London, R.I.L.U. Magazine for the ITUC-NW, 1931. (A Russian version of this book appeared as *Negry pod Gnetom Imperializma.* Moscow, Moskovskii Rabochii, 1931.)

——. *Negro Workers and the Imperialist War—Intervention in the Soviet Union.* Hamburg, ITUC-NW, 1931.

Pavlovich, M. P. [alias M. L. Vel'tman]. *Voprosy Kolonial'noi i Natsional'noi Politiki i IIIi Internatsional.* Moscow, Izd. Kommunisticheskogo Internatsionala, 1920.

RILU. *Mirovoe Revoliutsionnoe Profdvizhenie ot IV do V Kongressa Profinterna, 1928–1930.* Moscow, 1930.

——. *Report of the Fourth Congress of the RILU.* London, National Minority Movement, 1928.

——. *Rezoliutsii i Postanovleniia V Kongressa Krasnogo Internatsionala Profsoiuzov.* Moscow, 1930. (Published in English as *Resolutions of the Fifth World Congress of the RILU.* London, National Minority Movement, 1931.)

——. *The Tasks of the International Trade Union Movement (Resolutions and Decisions of the Third World Congress of the RILU).* London, National Minority Movement, 1924.

3. PERIODICALS PUBLISHED BY THE COMINTERN AND ITS AFFILIATES

Bulletin Colonial. Monthly newsletter of the Colonial Commission of the PCF. Paris, 1928–34.

Bulletin Colonial. Monthly newsletter of the French Section of the ILD. Paris, 1933–34.

Colonial Information Bulletin. Bi-monthly newsletter of the CPGB. London, 1937.

The Communist. Journal of the CPGB. London, 1920–23.

The Communist International. Bi-monthly theoretical journal of the ECCI, 1920–37. (Published in French as *L'Internationale Communiste* and in Russian as *Kommunisticheskii Internatsional.*)

The Communist Review. Monthly theoretical journal of the CPGB. London, 1921–27.

International Press Correspondence of the Comintern. Issued bi-weekly and weekly by Comintern headquarters, 1920–37. (Published in French as *La Correspondance Internationale.*)

The Negro Worker. Official organ of the ITUC-NW, published monthly and often semi-monthly, 1928–37. (Appeared in French as *L'Ouvrier Nègre.*)

C. OTHER BOOKS AND PAMPHLETS

Amter, Israel. *Mirovoe Osvoboditel'noe Dvizhenie Negrov.* Moscow, Gos. Izd., 1925.

Awoonor-Renner, Bankole. *This Africa* (with foreword by Kobina Sekyi and biographical note by J. B. Danquah). London, Central Books, 1943.

———. *West African Soviet Union.* London, WANS Press, 1946.

Beloff, Max. *The Foreign Policy of Soviet Russia, 1929–1941.* Vol. I (1929–36). London, Oxford University Press, 1947.

Boersner, Dmitri. *The Bolsheviks and the National and Colonial Question.* Geneva, Librairie Droz, 1957.

Botzaris, Alejandro. *Africa e o Comunismo.* Lisbon, Committee for Overseas Research of the Center for Political and Social Studies, 1961.

Bowen, Walter. *Colonial Trade Unions.* London, Fabian Publications, 1954.

Braginskii, M. and Lukonin, IU. *Aperçu d'Histoire du Mouvement de Libération Nationale dans les Pays d'Afrique Orientale.* Moscow, Eds. du Progrès, n.d.

Bruce, J. E. *A Tribute for the Negro Soldier.* New York, Bruce and Franklin, 1918.

Brzezinski, Zbigniew, ed. *Africa and the Communist World.* Stanford, Stanford University Press, 1963.

Buell, L. *The Native Problem in Africa.* 2 vols. New York, MacMillan, 1928.

Burns, M. E. *British Imperialism in West Africa.* London, Labour Research Department, 1927.

Coleman, J. S. *Nigeria: Background to Nationalism.* Berkeley, University of California Press, 1958.

—— and Rosberg, C. G., jr., eds. *Political Parties and National Integration in Tropical Africa.* Berkeley, University of California Press, 1964.

Coty, François. *Sauvons Nos Colonies: Le Péril Rouge en Pays Noir.* Paris, B. Grasset, 1931.

Cros, Charles, ed. *La Parole est à M. Blaise Diagne.* Paris, Chez l'Auteur, 1961.

Cunard, Nancy, ed. *Negro Anthology.* London, Lawrence and Wishart, 1934.

Deutscher, Isaac. *Stalin: A Political Biography.* Vintage Books. New York, Random House, 1960.

Doriot, Jacques. *Les Colonies et le Communisme.* Paris, Eds. Montaigne, 1929.

Draper, Theodore. *American Communism and Soviet Russia.* New York, Viking Press, 1960.

Fischer, Louis. *The Soviets in World Affairs.* Vintage Books. New York, Random House, 1960.

Gautherot, Gustave. *Le Bolchévisme aux Colonies et l'Impérialisme Rouge.* Paris, Librairie de la Revue Française, 1930.

Gavrilov, N. *Le Mouvement de Libération Nationale en Afrique Occidentale.* Moscow, Eds. du Progres, n.d.

Hooker, J. R. *Black Revolutionary: George Padmore's Path from Communism to Pan-Africanism.* New York, Praeger, 1967.

Italiaander, Rolf. *Schwarze Haut im Roten Griff.* Dusseldorf, Econ. Verlag, 1962.

K. Marx and F. Engels on Colonialism. Moscow, Foreign Languages Press, n. d.

Kitaigorodskii, P. V. *Ot Kolonial'nogo Rabstva k Natsional'noi Nezavisimosti* (with a preface by Pavlovich). Moscow, Moskovskii Rabochii, 1925.

——. *Ugroza Voiny na Sredizemnoe More.* Moscow, Moskovskii Rabochii, 1928.

Kolarz, Walter. *Communism and Colonialism.* (Essays for broadcast by the BBC.) London, MacMillan, 1964.

Kornilov, Boris. *Moia Afrika*. Leningrad, Molodaia Gvardiia, 1935.

Kreitner, G. *Abissiniia*. Moscow, Nauchno-Issledovatel'skaia Assotsiatsiia Instituta Vostokovedeniia pri TS. I.K. SSSR., 1932.

Legum, Colin. *Pan-Africanism*. New York, Praeger, 1965.

———. "Pan-Africanism and Communism." *The Soviet Bloc, China and Africa*. Edited by C. G. Widstrand and Sven Hamrell. Uppsala, Scandanavian Institute of African Studies, 1964.

Legvold, Robert. *Soviet Policy in West Africa*. Cambridge, Harvard University Press, 1970.

Lenin, V. I. *Imperialism: The Highest Stage of Capitalism*. New York, International Publishers, 1939.

———. *The National-Liberation Movement in the East*. Moscow, Foreign Languages Publishing House, 1957.

Lisovskii, P. *Abissinskaia Avantiura Italianskogo Fashizma*. Moscow, ANSSSR, Institut Mirovogo Khoziastva i Mirovoi Politiki, 1936.

McKay, Vernon. "Communist Exploitation of Anti-Colonialism and Nationalism in Africa." *The Threat of Soviet Imperialism*. Edited by C. Grove Haines. Baltimore, Johns Hopkins Press, 1954.

McKenzie, K. E. *The Comintern and World Revolution*. New York, Columbia University Press, 1963.

Markov, V. [V. I. Matvei]. *Iskusstvo Negrov*. Petrograd, Narodnyi Komissariat po Prosveshcheniiu, 1919.

Morganthau, Ruth. *Political Parties in French-Speaking West Africa*. London, Oxford University Press, 1964.

Morison, David. *The U.S.S.R. and Africa*. London, Oxford University Press, 1964.

Nelkin, Dorothy. "Socialist Sources of Pan-African Ideology." *African Socialism*. Edited by W. H. Friedland and C. G. Rosberg, jr. Stanford, Stanford University Press, 1964.

Nkrumah, Kwame. *The Autobiography of Kwame Nkrumah*. Edinburgh, Nelson, 1957.

Nolan, William. *Communism versus the Negro*. Chicago, Regency, 1951.

Ol'derogge, D. A., ed. *Abissiniia (Sbornik Statei)*. Moscow, ANSSSR, Institut Antropologii, 1936.

Ottley, Roi. *No Green Pastures*. New York, Scribner, 1951.

Padmore, George. *Africa and World Peace*. London, Martin, Secker and Warburg, 1937.

———. *Africa: Britain's Third Empire*. London, Dennis Dobson, 1949.

———. *The Gold Coast Revolution*. London, Dennis Dobson, 1953.

———. *How Russia Transformed Her Colonial Empire*. London, Dennis Dobson. 1946.

————. *Pan-Africanism or Communism?* London, Dennis Dobson, 1956.

————, ed. *History of the Pan-African Congress.* London, Hammersmith Book Shop, 1947.

Pavlovich, M. P. *Chto Dokazala Anglo-Burskaia Voina?* Odessa, Izd. It., 1901.

————. *Mirovaia Voina i Bor'ba za Razdel Chernogo Kontinenta.* Vol. IX of *Osnovy Imperialisticheskoi Politiki i Mirovaia Voina.* Petrograd, Izd. TSIK, 1918.

————. *Bor'ba za Aziiu i Afriku.* 2nd ed. Moscow, Vse-Rossiiskaia Nauchnaia Assotsiatsiia Vostokovedeniia, 1923.

————. *Frantsuzskii Imperializm i Ekonomicheskoe Razvitie Frantsii v XX Stoletii.* Vol. V of *Osnovy Imperialisticheskoe Politiki i Mirovaia Voina.* Petrograd, Zhizn i Znanie, 1918.

————. *Imperializm. (Kurs Lektsii Chitannykh v Akademii General'nogo Shtaba v 1922–3gg.)* Moscow, Krasnaia Nov'ia., 1923.

————. *Velikie Zheleznodorozhnye i Morskie Puti Budushchago.* St. Petersburg, B. M. Vol'fa, 1913.

————. *Sovetskaia Rossiia i Kapitalisticheskaia Angliia.* Moscow, Izd. Prometei, 1925.

————, et al. *Lenin i Vostok.* Moscow, Nauchnaia Assotsiatsiia Vostokovedeniia SSSR, 1925.

————, ed. *Sredizemnoe More: Politiko-Strategicheskii Ocherk.* Moscow, Voennyi Vestnik, 1927.

Potekhin, I. I. *Gana Segodnia (Dnevnik, 1957g.).* Moscow, Izd. Geograficheskoi Lit., 1959.

————. *Stanovlenie Novoi Gany.* Moscow, Izd. Nauka, 1965.

Record, Wilson. *The Negro and the Communist Party.* Chapel Hill, University of North Carolina Press, 1951.

Schatten, Fritz. *Communism in Africa.* New York, Praeger, 1966.

Sheng-Pao, Chin. *The Gold Coast Delegations to Britain in 1934: The Political Background. National Chengchi University Studies in African Affairs,* no. 2. Taipei, 1970.

Shiik, A. A. *Rasovaia Problema i Marksizm.* NIANKP, *Trudy,* no. 6. Moscow, 1930.

Sik, Endré. *Histoire de l'Afrique Noire.* 2 vols. Budapest, Akadémiai Kiadó, 1964.

Smith, Homer [alias Chatwood Hall]. *Black Man in Red Russia: A Memoir* (with introduction by Harrison Salisbury). Chicago, Johnson Publishing, 1964.

Stalin, J. *Marxism and the National Question.* Moscow, Foreign Languages Press, 1945.

Thwaite, Daniel. *The Seething African Pot: A Study of Black Nationalism, 1882–1935*. London, Constable, 1936.

Trotsky, Leon. *The First Five Years of the Comintern*. Vol. I. Edited and translated by J. G. Wright. New York, Pioneer Publishers, 1945.

Thompson, W. S. *Ghana's Foreign Policy, 1957–1966*. Princeton, Princeton University Press, 1969.

Valtin, Jan [Richard Krebs]. *Out of the Night*. New York, Alliance Book Corporation, 1941.

Vezeau, Roland. *L'Afrique Face au Communisme*. Paris, Edimpra Editeur, 1967.

Wallerstein, Immanuel. *Africa: The Politics of Independence*. Vintage Books. New York, Random House, 1961.

Yergan, Max. "The Communist Threat in Africa." *Africa Today*. Edited by C. Grove Haines. Baltimore, Johns Hopkins Press, 1955.

Zusmanovich, A. Z., ed. *Prinuditnel'nyi Trud i Profdvizhenie v Negritian- skoi Afrike*. Moscow, Profizdat, 1933.

D. OTHER PERIODICALS

I. PUBLISHED BY AFRICANS

Africa and the World. News bulletin of the IASB. London, 1937.

The African Morning Post. Nnamdi Azikiwe, Editor. Accra, 1935–37.

The African Sentinel. Edited by Wallace-Johnson for the IASB. London, 1937–38.

The African Standard. Organ of the WAYL—Sierra Leone Section. Freetown, 1939.

Les Continents. Bi-monthly organ of Houénou's LDRN. Paris, 1924.

Le Cri des Nègres. Monthly organ of Kouyaté's LDRN (continuation of Kouyaté's *La Race Nègre*). Edited by Stéphane Rosso. Paris, 1931–34.

La Dépêche Africaine. Nationalist monthly. Paris, 1930–36.

The Gambia Outlook. E. F. Small, Editor. Bathurst, 1930–36.

The Gold Coast Independent. Early nationalist weekly. Accra, 1895, 1918–24.

The Gold Coast Spectator. Nationalist weekly. Accra, 1932–36.

Le Libéré ("Tribune du Peuple Malgache"). Early Madagascan nationalist journal. (Merged with *Les Continents*, January, 1925.) Paris, 1923–25.

The New African. Organ of the WANS. London, 1946.

La Race Nègre. Monthly organ of the LDRN. (Edited by Senghor, Kouyaté.) Paris, 1927–31.

La Race Nègre. Organ of Faure faction of LDRN. Paris, 1931–36.

La Voix des Nègres. Monthly organ of the CDRN, Paris, 1927. Superseded by *La Race Nègre* (Kouyaté).

2. PUBLISHED BY SOVIET INSTITUTIONS OTHER THAN
   THE COMINTERN

Materialy po Natsional'no-Kolonial'nym Problemam. Collected papers of the NIANKP. Moscow, 1932–35.

Novyi Vostok. Journal of the All-Russian Association of Eastern Studies of the National Commissariat on Nationalities Affairs. M. P. Pavlovich, Editor. Moscow, 1922–30.

Revoliutsionnyi Vostok. Journal of the NIANKP, Moscow, 1927–37.

Vestnik Narkomindela. Journal of the Soviet Commissariat of Foreign Affairs. Moscow, 1922.

Zhizn Natsional'nostei. Issued by the National Commissariat on Nationalities Affairs, Moscow, 1918–24.

IV. ARCHIVAL SOURCES

France. Archives of the Ministère des Colonies at the Ministère des Affaires Culturelles, Archives Nationales, Section Outre-Mer, Paris. SLOTFOM (Service de Liaison avec les Originaires des Territoires de la France d'Outre-Mer), Série V; materials relating to the period 1927–34.

Great Britain. Colonial Office Archives at the Public Record Office, London. Files listed in the registers for the four colonies of British West Africa: Gambia, Gold Coast, Nigeria, and Sierra Leone; covering the period 1927–39.

V. INTERVIEWS AND UNPUBLISHED SOURCES

Allen, Christopher. "The Pathology of Gambian Trade Unionism, 1929–67." MSS, Nuffield College, Oxford, 1967.

Ballard, J. A. "The Development of Political Parties in French Equatorial Africa." Ph.D. dissertation, Fletcher School, 1963.

Denzer, L. R. E. "The National Congress of British West Africa, Gold Coast Section." M.A. thesis, Institute of African Studies, University of Ghana, 1965.

Drake, St. Clair. Interview, Washington, D.C., December, 1969.

Holdsworth, Mary. "Russian African Studies." MS, St. Mary's College, Durham, England, c. 1963.

Horton, Edna (former First Secretary of Wallace-Johnson's WAYL in Sierra Leone). Personal letters, January 9-10, 1970.

James, C. L. R. "Nkrumah Then and Now." MS, London, c. 1966.
———. "Notes on George Padmore." MS, George Padmore Library, Accra, n.d.

Jesman, Czeslaw. "African History through Soviet Eyes." MS, London, n.d.

Johns, S. W. "Marxism-Leninism in a Multi-Racial Environment." Ph.D. dissertation, Harvard University, 1965.

Kanet, Roger. "The Soviet Union and Sub-Saharan Africa: Communist Policy toward Africa, 1917–1965." Ph.D. dissertation, Princeton University, 1966.

Kottei, S. I. A. (Director, George Padmore Library, Accra). "George Padmore in the African Revolution." MS, Accra, c. 1965.

Ministère de la France d'Outre-Mer, Direction des Affairs Politiques, Deuxième Bureau. "Le Syndicalisme dans les Territoires Africains" (mimeographed). Paris, 1954.

Nicol, Dr. Davidson (former Chancellor, Fourah Bay College, and Ambassador of Sierra Leone to the United Nations). Interview, New York, November, 1969.

Nkrumah, Kwame. "Funeral Oration on the Occasion of the Internment of Ashes of the Late George Padmore at Christiansborg Castle." Copy of original MS at George Padmore Library, Accra.

Padmore-Sekyi correspondence. Copies of original letters at Ghana National Archives, Cape Coast. (All references in text are to Samuel Rohdie. "The Gold Coast Aborigines Abroad." *Journal of African History*, VI (1965), no. 3: 389–411.

RDA. "Charte de l'Organisation du RDA" (mimeographed). Bamako, c. 1947.

Schumacher, E. J. "A Political History of the RDA: 1946–58." M.S. thesis, London School of Economics, 1964.

INDEX